C# in Depth

C# in Depth

JON SKEET

MANNING

Greenwich
(74° w. long.)

For online information and ordering of this and other Manning books, please visit
www.manning.com. The publisher offers discounts on this book when ordered in quantity.
For more information, please contact:

Special Sales Department
Manning Publications Co.
Sound View Court 3B   fax: (609) 877-8256
Greenwich, CT 06830   email: orders@manning.com

Manning Publications Co.   Copyeditor: Liz Welch
Sound View Court 3B   Typesetter: Gordan Salinovic
Greenwich, CT 06830   Cover designer: Leslie Haimes

Second, corrected printing June 2009
ISBN 1933988363
Printed in the United States of America
   3 4 5 6 7 8 9 10 – MAL – 13 12 11 10 09

For family, friends, colleagues,
and all those who love C#

brief contents

contents

PART 1   PREPARING FOR THE JOURNEY 1

1   *The changing face of C# development   3*

foreword

There are two kinds of pianists.

There are some pianists who play not because they enjoy it, but because their parents force them to take lessons. Then there are those who play the piano because it pleases them to create music. They don't need to be forced; on the contrary, they sometimes don't know when to stop.

Of the latter kind, there are some who play the piano as a hobby. Then there are those who play for a living. That requires a whole new level of dedication, skill, and talent. They may have some degree of freedom about what genre of music they play and the stylistic choices they make in playing it, but fundamentally those choices are driven by the needs of the employer or the tastes of the audience.

Of the latter kind, there are some who do it primarily for the money. Then there are those professionals who would want to play the piano in public even if they weren't being paid. They enjoy using their skills and talents to make music for others. That they can have fun and get paid for it is so much the better.

Of the latter kind, there are some who are self-taught, who "play by ear," who might have great talent and ability but cannot communicate that intuitive understanding to others except through the music itself. Then there are those who have formal training in both theory and practice. They can explain what techniques the composer used to achieve the intended emotional effect, and use that knowledge to shape their interpretation of the piece.

Of the latter kind, there are some who have never looked inside their pianos. Then there are those who are fascinated by the clever escapements that lift the damper felts a fraction of a second before the hammers strike the strings. They own key levelers and capstan wrenches. They take delight and pride in being able to understand the mechanisms of an instrument that has five to ten thousand moving parts.

Of the latter kind, there are some who are content to master their craft and exercise their talents for the pleasure and profit it brings. Then there are those who are not just artists, theorists, and technicians; somehow they find the time to pass that knowledge on to others as mentors.

I have no idea if Jon Skeet is any kind of pianist. But from my email conversations with him as one of the C# team's Most Valuable Professionals over the years, from reading his blog and from reading every word of this book at least three times, it has become clear to me that Jon is that latter kind of software developer: enthusiastic, knowledgeable, talented, curious and analytical—a teacher of others.

C# is a highly pragmatic and rapidly evolving language. Through the addition of query comprehensions, richer type inference, a compact syntax for anonymous functions, and so on, I hope that we have enabled a whole new style of programming while still staying true to the statically typed, component-oriented approach that has made C# a success.

Many of these new stylistic elements have the paradoxical quality of feeling very old (lambda expressions go back to the foundations of computer science in the first half of the twentieth century) and yet at the same time feeling new and unfamiliar to developers used to a more modern object-oriented approach.

Jon gets all that. This book is ideal for professional developers who have a need to understand the "what" and "how" of the latest revision to C#. But it is also for those developers whose understanding is enriched by exploring the "why" of the language's design principles.

Being able to take advantage of all that new power will require new ways of thinking about data, functions, and the relationship between them. It's not unlike trying to play jazz after years of classical training—or vice versa. Either way, I am looking forward to finding out what sorts of functional compositions the next generation of C# programmers come up with. Happy composing, and thanks for choosing the key of C# to do it in.

ERIC LIPPERT
Senior Software Engineer, Microsoft

preface

I have a sneaking suspicion that many authors have pretty much stumbled into writing books. That's certainly true in my case. I've been writing about Java and C# on the Web and in newsgroups for a long time, but the leap from that to the printed page is quite a large one. From my perspective, it's been an "anti-Lemony Snicket"—a series of *fortunate* events.

I've been reviewing books for various publishers, including Manning, for a while. In April 2006 I asked whether it would be OK to write a blog entry on a book that looked particularly promising: *PowerShell in Action*. In the course of the ensuing conversation, I somehow managed to end up on the author team for *Groovy in Action*. I owe a huge debt of thanks to my wife for even allowing me to agree to this—which makes her sound like a control freak until you understand we were expecting twins at the time, and she had just gone into the hospital. It wasn't an ideal time to take on extra work, but Holly was as supportive as she's always been.

Contributing to the Groovy book took a lot of hard work, but the writing bug firmly hit me during the process. When talking with the principal author, Dierk König, I realized that I wanted to take on that role myself one day. So, when I heard later that Manning was interested in publishing a book about C#3, I started writing a proposal right away.

My relationship with C# itself goes further back. I started using it in 2002, and have kept up with it ever since. I haven't been using it professionally for all that time—I've been flitting back and forth between C# and Java, depending on what my employers wanted for the projects I was working on. However, I've never let my interest in it drop, posting on the newsgroups and developing code at home. Although I didn't start using C#2 until Visual Studio 2005 was close to release, I've tracked C#3 more closely.

While watching the gradual emergence of C#3, I've also been watching the developer reaction to C#2—and I think people are missing out. The adoption rate of C#2 has been quite slow for various reasons, but where it *is* being used, I believe its full potential isn't being realized. I want to fix that.

The proposal I made to Manning was narrow in focus, but deep in scope. My mission is a simple one: to take existing C#1 developers and turn them into confident and competent C#2 and 3 developers who understand the language at a deep level. At the time of this writing, I don't know of any other books that have a similar explicit aim. I'm immensely grateful to Manning for allowing me to write the book I really wanted to, without interfering and forcing it down a more conventional path. At the same time, the folks at Manning expertly guided the book and made it much more useful than it would have been otherwise.

I tried to write the book that *I* would want to read when learning C#2 and 3. To that extent, I think I've succeeded. Whether that means it's a book that anyone *else* will want to read remains to be seen—but if you, the reader, have even a fraction of the enjoyment when reading it that I've had writing it, you're in for a good time.

acknowledgments

I had a wonderful time writing this book, which is largely due to the skill and dedication of the people who worked with me on it and the patience of the people who put up with me. Those who fall into both camps are virtuous beyond words.

My family has borne the brunt of the time I spent writing when I should have been playing, sleeping, or just being more sociable. My wife Holly has been more supportive than I have any right to expect, and I'm both proud and slightly disturbed that the eyes of my sons Tom, William, and Robin light up as soon as a laptop is opened.

As well as the formal peer reviewers listed in a moment, I would like to mention Emma Middlebrook and Douglas Leeder, both of whom read significant portions of the original manuscript before it even reached my editor. Emma has the remarkable bad luck of having had to cope not only with reviewing my writing but also with working with me on a daily basis. Douglas freed himself from that drudgery a while ago, but was still kind enough to suggest improvements to the book *without even knowing C#*. You're both dear friends, and I thank you for that even more than for your efforts on the book.

The folks at Manning have been supportive right from the start—particularly Jackie Carter's original work with me, as well as Mike Stephens' help at a high level throughout the process and Jeff Bleiel's constant support and diligent editing. Liz Welch performed the near-impossible trick of making the copyediting process *fun* for both of us, and Karen Tegtmeyer kept me relatively sane during nail-biting peer reviews. These are only the people I got to know reasonably well during the last year; many other people were involved in the project, doing marvelous things: there's the production team of Gordan Salinovic, Dottie Marsico, Tiffany Taylor, Katie Tennant, and Mary Piergies; cover designer Leslie Haimes; webmaster Gabriel Dobrescu, marketing director Ron Tomich, and last but not least, publisher Marjan Bace.

The aforementioned peer reviewers are a picky bunch. There's no doubt in my mind that *my* life would have been easier without them—it's really you, the reader, who should thank them for a much better end result in the book that you are now reading. They pushed, prodded, pulled, commented, questioned, and generally made thorough nuisances of themselves—which is exactly what they were asked to do—as they read the manuscript in its many iterations. So on your behalf I thank Dave Corun, Anil Radhakrishna, Riccardo Audano, Will Morse, Christopher Haupt, Robin Shahan, Mark Seeman, Peter A. Bromberg, Fabio Angius, Massimo Perga, Chris Mullins, JD Conley, Marc Gravell, Ross Bradbury, Andrew Seimer, Alex Thissen, Keith J. Farmer, Fabrice Marguerie, Josh Cronemeyer, and Anthony Jones.

I've been very fortunate over the years to make acquaintances (both online and in person) with many people who are far smarter than I am, and I consulted some of them for pieces of information in this book. For keeping my facts straight, I'd like to thank Jon Jagger, Nigel Perry, Prashant Sridharan, Dan Fernandez, Tony Goodhew, Simon Tatham, Ben Voigt, and George Chrysanthakopoulos.

Finally, I need to thank the C# team. As well as creating such a fantastic language to write about, they were incredibly responsive to my questions. I don't know what's coming in C#4 (beyond the hints on blogs about *possible* features) or even a very rough timescale for it, but I wish the team the very best of luck.

I'd like to pay special tribute to Eric Lippert, first for being willing to enter into detailed conversations about all kinds of topics while I was writing the initial manuscript, and then for acting as the technical reviewer for the book, and finally for agreeing to write the foreword. I couldn't have asked for a more knowledgable and thorough reviewer—Eric is about as close to being the C# specification in human form as you can get! He's also a great source of trivia and recommendations on coding style. Many of the comments Eric made when reviewing the book didn't impact the text directly, but are pure gold nonetheless. Rather than keeping them to myself, I've incorporated them into the notes on the book's website. Think of them as the literary equivalent of a DVD commentary track.

about this book

This is a book about C#2 and 3—it's as simple as that. I barely cover C#1, and only cover the .NET Framework libraries and Common Language Runtime (CLR) when they're related to the language. This is a deliberate decision, and the result is quite a different book from most of the C# and .NET books I've seen.

By assuming a reasonable amount of knowledge of C#1, I avoided spending hundreds of pages covering material that I think most people already understand. That gave me much more room to expand on the *details* of C#2 and 3, which is what I hope you're reading the book for.

I believe that many developers would be less frustrated with their work if they had a deeper connection with the language they're writing in. I know it sounds geeky in the extreme to talk about having a "relationship" with a programming language, but that's the best way I can describe it. This book is my attempt to help you achieve that sort of understanding, or deepen it further. It won't be enough on its own—it should be a companion to your coding, guiding you and suggesting some interesting avenues to explore, as well as explaining why your code behaves the way it does.

Who should read this book?

During the course of the multiple rounds of reviewing this book underwent as I was writing it, one comment worried me more than most: "This is a book for C# experts." That was never the intention, and I hope that (partly thanks to that honest feedback) it's *not* an accurate reflection of who will get the most out of this book.

I don't particularly want to write for experts. Aside from anything else, I've got less to offer experts than I have "intermediate" developers. I want to write for people who *want* to become experts. That's what this book is about. If you feel passionately about computing, but happen not to have studied C#2 or 3 in much detail, this book is aimed squarely at you. If you want to immerse yourself in C# until it's part of your bloodstream, then I'd feel honored to be the one to push you under. If you feel frustrated when you arrive at working code, but don't quite know *why* it works, I want to help you to understand.

Having said all that, this book is not meant for complete beginners. If you haven't used C#1 before, you'll find this book very hard work. That doesn't mean it won't be useful to you—but *please* go and find a book (or at least a tutorial) on C#1 before you go much further. The first chapter will tease you with the joys of C#2 and 3, but you won't be able to appreciate them if you're worrying about how variables are declared and where the semicolons go.

I'm not going to claim that reading this book will make you a fabulous coder. There's so much more to software engineering than knowing the syntax of the language you happen to be using. I give some words of guidance here and there, but ultimately there's a lot more gut instinct in development than most of us would like to admit. What I *will* claim is that if you read and understand this book, you should feel comfortable with C#2 and 3, and free to follow your instincts without too much apprehension. It's not about being able to write code that no one else will understand because it uses unknown corners of the language: it's about being confident that you know the options available to you, and know which path the C# idioms are encouraging you to follow.

Roadmap

The book's structure is simple. There are three parts and a single appendix. The first part serves as an introduction, including a refresher on topics in C#1 that are important for understanding C#2 and 3, and that are often misunderstood. The second part covers the new features in C#2. The third part covers the new features in C#3.

There are occasions where organizing the material this way means we come back to a topic a couple of times—in particular delegates are improved in C#2 and then again in C#3—but there is method in my madness. I anticipate that a number of readers will *initially* only be using C#2 for the bulk of their professional work, but with an interest in learning C#3 for new projects and hobbies. That means that it is useful to clarify what is in which version. It also provides a feeling of context and evolution—it shows how the language has developed over time.

Chapter 1 sets the scene by taking a simple piece of C#1 code and evolving it, seeing how C#2 and 3 allow the source to become more readable and powerful. We look at the historical context in which C# has grown, and the technical context in which it operates as part of a complete platform: C# as a language builds on framework libraries and a powerful runtime to turn abstraction into reality.

Chapter 2 looks back at C#1, and three specific aspects: delegates, the type system characteristics, and the differences between value types and reference types. These topics are often understood "just well enough" by C#1 developers, but C#2 and 3 develop them significantly, so a solid grounding is required in order to make the most of the new features.

Chapter 3 tackles the biggest feature of C#2, and potentially the hardest to grasp: generics. Methods and types can be written generically, with type parameters standing in for real types which are specified in the calling code. Initially it's as confusing as this description makes it sound, but once you understand generics you'll wonder how you survived without them.

If you've ever wanted to represent a null integer, chapter 4 is for you. It introduces nullable types, a feature built on generics and taking advantage of support in the language, runtime, and framework.

Chapter 5 shows the improvements to delegates in C#2. You may have only used delegates for handling events such as button clicks before now. C#2 makes it easier to create delegates, and library support makes them more useful for situations other than events.

In chapter 6 we examine iterators, and the easy way to implement them in C#2. Few developers use iterator blocks, but as LINQ to Objects is built on iterators, they will become more and more important. The lazy nature of their execution is also a key part of LINQ.

Chapter 7 shows a number of smaller features introduced in C#2, each making life a little more pleasant. The language designers have smoothed over a few rough places in C#1, allowing more flexible interaction with code generators, better support for utility classes, more granular access to properties, and more.

Chapter 8 once again looks at a few relatively simple features—but this time in C#3. Almost all the new syntax is geared toward the common goal of LINQ but the building blocks are also useful in their own right. With anonymous types, automatically implemented properties, implicitly typed local variables, and greatly enhanced initialization support, C#3 gives a far richer language with which your code can express its behavior.

Chapter 9 looks at the first major topic of C#3—lambda expressions. Not content with the reasonably concise syntax we saw in chapter 5, the language designers have made delegates even easier to create than in C#2. Lambdas are capable of more—they can be converted into expression trees: a powerful way of representing code as data.

In chapter 10 we examine extension methods, which provide a way of fooling the compiler into believing that methods declared in one type actually belong to another. At first glance this appears to be a readability nightmare, but with careful consideration it can be an extremely powerful feature—and one which is vital to LINQ.

Chapter 11 combines the previous three chapters in the form of query expressions, a concise but powerful way of querying data. Initially we concentrate on LINQ to Objects, but see how the query expression pattern is applied in a way which allows other data providers to plug in seamlessly.

Chapter 12 reaps the rewards of query expressions combined with expression trees: it shows how LINQ to SQL is able to convert what appears to be normal C# into

SQL statements. We also take a speedy look at some other LINQ providers—those in the .NET Framework, some third-party ones which are gradually appearing, and a sneak peek at what Microsoft has in store.

We wind down in chapter 13 with a speculative glance at what the future might hold. We examine how the changes to C# will affect the flavor and texture of the code we write in it, as well as looking at some future trends in technology.

The appendix is a straightforward piece of reference material: the LINQ standard query operators, with some examples. Strictly speaking, this is not part of C#3—it's library material—but I believe it's so useful that readers will welcome its inclusion.

Terminology and typography

Most of the terminology of the book is explained as it goes along, but there are a few definitions that are worth highlighting here. I use C#1, C#2, and C#3 in a reasonably obvious manner—but you may see other books and websites referring to C#1.0, C#2.0, and C#3.0. The extra ".0" seems redundant to me, which is why I've omitted it—I hope the meaning is clear.

I've appropriated a pair of terms from a C# book by Mark Michaelis. To avoid the confusion between "runtime" being an execution environment (as in "the Common Language Runtime") and a point in time (as in "overriding occurs at runtime"), Mark uses "execution time" for the latter concept, usually in comparison with "compile time." This seems to me to be a thoroughly sensible idea, and one that I hope catches on in the wider community. I'm doing my bit by following his example in this book.

I frequently refer to "the language specification" or just "the specification"—unless I indicate otherwise, this means "the C# language specification." However, multiple versions of the specification are available, partly due to different versions of the language itself and partly due to the standardization process. Rather than clutter up the book with specific "chapter and verse" references, there's a page on the book's website that allows you to pick which version of the specification you're interested in and then see which part of the book refers to which area of the specification.

This book contains numerous pieces of code, which appear in a `fixed-width` font; output from the listings appears in the same way. Code annotations accompany some listings, and at other times particular sections of the code are highlighted in **bold**.

Almost all of the code appears in "snippet" form, allowing it to stay compact but still runnable—within the right environment. That environment is Snippy, a custom tool that is introduced in section 1.4. Snippy is available for download, along with all of the code from the book (in the form of snippets, full Visual Studio solutions, or more often both) from the book's website at www.manning.com/CSharpInDepth.

Author Online and the C# in Depth website

Purchase of *C# in Depth* includes free access to a private web forum run by Manning Publications where you can make comments about the book, ask technical questions, and receive help from the author and other users. To access the forum and subscribe to it, point your web browser to www.manning.com/CSharpInDepth or www.manning.com/skeet. This page provides information on how to get on the forum once you are registered, what kind of help is available, and the rules of conduct on the forum.

The Author Online forum and the archives of previous discussions will be accessible from the publisher's website as long as the book is in print.

In addition to Manning's own website, I have set up a companion website for the book at www.csharpindepth.com, containing information that didn't quite fit into the book, as well as downloadable source code for all the listings in the book and further examples.

About the author

In many books, you will find a very impressive list of business and technical achievements accomplished by the author(s). Sadly, I have little to boast of on that front. Microsoft has been kind enough to award me MVP (Most Valuable Professional) status since 2003 for my "work" in the C# newsgroups, but I have to put "work" in quotes as it's been such a fun ride. Beyond that, I run a modest website with some articles about C# and .NET, and a blog with some random thoughts about software development. I'm not the CTO of a wildly successful startup. I haven't given sell-out lecture tours across multiple continents with webcasts that brought the Internet to its knees. Instead, I've spent my time working as a developer, listening to the problems of other developers, and trying to gradually learn the best way to write code and design solutions.

I'd like to think that in some ways that makes me the *right* person to write a book about C#—because it's what I live and breathe from day to day, and it's what I love helping people with. I'm passionate about C# in a way which my wife has learned to tolerate, and I hope that passion comes through in this book. I thought I was mad about it *before* I started writing, and my appreciation has only grown as I've become more intimately familiar with the details.

I'm not so much in love with C# that I can't see any flaws—again, I hope that comes across in my writing. I've never met a language yet that didn't have its hidden traps: C# is better than most in that respect, but it's not perfect. When I see areas that have caused problems, either for me or for other developers who have posted in newsgroups or emailed me, I'm more than willing to point them out. I hope the designers will forgive the implied criticisms, and understand that I hold them in the highest regard for the beautiful and elegant language they created.

about the cover illustration

The caption on the illustration on the cover of *C# in Depth* is a "Musician." The illustration is taken from a collection of costumes of the Ottoman Empire published on January 1, 1802, by William Miller of Old Bond Street, London. The title page is missing from the collection and we have been unable to track it down to date. The book's table of contents identifies the figures in both English and French, and each illustration bears the names of two artists who worked on it, both of whom would no doubt be surprised to find their art gracing the front cover of a computer programming book...two hundred years later.

The collection was purchased by a Manning editor at an antiquarian flea market in the "Garage" on West 26th Street in Manhattan. The seller was an American based in Ankara, Turkey, and the transaction took place just as he was packing up his stand for the day. The Manning editor did not have on his person the substantial amount of cash that was required for the purchase and a credit card and check were both politely turned down. With the seller flying back to Ankara that evening the situation was getting hopeless. What was the solution? It turned out to be nothing more than an old-fashioned verbal agreement sealed with a handshake. The seller simply proposed that the money be transferred to him by wire and the editor walked out with the bank information on a piece of paper and the portfolio of images under his arm. Needless to say, we transferred the funds the next day, and we remain grateful and impressed by this unknown person's trust in one of us. It recalls something that might have happened a long time ago.

We at Manning celebrate the inventiveness, the initiative, and, yes, the fun of the computer business with book covers based on the rich diversity of regional life of two centuries ago, brought back to life by the pictures from this collection.

comments from the tech review

Technical proofreaders are a vital part of the book-publishing process. They read the final manuscript for technical accuracy and test all the code shortly before the book goes to typesetting.

A good proofreader will find and help correct all technical errors. A really good one will pick up incorrect implications and unhelpful nuances. A *great* technical proofreader will provide guidance in terms of style as well as content, helping to hone the manuscript and the author's point of view. In Eric Lippert we found such a person. As a member of the C# team, we knew from the start that he would provide accurate information—but he was also able to give Jon's excellent manuscript an extra layer of polish.

We always ask our technical proofreaders for feedback once they've completed the review, and for this book we wanted to share some of those comments with you:

This is a gem of a book, both in its details and its overall organization. Every bit of jargon from the specification is used correctly and in context; when Jon needs new terms he makes up good ones…

Where it needs to be simple it is simple, but never simplistic. The majority of my comments were not corrections; rather, they expanded on the history behind a particular design decision, giving ideas for further explorations, and so on.

Jon takes a sensible approach to presenting complex material. The book begins with an "ontogenic" approach, describing the evolution of the language over time. In the section on C#3, he switches to a more "constructivist" approach, describing how we built more complex features (such as query comprehensions) out of more basic features (such as extension methods and lambda expressions).

COMMENTS FROM THE TECH REVIEW

This choice of book organization is particularly well-suited to high-end users, like Jon himself, who are primarily looking to use the language, but who can do so better when they understand the parts from which it was built...

If I had time to write another book, this is the kind of book I would hope to write. Now I don't have to, and thank goodness for that!

To see more comments and margin notes made by Eric during the technical review process, as well as responses from Jon, please visit the book's web page at www.manning.com/CSharpInDepth or www.csharpindepth.com/Notes.aspx.

Part 1

Preparing for the journey

Every reader will come to this book with a different set of expectations and a different level of experience. Are you an expert looking to fill some holes, however small, in your present knowledge? Perhaps you consider yourself an "average" developer, beginning to migrate projects to .NET 2.0 but with an eye to the future. Maybe you're reasonably confident with C# 2 but have no C# 3 experience.

As an author, I can't make every reader the same—and I wouldn't want to even if I could. I hope that all readers have two things in common, however: the desire for a deeper relationship with C# as a language, and at least a basic knowledge of C# 1. If you can bring those elements to the party, I'll provide the rest.

The potentially huge range of skill levels is the main reason for this part of the book existing. You may already know what to expect from C# 2 and 3—or it could all be brand new to you. You could have a rock-solid understanding of C# 1, or you might be rusty on some of the details that didn't matter much before but that will become increasingly important as you learn C# 2 and then 3. By the end of part 1, I won't have leveled the playing field entirely, but you should be able to approach the rest of the book with confidence and an idea of what's coming later.

For the first two chapters, we will be looking both forward and back. One of the key themes of the book is *evolution*. Before introducing any feature into the language, the design team carefully considers that feature in the context of what's already present and the general aims of the future. This brings a feeling of consistency to the language even in the midst of change. To understand how and why the language is evolving, we need to see where we've come from and where we're going to.

Chapter 1 presents a bird's-eye view of the rest of the book, taking a brief look at some of the biggest features of both C# 2 and C# 3 and showing a progression of code from C# 1 onward. To bring more perspective and context to the new features, we'll also take a look at nearly 12 years of development history, from the first release of Java in January 1996 to the birth of C# 3 and .NET 3.5 in November 2007.

Chapter 2 is heavily focused on C# 1. If you're an expert in C# 1 you can skip this chapter, but it does tackle some of the areas of C# 1 that tend to be misunderstood. Rather than try to explain the whole of the language, the chapter concentrates on features that are fundamental to the later versions of C#. From this solid base, we can move on and look at C# 2 in part 2 of this book.

The changing face of C# development

This chapter covers

- An evolving example
- C#'s historical context
- The composition of .NET
- Snippy, the snippet compiler

The world is changing at a pace that is sometimes terrifying, and technology is one of the fastest-moving areas of that change. Computing in particular seems to push itself constantly, both in hardware and in software. Although many older computer languages are like bedrocks, rarely changing beyond being consolidated in terms of standardization, newer ones are still evolving. C# falls into the latter category, and the implications of this are double-edged. On the one hand, there's always more to learn—the feeling of having mastered the language is unlikely to last for long, with a "V next" always looming. However, the upside is that if you embrace the new features and you're willing to change your coding style to adopt the new idioms, you'll discover a more expressive, powerful way of developing software.

3

To get the most out of any new language feature, you need to understand it thoroughly. That's the point of this book—to delve into the very heart of C#, so you understand it at a deep level rather than just enough to get by. Without wishing to sound melodramatic or overly emotional, I want to put you in *harmony* with the language.

If you're anxious to get coding straight away, and if you're confident in your understanding of C# 1, feel free to skip to part 2 and dive in. However, there's always more to coding than just the technicalities, and in this part I will be providing background to the bigger picture: the reasons *why* both the C# language and the .NET Framework have changed in the ways that they have.

In this chapter, we'll have a sneak peek at a few of the features the rest of the book will cover. We'll see that while C# 2 fixed a lot of the issues people encountered when using C# 1, the ideas in C# 3 could significantly change the way we write and even think about code. I'll put the changes into historical context, guide you through the maze of terminology and version numbers, then talk about how the book is presented in order to help you get as much out of it as possible. Let's start by looking at how some code might evolve over time, taking advantage of new features as they become available.

1.1   *Evolution in action: examples of code change*

I've always dreamed of doing magic tricks, and for this one section I get to live that dream. This is the only time that I won't explain how things work, or try to go one step at a time. Quite the opposite, in fact—the plan is to impress rather than educate. If you read this entire section without getting at least a little excited about what C# 2 and 3 can do, maybe this book isn't for you. With any luck, though, you'll be eager to get to the details of how the tricks work—to slow down the sleight of hand until it's obvious what's going on—and that's what the rest of the book is for.

I should warn you that the example is very contrived—clearly designed to pack as many new features into as short a piece of code as possible. From C# 2, we'll see generics, properties with different access modifiers for getters and setters, nullable types, and anonymous methods. From C# 3, we'll see automatically implemented properties, enhanced collection initializers, enhanced object initializers, lambda expressions, extension methods, implicit typing, and LINQ query expressions. There are, of course, many other new features, but it would be impossible to demonstrate them all together in a meaningful way. Even though you usually wouldn't use even this select set of features in such a compact space, I'm sure you'll recognize the general tasks as ones that *do* crop up frequently in real-life code.

As well as being contrived, the example is also clichéd—but at least that makes it familiar. Yes, it's a product/name/price example, the e-commerce virtual child of "hello, world."

To keep things simple, I've split the code up into sections. Here's what we want to do:

- Define a `Product` type with a name and a price in dollars, along with a way of retrieving a hard-coded list of products
- Print out the products in alphabetical order

- Print out all the products costing more than $10
- Consider what would be required to represent products with unknown prices

We'll look at each of these areas separately, and see how as we move forward in versions of C#, we can accomplish the same tasks more simply and elegantly than before. In each case, the changes to the code will be in a **bold font**. Let's start with the Product type itself.

1.1.1 Defining the Product type

We're not looking for anything particularly impressive from the Product type—just encapsulation of a couple of properties. To make life simpler for demonstration purposes, this is also where we create a list of predefined products. We override ToString so that when we print out the products elsewhere, they show useful values. Listing 1.1 shows the type as it might be written in C# 1. We'll then move on to see how the same effect can be achieved in C# 2, then C# 3. This is the pattern we'll follow for each of the other pieces of code.

Listing 1.1 The Product type (C# 1)

```
using System.Collections;

public class Product
{
    string name;
    public string Name
    {
        get { return name; }
    }

    decimal price;
    public decimal Price
    {
        get { return price; }
    }

    public Product(string name, decimal price)
    {
        this.name = name;
        this.price = price;
    }

    public static ArrayList GetSampleProducts()
    {
        ArrayList list = new ArrayList();
        list.Add(new Product("Company", 9.99m));
        list.Add(new Product("Assassins", 14.99m));
        list.Add(new Product("Frogs", 13.99m));
        list.Add(new Product("Sweeney Todd", 10.99m));
        return list;
    }

    public override string ToString()
    {
```

```
        return string.Format("{0}: {1}", name, price);
    }
}
```

Nothing in listing 1.1 should be hard to understand—it's just C# 1 code, after all. There are four limitations that it demonstrates, however:

- An `ArrayList` has no compile-time information about what's in it. We could have accidentally added a string to the list created in `GetSampleProducts` and the compiler wouldn't have batted an eyelid.
- We've provided public "getter" properties, which means that if we wanted matching "setters," they would have to be public too. In this case it's not too much of a problem to use the fields directly, but it would be if we had validation that ought to be applied every time a value was set. A property setter would be natural, but we may not want to expose it to the outside world. We'd have to create a private `SetPrice` method or something similar, and that asymmetry is ugly.
- The variables themselves are available to the rest of the class. They're private, but it would be nice to encapsulate them within the properties, to make sure they're not tampered with other than *through* those properties.
- There's quite a lot of fluff involved in creating the properties and variables— code that complicates the simple task of encapsulating a string and a decimal.

Let's see what C# 2 can do to improve matters (see listing 1.2; changes are in bold).

Listing 1.2   Strongly typed collections and private setters (C# 2)

```
using System.Collections.Generic;

public class Product
{
    string name;
    public string Name
    {
        get { return name; }
        private set { name = value; }
    }

    decimal price;
    public decimal Price
    {
        get { return price; }
        private set { price = value; }
    }

    public Product(string name, decimal price)
    {
        Name = name;
        Price = price;
    }

    public static List<Product> GetSampleProducts()
```

```
    {
        List<Product> list = new List<Product>();
        list.Add(new Product("Company", 9.99m));
        list.Add(new Product("Assassins", 14.99m));
        list.Add(new Product("Frogs", 13.99m));
        list.Add(new Product("Sweeney Todd", 10.99m));
        return list;
    }

    public override string ToString()
    {
        return string.Format("{0}: {1}", name, price);
    }
}
```

The code hasn't changed much, but we've addressed two of the problems. We now have properties with private setters (which we use in the constructor), and it doesn't take a genius to guess that List<Product> is telling the compiler that the list contains products. Attempting to add a different type to the list would result in a compiler error. The change to C# 2 leaves only two of the original four difficulties unanswered. Listing 1.3 shows how C# 3 tackles these.

Listing 1.3　Automatically implemented properties and simpler initialization (C# 3)

```
using System.Collections.Generic;

class Product
{
    public string Name { get; private set; }
    public decimal Price { get; private set; }

    public Product(string name, decimal price)
    {
        Name = name;
        Price = price;
    }

    Product()
    {
    }

    public static List<Product> GetSampleProducts()
    {
        return new List<Product>
        {
            new Product { Name="Company", Price = 9.99m },
            new Product { Name="Assassins", Price=14.99m },
            new Product { Name="Frogs", Price=13.99m },
            new Product { Name="Sweeney Todd", Price=10.99m}
        };
    }

    public override string ToString()
    {
        return string.Format("{0}: {1}", Name, Price);
    }
}
```

The properties now don't have any code (or visible variables!) associated with them, and we're building the hard-coded list in a very different way. With no "name" and "price" variables to access, we're forced to use the properties everywhere in the class, improving consistency. We now have a private parameterless constructor for the sake of the new property-based initialization. In this example, we could actually have removed the public constructor completely, but it would make the class less useful in the real world.

Figure 1.1 shows a summary of how our `Product` type has evolved so far. I'll include a similar diagram after each task, so you can see the pattern of how C# 2 and 3 improve the code.

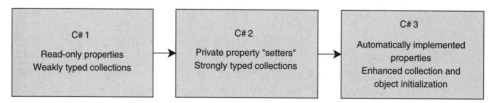

Figure 1.1   Evolution of the `Product` type, showing greater encapsulation, stronger typing, and ease of initialization over time

So far the changes are relatively minimal. In fact, the addition of generics (the `List<Product>` syntax) is probably the most important part of C# 2, but we've only seen part of its usefulness so far. There's nothing to get the heart racing yet, but we've only just started. Our next task is to print out the list of products in alphabetical order. That shouldn't be too hard...

1.1.2   *Sorting products by name*

The easiest way of displaying a list in a particular order is to sort the list and then run through it displaying items. In .NET 1.1, this involved using `ArrayList.Sort`, and in our case providing an `IComparer` implementation. We could have made the `Product` type implement `IComparable`, but we could only define one sort order that way, and it's not a huge stretch to imagine that we might want to sort by price at some stage as well as by name. Listing 1.4 implements `IComparer`, then sorts the list and displays it.

Listing 1.4   Sorting an `ArrayList` using `IComparer` (C# 1)

```
class ProductNameComparer : IComparer
{
    public int Compare(object x, object y)
    {
        Product first = (Product)x;
        Product second = (Product)y;
        return first.Name.CompareTo(second.Name);
    }
}

...

ArrayList products = Product.GetSampleProducts();
products.Sort(new ProductNameComparer());
```

```
foreach (Product product in products)
{
    Console.WriteLine (product);
}
```

The first thing to spot in listing 1.4 is that we've had to introduce an extra type to help us with the sorting. That's not a disaster, but it's a lot of code if we only want to sort by name in one place. Next, we see the casts in the `Compare` method. Casts are a way of telling the compiler that we know more information than it does—and that usually means there's a chance we're wrong. If the `ArrayList` we returned from `GetSample-Products` *had* contained a string, that's where the code would go bang—where the comparison tries to cast the string to a `Product`.

We've also got a cast in the code that displays the sorted list. It's not obvious, because the compiler puts it in automatically, but the `foreach` loop implicitly casts each element of the list to `Product`. Again, that's a cast we'd ideally like to get rid of, and once more generics come to the rescue in C# 2. Listing 1.5 shows the earlier code with the use of generics as the *only* change.

Listing 1.5　Sorting a `List<Product>` using `IComparer<Product>` (C# 2)

```
class ProductNameComparer : IComparer<Product>
{
    public int Compare(Product first, Product second)
    {
        return first.Name.CompareTo(second.Name);
    }
}

...

List<Product> products = Product.GetSampleProducts();
products.Sort(new ProductNameComparer());
foreach (Product product in products)
{
    Console.WriteLine(product);
}
```

The code for the comparer in listing 1.5 is simpler because we're given products to start with. No casting necessary. Similarly, the invisible cast in the `foreach` loop is gone. It's hard to tell the difference, given that it's invisible, but it really is gone. Honest. I wouldn't lie to you. At least, not in chapter 1…

That's an improvement, but it would be nice to be able to sort the products by simply specifying the comparison to make, without needing to implement an interface to do so. Listing 1.6 shows how to do precisely this, telling the `Sort` method how to compare two products using a delegate.

Listing 1.6　Sorting a `List<Product>` using `Comparison<Product>` (C# 2)

```
List<Product> products = Product.GetSampleProducts();
products.Sort(delegate(Product first, Product second)
    { return first.Name.CompareTo(second.Name); }
);
```

```
foreach (Product product in products)
{
    Console.WriteLine(product);
}
```

Behold the lack of the `ProductNameComparer` type. The statement in bold actually creates a delegate instance, which we provide to the `Sort` method in order to perform the comparisons. More on that feature (*anonymous methods*) in chapter 5. We've now fixed all the things we didn't like about the C# 1 version. That doesn't mean that C# 3 can't do better, though. First we'll just replace the anonymous method with an even more compact way of creating a delegate instance, as shown in listing 1.7.

Listing 1.7   Sorting using `Comparison<Product>` from a lambda expression (C# 3)

```
List<Product> products = Product.GetSampleProducts();
products.Sort(
    (first, second) => first.Name.CompareTo(second.Name)
);
foreach (Product product in products)
{
    Console.WriteLine(product);
}
```

We've gained even more strange syntax (a *lambda expression*), which still creates a `Comparison<Product>` delegate just the same as listing 1.6 did but this time with less fuss. We haven't had to use the `delegate` keyword to introduce it, or even specify the types of the parameters. There's more, though: with C# 3 we can easily print the names out in order without modifying the original list of products. Listing 1.8 shows this using the `OrderBy` method.

Listing 1.8   Ordering a `List<Product>` using an extension method (C# 3)

```
List<Product> products = Product.GetSampleProducts();

foreach (Product product in products.OrderBy(p => p.Name))
{
    Console.WriteLine (product);
}
```

We appear to be calling an `OrderBy` method, but if you look in MSDN you'll see that it doesn't even exist in `List<Product>`. We're able to call it due to the presence of an *extension method*, which we'll see in more detail in chapter 10. We're not actually sorting the list "in place" anymore, but just retrieving the contents of the list in a particular order. Sometimes you'll need to change the actual list; sometimes an ordering without any other side effects is better. The important point is that it's much more compact and readable (once you understand the syntax, of course). We wanted to order the list by name, and that's exactly what the code says. It doesn't say to sort by comparing the name of one product with the name of another, like the C# 2 code did, or to sort by using an instance of another type that knows how to compare one product with another. It just says to order by name. This simplicity of expression is one of the key benefits of C# 3. When the individual pieces of data querying and manipulation are so simple, larger transformations can still remain compact and readable in one piece of code. That in turn encourages a more "data-centric" way of looking at the world.

We've seen a bit more of the power of C# 2 and 3 in this section, with quite a lot of (as yet) unexplained syntax, but even without understanding the details we can see the progress toward clearer, simpler code. Figure 1.2 shows that evolution.

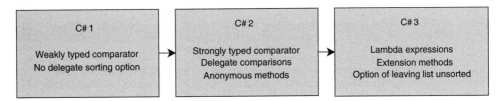

Figure 1.2   Features involved in making sorting easier in C# 2 and 3

That's it for sorting. Let's do a different form of data manipulation now—querying.

1.1.3   Querying collections

Our next task is to find all the elements of the list that match a certain criterion—in particular, those with a price greater than $10. In C# 1, we need to loop around, testing each element and printing it out where appropriate (see listing 1.9).

Listing 1.9   Looping, testing, printing out (C# 1)

```
ArrayList products = Product.GetSampleProducts();
foreach (Product product in products)
{
    if (product.Price > 10m)
    {
        Console.WriteLine(product);
    }
}
```

OK, this is *not* difficult code to understand. However, it's worth bearing in mind how intertwined the three tasks are—looping with `foreach`, testing the criterion with `if`, then displaying the product with `Console.WriteLine`. The dependency is obvious because of the nesting. C# 2 lets us flatten things out a bit (see listing 1.10).

Listing 1.10   Separating testing from printing (C# 2)

```
List<Product> products = Product.GetSampleProducts();
Predicate<Product> test = delegate(Product p)
    { return p.Price > 10m; };
List<Product> matches = products.FindAll(test);

Action<Product> print = delegate(Product p)
    { Console.WriteLine(p); };
matches.ForEach(print);
```

I'm not going to claim this code is simpler than the C# 1 code—but it *is* a lot more powerful.[1] In particular, it makes it *very* easy to change the condition we're testing for and the action we take on each of the matches independently. The delegate variables involved (test and print) could be passed into a method—that same method could end up testing radically different conditions and taking radically different actions. Of course, we could have put all the testing and printing into one statement, as shown in listing 1.11.

Listing 1.11   Separating testing from printing redux (C# 2)

```
List<Product> products = Product.GetSampleProducts();
products.FindAll (delegate(Product p) { return p.Price > 10;})
        .ForEach (delegate(Product p) { Console.WriteLine(p); });
```

That's a bit better, but the delegate(Product p) is getting in the way, as are the braces. They're adding noise to the code, which hurts readability. I still prefer the C# 1 version, in the case where we only ever want to use the same test and perform the same action. (It may sound obvious, but it's worth remembering that there's nothing stopping us from using the C# 1 version when using C# 2 or 3. You wouldn't use a bulldozer to plant tulip bulbs, which is the kind of overkill we're using here.) C# 3 improves matters dramatically by removing a lot of the fluff surrounding the actual *logic* of the delegate (see listing 1.12).

Listing 1.12   Testing with a lambda expression (C# 3)

```
List<Product> products = Product.GetSampleProducts();
foreach (Product product in products.Where(p => p.Price > 10))
{
    Console.WriteLine(product);
}
```

The combination of the lambda expression putting the test in just the right place and a well-named method means we can *almost* read the code out loud and understand it without even thinking. We still have the flexibility of C# 2—the argument to Where could come from a variable, and we could use an Action<Product> instead of the hard-coded Console.WriteLine call if we wanted to.

This task has emphasized what we already knew from sorting—anonymous methods make writing a delegate simple, and lambda expressions are even more concise. In both cases, that brevity means that we can include the query or sort operation inside the first part of the foreach loop without losing clarity. Figure 1.3 summarizes the changes we've just seen.

So, now that we've displayed the filtered list, let's consider a change to our initial assumptions about the data. What happens if we don't always know the price for a product? How can we cope with that within our Product class?

---

[1] In some ways, this is cheating. We could have defined appropriate delegates in C# 1 and called them within the loop. The FindAll and ForEach methods in .NET 2.0 just help to encourage you to consider separation of concerns.

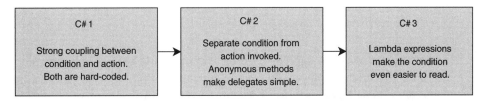

Figure 1.3 Anonymous methods and lambda expressions aid separation of concerns and readability for C# 2 and 3.

1.1.4 Representing an unknown price

I'm not going to present much code this time, but I'm sure it will be a familiar problem to you, especially if you've done a lot of work with databases. Let's imagine our list of products contains not just products on sale right now but ones that aren't available yet. In some cases, we may not know the price. If decimal were a reference type, we could just use null to represent the unknown price—but as it's a value type, we can't. How would you represent this in C# 1? There are three common alternatives:

- Create a reference type wrapper around decimal
- Maintain a separate Boolean flag indicating whether the price is known
- Use a "magic value" (decimal.MinValue, for example) to represent the unknown price

I hope you'll agree that none of these holds much appeal. Time for a little magic: we can solve the problem with the addition of a single extra character in the variable and property declarations. C# 2 makes matters a lot simpler by introducing the Nullable<T> structure and some syntactic sugar for it that lets us change the property declaration to

```
decimal? price;
public decimal? Price
{
    get { return price; }
    private set { price = value; }
}
```

The constructor parameter changes to decimal? as well, and then we can pass in null as the argument, or say Price = null; within the class. That's a lot more expressive than any of the other solutions. The rest of the code just works as is—a product with an unknown price will be considered to be less expensive than $10, which is probably what we'd want. To check whether or not a price is known, we can compare it with null or use the HasValue property—so to show all the products with unknown prices in C# 3, we'd write the code in listing 1.13.

Listing 1.13 Displaying products with an unknown price (C# 2 and 3)

```
List<Product> products = Product.GetSampleProducts();
foreach (Product product in products.Where(p => p.Price==null))
```

```
    {
          Console.WriteLine(product.Name);
    }
```

The C# 2 code would be similar to listing 1.11 but using `return p.Price == null;` as the body for the anonymous method. There's no difference between C# 2 and 3 in terms of nullable types, so figure 1.4 represents the improvements with just two boxes.

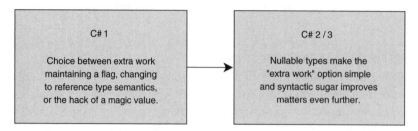

Figure 1.4   The options available for working around the lack of nullable types in C#1, and the benefits of C#2 and 3

So, is that it? Everything we've seen so far is useful and important (particularly generics), but I'm not sure it really counts as *exciting*. There are some cool things you can do with these features occasionally, but for the most part they're "just" making code a bit simpler, more reliable, and more expressive. I value these things immensely, but they rarely impress me enough to call colleagues over to show how much can be done so simply. If you've seen any C# 3 code already, you were probably expecting to see something rather different—namely LINQ. This is where the fireworks start.

1.1.5   *LINQ and query expressions*

LINQ (Language Integrated Query) is what C# 3 is all about at its heart. Whereas the features in C# 2 are arguably more about fixing annoyances in C# 1 than setting the world on fire, C# 3 is rather special. In particular, it contains *query expressions* that allow a declarative style for creating queries on various data sources. The reason none of the examples so far have used them is that they've all actually been simpler *without* using the extra syntax. That's not to say we couldn't use it anyway, of course—listing 1.12, for example, is equivalent to listing 1.14.

Listing 1.14   First steps with query expressions: filtering a collection

```
List<Product> products = Product.GetSampleProducts();
var filtered = from Product p in products
                where p.Price > 10
                select p;
foreach (Product product in filtered)
{
    Console.WriteLine(product);
}
```

Personally, I find the earlier listing easier to read—the only benefit to the query expression version is that the where clause is simpler.

So if query expressions are no good, why is everyone making such a fuss about them, and about LINQ in general? The first answer is that while query expressions are not particularly suitable for simple tasks, they're very, *very* good for more complicated situations that would be hard to read if written out in the equivalent method calls (and fiendish in C# 1 or 2). Let's make things just a little harder by introducing another type—Supplier. I haven't included the whole code here, but complete ready-to-compile code is provided on the book's website (www.csharpindepth.com). We'll concentrate on the fun stuff.

Each supplier has a Name (string) and a SupplierID (int). I've also added SupplierID as a property in Product and adapted the sample data appropriately. Admittedly that's not a very object-oriented way of giving each product a supplier—it's much closer to how the data would be represented in a database. It makes this particular feature easier to demonstrate for now, but we'll see in chapter 12 that LINQ allows us to use a more natural model too.

Now let's look at the code (listing 1.15) to join the sample products with the sample suppliers (obviously based on the supplier ID), apply the same price filter as before to the products, sort by supplier name and then product name, and print out the name of both supplier and product for each match. That was a mouthful (finger-ful?) to type, and in earlier versions of C# it would have been a nightmare to implement. In LINQ, it's almost trivial.

Listing 1.15 Joining, filtering, ordering, and projecting

```
List<Product> products = Product.GetSampleProducts();
List<Supplier> suppliers = Supplier.GetSampleSuppliers();
var filtered = from p in products
               join s in suppliers
               on p.SupplierID equals s.SupplierID
               where p.Price > 10
               orderby s.Name, p.Name
               select new {SupplierName=s.Name,
                           ProductName=p.Name};
foreach (var v in filtered)
{
    Console.WriteLine("Supplier={0}; Product={1}",
                v.SupplierName, v.ProductName);
}
```

The more astute among you will have noticed that it looks remarkably like SQL.[2] Indeed, the reaction of many people on first hearing about LINQ (but before examining it closely) is to reject it as merely trying to put SQL into the language for the sake of talking to databases. Fortunately, LINQ has borrowed the syntax and some ideas from SQL, but as we've seen, you needn't be anywhere near a database in order to use

---

[2] If you've ever worked with SQL in any form whatsoever but *didn't* notice the resemblance, I'm shocked.

it—none of the code we've run so far has touched a database at all. Indeed, we could be getting data from any number of sources: XML, for example. Suppose that instead of hard-coding our suppliers and products, we'd used the following XML file:

```xml
<?xml version="1.0"?>
<Data>
  <Products>
    <Product Name="Company" Price="9.99" SupplierID="1" />
    <Product Name="Assassins" Price="14.99" SupplierID="2" />
    <Product Name="Frogs" Price="13.99" SupplierID="1" />
    <Product Name="Sweeney Todd" Price="10.99" SupplierID="3" />
  </Products>

  <Suppliers>
    <Supplier Name="Solely Sondheim" SupplierID="1" />
    <Supplier Name="CD-by-CD-by-Sondheim" SupplierID="2" />
    <Supplier Name="Barbershop CDs" SupplierID="3" />
  </Suppliers>
</Data>
```

Well, the file is simple enough, but what's the best way of extracting the data from it? How do we query it? Join on it? Surely it's going to be somewhat harder than listing 1.14, right? Listing 1.16 shows how much work we have to do in LINQ to XML.

Listing 1.16   Complex processing of an XML file with LINQ to XML

```csharp
XDocument doc = XDocument.Load("data.xml");
var filtered = from p in doc.Descendants("Product")
               join s in doc.Descendants("Supplier")
               on (int)p.Attribute("SupplierID")
                  equals (int)s.Attribute("SupplierID")
               where (decimal)p.Attribute("Price") > 10
               orderby (string)s.Attribute("Name"),
                       (string)p.Attribute("Name")
               select new
               {
                   SupplierName = (string)s.Attribute("Name"),
                   ProductName = (string)p.Attribute("Name")
               };
foreach (var v in filtered)
{
    Console.WriteLine("Supplier={0}; Product={1}",
                      v.SupplierName, v.ProductName);
}
```

Well, it's not quite as straightforward, because we need to tell the system how it should understand the data (in terms of what attributes should be used as what types)—but it's not far off. In particular, there's an obvious relationship between each part of the two listings. If it weren't for the line length limitations of books, you'd see an exact line-by-line correspondence between the two queries.

Impressed yet? Not quite convinced? Let's put the data where it's much more likely to be—in a database. There's some work (much of which can be automated) to let

LINQ to SQL know about what to expect in what table, but it's all fairly straightforward. Listing 1.17 shows the querying code.

Listing 1.17   Applying a query expression to a SQL database

```
using (LinqDemoDataContext db = new LinqDemoDataContext())
{
    var filtered = from p in db.Products
                   join s in db.Suppliers
                   on p.SupplierID equals s.SupplierID
                   where p.Price > 10
                   orderby s.Name, p.Name
                   select new
                   {
                       SupplierName = s.Name,
                       ProductName = p.Name
                   };
    foreach (var v in filtered)
    {
        Console.WriteLine("Supplier={0}; Product={1}",
                          v.SupplierName, v.ProductName);
    }
}
```

Query is written in C#, but executes as SQL

By now, this should be looking incredibly familiar. Everything below the "join" line is cut and pasted directly from listing 1.14 with no changes. That's impressive enough, but if you're performance conscious you may be wondering why we would want to pull down all the data from the database and then apply these .NET queries and orderings. Why not get the database to do it? That's what it's good at, isn't it? Well, indeed—and that's exactly what LINQ to SQL does. The code in listing 1.17 issues a database request, which is basically the query translated into SQL. Even though we've *expressed* the query in C# code, it's been *executed* as SQL.

We'll see later that the way this query joins isn't how we'd normally use LINQ to SQL—there's a more relation-oriented way of approaching it when the schema and the entities know about the relationship between suppliers and products. The result is the same, however, and it shows just how similar LINQ to Objects (the in-memory LINQ operating on collections) and LINQ to SQL can be.

It's important to understand that LINQ is flexible, too: you can write your own query translators. It's not easy, but it can be well worth it. For instance, here's an example using Amazon's web service to query its available books:

```
var query =
  from book in new LinqToAmazon.AmazonBookSearch()
  where
    book.Title.Contains("ajax") &&
    (book.Publisher == "Manning") &&
    (book.Price <= 25) &&
    (book.Condition == BookCondition.New)
  select book;
```

This example was taken from the introduction[3] to "LINQ to Amazon," which is a LINQ provider written as an example for the *LINQ in Action* book (Manning, 2008). The query is easy to understand, and written in what appears to be "normal" C# 3—but the provider is translating it into a web service call. How cool is that?

Hopefully by now your jaw is suitably close to the floor—mine certainly was the first time I tried an exercise like the database one we've just seen, when it worked pretty much the first time. Now that we've seen a little bit of the evolution of the C# language, it's worth taking a little history lesson to see how other products and technologies have progressed in the same time frame.

1.2   *A brief history of C# (and related technologies)*

When I was learning French and German at school, the teachers always told me that I would never be proficient in those languages until I started *thinking* in them. Unfortunately I never achieved that goal, but I *do* think in C# (and a few other languages).[4] There are people who are quite capable of programming reasonably reliably in a computer language without ever getting *comfortable* (or even intimate) with it. They will always write their code with an accent, usually one reminiscent of whatever language they *are* comfortable in.

While you can learn the mechanics of C# without knowing anything about the context in which it was designed, you'll have a closer relationship with it if you understand why it looks the way it does—its ancestry, effectively. The technological landscape and its evolution have a significant impact on how both languages and libraries evolve, so let's take a brief walk through C#'s history, seeing how it fits in with the stories of other technologies, both those from Microsoft and those developed elsewhere. This is by no means a comprehensive history of computing at the end of the twentieth century and the start of the twenty-first—any attempt at such a history would take a whole (large) book in itself. However, I've included the products and technologies that I believe have most strongly influenced .NET and C# in particular.

1.2.1   *The world before C#*

We're actually going to start with Java. Although it would be a stretch to claim that C# and .NET definitely wouldn't have come into being without Java, it would also be hard to argue that it had no effect. Java 1.0 was released in January 1996 and the world went applet mad. Briefly. Java was very slow (at the time it was 100 percent interpreted) and most of the applets on the Web were fairly useless. The speed gradually improved as just-in-time compilers (JITs) were introduced, and developers started looking at using Java on the server side instead of on the client. Java 1.2 (or Java 2, depending on whether you talk developer version numbers or marketing version numbers) overhauled the core libraries significantly, the servlet API and JavaServer Pages took off, and Sun's Hotspot engine boosted the performance significantly.

---

[3]   http://linqinaction.net/blogs/main/archive/2006/06/26/Introducing-Linq-to-Amazon.aspx
[4]   Not all the time, I hasten to add. Only when I'm coding.

Java is reasonably portable, despite the "write once, debug everywhere" skit on Sun's catchphrase of "write once, run anywhere." The idea of letting coders develop enterprise Java applications on Windows with friendly IDEs and then deploy (without even recompiling) to powerful Unix servers was a compelling proposition—and clearly something of a threat to Microsoft.

Microsoft created their own Java Virtual Machine (JVM), which had reasonable performance and a *very* fast startup time, and even released an IDE for it, named J++. However, they introduced incompatible extensions into their platform, and Sun sued Microsoft for violating licensing terms, starting a *very* long (and frankly tedious) legal battle. The main impact of this legal battle was felt long before the case was concluded—while the rest of the world moved on to Java 1.2 and beyond, Microsoft's version of Java stayed at 1.1, which made it effectively obsolete pretty rapidly. It was clear that whatever Microsoft's vision of the future was, Java itself was unlikely to be a major part of it.

In the same period, Microsoft's Active Server Pages (ASP) gained popularity too. After an initial launch in December 1996, two further versions were released in 1997 and 2000. ASP made dynamic web development much simpler for developers on Microsoft servers, and eventually third parties ported it to non-Windows platforms. Despite being a great step forward in the Windows world, ASP didn't tend to promote the separation of presentation logic, business logic, and data persistence, which most of the vast array of Java web frameworks encouraged.

1.2.2   *C# and .NET are born*

C# and .NET were properly unveiled at the Professional Developers Conference (PDC) in July 2000, although some elements had been preannounced before then, and there had been talk about the same technologies under different names (including COOL, COM3, and Lightning) for a long time. Not that Microsoft hadn't been busy with other things, of course—that year also saw both Windows Me and Windows 2000 being released, with the latter being wildly successful compared with the former.

Microsoft didn't "go it alone" with C# and .NET, and indeed when the specifications for C# and the Common Language Infrastructure (CLI) were submitted to ECMA (an international standards body), they were co-sponsored by Hewlett-Packard and Intel along with Microsoft. ECMA ratified the specification (with some modifications), and later versions of C# and the CLI have gone through the same process. C# and Java are "open" in different ways, with Microsoft favoring the standardization path and Sun gradually open sourcing Java and allowing or even encouraging other Java runtime environments. There are alternative CLI and C# implementations, the most visible being the Mono project,[5] but they don't generally implement the whole of what we think of as the .NET Framework. Commercial reliance on and support

---

[5] http://www.mono-project.com

of non-Microsoft implementations is small, outside of Novell, which sponsors the Mono project.

Although C# and .NET weren't released until 2002 (along with Visual Studio .NET 2002), betas were available long before then, and by the time everything was official, C# was already a popular language. ASP.NET was launched as part of .NET 1.0, and it was clear that Microsoft had no plans to do anything more with either "ASP Classic" or "VB Classic"—much to the annoyance of many VB6 developers. While VB.NET *looks* similar to VB6, there are enough differences to make the transition a nontrivial one—not least of which is learning the .NET Framework. Many developers have decided to go straight from VB6 to C#, for various reasons.

1.2.3   *Minor updates with .NET 1.1 and the first major step: .NET 2.0*

As is often the case, the 1.0 release was fairly quickly followed by .NET 1.1, which launched with Visual Studio .NET 2003 and included C# 1.2. There were few significant changes to either the language or the framework libraries—in a sense, it was more of a service pack than a truly new release. Despite the small number of changes, it's rare to see anyone using .NET 1.0 at the time of this writing, although 1.1 is still very much alive and kicking, partly due to the OS requirements of 2.0.

Imitation is the sincerest form of flattery

While Microsoft was busy bringing its new platform to the world, Sun (and its other significant partners, including IBM) hadn't left Java stagnating. Not quite, anyway. Java 1.5 (Java 5 for the marketing folk among you) was launched in September 2004, with easily the largest set of language enhancements in any Java release, including generics, enums (supported in a very cool way—far more object-oriented than the "named numbers" that C# provides), an enhanced for loop (foreach to you and me), annotations (read: attributes), "varargs" (broadly equivalent to parameter arrays of C#—the params modifier), and automatic boxing/unboxing. It would be foolish to suggest that all of these enhancements were due to C# having taken off (after all, putting generics into the language had been talked about since 1997), but it's also worth acknowledging the competition for the mindshare of developers. For Sun, Microsoft, and other players, it's not just about coming up with a great language: it's about persuading developers to write software for their platform.

C# and Java have both been cautious when it comes to introducing powerful features such as templates and macros from C++. Every new feature has to earn its place in the language in terms of not just power, but also ease of use and readability—and sometimes that can take time. For example, both Java and C# shipped without anything like C++ templates to start with, and then worked out ways of providing much of their value with as few risks and drawbacks as possible. We'll see in chapter 3 that although Java and C# generics look quite similar on the most superficial level, they differ significantly under the surface.

NOTE *The pioneering role of Microsoft Research*—Microsoft Research is responsible for some of the new directions for .NET and C#. They published a paper on .NET generics as early as May 2001 (yes, even before .NET 1.0 had been released!) and worked on an extension called Cω (pronounced C omega), which included—among other things—some of the ideas which later formed LINQ. Another C# extension, Spec#, adds contracts to C#, allowing the compiler to do more verification automatically.[6] We will have to wait and see whether any or all of the ideas of Spec# eventually become part of C# itself.

C# 2 was released in November 2005, as part of .NET 2.0 and alongside Visual Studio 2005 and VB8. Visual Studio became more productive to work with as an IDE—particularly now that refactoring was finally included—and the significant improvements to both the language and the platform were warmly welcomed by most developers.

As a sign of just how quickly the world is moving on—and of how long it takes to actually bring a product to market—it's worth noting that the first announcements about C# 3 were made at the PDC in September 2005, which was two months *before* C# 2 was released. The sad part is that while it seems to take two years to bring a product from announcement to market, it appears that the industry takes another year or two—at least—to start widely embracing it. As mentioned earlier, many companies are only now transitioning from .NET 1.1 to 2.0. We can only hope that it will be a shorter path to widespread adoption of .NET 3.0 and 3.5. (C# 3 comes with .NET 3.5, although you can use many C# 3 features while still targeting .NET 2.0. I'll talk about the version numbers shortly.)

One of the reasons .NET 2.0 took so long to come out is that it was being embedded within SQL Server 2005, with the obvious robustness and reliability concerns that go hand in hand with such a system. This allows .NET code to execute right inside the database, with potential for much richer logic to sit so close to the data. Database folk tend to be rather cautious, and only time will tell how widely this ability is used—but it's a powerful tool to have available if you find you need it.

1.2.4 *"Next generation" products*

In November 2006 (a year after .NET 2.0 was released), Microsoft launched Windows Vista, Office 2007, and Exchange Server 2007. This included launching .NET 3.0, which comes preinstalled on Vista. Over time, this is likely to aid adoption of .NET client applications for two reasons. First, the old ".NET isn't installed on all computers" objection will become less relevant—you can safely assume that if the user is running Vista, they'll be able to run a .NET application. Second, Windows Presentation Foundation (WPF) is now the rich client platform of choice for developers in Microsoft's view—and it's only available from .NET.

---

[6] http://research.microsoft.com/specsharp/

Again, while Microsoft was busy with Vista and other products, the rest of the world was innovating too. Lightweight frameworks have been gaining momentum, and Object Relational Mapping (ORM) now has a significant developer mindshare, partly due to high-quality free frameworks such as Hibernate. The SQL aspect of LINQ is much more than just the querying side we've seen so far, and marks a more definite step from Microsoft than its previous lukewarm ventures into this area, such as ObjectSpaces. Only time will tell whether LINQ to SQL or perhaps its cousin the ADO.NET Entity Framework hits the elusive sweet spot of making database access truly simple—they're certainly very promising.

Visual Studio 2008 was released in November 2007, including .NET 3.5, C# 3, and VB9. It contains built-in support for many features that were previously only available as extensions to Visual Studio 2005, as well as the new language and framework features. Continuing the trend from Visual Studio 2005, a free Express edition is available for each language. With the ability to target multiple versions of the .NET Framework and only minimal solution and project changes when migrating existing code, there is little reason *not* to upgrade to Visual Studio 2008—I expect its adoption rate to be far faster than that of Visual Studio 2005.

Dynamic languages have become increasingly important, with many options vying for developers' attention. Ruby—and particularly the Ruby on Rails framework—has had a large impact (with ports for Java and .NET), and other projects such as Groovy on the Java platform and IronRuby and IronPython on .NET are gaining support. As part of Silverlight 2.0, Microsoft will release the Dynamic Language Runtime (DLR), which is a layer on top of the CLR to make it more amenable to dynamic languages. Silverlight is part of another battleground, but this time for rich Internet applications (RIAs), where Microsoft is competing with Adobe Flex and Sun's JavaFX. Silverlight 1.0 was released in September 2007, but this version was based on JavaScript. At the time of this writing, many developers are currently awaiting 1.1, which will ship with a "mini-CLR" and cater for multiple platforms.

1.2.5 *Historical perspective and the fight for developer support*

It's hard to describe all of these strands interweaving through history and yet keep a bird's-eye view of the period. Figure 1.5 shows a collection of timelines with some of the major milestones described earlier, within different technological areas. The list is not comprehensive, of course, but it gives some indication of which product versions were competing at different times.

There are many ways to look at technological histories, and many untold stories influencing events behind the scenes. It's possible that this retrospective overemphasizes the influence of Java on the development of .NET and C#, and that may well partly be due to my mixed allegiances to both technologies. However, it seems to me that the large wars for developer support are taking place among the following camps.

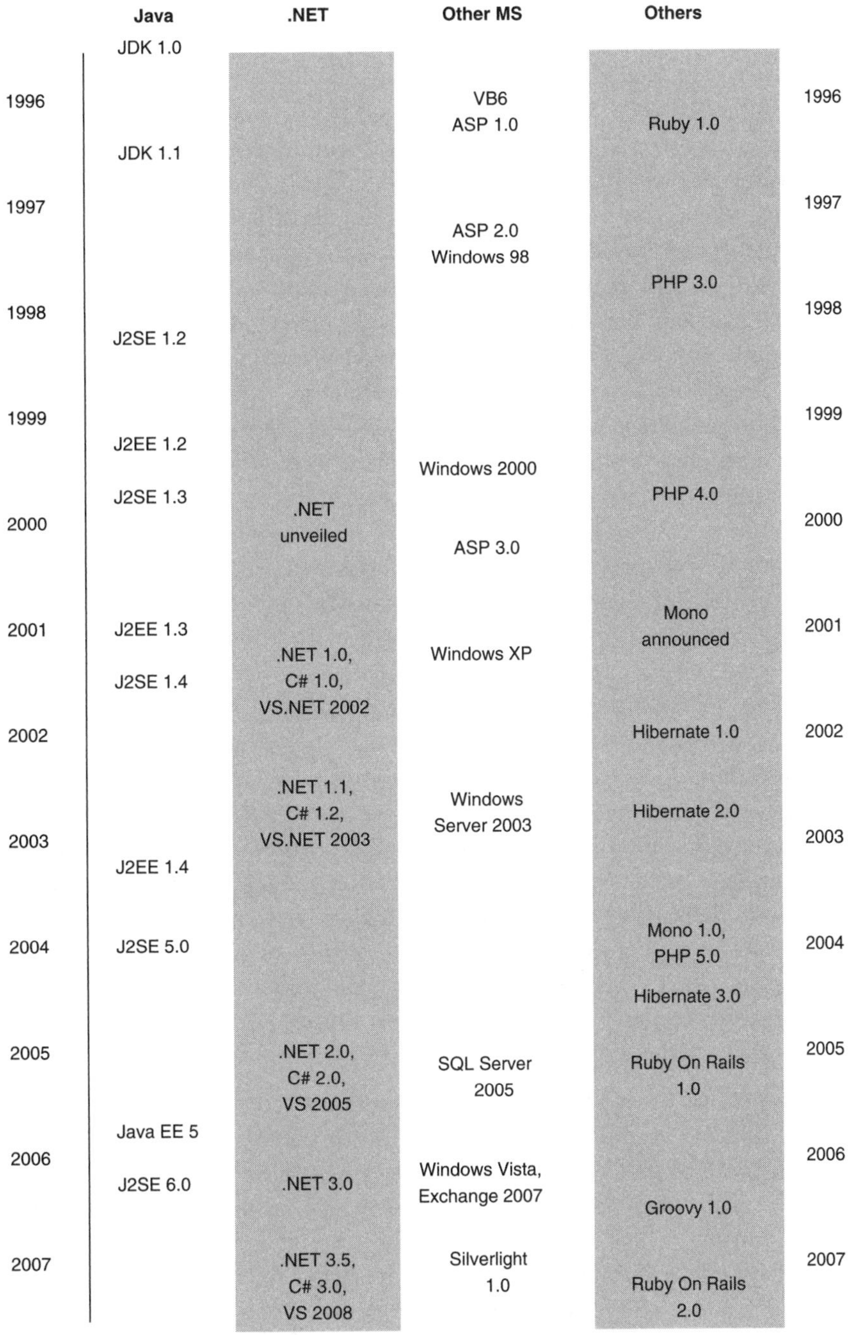

Year	Java	.NET	Other MS	Others	Year
	JDK 1.0				
1996			VB6 ASP 1.0	Ruby 1.0	1996
	JDK 1.1				
1997			ASP 2.0 Windows 98		1997
1998	J2SE 1.2			PHP 3.0	1998
1999	J2EE 1.2		Windows 2000		1999
2000	J2SE 1.3	.NET unveiled	ASP 3.0	PHP 4.0	2000
2001	J2EE 1.3 J2SE 1.4	.NET 1.0, C# 1.0, VS.NET 2002	Windows XP	Mono announced	2001
2002				Hibernate 1.0	2002
2003	J2EE 1.4	.NET 1.1, C# 1.2, VS.NET 2003	Windows Server 2003	Hibernate 2.0	2003
2004	J2SE 5.0			Mono 1.0, PHP 5.0 Hibernate 3.0	2004
2005		.NET 2.0, C# 2.0, VS 2005	SQL Server 2005	Ruby On Rails 1.0	2005
2006	Java EE 5 J2SE 6.0	.NET 3.0	Windows Vista, Exchange 2007	Groovy 1.0	2006
2007		.NET 3.5, C# 3.0, VS 2008	Silverlight 1.0	Ruby On Rails 2.0	2007

Figure 1.5 Timeline of releases for C#, .NET, and related technologies

- Native code (primarily C and C++) developers, who will have to be convinced about the reliability and performance of managed code before changing their habits. C++/CLI is the obvious way of dipping a toe in the water here, but its popularity may not be all that Microsoft had hoped for.

- VB6 developers who may have antipathy toward Microsoft for abandoning their preferred platform, but will need to decide which way to jump sooner or later—and .NET is the most obvious choice for most people at this stage. Some may cross straight to C#, with others making the smaller move to VB.NET.

- Scripting and dynamic language developers who value the immediacy of changes. Familiar languages running on managed platforms can act as Trojan horses here, encouraging developers to learn the associated frameworks for use in their dynamic code, which then lowers the barrier to entry for learning the traditional object-oriented languages for the relevant platform. The IronPython programmer of today may well become the C# programmer of tomorrow.

- "Traditional" managed developers, primarily writing C#, VB.NET, or Java. Here the war is not about whether or not running under some sort of managed environment is a good thing, but *which* managed environment to use. The battle-grounds are primarily in tools, portability, performance, and libraries, all of which have come on in leaps and bounds. Competition between different .NET languages is partly internal to Microsoft, with each team wanting its own language to have the best support—and features developed primarily for one language can often be used by another in the fullness of time.

- Web developers who have already had to move from static HTML, to dynamically generated content, to a nicer user experience with Ajax. Now the age of RIAs is upon us, with three very significant contenders in Microsoft, Adobe, and Sun. At the time of this writing, it's too early to tell whether there will be a clear winner here or whether the three can all garner enough support to make them viable for a long time to come. Although it's possible to use a .NET-based RIA solution with a Java-based server to some extent, the development process is significantly easier when technologies are aligned, so capturing the market here is important for all parties.

One thing is clear from all of this—it's a good time to be a developer. Companies are investing a lot of time and money in making software development a fun and profitable industry to be in. Given the changes we've seen over the last decade or so, it's difficult to predict what programming will look like in another decade, but it'll be a fantastic journey getting there.

   I mentioned earlier that C# 3 is effectively part of .NET 3.5. It's worth taking a bit of time to look at the different aspects that together make up .NET.

1.3   *The .NET platform*

When it was originally introduced, ".NET" was used as a catchall term for a vast range of technologies coming from Microsoft. For instance, Windows Live ID was called

.NET Passport despite there being no clear relationship between that and what we currently know as .NET. Fortunately things have calmed down somewhat since then. In this section we'll look at the various parts of .NET (at least the ones we're interested in) and how they have been separately versioned.

1.3.1 Distinguishing between language, runtime, and libraries

In several places in this book, I'll refer to three different kinds of features: features of C# as a *language,* features of the *runtime* that provides the "engine" if you will, and features of the .NET *framework libraries.* In particular, this book is heavily focused on the language of C#, only explaining runtime and framework features when they relate to features of C# itself. This only makes sense if there is a clear distinction between the three. Often features will overlap, but it's important to understand the principle of the matter.

LANGUAGE

The language of C# is defined by its specification, which describes the format of C# source code, including both syntax and behavior. It does *not* describe the platform that the compiler output will run on, beyond a few key points at which the two interact. For instance, the C# language requires a type called System.IDisposable, which contains a method called Dispose. These are required in order to define the using statement. Likewise, the platform needs to be able to support (in one form or other) both value types and reference types, along with garbage collection.

In theory, any platform that supports the required features could have a C# compiler targeting it. For example, a C# compiler could legitimately produce output in a form other than the Intermediate Language (IL), which is the typical output at the time of this writing. A runtime could legitimately interpret the output of a C# compiler rather than JIT-compiling it. In practice, although interpreting IL is possible (and indeed supported by Mono), we are unlikely to see widespread use of C# on platforms that are very different from .NET.

RUNTIME

The runtime aspect of the .NET platform is the relatively small amount of code that is responsible for making sure that programs written in IL execute according to the CLI specification, partitions I to III. The runtime part of the CLI is called the Common Language Runtime (CLR). When I refer to *the CLR* in the rest of the book, I mean Microsoft's implementation.

Some elements of language never appear at the runtime level, but others cross the divide. For instance, enumerators aren't defined at a runtime level, and neither is any particular meaning attached to the IDisposable interface—but arrays and delegates are important to the runtime.

FRAMEWORK LIBRARIES

Libraries provide code that is available to our programs. The framework libraries in .NET are largely built as IL themselves, with native code used only where necessary. This is a mark of the strength of the runtime: your own code isn't expected to be a second-class citizen—it can provide the same kind of power and performance as the libraries it utilizes. The amount of code in the library is much larger than that of the runtime, in the same way that there's much more to a car than the engine.

The .NET libraries are partially standardized. Partition IV of the CLI specification provides a number of different profiles (*compact* and *kernel*) and libraries. Partition IV comes in two parts—a general textual description of the libraries, including which libraries are required within which profiles, and another part containing the details of the libraries themselves in XML format. This is the same form of documentation produced when you use XML comments within C#.

There is much within .NET that is *not* within the base libraries. If you write a program that *only* uses libraries from the specification, and only uses them correctly, you should find your code works flawlessly on any implementation—Mono, .NET, or anything else. In practice, almost any program of any size will use libraries that aren't standardized—Windows Forms or ASP.NET, for instance. The Mono project has its own libraries that are not part of .NET as well, of course, such as GTK#, in addition to implementing many of the nonstandardized libraries.

The term *.NET* refers to the combination of the runtime and libraries provided by Microsoft, and it also includes compilers for C# and VB.NET. It can be seen as a whole *development platform* built on top of Windows.

Now that we know what term means what, we can look at different versions available of each. The subject of the version numbers chosen by Microsoft and what's in which version is a slightly convoluted one, but it's important that we all agree on what we mean when we talk about a particular version.

1.3.2   *Untangling version number chaos*

A newcomer to the industry might think that coming up with version numbers would be easy. You start with 1, then move on to 2, then 3 in a logical progression, right? If only that were the case... Software products and projects of all natures like to keep minor version changes distinct from major ones, and then there are patch levels, service packs, build numbers, and so forth. In addition, there are the *codenames*, which are widely used and then abandoned, much to the frustration of "bleeding edge" book authors and publishers. Fortunately from the point of view of C# *as a language* we can make life reasonably straightforward.

NOTE   *Keeping it simple: C# 1, C# 2, and C# 3*—Throughout this book, I'll refer to C# versions as just 1, 2, and 3. There's little point in distinguishing between the two 1.*x* versions, and no point in adding a cumbersome extra ".0" every time I refer to the different versions—which of course I'll be doing quite a lot.

We don't just need to keep track of the language, unfortunately. There are five things we're interested in, when it comes to versioning.

- The .NET Framework
- Framework libraries
- The CLR

- C# (the version of the compiler that comes with the framework)
- Visual Studio—version number and codename

Just for kicks, we'll throw in the Visual Basic numbering and naming too. (Visual Studio is abbreviated to VS and Visual Basic is abbreviated to VB for reasons of space.) Table 1.1 shows the different version numbers.

Table 1.1 Cross-reference table for versions of different products and technologies

.NET	Framework libraries (max)	CLR	C#	Visual Studio	Visual Basic
1.0	1.0	1.0	1.0	VS .NET 2002 (no codename)	VB.NET 7.0
1.1	1.1	1.1	1.2[a]	VS .NET 2003 (Everett)	VB.NET 7.1
2.0	2.0	2.0	2.0	VS 2005 (Whidbey)	VB 8.0
3.0	3.0	2.0	2.0	VS 2005 (extension previews), VS 2008 (full support)	VB 8.0
3.5	3.5	2.0	3.0	VS 2008 (Orcas)	VB 9.0

a. I've no idea why this isn't 1.1. I only discovered that it was 1.2 while researching this book. That's the numbering according to Microsoft's version of the specification, at least. I decided not to confuse matters further by also including the ECMA-334 edition number here, although that's another story in its own right.

Note how both Visual Studio and Visual Basic lost the ".NET" moniker between 2003 and 2005, indicating Microsoft's emphasis on this being *the* tool for Windows development, as far as they're concerned.

As you can see, so far the version of the overall framework has followed the libraries exactly. However, it would be possible for a new version of the CLR with more capabilities to still be released with the existing libraries, so we could (for instance) have .NET 4.0 with libraries from 3.5, a CLR 3.0, and a C# 3 compiler. Let's hope it doesn't come to that. As it is, Microsoft has already confounded developers somewhat with the last two lines of the table.

.NET 3.0 is really just the addition of four libraries: Windows Presentation Foundation (WPF), Windows Communication Foundation (WCF), Windows Workflow Foundation (WF[7]), and Windows CardSpace. None of the existing library classes were changed, and neither was the CLR, nor any of the languages targeting the CLR, so creating a whole new major version number for this feels a bit over the top.

Next comes .NET 3.5. This time, along with completely new classes (notably LINQ) there are many enhancements to the *base class libraries* (BCL—types within the namespaces such as System, System.IO; the core of the framework libraries). There's a new version of C#, without which this book would be considerably shorter, and a new version of Visual Studio to support that and VB 9.0. Apparently all of that isn't worth a major version number change, though. There are service packs for both .NET 2.0 and 3.0, and

---

[7] Not WWF due to wrestling and wildlife conflicts.

both service packs ship with Visual Studio 2008—so while you can target .NET 2.0 and 3.0 with the latest and greatest IDE (as well as 3.5, of course) you should be aware that what you'll *really* be compiling and running against is 2.0SP1, 3.0SP1 or 3.5.

OK, rant over. It's only version numbers, after all—but it *is* important to understand what each version means, if for no other reason than communication. If someone says they're using "3.0" you need to check whether they mean C# 3 or .NET 3.0.

If all this talk of history and versioning is making you want to get back onto the familiar ground of actual programming, don't worry—we're nearly there. Indeed, if you fancy writing some code right now, the next section invites you to do just that, as I introduce the style I'll be using for most of the examples in this book.

1.4   *Fully functional code in snippet form*

One of the challenges when writing a book about a computer language (other than scripting languages) is that complete programs—ones that the reader can compile and run with no source code other than what's presented—get pretty long pretty quickly. I wanted to get around this, to provide you with code that you could easily type in and experiment with: I believe that actually *trying* something is a much better way of learning about it than just reading.

The solution I've come up with isn't applicable to all situations, but it will serve us well for most of the example code. It would be awful to use for "real" development, but it's specifically tailored to the context we're working in: presenting and playing with code that can be compiled and run with the minimal amount of fuss. That's not to say you should only use it for experimentation when reading this book—I've found it useful as a general way of testing the behavior of small pieces of code.

1.4.1   *Snippets and their expansions*

With the right assembly references and the right `using` directives, you can accomplish quite a lot in a fairly short amount of C# code—but the killer is the fluff involved in writing those `using` directives, then declaring a class, then declaring a `Main` method before you've even written the first line of *useful* code. My examples are mostly in the form of *snippets*, which ignore the fluff that gets in the way of simple programs, concentrating on the important part. So, for example, suppose I presented the snippet in listing 1.18.

Listing 1.18   The first snippet, which simply displays two words on separate lines

```
foreach (string x in new string[] {"Hello", "There"})
{
    Console.WriteLine (x);
}
```

This code clearly won't compile on its own—there's no class declaration, for a start. The code from listing 1.18 corresponds to the full program shown in listing 1.19.

Listing 1.19   Expanded form of listing 1.18, creating a complete program

```
using System;
public class Snippet
```

```
    {
        [STAThread]
        static void Main(string[] args)
        {
            foreach (string x in new string[] {"Hello", "There"})
            {
                Console.WriteLine (x);
            }
        }
    }
```

Occasionally extra methods or even types are required, with a bit of code in the Main method to access them. I indicate this by listing the non-Main code, then an ellipsis (...) and then the Main code. So the code in listing 1.20 would turn into listing 1.21.

Listing 1.20 A code snippet with an extra method, called within the Main method

```
static string[] GetGreetingWords()
{
    return new string[] {"Hello", "There"};
}

...

foreach (string x in GetGreetingWords())
{
    Console.WriteLine (x);
}
```

Listing 1.21 Expanded form of listing 1.20

```
using System;
public class Snippet
{
    static string[] GetGreetingWords()
    {
        return new string[] {"Hello", "There"};
    }

    [STAThread]
    static void Main(string[] args)
    {
        foreach (string x in GetGreetingWords())
        {
            Console.WriteLine (x);
        }
    }
}
```

Types declared in snippets will be nested within the Snippet class, but that's very rarely a problem.

Now that we understand what snippets are and what they look like when they're expanded, let's make them a bit more user friendly.

1.4.2   *Introducing Snippy*

Just knowing what the code would look like isn't terribly helpful, so I've written a small tool that you can download from the book's website. It's written in WPF, so you'll need to have .NET 3.0 or higher installed in order to run it. Figure 1.6 shows a screenshot of it in action.

It's not a visual masterpiece, but it does the job. You can edit the code, compile it, and run it. There are different options available to use different using directives and references depending on which part of the book you are looking at, although the choice of ".NET 3.5" will compile anything that doesn't require extra custom references. Snippy doesn't try to work out which using directives are actually *required* by the code, so the full code is rather longer than the examples in the previous section, but having extra using directives is harmless.

Aside from the WPF requirement to run Snippy, everything in the C# 2 section of the book compiles and runs with only .NET 2.0 installed, and all the snippets compile and run with .NET 3.5 installed. There's a single button to compile and run, as you're unlikely to want to do anything after a successful compilation other than running the code.

As I mentioned earlier, not all examples work this way—the examples in this chapter, for instance, all require the Product type, which isn't included in every snippet. From this point on, however, I will give fair warning whenever a listing *isn't* a snippet—so unless you hear otherwise, you should be able to type it in and play around with it.

Of course, if you don't like manually typing in code from books, you can download all of the code from the book's website, including extra examples that don't appear directly in the text. All the code works in the Express editions of Visual C# 2005 and 2008, although of course the examples that are specific to C# 3 don't run in Visual C# 2005.[8]

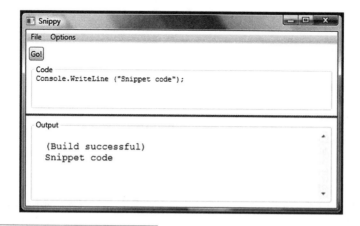

Figure 1.6   Snippy in action. The code in the top area is converted into a full program, then run. Its output is shown in the bottom area.

---

[8] Some of them may run in Visual Studio 2005 with the C# 3 extension Community Technology Preview (CTP) installed, but I make no guarantees. The language has changed in a few ways since the final CTP was released, and I haven't tested any of the code in this environment. Visual C# 2008 Express is free, though, so why not give it a try?

1.5   *Summary*

In this chapter, I've shown (but not explained) some of the features that are tackled in depth in the rest of the book. There are plenty more that haven't been shown here, and all the features we've seen so far have further "subfeatures" associated with them. Hopefully what you've seen here has whetted your appetite for the rest of the book.

After looking through some actual code, we took a step back to consider the history of C# and the .NET Framework. No technology is developed in a vacuum, and when it's commercial (whether or not it directly comes with a price tag) you can guarantee that the funding body sees a business opportunity in that development. I've not been through Microsoft's internal company memos, nor have I interviewed Bill Gates, but I've given my view on the reasons Microsoft has invested so much in .NET, and what the rest of the world has been doing in the same period. By talking *around* the language, I hope I've made you more comfortable *in* the language, and what it's trying to achieve.

We then performed a little detour by way of version numbers. This was mainly to make sure that you'll understand what I mean when I refer to particular .NET and C# version numbers (and how different those two can be!), but it might also help when talking with other people who may not have quite as clear a grasp on the matter as you now do. It's important to be able to get to the bottom of what people actually mean when they talk about a particular version, and with the information in this chapter you should be able to ask appropriate questions to get an accurate picture. This could be particularly useful if you ever talk to other developers in a support role—establishing the operating environment is always critical.

Finally, I described how code will be presented in this book, and introduced Snippy, the application you can use to run the code quickly if you don't want to download the full set of complete samples from the book's website. This system of code snippets is designed to pack the book with the really *interesting* parts of code samples—the bits that demonstrate the language features I'll be explaining—without removing the possibility of actually *running* the code yourself.

There's one more area we need to cover before we dive into the features of C# 2, and that's C# 1. Obviously as an author I have no idea how knowledgeable you are about C# 1, but I *do* have some understanding of which areas of C# 1 are typically understood fairly vaguely. Some of these areas are critical to getting the most out of C# 2 and 3, so in the next chapter I'll go over them in some detail.

Core foundations:
building on C#1

This is not a refresher on the whole of C# 1. Let's get that out of the way immediately. I couldn't do justice to *any* topic in C# if I had to cover the whole of the first version in a single chapter. I've written this book assuming that all my readers are at least reasonably competent in C# 1. What counts as "reasonably competent" is, of course, a somewhat subjective matter, but I'll assume you would *at least* be happy to walk into an interview for a junior C# developer role and answer technical questions appropriate to that job. My expectation is that many readers will have more experience, but that's the level of knowledge I'm assuming.

In this chapter we're going to focus on three areas of C# 1 that are particularly important for C# 2 and 3. This should raise the "lowest common denominator" a little, so that I can make slightly greater assumptions later on in the book. Given that it *is* a lowest common denominator, you may well find you already have a perfect understanding of all the concepts in this chapter. If you believe that's the case without even reading the chapter, then feel free to skip it. You can always come back later if it turns out something wasn't as simple as you thought. You might want to at least look at the summary at the end of each section, which highlights the important points—if any of those sound unfamiliar, it's worth reading that section in detail.

You may be wondering why I've included this chapter at all, if I've already assumed you know C# 1. Well, my experience is that some of the fundamental aspects of C# tend to be fudged over, both in books and tutorials. As a result, there's a lot of some-what hazy understanding of these concepts among developers—creating a lot of questions (and occasional well-intentioned but ill-informed answers) in the C# newsgroup, for instance.

The misunderstood concepts tend to be about the type system used by C# and .NET, and the details around it. If those concepts weren't important when learning about C# 2 and 3, I wouldn't have included this chapter, but as it happens they're absolutely crucial to the rest of the book. It's hard to come to grips with generics if you don't understand static typing, for instance, or to understand the problem solved by nullable types if the difference between value types and reference types is a bit of a blur. There's no shame in having an incomplete understanding of these concepts—often the details and differences are only important in certain rare situations or when discussing technicalities. Given that, a more thorough understanding of the language in which you're working is always a good thing.

In this chapter we'll be looking at three high-level concepts:

- Delegates
- Type system characteristics
- Value types and reference types

In each case I'll describe the ideas and behavior, as well as take the opportunity to define terms so that I can use them later on. After we've looked at how C# 1 works, I'll show you a quick preview of how many of the new features in C# 2 and 3 relate to the topics examined in this chapter.

2.1   Delegates

I'm sure you already have an instinctive idea about the concept of a delegate, hard as it can be to articulate. If you're familiar with C and had to describe delegates to another C programmer, the term "function pointer" would no doubt crop up. Essentially, delegates provide a way of giving a level of indirection, so that instead of specifying behavior directly, it can be in some way "contained" in an object, which can be used like any other object, where one available option is to execute the encapsulated behavior. Alternatively, you can think of a delegate type as a single-method interface, and a delegate instance as an object implementing that interface.

If that's just a lot of gobbledygook to you, maybe an example will help. It's slightly morbid, but it does capture what delegates are all about. Consider your will—that is, your last will and testament. It is a set of instructions—"pay the bills, make a donation to charity, leave the rest of my estate to the cat," for instance. You write it *before* your death, and leave it in an appropriately safe place. *After* your death, your attorney will (you hope!) act on those instructions.

A delegate in C# acts like your will does in the real world—as a sequence of actions to be executed at the appropriate time. Delegates are typically used when the code that wants to execute the actions doesn't know the details of what that action should be. For instance, the only reason that the Thread class knows what to run in a new thread when you start it is because you provide it with a ThreadStart delegate instance.

We'll start our tour of delegates with the four absolute basics, without which none of the rest would make sense.

2.1.1   *A recipe for simple delegates*

In order for delegates to do anything, four things need to happen:

- The *delegate type* needs to be declared.
- There must be a method containing the code to execute.
- A *delegate instance* must be created.
- The delegate instance must be *invoked.*

Let's take each of the steps of this recipe in turn.

DECLARING THE DELEGATE TYPE

A *delegate type* is effectively just a list of parameter types and a return type. It specifies what kind of action can be represented by instances of the type. For instance, consider a delegate type declared like this:

```
delegate void StringProcessor (string input);
```

The code says that if we want to create an instance of StringProcessor, we're going to need a method with one parameter (a string) and a void return type (the method doesn't return anything). It's important to understand that StringProcessor really is a type. It has methods, you can create instances of it, pass around references to instances, the whole works. There are obviously a few "special features," but if you're ever stuck wondering what will happen in a particular situation, first think about what would happen if you were just using a "normal" reference type.

NOTE   *Source of confusion: the ambiguous term "delegate"*—Delegates are often misunderstood because the word "delegate" is used to describe both a "delegate type" and a "delegate instance." The distinction between these two is exactly the same as the one that exists between any other type and instances of that type—the string type itself is different from a particular sequence of characters, for example. I've used the terms "delegate type" and "delegate instance" throughout this chapter to try to keep it clear exactly what I'm talking about at any point.

We'll use the StringProcessor delegate type when we consider the next ingredient.

FINDING AN APPROPRIATE METHOD FOR THE DELEGATE INSTANCE'S ACTION

In .NET, delegate instances always refer to methods. Our next ingredient is to find (or write, of course) a method that does what we want and has the same signature as the delegate type we're using. The idea is to make sure that when we try to invoke a delegate instance, the parameters we use will all match up and we'll be able to use the return value (if any) in the way we expect—just like a normal method call.

Now consider these five method signatures as candidates to be used for a String-Processor instance:

```
void PrintString (string x)
void PrintInteger (int x)
void PrintTwoStrings (string x, string y)
int  GetStringLength (string x)
void PrintObject (object x)
```

The first method has everything right, so we can use it to create a delegate instance. The second method takes one parameter, but it's not `string`, so it's incompatible with `StringProcessor`. The third method has the correct first parameter type, but it has another parameter as well, so it's still incompatible.

The fourth method has the right parameter list but a nonvoid return type. (If our delegate type had a return type, the return type of the method would have to match that too.) The fifth method is interesting—any time we invoke a `StringProcessor` instance we could call the `PrintObject` method with the same arguments, because `string` derives from `object`. It would make sense to be able to use it for an instance of `StringProcessor`, but C# 1 limits the delegate to have *exactly* the same parameter types.[1] C# 2 changes this situation—see chapter 5 for more details. In some ways the fourth method is similar, as you could always ignore the unwanted return value. However, void and nonvoid return types are currently always deemed to be incompatible.

Let's assume we've got a method body for the compatible signature (`PrintString`) and move on to our next ingredient—the delegate instance itself.

CREATING A DELEGATE INSTANCE

Now that we've got a delegate type and a method with the right signature, we can create an instance of that delegate type, specifying that this method be executed when the delegate instance is invoked. There's no good official terminology defined for this, but for this book I will call it the *action* of the delegate instance. The exact form of the expression used to create the delegate instance depends on whether the action uses an instance method or a static method. Suppose `PrintString` is a static method in a type called `StaticMethods` and an instance method in a type called `InstanceMethods`. Here are two examples of creating an instance of `StringProcessor`:

```
StringProcessor proc1, proc2;
proc1 = new StringProcessor(StaticMethods.PrintString);

InstanceMethods instance = new InstanceMethods();
proc2 = new StringProcessor(instance.PrintString);
```

---

[1] As well as the parameter types, you have to match whether the parameter is in (the default), `out`, or `ref`. It's reasonably rare to use `out`/`ref` parameters with delegates, though.

When the action is a static method, you only need to specify the type name. When the action is an instance method, you need an instance of the type (or a derived type)—just as if you were calling the method in the normal way. This object is called the *target* of the action, and when the delegate instance is invoked, the method will be called on that object. If the action is within the same class (as it often is, particularly when you're writing event handlers in UI code), you don't need to qualify it either way—the this reference is used implicitly for instance methods.[2] Again, these rules act just as if you were calling the method directly.

NOTE *Utter garbage! (Or not, as the case may be...)*—It's worth being aware that a delegate instance will prevent its target from being garbage collected, if the delegate instance itself can't be collected. This can result in apparent memory leaks, particularly when a "short-lived" object subscribes to an event in a "long-lived" object, using itself as the target. The long-lived object indirectly holds a reference to the short-lived one, prolonging its lifetime. **EXTRA** *code available*

There's not much point in creating a delegate instance if it doesn't get invoked at some point. Let's look at our last step—the invocation.

INVOKING A DELEGATE INSTANCE

This is the really easy bit[3]—it's just a case of calling a method on the delegate instance. The method itself is called Invoke, and it's always present in a delegate type with the same list of parameters and return type that the delegate type declaration specifies. So in our case, there's a method like this:

```
void Invoke (string input)
```

Calling Invoke will execute the action of the delegate instance, passing on whatever parameters you've specified in the call to Invoke, and (if the return type isn't void) returning the return value of the action.

Simple as this is, C# makes it even easier—if you have a variable[4] whose type is a delegate type, you can treat it as if it were a method itself. It's easiest to see this happening as a chain of events occurring at different times, as shown in figure 2.1.

So, that's simple too. All our ingredients are in place, so we can preheat our CLR to 220°F, stir everything together, and see what happens.

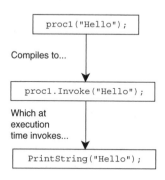

Figure 2.1 Processing a call to a delegate instance that uses the C# shorthand syntax

---

[2] Of course, if the action is an instance method and you're trying to create a delegate instance from within a static method, you'll still need to provide a reference to be the target.

[3] For synchronous invocation, anyway. You can use BeginInvoke and EndInvoke to invoke a delegate instance asynchronously, but that's beyond the scope of this chapter.

[4] Or any other kind of expression—but it's usually a variable.

A COMPLETE EXAMPLE AND SOME MOTIVATION

It's easiest to see all this in action in a complete example—finally, something we can actually run! As there are lots of bits and pieces going on, I've included the whole source code this time rather than using snippets. There's nothing mind-blowing in listing 2.1, so don't expect to be amazed—it's just useful to have concrete code to discuss.

Listing 2.1 Using delegates in a variety of simple ways

```
using System;

delegate void StringProcessor(string input);        ← ❶ Declares
                                                          delegate type
class Person
{
    string name;

    public Person(string name)
    {
        this.name = name;
    }
                                                   ❷ Declares compatible
    public void Say(string message)      ←            instance method
    {
        Console.WriteLine ("{0} says: {1}", name, message);
    }
}

class Background
{                                                  ❸ Declares compatible
    public static void Note(string note)   ←          static method
    {
        Console.WriteLine ("({0})", note);
    }
}

class SimpleDelegateUse
{
    static void Main()
    {
        Person jon = new Person("Jon");
        Person tom = new Person("Tom");

        StringProcessor jonsVoice, tomsVoice, background;      ❹ Creates
        jonsVoice = new StringProcessor(jon.Say);                three
        tomsVoice = new StringProcessor(tom.Say);                delegate
        background = new StringProcessor(Background.Note);       instances

        jonsVoice("Hello, son.");
        tomsVoice.Invoke("Hello, Daddy!");         ❺ Invokes delegate
        background("An airplane flies past.");        instances
    }
}
```

To start with, we declare the delegate type ❶. Next, we create two methods (❷ and ❸) that are both compatible with the delegate type. We've got one instance method (`Person.Say`) and one static method (`Background.Note`) so that we can see how they're used differently when we create the delegate instances ❹. We've created two instances of the Person class so that we can see the difference that the target of a delegate makes. When jonsVoice is invoked ❺, it calls the Say method on the Person object with the name *Jon*; likewise, when tomsVoice is invoked, it uses the object with the name *Tom*. I've included both the ways we've seen of invoking delegate instances—calling Invoke explicitly and using the C# shorthand—just for interest's sake. Normally you'd just use the shorthand. The output for listing 2.1 is fairly obvious:

```
Jon says: Hello, son.
Tom says: Hello, Daddy!
(An airplane flies past.)
```

Frankly, there's an awful lot of code in listing 2.1 to display three lines of output. Even if we wanted to use the Person class and the Background class, there's no real need to use delegates here. So what's the point? Why can't we just call methods directly? The answer lies in our original example of an attorney executing a will—just because you want something to happen, that doesn't mean you're always there at the right time and place to make it happen yourself. Sometimes you need to give instructions—to *delegate* responsibility, as it were.

I should stress that back in the world of software, this isn't a matter of objects leaving dying wishes. Often the object that first creates a delegate instance is still alive and well when the delegate instance is invoked. Instead, it's about specifying some code to be executed at a particular time, when you may not be able to (or may not want to) change the code that is running at that point. If I want something to happen when a button is clicked, I don't want to have to change the code of the *button*—I just want to tell the button to call one of my methods that will take the appropriate action. It's a matter of adding a level of *indirection*—as so much of object-oriented programming is. As we've seen, this adds complexity (look at how many lines of code it took to produce so little output!) but also flexibility.

Now that we understand a bit more about simple delegates, we'll take a brief look at combining delegates together to execute a whole bunch of actions instead of just one.

2.1.2 *Combining and removing delegates*

So far, all the delegate instances we've looked at have had a single action. The truth is a little bit more complicated: a delegate instance actually has a list of actions associated with it. This is called the *invocation list* of the delegate instance. The static Combine and Remove methods of the System.Delegate type are responsible for creating new delegate instances by respectively splicing together the invocation lists of two delegate instances or removing the invocation list of one delegate instance from another.

Before we look at the details, it's important to note that delegate instances are *immutable*. Once you've created a delegate instance, nothing about it can be changed. This makes it safe to pass around delegate instances and combine them with others without worrying about consistency, thread safety, or anyone trying to change their actions. This is just the same with delegate instances as it is with strings, which are also immutable. The reason for mentioning this is that `Delegate.Combine` is just like `String.Concat`—they both combine existing instances together to form a new one without changing the original objects at all. In the case of delegate instances, the original invocation lists are concatenated together. Note that if you ever try to combine `null` with a delegate instance, the `null` is treated as if it were a delegate instance with an empty invocation list.

You'll rarely see an explicit call to `Delegate.Combine` in C# code—usually the + and += operators are used. Figure 2.2 shows the translation process, where x and y are both variables of the same (or compatible) delegate types. All of this is done by the C# compiler.

As you can see, it's a straightforward transformation, but it does make the code a lot neater. Just as you can combine delegate instances, you can remove one from another with the `Delegate.Remove` method, and C# uses the short-

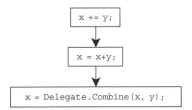

Figure 2.2 The transformation process used for the C# shorthand syntax for combining delegate instances

hand of the - and -= operators in the obvious way. `Delegate.Remove(source, value)` creates a new delegate whose invocation list is the one from `source`, with the list from `value` having been removed. If the result would have an empty invocation list, `null` is returned.

Table 2.1 shows some examples of the results of combining and removing delegate instances. I've used the notation [a, b, c] to indicate a delegate with an invocation list of actions a, b, and c (whatever they may happen to be).

Table 2.1 A selection of examples of combining and removing delegates, showing what the result is and why

Operation	Result	Notes
[a] + [b]	[a, b]	–
[a] + null	[a]	null counts as an empty invocation list.
null + [a]	[a]	–
[a] + [b, c]	[a, b, c]	–
[a, b] + [b, c]	[a, b, b, c]	Duplicates are allowed.
[a, b, c] - [b]	[a, c]	The removal list doesn't have to be at the end...
[a, b, c, d, b, c] - [b, c]	[a, b, c, d]	... but the *last occurrence* of the removal list is removed.
[a] - [b]	[a]	No-op removal of nonexistent list.

Table 2.1 A selection of examples of combining and removing delegates, showing what the result is and why *(continued)*

Operation	Result	Notes
[a, b, c, d, e] - [a, c, e]	[a, b, c, d, e]	The removal list must be present as a sublist; it's not just removing each element of the removal list.
[a, b] - [a, b]	null	null is returned for an empty invocation list.

When a delegate instance is invoked, all its actions are executed in order. If the delegate's signature has a nonvoid return type, the value returned by Invoke is the value returned by the *last* action executed. It's quite rare to see a nonvoid delegate instance with more than one action in its invocation list, because it means the return values of all the other actions are never seen.

If any of the actions in the invocation list throws an exception, that prevents any of the subsequent actions from being executed. For example, if a delegate instance with an action list [a, b, c] is invoked, and action b throws an exception, then the exception will be propagated immediately and action c won't be executed.

Combining and removing delegate instances is particularly useful when it comes to events. Now that we understand what combining and removing involves, we can sensibly talk about what events are.

2.1.3 *A brief diversion into events*

You probably have an instinctive idea about the overall *point* of events—particularly if you've written any UIs. The idea is that an event allows code to react when something happens—saving a file when the appropriate button is clicked, for example. In this case, the event is the button being clicked, and the action is the saving of the file. Understanding the reason for the concept isn't the same as understanding how C# defines events in language terms, however.

Developers often get confused between events and delegate instances, or between events and delegate type fields. The difference is important: *events aren't delegate type fields.* The reason for the confusion is that yet again, C# provides a shorthand, in the form of *field-like events.* We'll come to those in a minute, but first let's consider what events consist of as far as the C# compiler is concerned.

Events are like properties— both encapsulate data

I think it's helpful to think of events as being very similar to properties. To start with, both of them are declared to be of a certain type, which in the case of an event is forced to be a delegate type. When you use properties, it *looks* like you're fetching or assigning values directly to fields, but you're *actually* calling methods (getters and setters). The property implementation can do what it likes within those methods—it just happens that most properties are implemented with simple fields backing them, sometimes with some validation in the setter and sometimes with some thread safety thrown in for good measure.

Likewise, when you subscribe to or unsubscribe from an event, it *looks* like you're using a field whose type is a delegate type, with the += and -= operators. Again, though, you're actually calling methods (add and remove[5]). That's all you can do with a pure event—subscribe to it (add an event handler) or unsubscribe from it (remove an event handler). It's up to the event methods to do something useful—such as taking notice of the event handlers you're trying to add and remove, and making them available elsewhere within the class.

The reason for having events in the first place is very much like the reason for having properties—they add a layer of encapsulation. Just as you don't want other code to be able to set field values without the owner at least having the option of validating the new value, you often don't want code outside a class to be able to arbitrarily change (or call) the handlers for an event. Of course, a class *can* add methods to give extra access—for instance, to reset the list of handlers for an event, or to raise the event (in other words, call its event handlers). For example, Background-Worker.OnProgressChanged just calls the ProgressChanged event handlers. However, if you only expose the event itself, code outside the class only has the ability to add and remove handlers.

Field-like events make the implementation of all of this much simpler to look at—a single declaration and you're done. The compiler turns the declaration into both an event with default add/remove implementations, and a private delegate type field. Code inside the class sees the field; code outside the class only sees the event. This makes it *look* as if you can invoke an event—but what you actually do to call the event handlers is invoke the delegate instance stored in the field.

The details of events are outside the scope of this chapter—events themselves haven't changed significantly in C# 2 or 3—but I wanted to draw attention to the difference between delegate instances and events now, to prevent it causing confusion later on.

2.1.4   *Summary of delegates*

So, to summarize what we've covered on delegates:

- Delegates allow behavior to be encapsulated.
- The declaration of a delegate type controls which methods can be used to create delegate instances.
- Creating a delegate instance requires a method and (for instance methods) a target to call the method on.
- Delegate instances are immutable.
- Delegate instances each contain an invocation list—a list of actions.
- Delegate instances can be combined together and removed from each other.
- Events are not delegate instances—they're just add/remove method pairs (think property getters/setters).

---

[5] These aren't their names in the compiled code; otherwise you could only have one event per type. The compiler creates two methods with names that aren't used elsewhere, and a special piece of metadata to let other types know that there's an event with the given name, and what its add/remove methods are called.

Delegates are one very specific feature of C# and .NET—a detail, in the grand scheme of things. Both of the other "reminder" sections in this chapter deal with much broader topics. First, we will consider what it means to talk about C# being a *statically typed* language and the implications that has.

2.2   *Type system characteristics*

Almost every programming language has a type system of some kind. Over time, these have been classified as strong/weak, safe/unsafe, static/dynamic, and no doubt some more esoteric variations. It's obviously important to understand the type system with which one is working, and it's reasonable to expect that knowing the categories into which a language falls would give a lot of information to help on that front. However, because the terms are used to mean somewhat different things by different people, miscommunication is almost inevitable. I'll try to say *exactly* what I mean by each term to avoid confusion as much as possible.

One important thing to note is that this section is only applicable to "safe" code— which means all C# code that isn't explicitly within an unsafe context. As you might judge from the name, code within an unsafe context can do various things that safe code can't, and that may violate some aspects of normal type safety. Most developers are unlikely ever to need to write unsafe code, and the characteristics of the type system are far simpler to describe and understand when only safe code is considered.

This section shows what restrictions are and aren't enforced in C# 1 while defining some terms to describe that behavior. We'll then see a few things we can't do with C# 1—first from the point of view of what we *can't* tell the compiler, and then from the point of view of what we wish we didn't *have* to tell the compiler.

Let's start off with what C# 1 does, and what terminology is usually used to describe that kind of behavior.

2.2.1   *C#'s place in the world of type systems*

It's easiest to begin by making a statement, and then clarify what it actually means and what the alternatives might be:

> *C# 1's type system is static, explicit, and safe.*

You might well have expected the word *strong* to appear in the list, and I had half a mind to include it. However, while most people can reasonably agree on whether a language has the listed characteristics, deciding whether or not a language is *strongly typed* can cause heated debate because the definitions vary so wildly. Some meanings (those preventing any conversions, explicit or implicit) would clearly rule C# out— whereas others are quite close to (or even the same as) *statically typed*, which would include C#. Most of the articles and books I've read that describe C# as a strongly typed language are effectively using it to mean statically typed. I've used the word *static* here to try to minimize the potential for confusion—although it should be noted that it has little in common with the common understanding of the keyword `static` used within code itself as *related to the type rather than a particular instance*.

Let's take the terms in the definition one at a time and shed some light on them.

STATIC TYPING VS. DYNAMIC TYPING

C# is *statically typed:* each variable[6] is of a particular type, and that type is known at compile time. Only operations that are known about for that type are allowed, and this is enforced by the compiler. Consider this example of enforcement:

```
object o = "hello";
Console.WriteLine (o.Length);
```

Now as developers looking at the code, we obviously know that the value of o refers to a string, and that the string type has a Length property, but the compiler only thinks of o as being of type object. If we want to get to the Length property, we have to tell the compiler that the value of o *actually* refers to a string:

```
object o = "hello";
Console.WriteLine (((string)o).Length);
```

The alternative to static typing is *dynamic typing*, which can take a variety of guises. The essence of dynamic typing is to say that variables just have values—they aren't restricted to particular types, so the compiler can't perform the same sort of checks. Instead, the execution environment attempts to understand any given expression in an appropriate manner for the value involved. For example, if C# *were* dynamically typed, we could do this:

```
o = "hello";
Console.WriteLine (o.Length);
o = new string[] {"hi", "there"};
Console.WriteLine (o.Length);
```

This would be using two completely unrelated Length properties—String.Length and Array.Length—by examining the types dynamically at execution time. Like many areas of defining type systems, there are different levels of dynamic typing. Some languages allow you to specify types where you want to—possibly still treating them dynamically apart from assignment—but let you use untyped variables elsewhere.

EXPLICIT TYPING VS. IMPLICIT TYPING

The distinction between *explicit typing* and *implicit typing* is only relevant in statically typed languages. With explicit typing, the type of every variable must be explicitly stated in the declaration. Implicit typing allows the compiler to infer the type of the variable based on its use. For example, the language could dictate that the type of the variable is the type of the expression used to assign the initial value.

Consider a hypothetical language that uses the keyword var to indicate type inference.[7] Table 2.2 shows how code in such a language could be written in C# 1. The code in the left column is *not* allowed in C# 1, but the code in the right column is the equivalent valid code.

---

[6] This applies to most expressions too, but not quite all of them. There are certain expressions which don't have a type, such as void method invocations, but *this doesn't affect C#'s status of being statically typed.* I've used the word *variable* throughout this section to avoid unnecessary brain strain.

[7] OK, not so hypothetical. See section 8.2 for C# 3's implicitly typed local variable capabilities.

Invalid C#1—implicit typing	Valid C#1—explicit typing

`var s = "hello";`
`var x = s.Length;`
`var twiceX = x*2;`
	`string s = "hello";`
	`int x = s.Length;`
	`int twiceX = x*2;`

Table 2.2   An example showing the differences between implicit and explicit typing

Hopefully it's clear why this is only relevant for statically typed situations: for both implicit and explicit typing, the type of the variable is *known* at compile time, even if it's not explicitly stated. In a dynamic context, the variable doesn't even *have* a type to state or infer.

TYPE-SAFE VS. TYPE-UNSAFE

The easiest way of describing a type-safe system is to describe its opposite. Some languages (I'm thinking particularly of C and C++) allow you to do some really devious things. They're potentially powerful in the right situations, but with great power comes a free pack of donuts, or however the expression goes—and the right situations are relatively rare. Some of these devious things can shoot you in the foot if you get them wrong. Abusing the type system is one of them.

With the right voodoo rituals, you can persuade these languages to treat a value of one type as if it were a value of a *completely* different type without applying any conversions. I don't just mean calling a method that happens to be called the same thing, as in our dynamic typing example earlier. I mean some code that looks at the raw bytes within a value and interprets them in the "wrong" way. Listing 2.2 gives a simple C example of what I mean.

Listing 2.2   Demonstrating a type-unsafe system with C code

```
#include <stdio.h>

int main(int argc, char **argv)
{
    char *first_arg = argv[1];
    int *first_arg_as_int = (int *)first_arg;
    printf ("%d", *first_arg_as_int);
}
```

If you compile listing 2.2 and run it with a simple argument of `"hello"`, you will see a value of 1819043176—at least on a little-endian architecture with a compiler treating `int` as 32 bits and `char` as 8 bits, and where text is represented in ASCII or UTF-8. The code is treating the `char` pointer as an `int` pointer, so dereferencing it returns the first 4 bytes of text, treating them as a number.

In fact, this tiny example is quite tame compared with other potential abuses—casting between completely unrelated structs can easily result in total mayhem. It's not that this actually happens in real life very often, but some elements of the C typing system often mean you'll have to tell the compiler what to do, leaving it no option but to trust you even at execution time.

Fortunately, none of this occurs in C#. Yes, there are plenty of conversions available, but you can't pretend that data for one particular type of object is actually data for a different type. You can *try* by adding a cast to give the compiler this extra (and incorrect) information, but if the compiler spots that it's actually *impossible* for that cast to work, it will trigger a compilation error—and if it's theoretically allowed but actually incorrect at execution time, the CLR will throw an exception.

Now that we know a little about how C# 1 fits into the bigger picture of type systems, I'd like to mention a few downsides of its choices. That's not to say the choices are *wrong*—just limiting in some ways. Often language designers have to choose between different paths that add different limitations or have other undesirable consequences. I'll start with the case where you *want* to tell the compiler more information, but there's no way of doing so.

2.2.2 *When is C# 1's type system not rich enough?*

There are two common situations where you might want to expose more information to the caller of a method, or perhaps force the caller to limit what they provide in their arguments. The first involves collections, and the second involves inheritance and overriding methods or implementing interfaces. We'll examine each in turn.

COLLECTIONS, STRONG AND WEAK

Having avoided the terms *strong* and *weak* for the C# type system in general, I'll use them when talking about collections. They're used almost everywhere in this context, with little room for ambiguity. Broadly speaking, three kinds of collection types are built into .NET 1.1:

- Arrays—strongly typed—which are built into both the language and the runtime
- The weakly typed collections in the `System.Collections` namespace
- The strongly typed collections in the `System.Collections.Specialized` namespace

Arrays are strongly typed,[8] so at compile time you can't set an element of a `string[]` to be a `FileStream`, for instance. However, reference type arrays also support *covariance*, which provides an implicit conversion from one type of array to another, so long as there's a conversion between the element types. Checks occur at execution time to make sure that the wrong type of reference isn't actually stored, as shown in listing 2.3.

Listing 2.3 Demonstration of the covariance of arrays, and execution time type checking

```
string[] strings = new string[5];        ➊ Applies covariant
object[] objects = strings;       ◁──┐       conversion
objects[0] = new object();        ◁──┘
                                          Attempts to store
                                       ➋ a plain "object"
```

If you run listing 2.3, you will see an `ArrayTypeMismatchException` is thrown ➋. This is because the conversion from `string[]` to `object[]` ➊ returns the original reference—both `strings` and `objects` refer to the same array. The array itself "knows" it is

---

[8] At least, the language allows them to be. You can use the `Array` type for weakly typed access to arrays, though.

a string array, and will reject attempts to store references to nonstrings. Covariance is often useful, but comes at the cost of some of the type safety being implemented at execution time instead of compile time.

Let's compare this with the situation that the weakly typed collections such as `Array-List` and `Hashtable` put us in. The API of these collections uses `object` as the type of keys and values. When you are writing a method that takes an `ArrayList`, for example, there is no way of making sure at compile time that the caller will pass in a list of strings. You can document it, and the type safety of the runtime will enforce it if you cast each element of the list to `string`, but you don't get compile-time type safety. Likewise, if you return an `ArrayList`, you can indicate in the documentation that it will just contain strings, but callers will have to trust that you're telling the truth, and will have to insert casts when they access the elements of the list.

Finally, consider the strongly typed collections such as `StringCollection`. These provide an API that is strongly typed, so you can be confident that when you receive a `StringCollection` as a parameter or return value it will only contain strings, and you don't need to cast when fetching elements of the collection. It sounds ideal, but there are two problems. First, it implements `IList`, so you can still *try* to add non-strings to it (although you'll fail at runtime). Second, it only deals with strings. There are other specialized collections, but all told they don't cover much ground. There's the `CollectionBase` type, which can be used to build your own strongly typed collections, but that means creating a new collection type for each element type, which is also not ideal.

Now that we've seen the problem with collections, let's consider the issue that can occur when overriding methods and implementing interfaces. It's related to the idea of covariance, which we've already seen with arrays.

LACK OF COVARIANT RETURN TYPES
`ICloneable` is one of the simplest interfaces in the framework. It has a single method, `Clone`, which should return a copy of the object that the method is called on. Now, leaving aside the issue of whether this should be a deep or shallow copy, let's look at the signature of the `Clone` method:

```
object Clone()
```

It's a straightforward signature, certainly—but as I said, the method should return a copy of the object it's called on. That means it needs to return an object of the same type—or at least a compatible one (where that meaning will vary depending on the type). It would make sense to be able to override the method with a signature that gives a more accurate description of what the method actually returns. For example, in a `Person` class it would be nice to be able to implement `ICloneable` with

```
public Person Clone()
```

That wouldn't break anything—code expecting any old object would still work fine. This feature is called *return type covariance* but unfortunately, interface implementation and method overriding don't support it. Instead, the normal workaround for interfaces is to use *explicit interface implementation* to achieve the desired effect:

```
public Person Clone()
{

    [Implementation goes here]

}
object ICloneable.Clone()          ◁─── **Implements**
{                                        **interface explicitly**
    return Clone();    ◁───── **Calls noninterface**
}                                **method**
```

Any code that calls Clone() on an expression that the compiler knows is of type Person will call the top method; if the type of the expression is just ICloneable, it will call the bottom method. This works but is really ugly.

The mirror image of this situation also occurs with parameters, where if you had an interface or virtual method with a signature of, say void Process(string x), then it would seem logical to be able to implement or override the method with a less demanding signature, such as void Process(object x). This is called *parameter type contravariance*—and is just as unsupported as return type covariance, with the same workaround for interfaces and normal overloading for virtual methods. It's not a showstopper, but it's irritating.

Of course, C# 1 developers put up with all of these issues for a long time—and Java developers had a similar situation for far longer. While compile-time type safety is a great feature in general, I can't remember seeing many bugs where people *actually* put the wrong type of element in a collection. I can live with the workaround for the lack of covariance and contravariance. But there's such a thing as elegance and making your code clearly express what you mean, preferably *without* needing explanatory comments. We'll see later that C# 2 isn't flawless either, but it makes large improvements. As an aside, let's briefly go into an area that *isn't* improved upon in any way by C# 2 and is only tangentially touched on by C# 3—dynamic typing.

2.2.3 When does C# 1's type system get in the way?

I like static typing. Most of the time, it does what I want without much fuss, and it stops me from making silly mistakes. It also means the IDE has more information to help me with features such as IntelliSense.

Just occasionally, it's a real pain. If I've got two types that already have a particular method signature, but the types have nothing else in common or don't know about my code at all, *why* can't I "pretend" they implement an interface containing that signature? This feature is known as *duck typing* (and yet again, different people use the term to mean slightly different things) in that if something walks like a duck and quacks like a duck, you might as well treat it like a duck.

If I'm working with an API (usually through COM) that doesn't have strongly typed methods, why can't I ask the compiler to just stop using static typing for a while? Visual Basic has this feature, which is controlled with Option Strict; likewise, implicit typing is turned on and off using Option Explicit. Both of these features have received bad press, partly due to poor choices for default values in the past. It's also partly due to the overuse of these features by developers who decided to make their code compile at all costs (and then wondered why it failed at runtime). I can't say I would use this sort of feature particularly heavily in C# if it were there—but every so often, it would be welcome.

Of course, a dynamic type system doesn't have to stop there. More adventurous languages such as Ruby, Python, and Groovy allow methods to be added to types (or even individual objects) at execution time, and allow the type itself to determine what should happen if you try to call a method that doesn't exist. These powerful (though expensive in performance terms) features can lead to programs that appear to work almost by magic, and that certainly make C#'s static typing look positively antiquated. They have their costs in terms of understanding what's going on in your code, as well as reducing compile-time safety, but again, used in the right place they can be positive.

It's important that languages don't try too hard to be all things to all people. Such attempts always end in tears, and the cost in terms of the complexity of the language can be high. We'll see this balance between adding new features and limiting the cost of them time and time again throughout this book—the C# team has quite a high bar in terms of how useful a feature must be before it's considered for inclusion in the language.

2.2.4   *Summary of type system characteristics*

In this section we've learned some of the differences between type systems, and in particular which characteristics apply to C# 1:

- C# 1 is statically typed—the compiler knows what members to let you use.
- C# 1 is explicit—you have to tell the compiler what types variables have.
- C# 1 is safe—you can't treat one type as if it were another without the availability of a genuine conversion.
- Static typing still doesn't allow a single collection to be a strongly typed "list of strings" or "list of integers."
- Method overriding and interface implementation don't allow covariance/contravariance.

Our next section covers one of the most fundamental aspects of C#'s type system beyond its high-level characteristics—the differences between structs and classes.

2.3   *Value types and reference types*

It would be hard to overstate how important the subject of this section is. Everything you do in .NET will deal with either a value type or a reference type—and yet it's curiously possible to develop for a long time with only a vague idea of what the difference is. Worse yet, there are plenty of myths around to confuse things further. The unfortunate fact is that it's quite easy to make a short but incorrect statement that is close enough to the truth to be plausible but inaccurate enough to be misleading—but it's relatively tricky to come up with a concise but accurate description.

Once you "get it," the difference between value types and reference types is simple. It can take a while to reach that stage, and you may well have been able to write a lot of correct code without really understanding it. It's worth persevering, though: for one thing, a lot of seemingly complicated situations are *much* easier to understand when you're aware of what's really going on.

This section is not a complete breakdown of how types are handled, marshaling between application domains, interoperability with native code, and the like. Instead, it's a fairly brief look at the absolute basics of the topic (as applied to C# 1) that are crucial to understand in order to come to grips with C# 2 and 3.

We'll start off by seeing how the fundamental differences between value types and reference types appear naturally in the real world as well as in .NET.

2.3.1 Values and references in the real world

Suppose you're reading something really fantastic, and want a friend to read it too. Let's further suppose that it's a document in the public domain, just to avoid any accusations of supporting copyright violation. What do you need to give your friend so that he can read it too? It entirely depends on just what you're reading.

First we'll deal with the case where you've got real paper in your hands. To give your friend a copy, you'd need to photocopy all the pages and then give it to him. At that point, he has his own complete copy of the document. In this situation, we are dealing with *value type* behavior. All the information is directly in your hands—you don't need to go anywhere else to get it. Your copy of the information is also independent of your friend's after you've made the copy. You could add some notes to your pages, and his pages wouldn't be changed at all.

Compare that with the situation where you're actually reading a web page. This time, all you have to give your friend is the URL of the web page. This is *reference type* behavior, with the URL taking the place of the reference. In order to actually read the document, you have to navigate the reference by putting the URL in your browser and asking it to load the page. On the other hand, if the web page changes for some reason (imagine it's a wiki page and you've added your notes to the page) both you and your friend will see that change the next time each of you loads the page.

The differences we've seen in the real world form the heart of the distinction between value types and reference types in C# and .NET. Most types in .NET are reference types, and you're likely to create *far* more reference than value types. Aside from the special cases that follow, classes (declared using `class`) are reference types, and structures (declared using `struct`) are value types. The other cases are as follows:

- Array types are reference types, even if the element type is a value type (so `int[]` is still a reference type, even though `int` is a value type).
- Enumerations (declared using `enum`) are value types.
- Delegate types (declared using `delegate`) are reference types.
- Interface types (declared using `interface`) are reference types, but they can be implemented by value types.

Now that we've got the basic idea of what reference types and value types are about, we'll look at a few of the most important details.

2.3.2 Value and reference type fundamentals

The key concept to grasp when it comes to value types and reference types is what the value of a particular expression is. To keep things concrete, I'll use variables as the most common examples of expressions—but the same thing applies to properties, method calls, indexers, and other expressions.

As we discussed in section 2.2.1, most expressions have types associated with them. The value of a value type expression is the value, plain and simple. For instance, the value of the expression "2+3" is just 5. The value of a *reference* type expression, however, is a reference. It's *not* the object that the reference refers to. So, the value of the expression String. Empty is *not* an empty string—it's a reference to an empty string. In every-day discussions and even in documentation we tend to blur this distinction. For instance, we might describe String.Concat as returning "a string that is the concatenation of all the parameters." Using very precise terminology here would be time-consuming and distracting, and there's no problem so long as everyone involved understands that it's only a *reference* that is returned.

To demonstrate this further, consider a Point type that stores two integers, x and y. It could have a constructor that takes the two values. Now, this type could be implemented as either a struct or a class. Figure 2.3 shows the result of executing the following lines of code:

```
Point p1 = new Point(10, 20);
Point p2 = p1;
```

The left side of figure 2.3 indicates the values involved when Point is a class (a reference type), and the right side shows the situation when Point is a struct (a value type).

In both cases, p1 and p2 have the same value after the assignment. However, in the case where Point is a reference type, that value is a reference: both p1 and p2 refer to the same object. When Point is a value type, the value of p1 is the whole of the data for a point—the x and y values. Assigning the value of p1 to p2 copies all of that data.

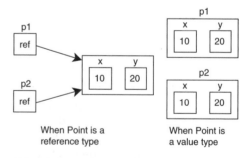

Figure 2.3 **Comparing value type and reference type behaviors, particularly with regard to assignment**

The values of variables are stored wherever they are declared. Local variable values are always stored on the stack,[9] and instance variable values are always stored wherever

---

[9] This is only totally true for C#1. We'll see later that local variables can end up on the heap in certain situations in C#2 and 3.

the instance itself is stored. Reference type instances (objects) are always stored on the heap, as are static variables.

Another difference between the two kinds of type is that value types cannot be derived from. One consequence of this is that the value doesn't need any extra information about what type that value *actually* is. Compare that with reference types, where each object contains a block of data at the start of it identifying the actual type of the object, along with some other information. You can never change the type of an object—when you perform a simple cast, the runtime just takes a reference, checks whether the object it refers to is a valid object of the desired type, and returns the original reference if it's valid or throws an exception otherwise. The reference itself doesn't know the type of the object—so the same reference value can be used for multiple variables of different types. For instance, consider the following code:

```
Stream stream = new MemoryStream();
MemoryStream memoryStream = (MemoryStream) stream;
```

The first line creates a new `MemoryStream` object, and sets the value of the `stream` variable to be a reference to that new object. The second line checks that the value of `stream` refers to a `MemoryStream` (or derived type) object and sets the value of `memoryStream` to the same value.

Once you understand these basic points, you can apply them when thinking about some of the falsehoods that are often stated about value types and reference types.

2.3.3 Dispelling myths

There are various myths that do the rounds on a regular basis. I'm sure the misinformation is almost always passed on with no malice and with no idea of the inaccuracies involved. In this section I'll tackle the most prominent myths, explaining the true situation as I go.

MYTH #1: "STRUCTS ARE LIGHTWEIGHT CLASSES"

This myth comes in a variety of forms. Some people believe that value types can't or shouldn't have methods or other significant behavior—they should be used as simple data transfer types, with just public fields or simple properties. The `DateTime` type is a good counterexample to this: it makes sense for it to be a value type, in terms of being a fundamental unit like a number or a character, and it *also* makes sense for it to be able to perform calculations to do with its value. Looking at things from the other direction, data transfer types should often be reference types anyway—the decision should be based on the desired value or reference type semantics, not the simplicity of the type.

Other people believe that value types are "lighter" than reference types in terms of performance. The truth is that in *some* cases value types are more performant—they don't require garbage collection, don't have the type identification overhead, and don't require dereferencing, for example. However, in other ways reference types are more performant—parameter passing, assignment, returning values and similar operations only require 4 or 8 bytes to be copied (depending on whether you're running the 32-bit or 64-bit CLR) rather than copying *all* the data. Imagine if `ArrayList` were somehow a "pure" value type, and passing an `ArrayList` expression to a method involved copying all its data!

MYTH #2: "REFERENCE TYPES LIVE ON THE HEAP, VALUE TYPES LIVE ON THE STACK"

This one is often caused just by laziness on the part of the person repeating it. The first part is correct—an instance of a reference type is always created on the heap. It's the second part that is problematic. As we've already noted, a variable's value lives wherever it's declared—so if you have a class with an instance variable of type `int`, that variable's value for any given object will always be where the rest of the data for the object is—on the heap. Only local variables (variables declared within methods) and method parameters live on the stack.

NOTE *Are these concepts relevant now?* It's arguable that if you're writing managed code, you should let the runtime worry about how memory is best used. Indeed, the language specification makes no guarantees about what lives where; a future runtime may be able to create some objects on the stack if it knows it could get away with it, or the C# compiler could generate code that hardly uses the stack at all.

The next myth is usually just a terminology issue.

MYTH #3: "OBJECTS ARE PASSED BY REFERENCE IN C# BY DEFAULT"

This is probably the most widely propagated myth. Again, the people who make this claim often (though not always) know what the actual C# behavior is, but they don't know what "pass by reference" really means. Unfortunately, this leads to people who *do* know what it means getting confused. The formal definition of "pass by reference" is relatively complicated, involving *l-values* and similar computer science terminology, but the important thing is that if you pass a variable by reference, the method you're calling can change the *value of the caller's variable* by changing its parameter value. Now remember that the value of a reference type variable is the *reference*, not the object itself. You can change the *contents* of the object that a parameter refers to without the parameter itself being passed by reference. For instance, the following method changes the contents of the `StringBuilder` object in question, but the caller's expression will still refer to the same object as before:

```
void AppendHello (StringBuilder builder)
{
    builder.Append("hello");
}
```

When this method is called, the parameter value (a reference to a `StringBuilder`) is passed by value. If I were to change the value of the `builder` variable within the method—for example with the statement `builder = null;`—*that* change wouldn't be seen by the caller, contrary to the myth.

It's interesting to note that not only is the "by reference" bit of the myth inaccurate, but so is the "objects are passed" bit. Objects themselves are *never* passed, either by reference or by value. When a reference type is involved, either the variable is passed by reference or the value of the argument (the reference) is passed by value. Aside from anything else, this answers the question of what happens when `null` is used as a by-value argument—if objects were being passed around, that would cause issues, as there wouldn't be an object to pass! Instead, the `null` reference is passed by value in just the same way as any other reference would be.

These myths aren't the only ones around. Boxing and unboxing come in for their fair share of misunderstanding, which I'll try to clear up next.

2.3.4 Boxing and unboxing

Sometimes, you just don't want a value type value. You want a reference. There are any number of reasons why this can happen, and fortunately C# and .NET provide a mechanism, called *boxing*, that lets you create an object from a value type value and use a reference to that new object. Before we leap straight into an example, let's start off by reviewing two important facts:

- The value of a reference type variable is always a reference.
- The value of a value type variable is always a value of that type.

Given those two facts, the following three lines of code don't seem to make much sense at first glance:

```
int i = 5;
object o = i;
int j = (int) o;
```

We have two variables: `i` is a value type variable, and `o` is a reference type variable. How does it make sense to assign the value of `i` to `o`? The value of `o` has to be a reference, and the number 5 isn't a reference—it's an integer value. What's actually happening is boxing: the runtime creates an object (on the heap—it's a normal object) that contains the value (5). The value of `o` is then a reference to that new object. The third line performs the reverse operation—*unboxing*. We have to tell the compiler which type to unbox the object as, and if we use the wrong type (if it's a boxed `uint` or `long`, for example, or not a boxed value at all) an `InvalidCastException` is thrown.[10]

That's it, really—boxing and unboxing in a nutshell. The only remaining problem is knowing when boxing and unboxing occur. Unboxing is usually obvious, because the cast is present in the code. Boxing can be more subtle. We've seen the simple version, but it can also occur if you call the `ToString`, `Equals`, or `GetHashCode` methods on the value of a type that doesn't override them, or if you use the value as an interface expression—assigning it to a variable whose type is an interface type or passing it as a parameter with an interface type. For example, the statement `IComparable x = 5;` would box the number 5.

It's worth being aware of boxing and unboxing because of the potential performance penalty involved. A single box or unbox operation is very cheap, but if you

---

[10] There are corner cases where the type doesn't have to be *exactly* right, mostly to do with enums. These are so fiddly that even the C# language specification hasn't got it quite right yet!

perform hundreds of thousands of them, you've not only got the cost of the operation yourself, but you're also creating a *lot* of objects, which gives the garbage collector more work to do.

2.3.5   *Summary of value types and reference types*

In this section we've looked at the differences between value types and reference types, as well as some of the myths surrounding them. Here are the key points:

- The value of a reference type expression (a variable for example) is a reference, not an object.
- References are like URLs—they are small pieces of data that let you access the real information.
- The value of a value type expression is the actual data.
- There are times when value types are more efficient than reference types, and vice versa.
- Reference type objects are always on the heap, but value type values can be on either the stack or the heap, depending on context.
- When a reference type is used as a method parameter, by default the parameter is passed *by value*—but the value itself is a reference.
- Value type values are boxed when reference type behavior is needed; unboxing is the reverse process.

Now that we've had a look at all the bits of C# 1 that you need to be comfortable with, it's time to take a quick look forward and see where each of the features will be enhanced by C# 2 and 3.

2.4   *C# 2 and 3: new features on a solid base*

The three topics covered in this chapter are all vital to C# 2 and 3. Almost all the new features relate to at least one of them, and they change the balance of how the language is used. Before we wrap up the chapter, let's explore how the new features relate to the old ones. I'm not going to give many details (for some reason the publisher didn't want a single 400-page section), but it's helpful to have an idea of where these areas are going before we get to the nitty-gritty. We'll look at them in the same order as we covered them earlier, starting with delegates.

2.4.1   *Features related to delegates*

Delegates of all kinds get a boost in C# 2, and then they're given even more special treatment in C# 3. Most of the features aren't new to the CLR, but are clever compiler tricks to make delegates work more smoothly within the language. This is where things are changing the most, not just in terms of syntax but also the idioms of how C# and the .NET Framework are best used. Over time, this will lead to a different way of approaching code.

C# 1 has pretty clumsy syntax when it comes to creating a delegate instance. For one thing, even if you need to accomplish something very straightforward, you've got to have a whole method dedicated to that job in order to create a delegate instance for it. C# 2 fixes this with anonymous methods, and introduces a simpler syntax for the cases where you still want to use a normal method to provide the action for the delegate. You can also create delegate instances using methods with *compatible* signatures—the method signature no longer has to be exactly the same as the delegate's declaration.

Listing 2.4 demonstrates all these improvements.

Listing 2.4   Improvements in delegate instantiation brought in by C#2

```
static void HandleDemoEvent(object sender, EventArgs e)
{
    Console.WriteLine ("Handled by HandleDemoEvent");
}
...

EventHandler handler;

handler = new EventHandler(HandleDemoEvent);           ❶ Specifies delegate
                                                          type and method

handler(null, EventArgs.Empty);

handler = HandleDemoEvent;                             ❷ Implicitly converts
                                                          to delegate instance

handler(null, EventArgs.Empty);

handler = delegate(object sender, EventArgs e)         ❸ Specifies action
    { Console.WriteLine ("Handled anonymously"); };       with anonymous
                                                          method

handler(null, EventArgs.Empty);

handler = delegate                                     ❹ Uses
    { Console.WriteLine ("Handled anonymously again"); };   anonymous
                                                          method
                                                          shortcut

handler(null, EventArgs.Empty);

MouseEventHandler mouseHandler = HandleDemoEvent;      ❺ Uses
mouseHandler(null, new MouseEventArgs(MouseButtons.None,   delegate
                    0, 0, 0, 0));                         contra-
                                                          variance
```

The first part of the main code ❶ is just C# 1 code, kept for comparison. The remaining delegates all use new features of C# 2. The conversion involved ❷ makes event subscription code read a lot more pleasantly—lines such as `saveButton.Click += SaveDocument;` are very straightforward, with no extra fluff to distract the eye. The anonymous method syntax ❸ is a little cumbersome, but does allow the action to be very clear at the point of creation, rather than being another method to look at before you understand what's going on. The shortcut used ❹ is another example of anonymous method syntax, but this form can only be used when you don't need the parameters. Anonymous methods have other powerful features as well, but we'll see those later.

The final delegate instance created ❺ is an instance of `MouseEventHandler` rather than just `EventHandler`—but the `HandleDemoEvent` method can still be used due to *contravariance*, which specifies parameter compatibility. *Covariance* specifies return type compatibility. We'll be looking at both of these in more detail in chapter 5. Event handlers are probably the biggest beneficiaries of this, as suddenly the Microsoft guideline to make all delegate types used in events follow the same convention makes a lot more sense. In C# 1, it didn't matter whether or not two different event handlers looked "quite similar"—you had to have a method with an *exactly* matching signature in order to create a delegate instance. In C# 2, you may well find yourself able to use the same method to handle many different kinds of events, particularly if the purpose of the method is fairly event independent, such as logging.

C# 3 provides special syntax for instantiating delegate types, using *lambda expressions*. To demonstrate these, we'll use a new delegate type. As part of the CLR gaining generics in .NET 2.0, generic delegate types became available and were used in a number of API calls in generic collections. However, .NET 3.5 takes things a step further, introducing a group of generic delegate types called Func that all take a number of parameters of specified types and return a value of another specified type. Listing 2.5 gives an example of the use of a Func delegate type as well as lambda expressions.

Listing 2.5   Lambda expressions, which are like improved anonymous methods

```
Func<int,int,string> func = (x,y) => (x*y).ToString();
Console.WriteLine (func(5, 20));
```

Func<int,int,string> is a delegate type that takes two integers and returns a string. The lambda expression in listing 2.5 specifies that the delegate instance (held in func) should multiply the two integers together and call ToString(). The syntax is much more straightforward than that of anonymous methods, and there are other benefits in terms of the amount of type inference the compiler is prepared to perform for you. Lambda expressions are absolutely crucial to LINQ, and you should get ready to make them a core part of your language toolkit. They're not restricted to working with LINQ, however—almost any use of anonymous methods from C# 2 can use lambda expressions in C# 3.

To summarize, the new features related to delegates are as follows:

- Generics (generic delegate types)—C# 2
- Delegate instance creation expressions—C# 2
- Anonymous methods—C# 2
- Delegate covariance/contravariance—C# 2
- Lambda expressions—C# 3

The use of generics extends well beyond delegates, of course—they're one of the principle enhancements to the type system, which we'll look at next.

2.4.2   *Features related to the type system*

The primary new feature in C# 2 regarding the type system is that of generics. It largely addresses the issues I raised in section 2.2.2 about strongly typed collections, although generic types are useful in a number of other situations too. As a feature, it's elegant, it solves a real problem, and despite a few wrinkles it generally works very well. We've seen examples of this in quite a few places already, and it's described fully in the next chapter, so I won't go into any more details here. It'll be a brief reprieve, though—generics form probably the most important feature in C# 2 with respect to the type system, and you'll see generic types throughout the rest of the book.

C# 2 doesn't tackle the issue of return type covariance and parameter contravariance for overriding members or implementing interfaces. However, it *does* improve the situation for delegate instance creation in certain situations, as we saw in section 2.4.1. C# 3 introduces a wealth of new concepts in the type system, most notably anonymous types, implicitly typed local variables, and extension methods. Anonymous types themselves are mostly present for the sake of LINQ, where it's useful to be able to effectively create a data transfer type with a bunch of read-only properties without having to actually write the code for them. There's nothing to stop them from being used outside LINQ, however, which makes life easier for demonstrations. Listing 2.6 shows both features in action.

Listing 2.6   Demonstration of anonymous types and implicit typing

```
var jon = new { Name="Jon", Age=31 };
var tom = new { Name="Tom", Age=4 };
Console.WriteLine ("{0} is {1}", jon.Name, jon.Age);
Console.WriteLine ("{0} is {1}", tom.Name, tom.Age);
```

The first two lines each show implicit typing (the use of var) and anonymous object initializers (the new {...} bit), which create instances of anonymous types.

There are two things worth noting at this stage, long before we get into the details—points that have caused people to worry needlessly before. The first is that C# is still statically typed. The C# compiler has declared jon and tom to be of a particular type, just as normal, and when we use the properties of the objects they are normal properties—there's no dynamic lookup going on. It's just that we (as source code authors) couldn't tell the compiler what type to use in the variable declaration because the compiler will be generating the type itself. The properties are also statically typed—here the Age property is of type int, and the Name property of type string.

The second point is that we haven't created two different anonymous types here. The variables jon and tom both have the same type because the compiler uses the property names, types, and order to work out that it can generate just one type and use it for both statements. This is done on a per-assembly basis, and makes life a lot simpler in terms of being able to assign the value of one variable to another (for example, jon=tom; would be permitted in the previous code) and similar operations.

Extension methods are also there for the sake of LINQ but can be useful outside it. Think of all the times you've wished that a framework type had a certain method, and you've had to write a static utility method to implement it. For instance, to create a new string by reversing an existing one you might write a static StringUtil.Reverse method. Well, the extension method feature effectively lets you call that static method as if it existed on the string type itself, so you could write

```
string x = "dlrow olleH".Reverse();
```

Extension methods also let you appear to add methods with implementations to interfaces—and indeed that's what LINQ relies on heavily, allowing calls to all kinds of methods on IEnumerable<T> that have never previously existed.

Here's the quick-view list of these features, along with which version of C# they're introduced in:

- Generics—C# 2
- Limited delegate covariance/contravariance—C# 2
- Anonymous types—C# 3
- Implicit typing—C# 3
- Extension methods—C# 3

After that fairly diverse set of features on the type system in general, let's look at the features added to one very specific part of typing in .NET—value types.

2.4.3 *Features related to value types*

There are only two features to talk about here, and C# 2 introduces them both. The first goes back to generics yet again, and in particular collections. One common complaint about using value types in collections with .NET 1.1 was that due to all of the "general purpose" APIs being specified in terms of the object type, every operation that added a struct value to a collection would involve boxing it, and when retrieving it you'd have to unbox it. While boxing is pretty cheap on a "per call" basis, it can cause a significant performance hit when it's used every time with frequently accessed collections. It also takes more memory than it needs to, due to the per-object overhead. Generics fix both the speed and memory deficiencies by using the *real* type involved rather than just a general-purpose object. As an example, it would have been madness to read a file and store each byte as an element in an ArrayList in .NET 1.1—but in .NET 2.0 it wouldn't be particularly crazy to do the same with a List<byte>.

The second feature addresses another common cause of complaint, particularly when talking to databases—the fact that you can't assign null to a value type variable. There's no such concept as an int value of null, for instance, even though a *database* integer field may well be nullable. At that point it can be hard to model the database table within a statically typed class without a bit of ugliness of some form or another. Nullable types are part of .NET 2.0, and C# 2 includes extra syntax to make them easy to use. Listing 2.7 gives a brief example of this.

Listing 2.7 Demonstration of a variety of nullable type features

```
int? x = null;        <--- Declares and sets nullable variable
x = 5;
if (x != null)        <--- Tests for presence of "real" value
{
    int y = x.Value;  <--- Obtains "real" value
    Console.WriteLine (y);
}
int z = x ?? 10;      <--- Uses null-coalescing operator
```

Listing 2.7 shows a number of the features of nullable types and the shorthand that C# provides for working with them. We'll get around to the details of each feature in chapter 4, but the important thing to think about is how much easier and cleaner all of this is than any of the alternative workarounds that have been used in the past.

The list of enhancements is smaller this time, but they're very important features in terms of both performance and elegance of expression:

- Generics—C# 2
- Nullable types—C# 2

2.5 Summary

This chapter has provided some revision of a few topics from C# 1. The aim wasn't to cover any of the topics in its entirety, but merely to get everyone on the same page so that I can describe the C# 2 and 3 features without worrying about the ground that I'm building on.

All of the topics we've covered are core to C# and .NET, but within community discussions, blogs, and even occasionally books often they're either skimmed over too quickly or not enough care is taken with the details. This has often left developers with a mistaken understanding of how things work, or with an inadequate vocabulary to express themselves. Indeed, in the case of characterizing type systems, computer science has provided such a variety of meanings for some terms that they've become almost useless. Although this chapter hasn't gone into much depth about any one point, it will hopefully have cleared up any confusion that would have made the rest of the book harder to understand.

The three core topics we've briefly covered in this chapter are all significantly enhanced in C# 2 and 3, and some features touch on more than one topic. In particular, generics has an impact on almost every area we've covered in this chapter—it's probably the most widely used and important feature in C# 2. Now that we've finished all our preparations, we can start looking at it properly in the next chapter.

Part 2

C# 2:
solving the issues
of C# 1

In part 1 we took a quick look at a few of the features of C# 2. Now it's time to do the job properly. We'll see how C# 2 fixes various problems that developers ran into when using C# 1, and how C# 2 makes existing features more useful by streamlining them. This is no mean feat, and life with C# 2 is *much* more pleasant than with C# 1.

The new features in C# 2 have a certain amount of independence. That's not to say they're not related at all, of course; many of the features are based on—or at least interact with—the *massive* contribution that generics make to the language. However, the different topics we'll look at in the next five chapters don't combine into one cohesive whole.

The first four chapters of this part cover the biggest new features. We'll look at the following:

- *Generics*—The most important new feature in C# 2 (and indeed in the CLR for .NET 2.0), generics allow type and method parameterization.
- *Nullable types*—Value types such as int and DateTime don't have any concept of "no value present"—nullable types allow you to represent the absence of a meaningful value.
- *Delegates*—Although delegates haven't changed at the CLR level, C# 2 makes them a lot easier to work with. As well as a few simple shortcuts, the introduction of anonymous methods begins the movement toward a more functional style of programming—this trend continues in C# 3.
- *Iterators*—While *using* iterators has always been simple in C# with the foreach statement, it's a pain to *implement* them in C# 1. The C# 2 compiler is happy to build a state machine for you behind the scenes, hiding a lot of the complexity involved.

Having covered the major, complex new features of C# 2 with a chapter dedicated to each one, chapter 7 rounds off our coverage by covering several simpler features. Simpler doesn't necessarily mean less useful, of course: partial types in particular are very important for better designer support in Visual Studio 2005.

As you can see, there's a lot to cover. Take a deep breath, and let's dive into the world of generics...

Parameterized typing with generics

This chapter covers
- Generic types and methods
- Generic collections in .NET 2.0
- Limitations of generics
- Comparisons with other languages

True[1] story: the other day my wife and I did our weekly grocery shopping. Just before we left, she asked me if I had the list. I confirmed that indeed I *did* have the list, and off we went. It was only when we got to the grocery store that our mistake made itself obvious. My wife had been asking about the *shopping* list whereas I'd actually brought the list of neat features in C# 2. When we asked an assistant whether we could buy any anonymous methods, we received a very strange look.

If only we could have expressed ourselves more clearly! If only she'd had some way of saying that she wanted me to bring the list of items we wanted to buy! If only we'd had generics…

---

[1] By which I mean "convenient for the purposes of introducing the chapter"—not, you know, *accurate* as such.

For most people, generics will be the most important new feature of C# 2. They enhance performance, make your code more expressive, and move a lot of safety from execution time to compile time. Essentially they allow you to *parameterize* types and methods—just as normal method calls often have parameters to tell them what *values* to use, generic types and methods have type parameters to tell them what *types* to use. It all sounds very confusing to start with—and if you're completely new to generics you can expect a certain amount of head scratching—but once you've got the basic idea, you'll come to love them.

In this chapter we'll be looking at how to use generic types and methods that others have provided (whether in the framework or as third-party libraries), and how to write your own. We'll see the most important generic types within the framework, and take a look just under the surface to understand some of the performance implications of generics. To conclude the chapter, I'll present some of the most frequently encountered limitations of generics, along with possible workarounds, and compare generics in C# with similar features in other languages.

First, though, we need to understand the problems that caused generics to be devised in the first place.

3.1 Why generics are necessary

Have you ever counted how many casts you have in your C# 1 code? If you use any of the built-in collections, or if you've written your own types that are designed to work with many different types of data, you've probably got plenty of casts lurking in your source, quietly telling the compiler not to worry, that everything's fine, just treat the expression over there as if it had *this* particular type. Using almost any API that has object as either a parameter type or a return type will probably involve casts at some point. Having a single-class hierarchy with object as the root makes things more straightforward, but the object type in itself is extremely dull, and in order to do anything genuinely useful with an object you almost always need to cast it.

Casts are bad, m'kay? Not bad in an "almost never do this" kind of way (like mutable structs and nonprivate fields) but bad in a "necessary evil" kind of way. They're an indication that you ought to give the compiler more information somehow, and that the way you're choosing is to get the compiler to trust you at compile time and generate a check to run at execution time, to keep you honest.

Now, if you need to tell the compiler the information somewhere, chances are that anyone *reading* your code is also going to need that same information. They can see it where you're casting, of course, but that's not terribly useful. The ideal place to keep such information is usually at the point of declaring a variable or method. This is even more important if you're providing a type or method which other people will call *without access to your code*. Generics allow library providers to prevent their users from compiling code that calls the library with bad arguments. Previously we've had to rely on manually written documentation—which is often incomplete or inaccurate, and is rarely read anyway. Armed with the extra information, everyone can work more productively: the compiler is able to do more checking; the IDE is able to present IntelliSense options based on the extra information (for instance, offering the members of string as next steps when you access an element of a list of strings); callers of methods can be more certain of correctness in terms of arguments passed in and values returned; and anyone maintaining your code can better understand what was running through your head when you originally wrote it in the first place.

> **NOTE** *Will generics reduce your bug count?* Every description of generics I've read (including my own) emphasizes the importance of compile-time type checking over execution-time type checking. I'll let you in on a secret: I can't remember ever fixing a bug in released code that was directly due to the lack of type checking. In other words, the casts we've been putting in our C# 1 code have always worked in my experience. Those casts have been like warning signs, forcing us to think about the type safety explicitly rather than it flowing naturally in the code we write. Although generics may not radically reduce the number of *type safety* bugs you encounter, the greater readability afforded can reduce the number of bugs across the board. Code that is simple to understand is simple to get right.

All of this would be enough to make generics worthwhile—but there are performance improvements too. First, as the compiler is able to perform more checking, that leaves less needing to be checked at execution time. Second, the JIT is able to treat value types in a particularly clever way that manages to eliminate boxing and unboxing in many situations. In some cases, this can make a huge difference to performance in terms of both speed and memory consumption.

Many of the benefits of generics may strike you as being remarkably similar to the benefits of static languages over dynamic ones: better compile-time checking, more information expressed directly in the code, more IDE support, better performance. The reason for this is fairly simple: when you're using a general API (for example, ArrayList) that can't differentiate between the different types, you effectively *are* in a dynamic situation in terms of access to that API. The reverse isn't generally true, by the way—there are plenty of benefits available from dynamic languages in many situations, but they rarely apply to the choice between generic/nongeneric APIs. When you *can* reasonably use generics, the decision to do so is usually a no-brainer.

So, those are the goodies awaiting us in C# 2—now it's time to actually start using generics.

3.2   *Simple generics for everyday use*

The topic of generics has a lot of dark corners if you want to know *everything* about it. The C# 2 language specification goes into a great deal of detail in order to make sure that the behavior is specified in pretty much every conceivable case. However, we don't need to understand most of those corner cases in order to be productive. (The same is true in other areas, in fact. For example, you don't need to know all the exact rules about definitely assigned variables—you just fix the code appropriately when the compiler complains.)

This section will cover most of what you'll need in your day-to-day use of generics, both consuming generic APIs that other people have created and creating your own. If you get stuck while reading this chapter but want to keep making progress, I suggest you concentrate on what you need to know in order to use generic types and methods within the framework and other libraries; writing your own generic types and methods crops up a lot less often than using the framework ones.

We'll start by looking at one of the collection classes from .NET 2.0—Dictionary<TKey,TValue>.

3.2.1   *Learning by example: a generic dictionary*

Using generic types can be very straightforward if you don't happen to hit some of the limitations and start wondering what's wrong. You don't need to know any of the terminology to have a pretty good guess as to what the code will do when reading it, and with a bit of trial and error you can experiment your way to writing your own working code too. (One of the benefits of generics is that more checking is done at compile time, so you're more likely to have working code by the time it all compiles—this makes the experimentation simpler.) Of course, the aim of this chapter is to give you the knowledge so that you *won't* be using guesswork—you'll know what's going on at every stage.

For now, though, let's look at some code that is straightforward even if the syntax is unfamiliar. Listing 3.1 uses a Dictionary<TKey,TValue> (roughly the generic equivalent of the Hashtable class you've almost certainly used with C# 1) to count the frequencies of words in a given piece of text.

Listing 3.1   Using a Dictionary<TKey,TValue> to count words in text

```
static Dictionary<string,int> CountWords(string text)
{
    Dictionary<string,int> frequencies;

    frequencies = new Dictionary<string,int>();      ❶ Creates new map from
                                                         word to frequency

    string[] words = Regex.Split(text, @"\W+");      ❷ Splits text
                                                         into words
    foreach (string word in words)
    {
        if (frequencies.ContainsKey(word))
        {
            frequencies[word]++;
        }
        else                                         ❸ Adds to or
        {                                               updates map
            frequencies[word] = 1;
        }
    }
    return frequencies;
}
...
string text = @"Do you like green eggs and ham?
          I do not like them, Sam-I-am.
```

```
                       I do not like green eggs and ham.";

        Dictionary<string,int> frequencies = CountWords(text);
        foreach (KeyValuePair<string,int> entry in frequencies)
        {
            string word = entry.Key;
            int frequency = entry.Value;
            Console.WriteLine ("{0}: {1}", word, frequency);
        }
```

❹ **Prints each key/value pair from map**

The CountWords method ❶ first creates an empty map from string to int. This will effectively count how often each word is used within the given text. We then use a regular expression ❷ to split the text into words. It's crude—we end up with an empty string due to the period at the end of the text, and I haven't worried about the fact that "do" and "Do" are counted separately. These issues are easily fixable, but I wanted to keep the code as simple as possible for this example. For each word, we check whether or not it's already in the map. If it is, we increment the existing count; otherwise, we give the word an initial count of 1 ❸. Notice how the incrementing code doesn't need to do a cast to int in order to perform the addition: the value we retrieve is known to be an int at compile time. The step incrementing the count is actually performing a get on the indexer for the map, then incrementing, then performing a set on the indexer. Some developers may find it easier to keep this explicit, using frequencies[word] = frequencies [word]+1; instead.

The final part of the listing is fairly familiar: enumerating through a Hashtable gives a similar (nongeneric) DictionaryEntry with Key and Value properties for each entry ❹. However, in C# 1 we would have needed to cast both the word and the frequency as the key and value would have been returned as just object. That also means that the frequency would have been boxed. Admittedly we don't really *have* to put the word and the frequency into variables—we could just have had a single call to Console.WriteLine and passed entry.Key and entry.Value as arguments. I've really just got the variables here to ram home the point that no casting is necessary.

There are some differences between Hashtable and Dictionary<TKey,TValue> beyond what you might expect. We're not looking at them right now, but we'll cover them when we look at all of the .NET 2.0 collections in section 3.4. For the moment, if you experiment beyond any of the code listed here (and please do—there's nothing like actually coding to get the hang of a concept) and if it doesn't do what you expect, just be aware that it might *not* be due to a lack of understanding of generics. Check the documentation before panicking!

Now that we've seen an example, let's look at what it means to talk about Dictionary<TKey,TValue> in the first place. What are TKey and TValue, and why do they have angle brackets round them?

3.2.2 *Generic types and type parameters*

There are two forms of generics: *generic types* (including classes, interfaces, delegates, and structures—there are no generic enums) and *generic methods*. Both are essentially a way of expressing an API (whether it's for a single generic method or a whole generic type) such that in some places where you'd expect to see a normal type, you see a *type parameter* instead.

A type parameter is a placeholder for a real type. Type parameters appear in angle brackets within a generic declaration, using commas to separate them. So in `Dictionary <TKey,TValue>` the type parameters are `TKey` and `TValue`. When you use a generic type or method, you specify the *real* types you want to use. These are called the *type arguments*—in listing 3.1, for example, the type arguments were `string` (for `TKey`) and `int` (for `TValue`).

There's a lot of detailed terminology involved in generics. I've included it for reference—and because very occasionally it makes it easier to talk about topics in a precise manner. It could well be useful if you ever need to consult the language specification, but you're unlikely to need to use this terminology in day-to-day life. Just grin and bear it for the moment.

The form where none of the type parameters have been provided with type arguments is called an *unbound generic type*. When type arguments are specified, the type is said to be a *constructed type*. Unbound generic types are effectively blueprints for constructed types, in a way similar to how types (generic or not) can be regarded as blueprints for objects. It's a sort of extra layer of abstraction. Figure 3.1 shows this graphically.

As a further complication, constructed types can be open or closed. An *open type* is one that involves a type parameter from elsewhere (the enclosing generic method or

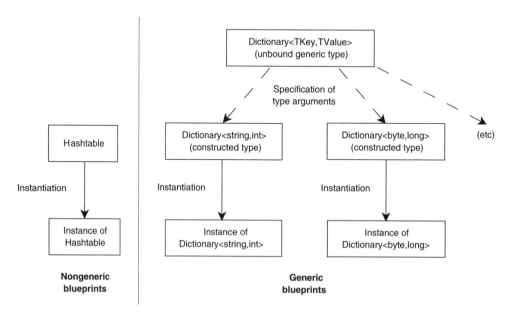

Figure 3.1   Unbound generic types act as blueprints for constructed types, which then act as blueprints for actual objects, just as nongeneric types do.

type), whereas for a *closed type* all the types involved are completely known about. All code actually *executes* in the context of a closed constructed type. The only time you see an unbound generic type appearing within C# code (other than as a declaration) is within the typeof operator, which we'll meet in section 3.4.4.

The idea of a type parameter "receiving" information and a type argument "providing" the information—the dashed lines in figure 3.1—is exactly the same as with method parameters and arguments, although type arguments are always just names of types or type parameters.

You can think of a closed type as having the API of the open type, but with the type parameters being replaced with their corresponding type arguments.[2] Table 3.1 shows some method and property declarations from the open type Dictionary<TKey,TValue> and the equivalent member in closed type we built from it—Dictionary<string,int>.

Table 3.1 Examples of how method signatures in generic types contain placeholders, which are replaced when the type arguments are specified

Method signature in generic type	Method signature after type parameter replacement

public void Add
    (TKey key, TValue value)
	public void Add
	    (string key, int value)

public TValue this [TKey key]
    { get; set; }
	public int this [string key]
	    { get; set; }

public bool ContainsValue
    (TValue value)
	public bool ContainsValue
	    (int value)

public bool ContainsKey
    (TKey key)
	public bool ContainsKey
	    (string key)

One important thing to note is that none of the methods in table 3.1 are actually generic methods. They're just "normal" methods within a generic type, and they happen to use the type parameters declared as part of the type.

Now that you know what TKey and TValue mean, and what the angle brackets are there for, we can have a look at how Dictionary<TKey,TValue> might be implemented, in terms of the type and member declarations. Here's part of it—although the actual method implementations are all missing, and there are more members in reality:

```
namespace System.Collections.Generic
{
    public class Dictionary<TKey,TValue>          Declares
                                                  generic class
```

---

[2] It doesn't always work *exactly* that way—there are corner cases that break when you apply that simple rule—but it's an easy way of thinking about generics that works in the vast majority of situations.

```
        : IEnumerable<KeyValuePair<TKey,TValue>>        ◁─┐  Implements
    {                                                     │  generic interface
        public Dictionary()    ◁─┐ Declares
        {                        │ parameterless            Declares method
            [...]                │ constructor              using type
        }                                              ◁─┘  parameters
        public void Add (TKey key, TValue value)
        {
            [...]
        }
        public TValue this [TKey key]
        {
            get { [...] }
            set { [...] }
        }
        public bool ContainsValue (TValue value)
        {
            [...]
        }
        public bool ContainsKey (TKey key)
        {
            [...]
        }
        [... other members ...]
    }
}
```

Notice how `Dictionary<TKey,TValue>` implements the generic interface `IEnumerable<KeyValuePair<TKey,TValue>>` (and many other interfaces in real life). Whatever type arguments you specify for the class are applied to the interface where the same type parameters are used—so in our example, `Dictionary<string,int>` implements `IEnumerable<KeyValuePair<string,int>>`. Now that's actually sort of a "doubly generic" interface—it's the `IEnumerable<T>` interface, with the structure `KeyValue-Pair <string,int>` as the type argument. It's because it implements that interface that listing 3.1 was able to enumerate the keys and values in the way that it did. It's also worth pointing out that the constructor doesn't list the type parameters in angle brackets. The type parameters belong to the *type* rather than to the particular constructor, so that's where they're declared.

Generic types can effectively be overloaded on the number of type parameters—so you could define `MyType`, `MyType<T>`, `MyType<T,U>`, `MyType<T,U,V>`, and so forth, all within the same namespace. The names of the type parameters aren't used when considering this—just how many there are of them. These types are unrelated except in name—there's no default conversion from one to another, for instance. The same is true for generic methods: two methods can be exactly the same in signature other than the number of type parameters.

NOTE   *Naming conventions for type parameters*—Although you *could* have a type with
type parameters T, U, and V, it wouldn't give much indication of what they
actually meant, or how they should be used. Compare this with Dictionary
<TKey,TValue>, where it's obvious that TKey represents the type of the keys
and TValue represents the type of the values. Where you have a single type
parameter and it's clear what it means, T is conventionally used (List<T>
is a good example of this). Multiple type parameters should usually be
named according to meaning, using the prefix T to indicate a type parameter. Every so often you *may* run into a type with multiple single-letter type
parameters (SynchronizedKeyedCollection<K,T>, for example), but you
should try to avoid creating the same situation yourself.

Now that we've got an idea of what generic types do, let's look at generic methods.

3.2.3   *Generic methods and reading generic declarations*

We've mentioned generic methods a few times, but we haven't actually met one yet.
You may find the overall idea of generic methods more confusing than generic
types—they're somehow less natural for the brain—but it's the same basic principle.
We're used to the parameters and return value of a method having firmly specified
types—and we've seen how a generic type can use its type parameters in method declarations. Well, generic methods go one step further—even if you know exactly which
constructed type you're dealing with, an individual method can have type parameters
too. Don't worry if you're still none the wiser—the concept is likely to "click" at some
point after you've seen enough examples.

   Dictionary<TKey,TValue> doesn't have any generic methods, but its close neigh-
bor List<T> does. As you can imagine, List<T> is just a list of items of whatever type
is specified—so List<string> is just a list of strings, for instance. Remembering that
T is the type parameter for the whole *class*, let's dissect a generic method declaration. Figure 3.2 shows what the different parts of the declaration of the ConvertAll
method mean.[3]

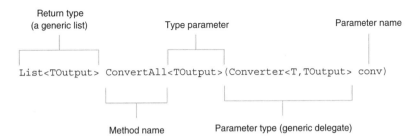

Figure 3.2   The anatomy of a generic method declaration

---

[3]   I've renamed the parameter from converter to conv so that it fits on one line, but everything else is as doc-
umented.

When you look at a generic declaration—whether it's for a generic type or a generic method—it can be a bit daunting trying to work out what it means, particularly if you have to deal with generic types of generic types, as we did when we looked at the interface implemented by the dictionary. The key is not to panic—just take things calmly, and pick an example situation. Use a different type for each type parameter, and apply them all consistently.

In this case, let's start off by replacing the type parameter of the type containing the method (the `<T>` part of `List<T>`). We've used `List<string>` as an example before, so let's continue to do so and replace `T` with `string` everywhere:

```
List<TOutput> ConvertAll<TOutput>(Converter<string,TOutput> conv)
```

That looks a bit better, but we've still got `TOutput` to deal with. We can tell that it's a method's type parameter (apologies for the confusing terminology) because it's in angle brackets directly after the name of the method. So, let's try to use another familiar type—`Guid`—as the type argument for `TOutput`. The method declaration becomes

```
List<Guid> ConvertAll<Guid>(Converter<string,Guid> conv)
```

To go through the bits of this from left to right:

- The method returns a `List<Guid>`.
- The method's name is `ConvertAll`.
- The method has a single type parameter, and the type argument we're using is `Guid`.
- The method takes a single parameter, which is a `Converter<string,Guid>` and is called `conv`.

Now we just need to know what `Converter<string,Guid>` is and we're all done. Not surprisingly, `Converter<string,Guid>` is a constructed *generic delegate type* (the unbound type is `Converter<TInput,TOutput>`), which is used to convert a string to a GUID.

So, we have a method that can operate on a list of strings, using a converter to produce a list of GUIDs. Now that we understand the method's signature, it's easier to understand the documentation, which confirms that this method does the obvious thing and converts each element in the original list into the target type, and adds it to a list, which is then returned. Thinking about the signature in concrete terms gives us a clearer mental model, and makes it simpler to think about what we might expect the method to do.

Just to prove I haven't been leading you down the garden path, let's take a look at this method in action. Listing 3.2 shows the conversion of a list of integers into a list of floating-point numbers, where each element of the second list is the square root of the corresponding element in the first list. After the conversion, we print out the results.

Listing 3.2 The `List<T>.ConvertAll<TOutput>` method in action

```
static double TakeSquareRoot (int x)
{
    return Math.Sqrt (x);
```

```
}
...
List<int> integers = new List<int>();
integers.Add(1);
integers.Add(2);                              ❶ Creates and
integers.Add(3);                                populates list
integers.Add(4);                                of integers

Converter<int,double> converter = TakeSquareRoot;   ❷ Creates delegate
                                                       instance
List<double> doubles;
doubles = integers.ConvertAll<double>(converter);   Calls generic
                                                    method to
foreach (double d in doubles)                     ❸ convert list
{
    Console.WriteLine (d);
}
```

The creation and population of the list ❶ is straightforward enough—it's just a strongly typed list of integers. ❷ uses a feature of delegates (method group conversions), which is new to C# 2 and which we'll discuss in more detail in section 5.2. Although I don't like using a feature before describing it fully, the line would just have been too long to fit on the page with the full version. It does what you expect it to, though. At ❸ we call the generic method, specifying the type argument for the method in the same way as we've seen for generic types. We'll see later (section 3.3.2) that you don't always need to specify the type argument—often the compiler can work it out itself, making the code that bit more compact. We could have omitted it this time, but I wanted to show the full syntax. Writing out the list that has been returned is simple, and when you run the code you'll see it print 1, 1.414..., 1.732..., and 2, as expected.

So, what's the point of all of this? We could have just used a foreach loop to go through the integers and printed out the square root immediately, of course, but it's not at all uncommon to want to convert a list of one type to a list of another by performing some logic on it. The code to do it manually is still simple, but it's easier to read a version that just does it in a single method call. That's often the way with generic methods—they often do things that previously you'd have happily done "longhand" but that are just simpler with a method call. Before generics, there could have been a similar operation to ConvertAll on ArrayList converting from object to object, but it would have been a lot less satisfactory. Anonymous methods (see section 5.4) also help here—if we hadn't wanted to introduce an extra method, we could just have specified the conversion "inline."

Note that just because a method is generic doesn't mean it has to be part of a generic type. Listing 3.3 shows a generic method being declared and used within a perfectly normal class.

Listing 3.3 Implementing a generic method in a nongeneric type

```
static List<T> MakeList<T> (T first, T second)
{
    List<T> list = new List<T>();
    list.Add (first);
```

```
        list.Add (second);
        return list;
    }
    ...
    List<string> list = MakeList<string> ("Line 1", "Line 2");
    foreach (string x in list)
    {
        Console.WriteLine (x);
    }
```

The MakeList<T> generic method only needs one type parameter (T). All it does is build a list containing the two parameters. It's worth noting that we can use T as a type argument when we create the List<T> in the method, however. Just as when we were looking at generic declarations, think of the implementation as (roughly speaking) replacing all of the places where it says T with string. When we call the method, we use the same syntax we've seen before. In case you were wondering, a generic method within a generic type doesn't *have* to use the generic type's type parameters—although most do.

All OK so far? You should now have the hang of "simple" generics. There's a bit more complexity to come, I'm afraid, but if you're happy with the fundamental idea of generics, you've jumped the biggest hurdle. Don't worry if it's still a bit hazy—particularly when it comes to the open/closed/unbound/constructed terminology—but now would be a good time to do some experimentation so you can see generics in action before we go any further.

The most important types to play with are List<T> and Dictionary<TKey,TValue>. A lot of the time you can get by just by instinct and experimentation, but if you want more details of these types, you can skip ahead to sections 3.5.1 and 3.5.2. Once you're confident using these types, you should find that you rarely want to use ArrayList or Hashtable anymore.

One thing you may find when you experiment is that it's hard to only go part of the way. Once you make one part of an API generic, you often find that you need to rework other code to either *also* be generic or to put in the casts required by the more strongly typed method calls you have now. An alternative can be to have a strongly typed implementation, using generic classes under the covers, but leaving a weakly typed API for the moment. As time goes on, you'll become more confident about when it's appropriate to use generics.

3.3   *Beyond the basics*

While the relatively simple uses of generics we've seen can get you a long way, there are some more features available that can help you further. We'll start off by examining *type constraints*, which allow you more control over which type arguments can be specified. They are useful when creating your own generic types and methods, and you'll need to understand them in order to know what options are available when using the framework, too.

We'll then examine *type inference*—a handy compiler trick that means that when you're using generic methods, you don't always have to explicitly state the type parameters. You don't have to use it, but it can make your code a lot easier to read when used appropriately. We'll see in part 3 that the C# compiler is gradually being allowed to infer a lot more information from your code, while still keeping the language safe and statically typed.

The last part of this section deals with obtaining the default value of a type parameter and what comparisons are available when you're writing generic code. We'll wrap up with an example demonstrating most of the features we've covered, as well as being a useful class in itself.

Although this section delves a bit deeper into generics, there's nothing *really* hard about it. There's plenty to remember, but all the features serve a purpose, and you'll be grateful for them when you need them. Let's get started.

3.3.1 *Type constraints*

So far, all the type parameters we've seen can be applied to any type at all—they are *unconstrained*. We can have a `List<int>`, a `Dictionary<object,FileMode>`, anything. That's fine when we're dealing with collections that don't have to interact with what they store—but not all uses of generics are like that. Often you want to call methods on instances of the type parameter, or create new instances, or make sure you only accept reference types (or only accept value types). In other words, you want to specify rules to say which type arguments are considered valid for your generic type or method. In C# 2, you do this with *constraints*.

Four kinds of constraints are available, and the general syntax is the same for all of them. Constraints come at the end of the declaration of a generic method or type, and are introduced by the contextual keyword `where`. They can be combined together in sensible ways, as we'll see later. First, however, we'll explore each kind of constraint in turn.

REFERENCE TYPE CONSTRAINTS

The first kind of constraint (which is expressed as `T : class` and must be the first constraint specified for that type parameter) simply ensures that the type argument used is a reference type. This can be any class, interface, array, or delegate—or another type parameter that is already known to be a reference type. For example, consider the following declaration:

```
struct RefSample<T> where T : class
```

Valid closed types include

- `RefSample<IDisposable>`
- `RefSample<string>`
- `RefSample<int[]>`

Invalid closed types include

- `RefSample<Guid>`
- `RefSample<int>`

I deliberately made `RefSample` a `struct` (and therefore a value type) to emphasize the difference between the constrained type parameter and the type itself. `RefSample` `<string>` is still a value type with value semantics everywhere—it just happens to use the string type wherever `T` is specified in its API.

When a type parameter is constrained this way, you can compare references (including `null`) with `==` and `!=`, but be aware that unless there are any other constraints, only references will be compared, even if the type in question overloads those operators (as `string` does, for example). With a derivation type constraint (described in a little while), you can end up with "compiler guaranteed" overloads of `==` and `!=`, in which case those overloads are used—but that's a relatively rare situation.

VALUE TYPE CONSTRAINTS

This constraint (expressed as `T : struct`) ensures that the type argument used is a value type, including enums. It excludes nullable types (as described in chapter 4), however. Let's look at an example declaration:

```
class ValSample<T> where T : struct
```

Valid closed types include

- `ValSample<int>`
- `ValSample<FileMode>`

Invalid closed types include

- `ValSample<object>`
- `ValSample<StringBuilder>`

This time `ValSample` is a reference type, despite `T` being constrained to be a value type. Note that `System.Enum` and `System.ValueType` are both reference types in themselves, so aren't allowed as valid type arguments for `ValSample`. Like reference type constraints, when there are multiple constraints for a particular type parameter, a value type constraint must be the first one specified. When a type parameter is constrained to be a value type, comparisons using `==` and `!=` are prohibited.

I rarely find myself using value or reference type constraints, although we'll see in the next chapter that nullable types rely on value type constraints. The remaining two constraints are likely to prove more useful to you when writing your own generic types.

CONSTRUCTOR TYPE CONSTRAINTS

The third kind of constraint (which is expressed as `T : new()` and must be the last constraint for any particular type parameter) simply checks that the type argument used has a parameterless constructor, which can be used to create an instance. This applies to any value type; any nonstatic, nonabstract class without any explicitly declared constructors; and any nonabstract class with an explicit public parameterless constructor.

NOTE *C# vs. CLI standards*—There is a discrepancy between the C# and CLI standards when it comes to value types and constructors. The CLI specification states that value types can't have parameterless constructors, but there's a special instruction to create a value without specifying any parameters. The C# specification states that *all* value types have a default parameterless constructor, and it uses the same syntax to call both explicitly declared constructors and the parameterless one, relying on the compiler to do the right thing underneath. You can see this discrepancy at work when you use reflection to find the constructors of a value type—you won't see a parameterless one.

Again, let's look at a quick example, this time for a method. Just to show how it's useful, I'll give the implementation of the method too.

```
public T CreateInstance<T>() where T : new()
{
    return new T();
}
```

This method just returns a new instance of whatever type you specify, providing that it has a parameterless constructor. So `CreateInstance<int>();` and `CreateInstance<object>();` are OK, but `CreateInstance<string>();` isn't, because `string` doesn't have a parameterless constructor.

There is no way of constraining type parameters to force other constructor signatures—for instance, you can't specify that there has to be a constructor taking a single string parameter. It can be frustrating, but that's unfortunately just the way it is.

Constructor type constraints can be useful when you need to use factory-like patterns, where one object will create another one as and when it needs to. Factories often need to produce objects that are compatible with a certain interface, of course—and that's where our last type of constraint comes in.

DERIVATION TYPE CONSTRAINTS

The final (and most complicated) kind of constraint lets you specify another type that the type argument must derive from (in the case of a class) or implement (in the case of an interface).[4] For the purposes of constraints, types are deemed to derive from themselves. You can specify that one type argument must derive from another, too—this is called a *type parameter constraint* and makes it harder to understand the declaration, but can be handy every so often. Table 3.2 shows some examples of generic type declarations with derivation type constraints, along with valid and invalid examples of corresponding constructed types.

The third constraint of `T : IComparable<T>` is just one example of using a generic type as the constraint. Other variations such as `T : List<U>` (where `U` is another type

---

[4] Strictly speaking, an implicit reference conversion is OK too. This allows for a constraint such as where `T : IList<Shape>` to be satisfied by `Circle[]`. Even though `Circle[]` doesn't actually implement `IList<Shape>`, there is an implicit reference conversion available.

Table 3.2   Examples of derivation type constraints

Declaration	Constructed type examples

`class Sample<T>`
`   where T : Stream`
	Valid: `Sample<Stream>`
	`         Sample<MemoryStream>`
	Invalid: `Sample<object>`
	`           Sample<string>`

`struct Sample<T>` `   where T : IDisposable`	Valid: `Sample<IDisposable>` `         Sample<DataTable>` Invalid: `Sample<StringBuilder>`
`class Sample<T>` `   where T : IComparable<T>`	Valid: `Sample<string>` Invalid: `Sample<FileInfo>`
`class Sample<T,U>` `   where T : U`	Valid: `Sample<Stream,IDisposable>` `         Sample<string,string>` Invalid: `Sample<string,IDisposable>`

parameter) and `T : IList<string>` are also fine. You can specify multiple interfaces, but only one class. For instance, this is fine (if hard to satisfy):

```
class Sample<T> where T : Stream,
                         IEnumerable<string>,
                         IComparable<int>
```

But this isn't:

```
class Sample<T> where T : Stream,
                         ArrayList,
                         IComparable<int>
```

No type can derive directly from more than one class anyway, so such a constraint would usually either be impossible (like this one) or part of it would be redundant (specifying that the type had to derive from both `Stream` and `MemoryStream`, for example). One more set of restrictions: the class you specify can't be a struct, a sealed class (such as `string`), or any of the following "special" types:

- `System.Object`
- `System.Enum`
- `System.ValueType`
- `System.Delegate`

Derivation type constraints are probably the most useful kind, as they mean you can use members of the specified type on instances of the type parameter. One particularly handy example of this is `T : IComparable<T>`, so that you know you can compare two instances of `T` meaningfully and directly. We'll see an example of this (as well as discuss other forms of comparison) in section 3.3.3.

COMBINING CONSTRAINTS

I've mentioned the possibility of having multiple constraints, and we've seen them in action for derivation constraints, but we haven't seen the different kinds being combined together. Obviously no type can be both a reference type and a value type, so that combination is forbidden, and as *every* value type has a parameterless constructor, specifying the construction constraint when you've already got a value type constraint is also not allowed (but you can still use `new T()` within methods if T is constrained to be a value type). Different type parameters can have different constraints, and they're each introduced with a separate `where`.

Let's see some valid and invalid examples:

Valid:

```
class Sample<T> where T : class, IDisposable, new()
class Sample<T> where T : struct, IDisposable
class Sample<T,U> where T : class where U : struct, T
class Sample<T,U> where T : Stream where U : IDisposable
```

Invalid:

```
class Sample<T> where T : class, struct
class Sample<T> where T : Stream, class
class Sample<T> where T : new(), Stream
class Sample<T,U> where T : struct where U : class, T
class Sample<T,U> where T : Stream, U : IDisposable
```

I included the last example on each list because it's so easy to try the invalid one instead of the valid version, and the compiler error is not at all helpful. Just remember that each list of type parameter constraints needs its own introductory `where`. The third valid example is interesting—if U is a value type, how can it derive from T, which is a reference type? The answer is that T could be `object` or an interface that U implements. It's a pretty nasty constraint, though.

Now that you've got all the knowledge you need to read generic type declarations, let's look at the type argument inference that I mentioned earlier. In listing 3.2 we explicitly stated the type arguments to `List.ConvertAll`—but let's now ask the compiler to work them out when it can, making it simpler to call generic methods.

3.3.2 Type inference for type arguments of generic methods

Specifying type arguments when you're calling a generic method can often seem pretty redundant. Usually it's obvious what the type arguments should be, based on the method arguments themselves. To make life easier, the C# 2 compiler is allowed to be smart in tightly defined ways, so you can call the method without explicitly stating the type arguments.

Before we go any further, I should stress that this is only true for generic *methods*. It doesn't apply to generic *types*. Now that we've got that cleared up, let's look at the relevant lines from listing 3.3, and see how things can be simplified. Here are the lines declaring and invoking the method:

```
static List<T> MakeList<T> (T first, T second)
...
List<string> list = MakeList<string> ("Line 1", "Line 2");
```

Now look at the arguments we've specified—they're both strings. Each of the parameters in the method is declared to be of type T. Even if we hadn't got the <string> part of the method invocation expression, it would be fairly obvious that we meant to call the method using `string` as the type argument for T. The compiler allows you to omit it, leaving this:

```
List<string> list = MakeList ("Line 1", "Line 2");
```

That's a bit neater, isn't it? At least, it's shorter. That doesn't always mean it's more readable, of course—in some cases it'll make it harder for the reader to work out what type arguments you're trying to use, even if the compiler can do it easily. I recommend that you judge each case on its merits.

Notice how the compiler definitely knows that we're using `string` as the type parameter, because the assignment to `list` works too, and that still *does* specify the type argument (and has to). The assignment has no influence on the type parameter inference process, however. It just means that if the compiler works out what type arguments it thinks you want to use but gets it wrong, you're still likely to get a compile-time error.

How could the compiler get it wrong? Well, suppose we actually wanted to use `object` as the type argument. Our method parameters are still valid, but the compiler thinks we actually meant to use `string`, as they're both strings. Changing one of the parameters to explicitly be cast to `object` makes type inference fail, as one of the method arguments would suggest that T should be `string`, and the other suggests that T should be `object`. The compiler *could* look at this and say that setting T to `object` would satisfy everything but setting T to `string` wouldn't, but the specification only gives a limited number of steps to follow. This area is already fairly complicated in C# 2, and C# 3 takes things even further. I won't try to give all of the nuts and bolts of the C# 2 rules here, but the basic steps are as follows.

1 For each method argument (the bits in normal parentheses, not angle brackets), try to infer some of the type arguments of the generic method, using some fairly simple techniques.

2 Check that all the results from the first step are consistent—in other words, if one argument implied one type argument for a particular type parameter, and another implied a different type argument for the same type parameter, then inference fails for the method call.

3 Check that all the type parameters needed for the generic method have been inferred. You can't let the compiler infer some while you specify others explicitly—it's all or nothing.

To avoid learning all the rules (and I wouldn't recommend it unless you're particularly interested in the fine details), there's one simple thing to do: try it to see what happens. If you think the compiler *might* be able to infer all the type arguments, try calling the method without specifying any. If it fails, stick the type arguments in explicitly. You lose nothing more than the time it takes to compile the code once, and you don't have to have all the extra language-lawyer garbage in your head.

3.3.3 *Implementing generics*

Although you're likely to spend more time using generic types and methods than writing them yourself, there are a few things you should know for those occasions where you're providing the implementation. Most of the time you can just pretend T (or whatever your type parameter is called) is just the name of a type and get on with writing code as if you weren't using generics at all. There are a few extra things you should know, however.

DEFAULT VALUE EXPRESSIONS
When you know exactly what type you're working with, you know its "default" value—the value an otherwise uninitialized field would have, for instance. When you don't know what type you're referring to, you can't specify that default value directly. You can't use null because it might not be a reference type. You can't use 0 because it might not be a numeric type. While it's fairly rare to need the default value, it can be useful on occasion. Dictionary<TKey,TValue> provides a good example—it has a TryGetValue method that works a bit like the TryParse methods on the numeric types: it uses an output parameter for the value you're trying to fetch, and a Boolean return value to indicate whether or not it succeeded. This means that the method *has* to have some value of type TValue to populate the output parameter with. (Remember that output parameters must be assigned before the method returns normally.)

NOTE *The TryXXX pattern*—There are a few patterns in .NET that are easily identifiable by the names of the methods involved—BeginXXX and EndXXX suggest an asynchronous operation, for example. The TryXXX pattern is one that has had its use expanded between .NET 1.1 and 2.0. It's designed for situations that might normally be considered to be errors (in that the method can't perform its primary duty) but where failure could well occur without this indicating a serious issue, and shouldn't be deemed exceptional. For instance, users can often fail to type in numbers correctly, so being able to *try* to parse some text without having to catch an exception and swallow it is very useful. Not only does it improve performance in the failure case, but more importantly, it saves exceptions for genuine error cases where something is wrong in the *system* (however widely you wish to interpret that). It's a useful pattern to have up your sleeve as a library designer, when applied appropriately.

C# 2 provides the *default value expression* to cater for just this need. The specification doesn't refer to it as an operator, but you can think of it as being similar to the typeof operator, just returning a different value. Listing 3.4 shows this in a generic method, and also gives an example of type inference and a derivation type constraint in action.

Listing 3.4 Comparing a given value to the default in a generic way

```
static int CompareToDefault<T> (T value)
    where T : IComparable<T>
{
    return value.CompareTo(default(T));
```

```
}
...
Console.WriteLine(CompareToDefault("x"));
Console.WriteLine(CompareToDefault(10));
Console.WriteLine(CompareToDefault(0));
Console.WriteLine(CompareToDefault(-10));
Console.WriteLine(CompareToDefault(DateTime.MinValue));
```

Listing 3.4 shows a generic method being used with three different types: string, int, and DateTime. The CompareToDefault method dictates that it can only be used with types implementing the IComparable<T> interface, which allows us to call CompareTo(T) on the value passed in. The other value we use for the comparison is the default value for the type. As string is a reference type, the default value is null—and the documentation for CompareTo states that for reference types, everything should be greater than null so the first result is 1. The next three lines show comparisons with the default value of int, demonstrating that the default value is 0. The output of the last line is 0, showing that DateTime.MinValue is the default value for DateTime.

Of course, the method in listing 3.4 will fail if you pass it null as the argument—the line calling CompareTo will throw NullReferenceException in the normal way. Don't worry about it for the moment—there's an alternative using IComparer<T>, as we'll see soon.

DIRECT COMPARISONS

Although listing 3.4 showed how a comparison is possible, we don't always want to constrain our types to implement IComparable<T> or its sister interface, IEquatable<T>, which provides a strongly typed Equals(T) method to complement the Equals(object) method that all types have. Without the extra information these interfaces give us access to, there is little we can do in terms of comparisons, other than calling Equals(object), which will result in boxing the value we want to compare with when it's a value type. (In fact, there are a couple of types to help us in some situations—we'll come to them in a minute.)

When a type parameter is unconstrained (in other words, no constraints are applied to it), you can use == and != operators but *only* to compare a value of that type with null. You can't compare two values of type T with each other. In the case where the type argument provided for T is a value type (other than a nullable type), a comparison with null will always decide they are unequal (so the comparison can be removed by the JIT compiler). When the type argument is a reference type, the normal reference comparison will be used. When the type argument is a nullable type, the comparison will do the obvious thing, treating an instance without a value as null. (Don't worry if this last bit doesn't make sense yet—it will when you've read the next chapter. Some features are too intertwined to allow me to describe either of them completely without referring to the other, unfortunately.)

When a type parameter is constrained to be a value type, == and != can't be used with it at all. When it's constrained to be a reference type, the kind of comparison performed depends on *exactly* what the type parameter is constrained to be. If it's *just* a reference type, simple reference comparisons are performed. If it's further constrained to derive from a particular type that overloads the `==` and `!=` operators, those overloads are used. Beware, however—extra overloads that happen to be made available by the type argument specified by the caller are *not* used. Listing 3.5 demonstrates this with a simple reference type constraint and a type argument of `string`.

Listing 3.5 Comparisons using == and != using reference comparisons

```
static bool AreReferencesEqual<T> (T first, T second)
   where T : class
{                                         ❶ Compares
   return first==second;      ◁────────     references
}
...
string name = "Jon";
string intro1 = "My name is "+name;
string intro2 = "My name is "+name;       ❷ Compares using
Console.WriteLine (intro1==intro2);    ◁───  string overload
Console.WriteLine (AreReferencesEqual(intro1, intro2));
```

Even though `string` overloads `==` (as demonstrated by ❷ printing `True`), this overload is not used by the comparison at ❶. Basically, when `AreReferencesEqual<T>` is compiled the compiler doesn't know what overloads will be available—it's as if the parameters passed in were just of type `object`.

This is not just specific to operators—when the compiler encounters a generic type, it resolves all the method overloads when compiling the unbound generic type, rather than reconsidering each possible method call for more specific overloads at execution time. For instance, a statement of `Console.WriteLine (default(T));` will always resolve to call `Console.WriteLine(object value)`—it doesn't call `Console.WriteLine (string value)` when `T` happens to be `string`. This is similar to the normal situation of overloads being chosen at compile time rather than execution time, but readers familiar with templates in C++ may be surprised nonetheless.

Two classes that are *extremely* useful when it comes to comparing values are `Equality-Comparer<T>` and `Comparer<T>`, both in the `System.Collections.Generic` namespace. They implement `IEqualityComparer<T>` (useful for comparing and hashing dictionary keys) and `IComparer<T>` (useful for sorting) respectively, and the `Default` property returns an implementation that generally does the right thing for the appropriate type. See the documentation for more details, but consider using these (and similar types such as `StringComparer`) when performing comparisons. We'll use `Equality-Comparer<T>` in our next example.

FULL COMPARISON EXAMPLE: REPRESENTING A PAIR OF VALUES

To finish off our section on implementing generics—and indeed "medium-level" generics—here's a complete example. It implements a useful generic type—a `Pair <TFirst,TSecond>`, which just holds two values together, like a key/value pair, but with no expectations as to the relationship between the two values. As well as providing properties to access the values themselves, we'll override `Equals` and `GetHashCode` to allow instances of our type to play nicely when used as keys in a dictionary. Listing 3.6 gives the complete code.

Listing 3.6   Generic class representing a pair of values

```csharp
using System;
using System.Collections.Generic;

public sealed class Pair<TFirst, TSecond>
    : IEquatable<Pair<TFirst, TSecond>>
{
    private readonly TFirst first;
    private readonly TSecond second;

    public Pair(TFirst first, TSecond second)
    {
        this.first = first;
        this.second = second;
    }

    public TFirst First
    {
        get { return first; }
    }

    public TSecond Second
    {
        get { return second; }
    }

    public bool Equals(Pair<TFirst, TSecond> other)
    {
        if (other == null)
        {
            return false;
        }
        return EqualityComparer<TFirst>.Default
                .Equals(this.First, other.First) &&
               EqualityComparer<TSecond>.Default
                .Equals(this.Second, other.Second);
    }

    public override bool Equals(object o)
    {
        return Equals(o as Pair<TFirst, TSecond>);
    }

    public override int GetHashCode()
    {
        return EqualityComparer<TFirst>.Default
                .GetHashCode(first) * 37 +
               EqualityComparer<TSecond>.Default
                .GetHashCode(second);
    }
}
```

Listing 3.6 is very straightforward. The constituent values are stored in appropriately typed member variables, and access is provided by simple read-only properties. We implement IEquatable<Pair<TFirst,TSecond>> to give a strongly typed API that will avoid unnecessary execution time checks. The equality and hash-code computations both use the default equality comparer for the two type parameters—these handle nulls for us automatically, which makes the code somewhat simpler.[5]

If we wanted to support sorting, we could implement IComparer <Pair <TFirst,TSecond>>, perhaps ordering by the first component and then the second. This kind of type is a good candidate for bearing in mind what functionality you *might* want, but not actually implementing until you need it.

We've finished looking at our "intermediate" features now. I realize it can all seem complicated at first sight, but don't be put off: the benefits far outweigh the added complexity. Over time they become second nature. Now that you've got the Pair class as an example, it might be worth looking over your own code base to see whether there are some patterns that you keep reimplementing solely to use different types.

With any large topic there is always more to learn. The next section will take you through the most important advanced topics in generics. If you're feeling a bit over-whelmed by now, you might want to skip to the relative comfort of section 3.5, where we explore the generic collections provided in the framework. It's well worth understanding the topics in the next section *eventually*, but if everything so far has been new to you it wouldn't hurt to skip it for the moment.

3.4 *Advanced generics*

You may be expecting me to claim that in the rest of this chapter we'll be covering every aspect of generics that we haven't looked at so far. However, there are *so many* little nooks and crannies involving generics, that's simply not possible—or at least, I certainly wouldn't want to even read about all the details, let alone write about them. Fortunately the nice people at Microsoft and ECMA have written all the details in the freely available language specification,[6] so if you ever want to check some obscure situation that isn't covered here, that should be your next port of call. Arguably if your code ends up in a corner case complicated enough that you need to consult the specification to work out what it should do, you should refactor it into a more obvious form anyway; you don't want each maintenance engineer from now until eternity to have to read the specification.

My aim with this section is to cover everything you're *likely* to want to know about generics. It talks more about the CLR and framework side of things than the particular syntax of the C# 2 language, although of course it's all relevant when developing in C# 2. We'll start by considering static members of generic types, including type initialization. From there, it's a natural step to wonder just how all this is implemented

---

[5] The formula used for calculating the hash code based on the two "part" results comes from reading *Effective Java* (Prentice Hall PTR, 2001) by Joshua Bloch. It certainly doesn't guarantee a good distribution of hash codes, but in my opinion it's better than using a bitwise exclusive OR. See *Effective Java* for more details, and indeed for many other useful tips.

[6] http://www.ecma-international.org/publications/standards/Ecma-334.htm

under the covers—although we won't be going so deep that you need a flashlight. We'll have a look at what happens when you enumerate a generic collection using foreach in C# 2, and round off the section by seeing how reflection in the .NET Framework is affected by generics.

3.4.1 Static fields and static constructors

Just as instance fields belong to an instance, static fields belong to the type they're declared in. That is, if you declare a static field x in class SomeClass, there's exactly one SomeClass.x field, no matter how many instances of SomeClass you create, and no matter how many types derive from SomeClass.[7] That's the familiar scenario from C# 1—so how does it map across to generics?

The answer is that each *closed* type has its own set of static fields. This is easiest to see with an example. Listing 3.7 creates a generic type including a static field. We set the field's value for different closed types, and then print out the values to show that they are separate.

> **Listing 3.7 Proof that different closed types have different static fields**

```
class TypeWithField<T>
{
    public static string field;

    public static void PrintField()
    {
        Console.WriteLine(field+": "+typeof(T).Name);
    }
}
...
TypeWithField<int>.field = "First";
TypeWithField<string>.field = "Second";
TypeWithField<DateTime>.field = "Third";

TypeWithField<int>.PrintField();
TypeWithField<string>.PrintField();
TypeWithField<DateTime>.PrintField();
```

We set the value of each field to a different value, and print out each field along with the name of the type argument used for that closed type. Here's the output from listing 3.7:

```
First: Int32
Second: String
Third: DateTime
```

So the basic rule is "one static field per closed type." The same applies for static initializers and static constructors. However, it's possible to have one generic type nested

---

[7] Well, one per application domain. For the purposes of this section, we'll assume we're only dealing with one application domain. The concepts for different application domains work the same with generics as with non-generic types.

within another, and types with multiple generic parameters. This *sounds* a lot more complicated, but it works as you probably think it should. Listing 3.8 shows this in action, this time using static constructors to show just how many types there are.

Listing 3.8 Static constructors with nested generic types

```
public class Outer<T>
{
   public class Inner<U,V>
   {
      static Inner()
      {
         Console.WriteLine("Outer<{0}>.Inner<{1},{2}>",
                     typeof(T).Name,
                     typeof(U).Name,
                     typeof(V).Name);
      }

      public static void DummyMethod()
      {
      }
   }
}
...
Outer<int>.Inner<string,DateTime>.DummyMethod();
Outer<string>.Inner<int,int>.DummyMethod();
Outer<object>.Inner<string,object>.DummyMethod();
Outer<string>.Inner<string,object>.DummyMethod();
Outer<object>.Inner<object,string>.DummyMethod();
Outer<string>.Inner<int,int>.DummyMethod();
```

Note! Only 5 lines of output…

Each different list of type arguments counts as a different closed type, so the output of listing 3.8 looks like this:

```
Outer<Int32>.Inner<String,DateTime>
Outer<String>.Inner<Int32,Int32>
Outer<Object>.Inner<String,Object>
Outer<String>.Inner<String,Object>
Outer<Object>.Inner<Object,String>
```

Just as with nongeneric types, the static constructor for any closed type is only executed once, which is why the last line of listing 3.8 doesn't create a sixth line of output—the static constructor for Outer<string>.Inner<int,int> executed earlier, producing the second line of output. To clear up any doubts, if we had a nongeneric PlainInner class inside Outer, there would still have been one possible Outer<T>.PlainInner type per closed Outer type, so Outer<int>.PlainInner would be separate from Outer<long>.PlainInner, with a separate set of static fields as seen earlier.

Now that we've seen just what constitutes a different type, we should think about what the effects of that might be in terms of the amount of native code generated. And no, it's not as bad as you might think…

3.4.2 How the JIT compiler handles generics

Given that we have all of these different closed types, the JIT's job is to convert the IL of the generic type into native code so it can actually be run. In some ways, we shouldn't care exactly how it does that—beyond keeping a close eye on memory and CPU time, we wouldn't see much difference if the JIT did the obvious thing and generated native code for each closed type separately, as if each one had nothing to do with any other type. However, the JIT authors are clever enough that it's worth seeing just what they've done.

Let's start with a simple situation first, with a single type parameter—we'll use List<T> for the sake of convenience. The JIT creates different code for each value type argument—int, long, Guid, and the like—that we use. However, it shares the native code generated for all the closed types that use a reference type as the type argument, such as string, Stream, and StringBuilder. It can do this because all references are the same size (they are 4 bytes on a 32-bit CLR and 8 bytes on a 64-bit CLR, but within any one CLR all references are the same size). An array of references will always be the same size whatever the references happen to be. The space required on the stack for a reference will always be the same. It can use the same register optimizations whatever type is being used—the List<Reason> goes on.

Each of the types still has its own static fields as described in section 3.4.1, but the code that is executed is reused. Of course, the JIT still does all of this lazily—it won't generate the code for List<int> before it needs to, and it will cache that code for all future uses of List<int>. In theory, it's possible to share code for at least *some* value types. The JIT would have to be careful, not just due to size but also for garbage collection reasons—it has to be able to quickly identify areas of a struct value that are live references. However, value types that are the same size and have the same in-memory footprint as far as the GC is concerned *could* share code. At the time of this writing, that's been of sufficiently low priority that it hasn't been implemented and it may well stay that way.

High performance— avoids boxing

This level of detail is primarily of academic interest, but it does have a slight performance impact in terms of more code being JIT compiled. However, the performance *benefits* of generics can be huge, and again that comes down to having the opportunity to JIT to different code for different types. Consider a List<byte>, for instance. In .NET 1.1, adding individual bytes to an ArrayList would have meant boxing each one of them, and storing a reference to each boxed value. Using List<byte> has no such impact—List<T> has a member of type T[] to replace the object[] within ArrayList, and that array is of the appropriate type, taking the appropriate space. So List<byte> has a straight byte[] within it used to store the elements of the array. (In many ways this makes a List<byte> behave like a MemoryStream.)

Figure 3.3 shows an ArrayList and a List<byte>, each with the same six values. (The arrays themselves have more than six elements, to allow for growth. Both

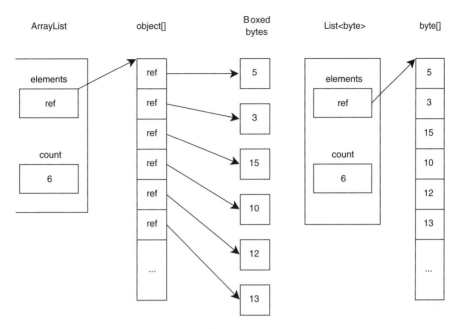

Figure 3.3   Visual demonstration of why `List<T>` takes up a lot less space than `ArrayList` when storing value types

`List<T>` and `ArrayList` have a buffer, and they create a larger buffer when they need to.)

The difference in efficiency here is incredible. Let's look at the `ArrayList` first, considering a 32-bit CLR.[8] Each of the boxed bytes will take up 8 bytes of object overhead, plus 4 bytes (1 byte, rounded up to a word boundary) for the data itself. On top of that, you've got all the references themselves, each of which takes up 4 bytes. So for each byte of useful data, we're paying at least 16 bytes—and then there's the extra unused space for references in the buffer.

Compare this with the `List<byte>`. Each byte in the list takes up a single byte within the elements array. There's still "wasted" space in the buffer, waiting to be used potentially by new items—but at least we're only wasting a single byte per unused element there.

We don't just gain space, but execution speed too. We don't need the time taken to allocate the box, the type checking involved in unboxing the bytes in order to get at them, or the garbage collection of the boxes when they're no longer referenced.

We don't have to go down to the CLR level to find things happening transparently on our behalf, however. C# has always made life easier with syntactic shortcuts, and our next section looks at a familiar example but with a generic twist: iterating with `foreach`.

---

[8] When running on a 64-bit CLR, the overheads are bigger.

3.4.3   *Generic iteration*

One of the most common operations you'll want to perform on a collection (usually an array or a list) is to iterate through all its elements. The simplest way of doing that is usually to use the foreach statement. In C# 1 this relied on the collection either implementing the System.Collections.IEnumerable interface or having a similar GetEnumerator() method that returned a type with a suitable MoveNext() method and Current property. The Current property didn't have to be of type object—and that was the whole point of having these extra rules, which look odd on first sight. Yes, even in C# 1 you could avoid boxing and unboxing during iteration if you had a custom-made enumeration type.

C# 2 makes this somewhat easier, as the rules for the foreach statement have been extended to also use the System.Collections.Generic.IEnumerable<T> interface along with its partner, IEnumerator<T>. These are simply the generic equivalents of the old enumeration interfaces, and they're used in preference to the nongeneric versions. That means that if you iterate through a generic collection of value type elements—List<int>, for example—then no boxing is performed at all. If the old interface had been used instead, then although we wouldn't have incurred the boxing cost while *storing* the elements of the list, we'd still have ended up boxing them when we retrieved them using foreach!

All of this is done for you under the covers—all you need to do is use the foreach statement in the normal way, using the type argument of the collection as the type of the iteration variable, and all will be well. That's not the end of the story, however. In the relatively rare situation that you need to implement iteration over one of your own types, you'll find that IEnumerable<T> extends the old IEnumerable interface, which means you've got to implement two different methods:

```
IEnumerator<T> GetEnumerator();
IEnumerator GetEnumerator();
```

Can you see the problem? The methods differ only in return type, and the rules of C# prevent you from writing two such methods normally. If you think back to section 2.2.2, we saw a similar situation—and we can use the same workaround. If you implement IEnumerable using explicit interface implementation, you can implement IEnumerable<T> with a "normal" method. Fortunately, because IEnumerator<T> extends IEnumerator, you can use the same return value for both methods, and implement the nongeneric method by just calling the generic version. Of course, now you need to implement IEnumerator<T> and you quickly run into similar problems, this time with the Current property.

Listing 3.9 gives a full example, implementing an enumerable class that always just enumerates to the integers 0 to 9.

> **Listing 3.9   A full generic enumeration—of the numbers 0 to 9**

```
class CountingEnumerable: IEnumerable<int>                ❶ Implements
{                                                            IEnumerable<T>
    public IEnumerator<int> GetEnumerator()      ◄──┘        implicitly
```

```
    {
        return new CountingEnumerator();
    }
    IEnumerator IEnumerable.GetEnumerator()
    {
        return GetEnumerator();
    }
}
class CountingEnumerator : IEnumerator<int>
{
    int current = -1;

    public bool MoveNext()
    {
        current++;
        return current < 10;
    }

    public int Current
    {
        get { return current; }
    }

    object IEnumerator.Current
    {
        get { return Current; }
    }

    public void Reset()
    {
            current = -1;
    }

    public void Dispose()
    {
    }
}
...
CountingEnumerable counter = new CountingEnumerable();
foreach (int x in counter)
{
    Console.WriteLine(x);
}
```

2 Implements IEnumerable explicitly

3 Implements IEnumerator<T>.Current implicitly

4 Implements IEnumerator.Current explicitly

5 Proves that enumerable type works

Clearly this isn't useful in terms of the result, but it shows the little hoops you have to go through in order to implement generic enumeration appropriately—at least if you're doing it all longhand. (And that's without making an effort to throw exceptions if Current is accessed at an inappropriate time.) If you think that listing 3.9 looks like a lot of work just to print out the numbers 0 to 9, I can't help but agree with you—and there'd be even more code if we wanted to iterate through anything useful. Fortunately we'll see in chapter 6 that C# 2 takes a large amount of the work away from enumerators in many cases. I've shown the "full" version so you can appreciate the slight wrinkles that have been introduced by the design decision for IEnumerable<T> to extend IEnumerable.

We only need the trick of using explicit interface implementation twice—once for `IEnumerable.GetEnumerator` ❷, and once at `IEnumerator.Current` ❹. Both of these call their generic equivalents (❶ and ❸ respectively). Another addition to `IEnumerator<T>` is that it extends `IDisposable`, so you have to provide a `Dispose` method. The `foreach` statement in C# 1 already called `Dispose` on an enumerator if it implemented `IDisposable`, but in C# 2 there's no execution time testing required—if the compiler finds that you've implemented `IEnumerable<T>`, it creates an unconditional call to `Dispose` at the end of the loop (in a `finally` block). Many enumerators won't actually need to dispose of anything, but it's nice to know that when it *is* required, the most common way of working through an enumerator (the `foreach` statement ❺) handles the calling side automatically.

We'll now go from compile-time efficiency to execution-time flexibility: our final advanced topic is reflection. Even in .NET 1.0/1.1 reflection could be a little tricky, but generic types and methods introduce an extra level of complexity. The framework provides everything we need (with a bit of helpful syntax from C# 2 as a language), and although the additional considerations can be daunting, it's not too bad if you take it one step at a time.

3.4.4 *Reflection and generics*

Reflection is used by different people for all sorts of things. You might use it for execution-time introspection of objects to perform a simple form of data binding. You might use it to inspect a directory full of assemblies to find implementations of a plug-in interface. You might write a file for an Inversion of Control[9] framework to load and dynamically configure your application's components. As the uses of reflection are so diverse, I won't focus on any particular one but give you more general guidance on performing common tasks. We'll start by looking at the extensions to the `typeof` operator.

USING TYPEOF WITH GENERIC TYPES

Reflection is all about examining objects and their types. As such, one of the most important things you need to be able to do is obtain a reference to the `System.Type` object, which allows access to all the information about a particular type. C# uses the `typeof` operator to obtain such a reference for types known at compile time, and this has been extended to encompass generic types.

There are two ways of using `typeof` with generic types—one retrieves the *generic type definition* (in other words, the unbound generic type) and one retrieves a particular constructed type. To obtain the generic type definition—that is, the type with none of the type arguments specified—you simply take the name of the type as it would have been declared and remove the type parameter names, keeping any commas. To retrieve constructed types, you specify the type arguments in the same way as you would to declare a variable of the generic type. Listing 3.10 gives an example of both uses. It uses a generic method so we can revisit how `typeof` can be used with a type parameter, which we previously saw in listing 3.7.

---

[9] . See http://www.martinfowler.com/articles/injection.html

Listing 3.10 Using the `typeof` operator with type parameters

```
static void DemonstrateTypeof<X>()          Displays method's
{                                           type parameter
    Console.WriteLine(typeof(X));        ◁

    Console.WriteLine(typeof(List<>));          Displays
    Console.WriteLine(typeof(Dictionary<,>));   generic      ❶ Displays closed
                                                types           types (despite
    Console.WriteLine(typeof(List<X>));                         using type
    Console.WriteLine(typeof(Dictionary<string,X>));            parameter)

    Console.WriteLine(typeof(List<long>));          Displays
    Console.WriteLine(typeof(Dictionary<long,Guid>)); closed types
}
...
DemonstrateTypeof<int>();
```

Most of listing 3.10 is as you might naturally expect, but it's worth pointing out two things. First, look at the syntax for obtaining the generic type definition of `Dictionary <TKey,TValue>`. The comma in the angle brackets is required to effectively tell the compiler to look for the type with two type parameters: remember that there can be several generic types with the same name, as long as they vary by the number of type parameters they have. Similarly, you'd retrieve the generic type definition for `MyClass<T,U,V,W>` using `typeof(MyClass<,,,>)`. The number of type parameters is specified in IL (and in full type names as far as the framework is concerned) by putting a back tick after the first part of the type name and then the number. The type parameters are then indicated in square brackets instead of the angle brackets we're used to. For instance, the second line printed ends with `List`1[T]`, showing that there is one type parameter, and the third line includes `Dictionary`2[TKey,TValue]`.

Second, note that wherever the method's type parameter is used, the actual value of the type argument is used at execution time. So the first line ❶ prints `List`1 <System.Int32>` rather than `List`1<X>`, which you might have expected. In other words, a type that is open at compile time may be closed at execution time. *This is very confusing. You should be aware of it in case you don't get the results you expect, but otherwise don't worry.* To retrieve a truly open constructed type at execution time, you need to work a bit harder. See the MSDN documentation for `Type.IsGenericType` for a suitably convoluted example.

For reference, here's the output of listing 3.10:

```
System.Int32
System.Collections.Generic.List`1[T]
System.Collections.Generic.Dictionary`2[TKey,TValue]
System.Collections.Generic.List`1[System.Int32]
System.Collections.Generic.Dictionary`2[System.String,System.Int32]
System.Collections.Generic.List`1[System.Int64]
System.Collections.Generic.Dictionary`2[System.Int64,System.Guid]
```

Having retrieved an object representing a generic type, there are many "next steps" you can take. All the previously available ones (finding the members of the type, creating an instance, and so on) are still present—although some are not applicable for generic type definitions—and there are new ones as well that let you inquire about the generic nature of the type.

METHODS AND PROPERTIES OF SYSTEM.TYPE

There are far too many new methods and properties to look at them all in detail, but there are two particularly important ones: GetGenericTypeDefinition and MakeGenericType. They are effectively opposites—the first acts on a constructed type, retrieving the generic type definition; the second acts on a generic type definition and returns a constructed type. Arguably it would have been clearer if this method had been called ConstructGenericType, MakeConstructedType, or some other name with *construct* or *constructed* in it, but we're stuck with what we've got.

Just like normal types, there is only one Type object for any particular type—so calling MakeGenericType twice with the same types as parameters will return the same reference twice, and calling GetGenericTypeDefinition on two types constructed from the same generic type definition will likewise give the same result for both calls.

Another method—this time one which already existed in .NET 1.1—that is worth exploring is Type.GetType, and its related Assembly.GetType method, both of which provide a dynamic equivalent to typeof. You might expect to be able to feed each line of the output of listing 3.10 to the GetType method called on an appropriate assembly, but unfortunately life isn't quite that straightforward. It's fine for closed constructed types—the type arguments just go in square brackets. For generic type definitions, however, you need to remove the square brackets entirely—otherwise GetType thinks you mean an array type. Listing 3.11 shows all of these methods in action.

Listing 3.11   Various ways of retrieving generic and constructed Type objects

```
string listTypeName = "System.Collections.Generic.List`1";

Type defByName = Type.GetType(listTypeName);

Type closedByName = Type.GetType(listTypeName+"[System.String]");
Type closedByMethod = defByName.MakeGenericType(typeof(string));
Type closedByTypeof = typeof(List<string>);

Console.WriteLine(closedByMethod==closedByName);
Console.WriteLine(closedByName==closedByTypeof);

Type defByTypeof = typeof(List<>);
Type defByMethod = closedByName.GetGenericTypeDefinition();

Console.WriteLine(defByMethod==defByName);
Console.WriteLine(defByName==defByTypeof);
```

The output of listing 3.11 is just True four times, validating that however you obtain a reference to a particular type object, there is only one such object involved.

As I mentioned earlier, there are many new methods and properties on Type, such as GetGenericArguments, IsGenericTypeDefinition, and IsGenericType. The documentation for IsGenericType is probably the best starting point for further exploration.

REFLECTING GENERIC METHODS

Generic methods have a similar (though smaller) set of additional properties and methods. Listing 3.12 gives a brief demonstration of this, calling a generic method by reflection.

Listing 3.12 Retrieving and invoking a generic method with reflection

```
public static void PrintTypeParameter<T>()
{
    Console.WriteLine (typeof(T));
}
...
Type type = typeof(Snippet);
MethodInfo definition = type.GetMethod("PrintTypeParameter");
MethodInfo constructed;
constructed = definition.MakeGenericMethod(typeof(string));
constructed.Invoke(null, null);
```

First we retrieve the generic method definition, and then we make a constructed generic method using MakeGenericMethod. As with types, we could go the other way if we wanted to—but unlike Type.GetType, there is no way of specifying a constructed method in the GetMethod call. The framework also has a problem if there are methods that are overloaded purely by number of type parameters—there are no methods in Type that allow you to specify the number of type parameters, so instead you'd have to call Type.GetMethods and find the right one by looking through *all* the methods.

After retrieving the constructed method, we invoke it. The arguments in this example are both null as we're invoking a static method that doesn't take any "normal" parameters. The output is System.String, as we'd expect.

Note that the methods retrieved from generic type definitions cannot be invoked directly—instead, you must get the method from a constructed type. This applies to both generic methods and nongeneric methods.

Again, more methods and properties are available on MethodInfo, and IsGeneric-Method is a good starting point in MSDN. Hopefully the information in this section will have been enough to get you going, though—and to point out some of the added complexities you might not have otherwise anticipated when first starting to access generic types and methods with reflection.

That's all we're going to cover in the way of advanced features. Just to reiterate, this is not meant to have been an absolutely complete guide by any means—but most developers are unlikely to need to know the more obscure areas. I hope for your sake that you fall into this camp, as specifications tend to get harder to read the deeper you go into them. Remember that unless you're working alone and just for yourself, you're unlikely to be the only one to work on your code. If you need features that are more complex than the ones demonstrated here, you almost certainly shouldn't assume that anyone reading your code will understand it without help. On the other hand, if you find that your coworkers don't know about some of the topics we've covered so far, please feel free to direct them to the nearest bookshop...

The next section is much more down to earth than our investigations into reflection and the bowels of the JIT. It covers the most common use of generics: the standard collection classes.

3.5   *Generic collection classes in .NET 2.0*

Although this book is primarily about C# as a *language*, it would be foolish to ignore the fact that C# is almost always used within the .NET Framework, and that in order to use the language effectively you'll need to have a certain amount of knowledge of the libraries too. I won't be going into the details of ADO.NET, ASP.NET, and the like, but you're bound to use collections in almost *any* .NET program of any size. This section will cover the core collections found in the System.Collections.Generic namespace. We'll start in familiar territory with List<T>.

3.5.1   *List<T>*

We've already seen List<T> several times. Broadly speaking, it's the generic equivalent of the nongeneric ArrayList type, which has been a part of .NET from the word go. There are some new features, and a few operations in ArrayList didn't make it to List<T>. Most of the features that have been removed from List<T> have also been removed from other collections, so we'll cover them here and then just refer to them later on when talking about the other collections. Many of the new features in List<T> (beyond "being generic") *aren't* available in the other generic collections. The combination of these factors leads to our discussion of List<T> being the longest in this section—but then it's probably the most widely used collection in real-life code, too. When you think of using a list of data items in your code, List<T> is the default choice.

I won't bore you with the most common operations (adding, removing, fetching, and replacing items) but will merely point out that List<T> makes itself available in a large number of situations using old APIs by implementing IList as well as IList<T>. Enough of looking backward, though—let's see what's new.

NEW FEATURES OF LIST<T>
The new methods available within List<T> are all powered by generics—in particular, generic delegates. This is part of a general trend toward using delegates more heavily in the framework, which has been made simpler by the improvements in delegate syntax available in C# 2. (There would have been little point in adding lots of delegate-specific features into the framework with the syntax being as clunky as it was in C# 1.) We can now do the following:

- Convert each element of the list to a different type, resulting in a new list (ConvertAll).
- Check whether *any* of the elements in the list match a given predicate (Exists).
- Check whether *all* of the elements in the list match a given predicate (TrueForAll).
- Find the first, last, or all elements in the list matching a predicate (FindXXX).

- Remove all elements in the list matching a given predicate (RemoveAll).
- Perform a given action on each element on the list (ForEach).[10]

We've already seen the ConvertAll method in listing 3.2, but there are two more delegate types that are very important for this extra functionality: Predicate<T> and Action<T>, which have the following signatures:

```
public delegate bool Predicate<T> (T obj)
public delegate void Action<T> (T obj)
```

A *predicate* is a way of testing whether a value matches a criterion. For instance, you could have a predicate that tested for strings having a length greater than 5, or one that tested whether an integer was even. An *action* does exactly what you might expect it to—performs an action with the specified value. You might print the value to the console, add it to another collection—whatever you want.

For simple examples, most of the methods listed here are easily achieved with a foreach loop. However, using a delegate allows the behavior to come from somewhere other than the immediate code in the foreach loop. With the improvements to delegates in C# 2, it can also be a bit simpler than the loop.

Listing 3.13 shows the last two methods—ForEach and RemoveAll—in action. We take a list of the integers from 2 to 100, remove multiples of 2, then multiples of 3, and so forth up to 10, finally listing the numbers. You may well recognize this as a slight variation on the "Sieve of Eratosthenes" method of finding prime numbers. I've used the streamlined method of creating delegates to make the example more realistic. Even though we haven't covered the syntax yet (you can peep ahead to chapter 5 if you want to get the details), it should be fairly obvious what's going on here.

Listing 3.13 Printing primes using RemoveAll and ForEach from List<T>

```
List<int> candidates = new List<int>();          ❶ Populates list
for (int i=2; i <= 100; i++)                         of candidate
{                                                    primes
    candidates.Add(i);
}

for (int factor=2; factor <= 10; factor++)
{
    candidates.RemoveAll (delegate(int x)         ❷ Removes
        { return x>factor && x%factor==0; }          nonprimes
    );
}

candidates.ForEach (delegate(int prime)           ❸ Prints out
    { Console.WriteLine(prime); }                    remaining
);                                                   elements
```

---

[10] Not to be confused with the foreach statement, which does a similar thing but requires the actual code in place, rather than being a method with an Action<T> parameter.

Listing 3.13 starts off by just creating a list of all the integers between 2 and 100 inclusive ❶—nothing spectacular here, although once again I should point out that there's no boxing involved. The delegate used in step ❷ is a `Predicate <int>`, and the one used in ❸ is an `Action<int>`. One point to note is how simple the use of `RemoveAll` is. Because you can't change the contents of a collection while iterating over it, the typical ways of removing multiple elements from a list have previously been as follows:

- Iterate using the index in ascending order, decrementing the index variable whenever you remove an element.
- Iterate using the index in descending order to avoid excessive copying.
- Create a new list of the elements to remove, and then iterate through the new list, removing each element in turn from the old list.

None of these is particularly satisfactory—the predicate approach is much neater, giving emphasis to what you want to achieve rather than how exactly it should happen. It's a good idea to experiment with predicates a bit to get comfortable with them, particularly if you're likely to be using C# 3 in a production setting any time in the near future—this more functional style of coding is going to be increasingly important over time.

Next we'll have a brief look at the methods that are present in `ArrayList` but not `List<T>`, and consider why that might be the case.

FEATURES "MISSING" FROM LIST<T>

A few methods in `ArrayList` have been shifted around a little—the static `ReadOnly` method is replaced by the `AsReadOnly` instance method, and `TrimToSize` is *nearly* replaced by `TrimExcess` (the difference is that `TrimExcess` won't do anything if the size and capacity are nearly the same anyway). There are a few genuinely "missing" pieces of functionality, however. These are listed, along with the suggested workaround, in table 3.3.

Table 3.3   Methods from `ArrayList` with no direct equivalent in `List<T>`

ArrayList method	Way of achieving similar effect
Adapter	None provided
Clone	`list.GetRange (0, list.Count)` or `new List<T>(list)`
FixedSize	None
Repeat	for loop or write a replacement generic method
SetRange	for loop or write a replacement generic method
Synchronized	`SynchronizedCollection`

The `Synchronized` method was a bad idea in `ArrayList` to start with, in my view. Making individual calls to a collection thread-safe doesn't make the collection itself thread-safe, because so many operations (e.g., iterating over the collection) involve *multiple* calls. To make those operations thread-safe, the collection needs to be locked for the duration of the operation. (It requires cooperation from other code using the same collection, of course.) In short, the Synchronized method gave the appearance of safety without the reality. It's better not to give the wrong impression in the first place—developers just have to be careful when working with collections accessed in multiple threads. SynchronizedCollection<T> performs broadly the same role as a synchronized ArrayList. I would argue that it's still not a good idea to use this, for the reasons outlined in this paragraph—the safety provided is largely illusory. Ironically, this would be a great collection to support a ForEach method, where it could automatically hold the lock for the duration of the iteration over the collection—but there's no such method.

That completes our coverage of List<T>. The next collection under the microscope is Dictionary<TKey,TValue>, which we've already seen so much of.

3.5.2 *Dictionary<TKey,TValue>*

There is less to say about Dictionary<TKey,TValue> (just called Dictionary<,> for the rest of this section, for simplicity) than there was about List<T>, although it's another heavily used type. As stated earlier, it's the generic replacement for Hashtable and the related classes, such as StringDictionary. There aren't many features present in Dictionary<,> that aren't in Hashtable, although this is partly because the ability to specify a comparison in the form of an IEqualityComparer was added to Hashtable in .NET 2.0. This allows for things like case-insensitive comparisons of strings without using a separate type of dictionary. IEqualityComparer and its generic equivalent, IEqualityComparer<T>, have both Equals and GetHashCode. Prior to .NET 2.0 these were split into IComparer (which had to give an ordering, not just test for equality) and IHashCodeProvider. This separation was awkward, hence the move to IEquality-Comparer<T> for 2.0. Dictionary<,> exposes its IEqualityComparer<T> in the public Comparer property.

The most important difference between Dictionary and Hashtable (beyond the normal benefits of generics) is their behavior when asked to fetch the value associated with a key that they don't know about. When presented with a key that isn't in the map, the indexer of Hashtable will just return null. By contrast, Dictionary<,> will throw a KeyNotFoundException. Both of them support the ContainsKey method to tell beforehand whether a given key is present. Dictionary<,> also provides TryGetValue, which retrieves the value if a suitable entry is present, storing it in the output parameter and returning true. If the key is not present, TryGetValue will set the output parameter to the default value of TValue and return false. This avoids having to search for the key twice, while still allowing the caller to distinguish between the situation where a key isn't present at all, and the one where it's present but its associated value is the default value of TValue. Making the indexer throw an exception is of more debatable merit, but it does make it very clear when a lookup has failed instead of masking the failure by returning a potentially valid value.

Just as with `List<T>`, there is no way of obtaining a synchronized `Dictionary<,>`, nor does it implement `ICloneable`. The dictionary equivalent of `Synchronized-Collection<T>` is `SynchronizedKeyedCollection<K,T>` (which in fact derives from `SynchronizedCollection<T>`).

With the lack of additional functionality, another example of `Dictionary<,>` would be relatively pointless. Let's move on to two types that are closely related to each other: `Queue<T>` and `Stack<T>`.

3.5.3   *Queue<T> and Stack<T>*

The generic queue and stack classes are essentially the same as their nongeneric counterparts. The same features are "missing" from the generic versions as with the other collections—lack of cloning, and no way of creating a synchronized version. As before, the two types are closely related—both act as lists that don't allow random access, instead only allowing elements to be removed in a certain order. Queues act in a *first in, first out* (FIFO) fashion, while stacks have *last in, first out* (LIFO) semantics. Both have `Peek` methods that return the next element that would be removed but without actually removing it. This behavior is demonstrated in listing 3.14.

> **Listing 3.14   Demonstration of `Queue<T>` and `Stack<T>`**

```
Queue<int> queue = new Queue<int>();
Stack<int> stack = new Stack<int>();

for (int i=0; i < 10; i++)
{
    queue.Enqueue(i);
    stack.Push(i);
}

for (int i=0; i < 10; i++)
{
    Console.WriteLine ("Stack:{0} Queue:{1}",
                    stack.Pop(), queue.Dequeue());
}
```

The output of listing 3.14 is as follows:

```
Stack:9 Queue:0
Stack:8 Queue:1
Stack:7 Queue:2
Stack:6 Queue:3
Stack:5 Queue:4
Stack:4 Queue:5
Stack:3 Queue:6
Stack:2 Queue:7
Stack:1 Queue:8
Stack:0 Queue:9
```

You can enumerate `Stack<T>` and `Queue<T>` in the same way as with a list, but in my experience this is used relatively rarely. Most of the uses I've seen have involved a thread-safe wrapper being put around either class, enabling a producer/consumer pattern for multithreading. This is not particularly hard to write, and third-party implementations are available, but having these classes directly available in the framework would be more welcome.

Next we'll look at the generic versions of `SortedList`, which are similar enough to be twins.

3.5.4 *SortedList<TKey,TValue> and SortedDictionary<TKey,TValue>*

The naming of `SortedList` has always bothered me. It feels more like a map or dictionary than a list. You can access the elements by index as you can for other lists (although not with an indexer)—but you can also access the value of each element (which is a key/value pair) by key. The important part of `SortedList` is that when you enumerate it, the entries come out sorted by key. Indeed, a common way of using `SortedList` is to access it as a map when writing to it, but then enumerate the entries in order.

There are two generic classes that map to the same sort of behavior: `Sorted-List<TKey,TValue>` and `SortedDictionary<TKey,TValue>`. (From here on I'll just call them `SortedList<,>` and `SortedDictionary<,>` to save space.) They're very similar indeed—it's mostly the performance that differs. `SortedList<,>` uses less memory, but `SortedDictionary<,>` is faster in the *general* case when it comes to adding entries. However, if you add them in the sort order of the keys to start with, `SortedList<,>` will be faster.

NOTE *A difference of limited benefit*—`SortedList<,>` allows you to find the index of a particular key or value using `IndexOfKey` and `IndexOfValue`, and to remove an entry by index with `RemoveAt`. To retrieve an entry by index, however, you have to use the `Keys` or `Values` properties, which implement `IList<TKey>` and `IList<TValue>`, respectively. The nongeneric version supports more direct access, and a private method exists in the generic version, but it's not much use while it's private. `SortedDictionary<,>` doesn't support any of these operations.

If you want to see either of these classes in action, use listing 3.1 as a good starting point. Just changing `Dictionary` to `SortedDictionary` or `SortedList` will ensure that the words are printed in alphabetical order, for example.

Our final collection class is genuinely new, rather than a generic version of an existing nongeneric type. It's that staple of computer science courses everywhere: the linked list.

3.5.5 *LinkedList<T>*

I suspect you know what a linked list is. Instead of keeping an array that is quick to access but slow to insert into, a linked list stores its data by building up a chain of nodes, each of which is linked to the next one. Doubly linked lists (like `LinkedList<T>`) store a link to the *previous* node as well as the next one, so you can easily iterate backward as well as forward.

Linked lists make it easy to insert another node into the chain—as long as you already have a handle on the node representing the insertion position. All the list needs to do is create a new node, and make the appropriate links between that node and the ones that will be before and after it. Lists storing all their data in a plain array (as `List<T>` does) need to move all the entries that will come after the new one, which can be very expensive—and if the array runs out of spare capacity, the whole lot must be copied. Enumerating a linked list from start to end is also cheap—but random access (fetching the fifth element, then the thousandth, then the second) is slower than using an array-backed list. Indeed, `LinkedList<T>` doesn't even provide a random access method or indexer. Despite its name, it doesn't implement `IList<T>`. Linked lists are usually more expensive in terms of memory than their array-backed cousins due to the extra link node required for each value. However, they don't have the "wasted" space of the spare array capacity of `List<T>`.

The linked list implementation in .NET 2.0 is a relatively plain one—it doesn't support chaining two lists together to form a larger one, or splitting an existing one into two, for example. However, it can still be useful if you want fast insertions at both the start and end of the list (or in between if you keep a reference to the appropriate node), and only need to read the values from start to end, or vice versa.

Our final main section of the chapter looks at some of the limitations of generics in C# and considers similar features in other languages.

3.6   *Limitations of generics in C# and other languages*

There is no doubt that generics contribute a great deal to C# in terms of expressiveness, type safety, and performance. The feature has been carefully designed to cope with most of the tasks that C++ programmers typically used templates for, but without some of the accompanying disadvantages. However, this is not to say limitations don't exist. There are some problems that C++ templates solve with ease but that C# generics can't help with. Similarly, while generics in Java are generally less powerful than in C#, there are some concepts that can be expressed in Java but that don't have a C# equivalent. This section will take you through some of the most commonly encountered weaknesses, as well as briefly compare the C#/.NET implementation of generics with C++ templates and Java generics.

It's important to stress that pointing out these snags does not *imply* that they should have been avoided in the first place. In particular, I'm in no way saying that I could have done a better job! The language and platform designers have had to balance power with complexity (and the small matter of achieving both design and implementation within a reasonable timescale). It's possible that future improvements will either remove some of these issues or lessen their impact. Most likely, you won't encounter problems, and if you do, you'll be able to work around them with the guidance given here.

We'll start with the answer to a question that almost everyone raises sooner or later: why can't I convert a `List<string>` to `List<object>`?

3.6.1 Lack of covariance and contravariance

In section 2.3.2, we looked at the *covariance* of arrays—the fact that an array of a reference type can be viewed as an array of its base type, or an array of any of the interfaces it implements. Generics don't support this—they are *invariant*. This is for the sake of type safety, as we'll see, but it can be annoying.

WHY DON'T GENERICS SUPPORT COVARIANCE?

Let's suppose we have two classes, Animal and Cat, where Cat derives from Animal. In the code that follows, the array code (on the left) is valid C# 2; the generic code (on the right) isn't:

Valid (at compile-time):	Invalid:
`Animal[] animals = new Cat[5];`	`List<Animal> animals=new List<Cat>();`
`animals[0] = new Animal();`	`animals.Add(new Animal());`

The compiler has no problem with the second line in either case, but the first line on the right causes the error:

```
error CS0029: Cannot implicitly convert type
    'System.Collections.Generic.List<Cat>' to
    'System.Collections.Generic.List<Animal>'
```

This was a deliberate choice on the part of the framework and language designers. The obvious question to ask is *why* this is prohibited—and the answer lies on the second line. There is nothing about the second line that should raise any suspicion. After all, List<Animal> effectively has a method with the signature void Add(Animal value)— you should be able to put a Turtle into any list of animals, for instance. However, the *actual* object referred to by animals is a Cat[] (in the code on the left) or a List<Cat> (on the right), both of which require that only references to instances of Cat are stored in them. Although the array version will compile, it will fail at execution time. This was deemed by the designers of generics to be worse than failing at compile time, which is reasonable—the whole point of static typing is to find out about errors before the code ever gets run.

NOTE   *So why are arrays covariant?* Having answered the question about why generics are invariant, the *next* obvious step is to question why arrays are covariant. According to the Common Language Infrastructure Annotated Standard (Addison-Wesley Professional, 2003), for the first edition the designers wished to reach as broad an audience as possible, which included being able to run code compiled from Java source. In other words, .NET has covariant arrays because Java has covariant arrays—despite this being a known "wart" in Java.

So, that's why things are the way they are—but why should you care, and how can you get around the restriction?

WHERE COVARIANCE WOULD BE USEFUL

Suppose you are implementing a platform-agnostic storage system,[11] which could run across WebDAV, NFS, Samba, NTFS, ReiserFS, files in a database, you name it. You may have the idea of storage locations, which may contain sublocations (think of directories containing files and more directories, for instance). You could have an interface like this:

```
public interface IStorageLocation
{
    Stream OpenForRead();
    ...
    IEnumerable<IStorageLocation> GetSublocations();
}
```

That all seems reasonable and easy to implement. The problem comes when your implementation (FabulousStorageLocation for instance) stores its list of sublocations for any particular location as List<FabulousStorageLocation>. You might expect to be able to either return the list reference directly, or possibly call AsRead-Only to avoid clients tampering with your list, and return the result—but that would be an implementation of IEnumerable<FabulousStorageLocation> instead of an IEnumerable<IStorageLocation>.

Here are some options:

- Make your list a List<IStorageLocation> instead. This is likely to mean you need to cast every time you fetch an entry in order to get at your implementation-specific behavior. You might as well not be using generics in the first place.
- Implement GetSublocations using the funky new iteration features of C# 2, as described in chapter 6. That happens to work in this example, because the interface uses IEnumerable<IStorageLocation>. It wouldn't work if we had to return an IList<IStorageLocation> instead. It also requires each implementation to have the same kind of code. It's only a few lines, but it's still inelegant.
- Create a new copy of the list, this time as List<IStorageLocation>. In some cases (particularly if the interface *did* require you to return an IList<IStorageLocation>), this would be a good thing to do anyway—it keeps the list returned separate from the internal list. You could even use List.Convert-All to do it in a single line. It involves copying everything in the list, though, which may be an unnecessary expense if you trust your callers to use the returned list reference appropriately.
- Make the interface generic, with the type parameter representing the actual type of storage sublocation being represented. For instance, FabulousStorage-Location might implement IStorageLocation<FabulousStorageLocation>. It looks a little odd, but this recursive-looking use of generics can be quite useful at times.[12]
- Create a generic helper method (preferably in a common class library) that converts IEnumerator<TSource> to IEnumerator<TDest>, where TSource derives from TDest.

---

[11] Yes, another one.

[12] For instance, you might have a type parameter T with a constraint that any instance can be compared to another instance of T for equality—in other words, something like MyClass<T> where T : IEquatable<T>.

When you run into covariance issues, you may need to consider all of these options and anything else you can think of. It depends heavily on the exact nature of the situation. Unfortunately, covariance isn't the only problem we have to consider. There's also the matter of *contravariance*, which is like covariance in reverse.

WHERE CONTRAVARIANCE WOULD BE USEFUL

Contravariance feels slightly less intuitive than covariance, but it does make sense. Where covariance is about declaring that we will return a *more specific* object from a method than the interface requires us to, contravariance is about being willing to accept a *more general* parameter.

For instance, suppose we had an IShape interface[13] that contained the Area property. It's easy to write an implementation of IComparer<IShape> that sorts by area. We'd then *like* to be able to write the following code:

```
IComparer<IShape> areaComparer = new AreaComparer();
List<Circle> circles = new List<Circle>();
circles.Add(new Circle(20));
circles.Add(new Circle(10));
circles.Sort(areaComparer);
```

> **INVALID**

That won't work, though, because the Sort method on List<Circle> effectively takes an IComparer<Circle>. The fact that our AreaComparer can compare *any* shape rather than just circles doesn't impress the compiler at all. It considers IComparer <Circle> and IComparer<IShape> to be completely different types. Maddening, isn't it? It would be nice if the Sort method had this signature instead:

> **INVALID**

```
void Sort<S>(IComparer<S> comparer) where T : S
```

Unfortunately, not only is that not the signature of Sort, but it *can't* be—the constraint is invalid, because it's a constraint on T instead of S. We want a derivation type constraint but in the other direction, constraining the S to be somewhere *up* the inheritance tree of T instead of down.

Given that this isn't possible, what *can* we do? There are fewer options this time than before. First, you could create a generic class with the following declaration:

```
ComparisonHelper<TBase,TDerived> : IComparer<TDerived>
    where TDerived : TBase
```

You'd then create a constructor that takes (and stores) an IComparer<TBase> as a parameter. The implementation of IComparer<TDerived> would just return the result of calling the Compare method of the IComparer<TBase>. You could then sort the List<Circle> by creating a new ComparisonHelper<IShape,Circle> that uses the area comparison.

The second option is to make the area comparison class generic, with a derivation constraint, so it can compare any two values of the same type, as long as that type implements IShape. Of course, you can only do this when you're able to change the comparison class—but it's a nice solution when it's available.

---

[13] You didn't really expect to get through the whole book without seeing a shape-related example, did you?

Notice that the various options for both covariance and contravariance use more generics and constraints to express the interface in a more general manner, or to provide generic "helper" methods. I know that adding a constraint makes it sound *less* general, but the generality is added by first making the type or method generic. When you run into a problem like this, adding a level of genericity somewhere with an appropriate constraint should be the first option to consider. Generic *methods* (rather than generic types) are often helpful here, as type inference can make the lack of variance invisible to the naked eye. This is particularly true in C# 3, which has stronger type inference capabilities than C# 2.

NOTE   *Is this really the best we can do?*—As we'll see later, Java supports covariance and contravariance within its generics—so why can't C#? Well, a lot of it boils down to the implementation—the fact that the Java runtime doesn't get involved with generics; it's basically a compile-time feature. However, the CLR *does* support limited generic covariance and contravariance, just on interfaces and delegates. C# doesn't expose this feature (neither does VB.NET), and none of the framework libraries use it. The C# compiler consumes covariant and contravariant interfaces as if they were invariant. Adding variance is under consideration for C# 4, although no firm commitments have been made. Eric Lippert has written a whole series of blog posts about the general problem, and what *might* happen in future versions of C#: http://blogs.msdn.com/ericlippert/archive/tags/Covariance+and+Contravariance/default.aspx.

This limitation is a *very* common cause of questions on C# discussion groups. The remaining issues are either relatively academic or affect only a moderate subset of the development community. The next one mostly affects those who do a lot of calculations (usually scientific or financial) in their work.

3.6.2   *Lack of operator constraints or a "numeric" constraint*

C# is not without its downside when it comes to heavily mathematical code. The need to explicitly use the Math class for every operation beyond the simplest arithmetic and the lack of C-style typedefs to allow the data representation used throughout a program to be easily changed have always been raised by the scientific community as barriers to C#'s adoption. Generics weren't likely to fully solve either of those issues, but there's a common problem that stops generics from helping as much as they could have. Consider this (illegal) generic method:

```
public T FindMean<T>(IEnumerable<T> data)
{
    T sum = default(T);
    int count = 0;
    foreach (T datum in data)
    {
        sum += datum;
        count++;
    }
}
```

INVALID

```
        return sum/count;
    }
```

Obviously that could never work for *all* types of data—what could it mean to add one `Exception` to another, for instance? Clearly a constraint of some kind is called for… something that is able to express what we need to be able to do: add two instances of `T` together, and divide a `T` by an integer. If that were available, even if it were limited to built-in types, we could write generic algorithms that wouldn't care whether they were working on an `int`, a `long`, a `double`, a `decimal`, and so forth. Limiting it to the built-in types would have been disappointing but better than nothing. The ideal solution would have to also allow user-defined types to act in a numeric capacity—so you could define a `Complex` type to handle complex numbers, for instance. That complex number could then store each of its components in a generic way as well, so you could have a `Complex<float>`, a `Complex<double>`, and so on.[14]

Two related solutions present themselves. One would be simply to allow constraints on operators, so you could write a set of constraints such as

```
where T : T operator+ (T,T), T operator/ (T, int)
```

This would require that `T` have the operations we need in the earlier code. The other solution would be to define a few operators and perhaps conversions that must be supported in order for a type to meet the extra constraint—we could make it the "numeric constraint" written `where T : numeric`.

One problem with both of these options is that they can't be expressed as normal interfaces, because operator overloading is performed with *static* members, which can't implement interfaces. It would require a certain amount of shoehorning, in other words.

Various smart people (including Eric Gunnerson and Anders Hejlsberg, who ought to be able to think of C# tricks if anyone can) have thought about this, and with a bit of extra code, some solutions have been found. They're slightly clumsy, but they work. Unfortunately, due to current JIT optimization limitations, you have to pick between pleasant syntax (x=y+z) that reads nicely but performs poorly, and a method-based syntax (x=y.Add(z)) that performs without significant overhead but looks like a dog's dinner when you've got anything even moderately complicated going on.

The details are beyond the scope of this book, but are very clearly presented at http://www.lambda-computing.com/publications/articles/generics2/ in an article on the matter.

The two limitations we've looked at so far have been quite practical—they've been issues you may well run into during actual development. However, if you're generally curious like I am, you may also be asking yourself about other limitations that don't necessarily slow down development but are intellectual curiosities. In particular, just why are generics limited to types and methods?

---

[14] More mathematically minded readers might want to consider what a `Complex<Complex<double>>` would mean. You're on your own there, I'm afraid.

3.6.3   *Lack of generic properties, indexers, and other member types*

We've seen generic types (classes, structs, delegates, and interfaces) and we've seen generic methods. There are plenty of other members that *could* be parameterized. However, there are no generic properties, indexers, operators, constructors, finalizers, or events. First let's be clear about what we mean here: clearly an indexer can have a return type that is a type parameter—List<T> is an obvious example. KeyValue-Pair<TKey,TValue> provides similar examples for properties. What you *can't* have is an indexer or property (or any of the other members in that list) with *extra* type parameters. Leaving the possible syntax of declaration aside for the minute, let's look at how these members might have to be called:

```
SomeClass<string> instance = new SomeClass<string><Guid>("x");
int x = instance.SomeProperty<int>;
byte y = instance.SomeIndexer<byte>["key"];
instance.Click<byte> += ByteHandler;
instance = instance +<int> instance;
```

INVALID

I hope you'll agree that all of those look somewhat silly. Finalizers can't even be called explicitly from C# code, which is why there isn't a line for them. The fact that we can't do any of these isn't going to cause significant problems anywhere, as far as I can see—it's just worth being aware of it as an academic limitation.

The one exception to this is *possibly* the constructor. However, a static generic method in the class is a good workaround for this, and the syntax with two lists of type arguments is horrific.

These are by no means the *only* limitations of C# generics, but I believe they're the ones that you're most likely to run up against, either in your daily work, in community conversations, or when idly considering the feature as a whole. In our next two sections we'll see how some aspects of these aren't issues in the two languages whose features are most commonly compared with C#'s generics: C++ (with templates) and Java (with generics as of Java 5). We'll tackle C++ first.

3.6.4   *Comparison with C++ templates*

C++ templates are a bit like macros taken to an extreme level. They're incredibly powerful, but have costs associated with them both in terms of code bloat and ease of understanding.

When a template is used in C++, the code is compiled for that particular set of template arguments, as if the template arguments were in the source code. This means that there's not as much need for constraints, as the compiler will check whether you're allowed to do everything you want to with the type anyway while it's compiling the code for this particular set of template arguments. The C++ standards committee has recognized that constraints are still useful, though, and they will be present in C++0x (the next version of C++) under the name of *concepts*.

The C++ compiler is smart enough to compile the code only once for any given set of template arguments, but it isn't able to share code in the way that the CLR does with reference types. That lack of sharing does have its benefits, though—it allows type-specific optimizations, such as inlining method calls for some type parameters but not others, from the same template. It also means that overload resolution can be performed separately for each set of type parameters, rather than just once based solely on the limited knowledge the C# compiler has due to any constraints present.

Don't forget that with "normal" C++ there's only one compilation involved, rather than the "compile to IL" then "JIT compile to native code" model of .NET. A program using a standard template in ten different ways will include the code ten times in a C++ program. A similar program in C# using a generic type from the framework in ten different ways won't include the code for the generic type at all—it will refer to it, and the JIT will compile as many different versions as required (as described in section 3.4.2) at execution time.

One significant feature that C++ templates have over C# generics is that the template arguments don't have to be type names. Variable names, function names, and constant expressions can be used as well. A common example of this is a buffer type that has the size of the buffer as one of the template arguments—so a buffer<int,20> will always be a buffer of 20 integers, and a buffer<double,35> will always be a buffer of 35 doubles. This ability is crucial to *template metaprogramming*[15]—an advanced C++ technique the very idea of which scares me, but that can be very powerful in the hands of experts.

C++ templates are more flexible in other ways, too. They don't suffer from the problem described in 3.6.2, and there are a few other restrictions that don't exist in C++: you can derive a class from one of its type parameters, and you can specialize a template for a particular set of type arguments. The latter ability allows the template author to write general code to be used when there's no more knowledge available but specific (often highly optimized) code for particular types.

The same variance issues of .NET generics exist in C++ templates as well—an example given by Bjarne Stroustrup[16] is that there are no implicit conversions between Vector<shape*> and Vector<circle*> with similar reasoning—in this case, it might allow you to put a square peg in a round hole.

For further details of C++ templates, I recommend Stroustrup's *The C++ Programming Language* (Addison-Wesley, 1991). It's not always the easiest book to follow, but the templates chapter is fairly clear (once you get your mind around C++ terminology and syntax). For more comparisons with .NET generics, look at the blog post by the Visual C++ team on this topic: http://blogs.msdn.com/branbray/archive/2003/11/19/51023.aspx.

The other obvious language to compare with C# in terms of generics is Java, which introduced the feature into the mainstream language for the 1.5 release,[17] several years after other projects had created Java-like languages including generics.

---

[15] http://en.wikipedia.org/wiki/Template_metaprogramming
[16] The inventor of C++.
[17] Or 5.0, depending on which numbering system you use. Don't get me started.

3.6.5 *Comparison with Java generics*

Where C++ includes *more* of the template in the generated code than C# does, Java includes *less*. In fact, the Java runtime doesn't know about generics at all. The Java bytecode (roughly equivalent terminology to IL) for a generic type includes some extra metadata to say that it's generic, but after compilation the calling code doesn't have much to indicate that generics were involved at all—and certainly an instance of a generic type only knows about the nongeneric side of itself. For example, an instance of HashSet<T> doesn't know whether it was created as a HashSet<String> or a HashSet<Object>. The compiler effectively just adds casts where necessary and performs more sanity checking. Here's an example—first the generic Java code:

```
ArrayList<String> strings = new ArrayList<String>();
strings.add("hello");
String entry = strings.get(0);
strings.add(new Object());
```

and now the equivalent nongeneric code:

```
ArrayList strings = new ArrayList();
strings.add("hello");
String entry = (String) strings.get(0);
strings.add(new Object());
```

They would generate the same Java bytecode, except for the last line—which is valid in the nongeneric case but caught by the compiler as an error in the generic version. You can use a generic type as a "raw" type, which is equivalent to using java.lang.Object for each of the type arguments. This rewriting—and loss of information—is called *type erasure*. Java doesn't have user-defined value types, but you can't even use the built-in ones as type arguments. Instead, you have to use the boxed version—ArrayList<Integer> for a list of integers, for example.

You may be forgiven for thinking this is all a bit disappointing compared with generics in C#, but there are some nice features of Java generics too:

- The runtime doesn't know anything about generics, so you can use code compiled using generics on an older version, as long as you don't use any classes or methods that aren't present on the old version. Versioning in .NET is much stricter in general—for each assembly you reference, you can specify whether or not the version number has to match exactly. Also, code built to run on the 2.0 CLR will not run on .NET 1.1.

- You don't need to learn a new set of classes to use Java generics—where a nongeneric developer would use ArrayList, a generic developer just uses ArrayList<T>. Existing classes can reasonably easily be "upgraded" to generic versions.

- The previous feature has been utilized quite effectively with the reflection system—java.lang.Class (the equivalent of System.Type) is generic, which allows compile-time type safety to be extended to cover many situations involving reflection. In some other situations it's a pain, however.

- Java has support for covariance and contravariance using wildcards. For instance, ArrayList<? extends Base> can be read as "this is an ArrayList of some type that derives from Base, but we don't know which exact type."

My personal opinion is that .NET generics are superior in almost every respect, although every time I run into a covariance/contravariance issue I suddenly wish I had wildcards. Java with generics is still much better than Java without generics, but there are no performance benefits and the safety only applies at compile time. If you're interested in the details, they're in the Java language specification, or you could read Gilad Bracha's excellent guide to them at http://java.sun.com/j2se/1.5/pdf/generics-tutorial.pdf.

3.7 *Summary*

Phew! It's a good thing generics are simpler to use in reality than they are in description. Although they *can* get complicated, they're widely regarded as the most important addition to C# 2 and are incredibly useful. The worst thing about writing code using generics is that if you ever have to go back to C# 1, you'll miss them terribly.

In this chapter I haven't tried to cover absolutely every detail of what is and isn't allowed when using generics—that's the job of the language specification, and it makes for very dry reading. Instead, I've aimed for a practical approach, providing the information you'll need in everyday use, with a smattering of theory for the sake of academic interest.

We've seen three main benefits to generics: compile-time type safety, performance, and code expressiveness. Being able to get the IDE and compiler to validate your code early is certainly a good thing, but it's arguable that more is to be gained from tools providing intelligent options based on the types involved than the actual "safety" aspect.

Performance is improved most radically when it comes to value types, which no longer need to be boxed and unboxed when they're used in strongly typed generic APIs, particularly the generic collection types provided in .NET 2.0. Performance with reference types is usually improved but only slightly.

Your code is able to express its intention more clearly using generics—instead of a comment or a long variable name required to describe exactly what types are involved, the details of the type itself can do the work. Comments and variable names can often become inaccurate over time, as they can be left alone when code is changed—but the type information is "correct" by definition.

Generics aren't capable of doing *everything* we might sometimes like them to do, and we've studied some of their limitations in the chapter, but if you truly embrace C# 2 and the generic types within the .NET 2.0 Framework, you'll come across good uses for them incredibly frequently in your code.

This topic will come up time and time again in future chapters, as other new features build on this key one. Indeed, the subject of our next chapter would be very different without generics—we're going to look at nullable types, as implemented by `Nullable<T>`.

Saying nothing
with nullable types

This chapter covers
- Motivation for null values
- Framework and runtime support
- Language support in C# 2
- Patterns using nullable types

Nullity is a concept that has provoked a certain amount of debate over the years. Is a null reference a value, or the absence of a value? Is "nothing" a "something"? In this chapter, I'll try to stay more practical than philosophical. First we'll look at why there's a problem in the first place—why you can't set a value type variable to `null` in C# 1 and what the traditional alternatives have been. After that I'll introduce you to our knight in shining armor—`System.Nullable<T>`—before we see how C# 2 makes working with nullable types a bit simpler and more compact. Like generics, nullable types sometimes have some uses beyond what you might expect, and we'll look at a few examples of these at the end of the chapter.

So, when is a value not a value? Let's find out.

4.1 *What do you do when you just don't have a value?*

The C# and .NET designers don't add features just for kicks. There has to be a real, significant problem to be fixed before they'll go as far as changing C# as a language or .NET at the platform level. In this case, the problem is best summed up in one of the most frequently asked questions in C# and .NET discussion groups:

> *I need to set my* DateTime[1] *variable to* null, *but the compiler won't let me.*
> *What should I do?*

It's a question that comes up fairly naturally—a simple example might be in an e-commerce application where users are looking at their account history. If an order has been placed but not delivered, there may be a purchase date but no dispatch date—so how would you represent that in a type that is meant to provide the order details?

The answer to the question is usually in two parts: first, why you can't just use null in the first place, and second, which options are available. Let's look at the two parts separately—assuming that the developer asking the question is using C# 1.

4.1.1 *Why value type variables can't be null*

As we saw in chapter 2, the value of a reference type variable is a reference, and the value of a value type variable is the "real" value itself. A "normal" reference value is some way of getting at an object, but null acts as a special value that means "I don't refer to any object." If you want to think of references as being like URLs, null is (*very* roughly speaking) the reference equivalent of about:blank. It's represented as all zeroes in memory (which is why it's the default value for all reference types—clearing a whole block of memory is cheap, so that's the way objects are initialized), but it's still basically stored in the same way as other references. There's no "extra bit" hidden somewhere for each reference type variable. That means we can't use the "all zeroes" value for a "real" reference, but that's OK—our memory is going to run out long before we have that many live objects anyway.

The last sentence is the key to why null isn't a valid *value* type value, though. Let's consider the byte type as a familiar one that is easy to think about. The value of a variable of type byte is stored in a single byte—it may be padded for alignment purposes, but the value itself is conceptually only made up of one byte. We've *got* to be able to store the values 0–255 in that variable; otherwise it's useless for reading arbitrary binary data. So, with the 256 "normal" values and one null value, we'd have to cope with a total of 257 values, and there's no way of squeezing that many values into a single byte. Now, the designers could have decided that every value type would have an extra flag bit somewhere determining whether a value was null or a "real" value, but the memory usage implications are horrible, not to mention the fact that we'd have to check the flag every time we wanted to use the value. So in a nutshell, with value types

---

[1] It's almost always DateTime rather than any other value type. I'm not entirely sure why—it's as if developers inherently understand why a byte shouldn't be null, but feel that dates are more "inherently nullable."

you often care about having the whole range of possible bit patterns available as real values, whereas with reference types we're happy enough to lose one potential value in order to gain the benefits of having a null value.

That's the usual situation—now why would you *want* to be able to represent null for a value type anyway? The most common immediate reason is simply because databases typically support NULL as a value for every type (unless you specifically make the field non-nullable), so you can have nullable character data, nullable integers, nullable Booleans—the whole works. When you fetch data from a database, it's generally not a good idea to lose information, so you want to be able to represent the nullity of whatever you read, somehow.

That just moves the question one step further on, though. Why do databases allow null values for dates, integers and the like? Null values are typically used for unknown or missing values such as the dispatch date in our earlier e-commerce example. Nullity represents an absence of definite information, which can be important in many situations.

That brings us to options for representing null values in C# 1.

4.1.2   *Patterns for representing null values in C# 1*

There are three basic patterns commonly used to get around the lack of nullable value types in C# 1. Each of them has its pros and cons—mostly cons—and all of them are fairly unsatisfying. However, it's worth knowing them, partly to more fully appreciate the benefits of the integrated solution in C# 2.

PATTERN 1: THE MAGIC VALUE

The first pattern tends to be used as the solution for DateTime, because few people expect their databases to *actually* contain dates in 1AD. In other words, it goes against the reasoning I gave earlier, expecting every possible value to be available. So, we sacrifice one value (typically DateTime.MinValue) to mean a null value. The *semantic* meaning of that will vary from application to application—it may mean that the user hasn't entered the value into a form yet, or that it's inappropriate for that record, for example.

The good news is that using a magic value doesn't waste any memory or need any new types. However, it does rely on you picking an appropriate value that will never be one you actually want to use for real data. Also, it's basically inelegant. It just doesn't feel right. If you ever find yourself needing to go down this path, you should at least have a constant (or static read-only value for types that can't be expressed as constants) representing the magic value—comparisons with DateTime.MinValue everywhere, for instance, don't express the meaning of the magic value.

ADO.NET has a variation on this pattern where the same magic value—DBNull.Value—is used for *all* null values, of whatever type. In this case, an extra value and indeed an extra type have been introduced to indicate when a database has returned null. However, it's only applicable where compile-time type safety isn't important (in other words when you're happy to use object and cast after testing for nullity), and again it doesn't feel quite right. In fact, it's a mixture of the "magic value" pattern and the "reference type wrapper" pattern, which we'll look at next.

PATTERN 2: A REFERENCE TYPE WRAPPER

The second solution can take two forms. The simpler one is to just use `object` as the variable type, boxing and unboxing values as necessary. The more complex (and rather more appealing) form is to have a reference type for each value type you need in a nullable form, containing a single instance variable of that value type, and with implicit conversion operators to and from the value type. With generics, you *could* do this in one generic type—but if you're using C# 2 anyway, you might as well use the nullable types described in this chapter instead. If you're stuck in C# 1, you have to create extra source code for each type you wish to wrap. This isn't hard to put in the form of a template for automatic code generation, but it's still a burden that is best avoided if possible.

Both of these forms have the problem that while they allow you to use `null` directly, they *do* require objects to be created on the heap, which can lead to garbage collection pressure if you need to use this approach very frequently, and adds memory use due to the overheads associated with objects. For the more complex solution, you could make the reference type mutable, which may reduce the number of instances you need to create but could also make for some very unintuitive code.

PATTERN 3: AN EXTRA BOOLEAN FLAG

The final pattern revolves around having a normal value type value available, and another value—a Boolean flag—indicating whether the value is "real" or whether it should be disregarded. Again, there are two ways of implementing this solution. Either you could maintain two separate variables in the code that uses the value, or you could encapsulate the "value plus flag" into another value type.

This latter solution is quite similar to the more complicated reference type idea described earlier, except that you avoid the garbage-collection issue by using a value type, and indicate nullity within the encapsulated value rather than by virtue of a null reference. The downside of having to create a new one of these types for every value type you wish to handle is the same, however. Also, if the value is ever boxed for some reason, it will be boxed in the normal way whether it's considered to be null or not.

The last pattern (in the more encapsulated form) is effectively how nullable types work in C# 2. We'll see that when the new features of the framework, CLR, and language are all combined, the solution is significantly neater than anything that was possible in C# 1. Our next section deals with just the support provided by the framework and the CLR: if C# 2 *only* supported generics, the whole of section 4.2 would still be relevant and the feature would still work and be useful. However, C# 2 provides extra syntactic sugar to make it even better—that's the subject of section 4.3.

4.2   *System.Nullable<T> and System.Nullable*

The core structure at the heart of nullable types is `System.Nullable<T>`. In addition, the `System.Nullable` static class provides utility methods that occasionally make nullable types easier to work with. (From now on I'll leave out the namespace, to make life simpler.) We'll look at both of these types in turn, and for this section I'll avoid any extra features provided by the language, so you'll be able to understand what's going on in the IL code when we *do* look at the C# 2 syntactic sugar.

4.2.1   *Introducing Nullable<T>*

As you can tell by its name, `Nullable<T>` is a generic type. The type parameter T has the value type constraint on it. As I mentioned in section 3.3.1, this also means you can't use another nullable type as the argument—so `Nullable<Nullable<int>>` is forbidden, for instance, even though `Nullable<T>` is a value type in every other way. The type of T for any particular nullable type is called the *underlying type* of that nullable type. For example, the underlying type of `Nullable<int>` is int.

The most important parts of `Nullable<T>` are its properties, `HasValue` and `Value`. They do the obvious thing: `Value` represents the non-nullable value (the "real" one, if you will) when there is one, and throws an `InvalidOperation-Exception` if (conceptually) there is no real value. `HasValue` is simply a Boolean property indicating whether there's a real value or whether the instance should be regarded as null. For now, I'll talk about an "instance with a value" and an "instance without a value," which mean instances where the `HasValue` property returns true or false, respectively.

Now that we know what we want the properties to achieve, let's see how to create an instance of the type. `Nullable<T>` has two constructors: the default one (creating an instance without a value) and one taking an instance of T as the value. Once an instance has been constructed, it is immutable.

NOTE   *Value types and mutability*—A type is said to be *immutable* if it is designed so that an instance can't be changed after it's been constructed. Immutable types often make life easier when it comes to topics such as multithreading, where it helps to know that nobody can be changing values in one thread while you're reading them in a different one. However, immutability is also important for value types. As a general rule, value types should almost always be immutable. If you need a way of basing one value on another, follow the lead of `DateTime` and `TimeSpan`—provide methods that return a new value rather than modifying an existing one. That way, you avoid situations where you *think* you're changing a variable but *actually* you're changing the value returned by a property or method, which is just a copy of the variable's value. The compiler is usually smart enough to warn you about this, but it's worth trying to avoid the situation in the first place. Very few value types in the framework are mutable, fortunately.

`Nullable<T>` introduces a single new method, `GetValueOrDefault`, which has two overloads. Both return the value of the instance if there is one, or a default value otherwise. One overload doesn't have any parameters (in which case the generic default value of the underlying type is used), and the other allows you to specify the default value to return if necessary.

The other methods implemented by `Nullable<T>` all override existing methods: `GetHashCode`, `ToString`, and `Equals`. `GetHashCode` returns 0 if the instance doesn't have a value, or the result of calling `GetHashCode` on the value if there is one. `ToString` returns an empty string if there isn't a value, or the result of calling

ToString on the value if there is. Equals is slightly more complicated—we'll come back to it when we've discussed boxing.

Finally, two conversions are provided by the framework. First, there is an implicit conversion from T to Nullable<T>. This always results in an instance where HasValue returns true. Likewise, there is an explicit operator converting from Nullable<T> to T, which behaves exactly the same as the Value property, including throwing an exception when there is no real value to return.

NOTE *Wrapping and unwrapping*—The C# specification names the process of converting an instance of T to an instance of Nullable<T> *wrapping*, with the obvious opposite process being called *unwrapping*. The C# specification actually defines these terms with reference to the constructor taking a parameter and the Value property, respectively. Indeed these calls are generated by the C# code, even when it otherwise *looks* as if you're using the conversions provided by the framework. The results are the same either way, however. For the rest of this chapter, I won't distinguish between the two implementations available.

Before we go any further, let's see all this in action. Listing 4.1 shows everything you can do with Nullable<T> directly, leaving Equals aside for the moment.

Listing 4.1 Using various members of Nullable<T>

```
static void Display (Nullable<int> x)
{
    Console.WriteLine ("HasValue: {0}", x.HasValue);
    if (x.HasValue)
    {
        Console.WriteLine ("Value: {0}", x.Value);
        Console.WriteLine ("Explicit conversion: {0}", (int)x);
    }
    Console.WriteLine ("GetValueOrDefault(): {0}",
                       x.GetValueOrDefault());
    Console.WriteLine ("GetValueOrDefault(10): {0}",
                       x.GetValueOrDefault(10));
    Console.WriteLine ("ToString(): \"{0}\"", x.ToString());
    Console.WriteLine ("GetHashCode(): {0}", x.GetHashCode());
    Console.WriteLine ();
}
...
Nullable<int> x = 5;
x = new Nullable<int>(5);
Console.WriteLine("Instance with value:");
Display(x);

x = new Nullable<int>();
Console.WriteLine("Instance without value:");
Display(x);
```

In listing 4.1 we first show the two different ways (in terms of C# source code) of wrapping a value of the underlying type, and then we use various different members on the instance. Next, we create an instance that *doesn't* have a value, and use the same members in the same order, just omitting the Value property and the explicit conversion to int since these would throw exceptions. The output of listing 4.1 is as follows:

```
Instance with value:
HasValue: True
Value: 5
Explicit conversion: 5
GetValueOrDefault(): 5
GetValueOrDefault(10): 5
ToString(): "5"
GetHashCode(): 5

Instance without value:
HasValue: False
GetValueOrDefault(): 0
GetValueOrDefault(10): 10
ToString(): ""
GetHashCode(): 0
```

So far, you could probably have predicted all of the results just by looking at the members provided by Nullable<T>. When it comes to boxing and unboxing, however, there's special behavior to make nullable types behave how we'd really *like* them to behave, rather than how they'd behave if we slavishly followed the normal boxing rules.

4.2.2 *Boxing and unboxing*

It's important to remember that Nullable<T> is a struct—a value type. This means that if you want to convert it to a reference type (object is the most obvious example), you'll need to box it. It is only with respect to boxing and unboxing that the CLR itself has any special behavior regarding nullable types—the rest is "standard" generics, conversions, method calls, and so forth. In fact, the behavior was only changed shortly before the release of .NET 2.0, as the result of community requests.

An instance of Nullable<T> is boxed to either a null reference (if it doesn't have a value) or a boxed value of T (if it does). You can unbox from a boxed value either to its normal type or to the corresponding nullable type. Unboxing a null reference will throw a NullReferenceException if you unbox to the normal type, but will unbox to an instance without a value if you unbox to the appropriate nullable type. This behavior is shown in listing 4.2.

Listing 4.2 Boxing and unboxing behavior of nullable types

```
Nullable<int> nullable = 5;

object boxed = nullable;                      Boxes a nullable
Console.WriteLine(boxed.GetType());           with value

int normal = (int)boxed;                      Unboxes to non-
Console.WriteLine(normal);                    nullable variable

nullable = (Nullable<int>)boxed;              Unboxes to
Console.WriteLine(nullable);                  nullable variable
```

```
nullable = new Nullable<int>();
boxed = nullable;                          ◁            Boxes a nullable
Console.WriteLine (boxed==null);                        without value

nullable = (Nullable<int>)boxed;            ◁           Unboxes to
Console.WriteLine(nullable.HasValue);                   nullable variable
```

The output of listing 4.2 shows that the type of the boxed value is printed as `System.Int32` (not `System.Nullable<System.Int32>`). It then confirms that we can retrieve the value by unboxing to either just `int` or to `Nullable<int>`. Finally, the output demonstrates we can box from a nullable instance without a value to a null reference and successfully unbox again to another value-less nullable instance. If we'd tried unboxing the last value of `boxed` to a non-nullable `int`, the program would have blown up with a `NullReferenceException`.

Now that we understand the behavior of boxing and unboxing, we can begin to tackle the behavior of `Nullable<T>.Equals`.

4.2.3 *Equality of Nullable<T> instances*

`Nullable<T>` overrides `object.Equals(object)` but doesn't introduce any equality operators or provide an `Equals(Nullable<T>)` method. Since the framework has supplied the basic building blocks, languages can add extra functionality on top, including making existing operators work as we'd expect them to. We'll see the details of that in section 4.3.3, but the basic equality as defined by the vanilla `Equals` method follows these rules for a call to `first.Equals(second)`:

- If `first` has no value and `second` is `null`, they are equal.
- If `first` has no value and `second` isn't `null`, they aren't equal.
- If `first` has a value and `second` is `null`, they aren't equal.
- Otherwise, they're equal if `first`'s value is equal to `second`.

Note that we don't have to consider the case where `second` is another `Nullable<T>` because the rules of boxing prohibit that situation. The type of `second` is `object`, so in order to be a `Nullable<T>` it would have to be boxed, and as we have just seen, boxing a nullable instance creates a box of the non-nullable type or returns a null reference.

The rules are consistent with the rules of equality elsewhere in .NET, so you can use nullable instances as keys for dictionaries and any other situations where you need equality. Just don't expect it to differentiate between a non-nullable instance and a nullable instance with a value—it's all been carefully set up so that those two cases *are* treated the same way as each other.

That covers the `Nullable<T>` structure itself, but it has a shadowy partner: the `Nullable` class.

4.2.4 *Support from the nongeneric Nullable class*

The `System.Nullable<T>` struct does almost everything you want it to. However, it receives a little help from the `System.Nullable` class. This is a static class—it only contains static methods, and you can't create an instance of it.[2] In fact, everything it does could have been done equally well by other types, and if Microsoft had seen where they were going right from the beginning, it might not have even existed—which would have saved a little confusion over what the two types are there for, aside from anything else. However, this accident of history has three methods to its name, and they're still useful.

The first two are comparison methods:

```
public static int Compare<T>(Nullable<T> n1, Nullable<T> n2)
public static bool Equals<T>(Nullable<T> n1, Nullable<T> n2)
```

Compare uses Comparer<T>.Default to compare the two underlying values (if they exist), and Equals uses EqualityComparer<T>.Default. In the face of instances with no values, the values returned from each method comply with the .NET conventions of nulls comparing equal to each other and less than anything else.

Both of these methods could quite happily be part of Nullable<T> as static but nongeneric methods. The one small advantage of having them as generic methods in a nongeneric type is that generic type inference can be applied, so you'll rarely need to explicitly specify the type parameter.

The final method of System.Nullable isn't generic—indeed, it absolutely couldn't be. Its signature is as follows:

```
public static Type GetUnderlyingType (Type nullableType)
```

If the parameter is a nullable type, the method returns its underlying type; otherwise it returns null. The reason this couldn't be a generic method is that if you knew the underlying type to start with, you wouldn't have to call it!

We've now seen what the framework and the CLR provide to support nullable types—but C# 2 adds language features to make life a lot more pleasant.

4.3   *C# 2's syntactic sugar for nullable types*

The examples so far have shown nullable types doing their job, but they've not been particularly pretty to look at. Admittedly it makes it obvious that you *are* using nullable types when you have to type Nullable<> around the name of the type you're really interested in, but it makes the nullability more prominent than the name of the type itself, which is surely not a good idea.

In addition, the very name "nullable" suggests that we should be able to assign null to a variable of a nullable type, and we haven't seen that—we've always used the default constructor of the type. In this section we'll see how C# 2 deals with these issues and others.

Before we get into the details of what C# 2 provides as a language, there's one definition I can finally introduce. The *null value* of a nullable type is the value where HasValue returns false—or an "instance without a value," as I've referred to it in section 4.2. I didn't use it before because it's specific to C#. The CLI specification

---

[2] You'll learn more about static classes in chapter 7.

doesn't mention it, and the documentation for `Nullable<T>` itself doesn't mention it. I've honored that difference by waiting until we're specifically talking about C# 2 itself before introducing the term.

With that out of the way, let's see what features C# 2 gives us, starting by reducing the clutter in our code.

4.3.1 The ? modifier

There are some elements of syntax that may be unfamiliar at first but have an appropriate *feel* to them. The conditional operator (a ? b : c) is one of them for me—it asks a question and then has two corresponding answers. In the same way, the ? operator for nullable types just feels right to me.

It's a shorthand way of using a nullable type, so instead of using `Nullable <byte>` we can use `byte?` throughout our code. The two are interchangeable and compile to exactly the same IL, so you can mix and match them if you want to, but on behalf of whoever reads your code next, I'd urge you to pick one way or the other and use it consistently. Listing 4.3 is exactly equivalent to listing 4.2 but uses the ? modifier.

Listing 4.3   The same code as listing 4.2 but using the ? modifier

```
int? nullable = 5;

object boxed = nullable;
Console.WriteLine(boxed.GetType());

int normal = (int)boxed;
Console.WriteLine(normal);

nullable = (int?)boxed;
Console.WriteLine(nullable);

nullable = new int?();
boxed = nullable;
Console.WriteLine (boxed==null);

nullable = (int?)boxed;
Console.WriteLine(nullable.HasValue);
```

I won't go through what the code does or how it does it, because the result is exactly the same as listing 4.2. The two listings compile down to the same IL—they're just using different syntax, just as using int is interchangeable with `System.Int32`. The only changes are the ones in bold. You can use the shorthand version everywhere, including in method signatures, `typeof` expressions, casts, and the like.

The reason I feel the modifier is very well chosen is that it adds an air of uncertainty to the nature of the variable. Does the variable `nullable` in listing 4.3 have an integer value? Well, at any particular time it might, or it might be the null value. From now on, we'll use the ? modifier in all the examples—it's neater, and it's arguably the idiomatic way to use nullable types in C# 2. However, you may feel that it's too easy to miss when reading the code, in which case there's certainly nothing to stop you from using the longer syntax. You may wish to compare the listings in this section and the previous one to see which you find clearer.

Given that the C# 2 specification defines the null value, it would be pretty odd if we couldn't use the `null` literal we've already got in the language in order to represent it. Fortunately we can, as our next section will show.

4.3.2   *Assigning and comparing with null*

A very concise author could cover this whole section in a single sentence: "The C# compiler allows the use of `null` to represent the null value of a nullable type in both comparisons and assignments." I prefer to show you what it means in real code, as well as think about *why* the language has been given this feature.

You may have felt a bit uncomfortable every time we've used the default constructor of `Nullable<T>`. It achieves the desired behavior, but it doesn't express the *reason* we want to do it—it doesn't leave the right impression with the reader. We want to give the same sort of feeling that using `null` does with reference types. If it seems odd to you that I've talked about feelings in both this section and the last one, just think about who writes code, and who reads it. Sure, the compiler has to understand the code, and it couldn't care less about the subtle nuances of style—but very few pieces of code used in production systems are written and then never read again. Anything you can do to get the reader into the mental process you were going through when you originally wrote the code is good—and using the familiar `null` literal helps to achieve that.

With that in mind, we're going to change the example we're using from one that just shows syntax and behavior to one that gives an impression of how nullable types might be used. We'll consider modeling a `Person` class where you need to know the name, date of birth, and date of death of a person. We'll only keep track of people who have definitely been born, but some of those people may still be alive—in which case our date of death is represented by `null`. Listing 4.4 shows some of the possible code. Although a real class would clearly have more operations available, we're just looking at the calculation of age for this example.

Listing 4.4   Part of a `Person` class including calculation of age

```
class Person
{
    DateTime birth;
    DateTime? death;
    string name;

    public TimeSpan Age
    {
        get
        {
            if (death==null)                    ❶ Checks
            {                                       HasValue
                return DateTime.Now-birth;
            }
            else
            {                                   ❷ Unwraps for
                return death.Value-birth;           calculation
```

```
            }
        }
    }

    public Person(string name,
                  DateTime birth,
                  DateTime? death)
    {
        this.birth = birth;
        this.death = death;
        this.name = name;
    }
}
...
Person turing = new Person("Alan Turing",
                     new DateTime(1912, 6, 23),
                     new DateTime(1954, 6, 7));
Person knuth  = new Person("Donald Knuth",
                     new DateTime(1938, 1, 10),
                     null);
```

❸ **Wraps DateTime as a nullable**

❹ **Specifies a null date of death**

Listing 4.4 doesn't produce any output, but the very fact that it compiles might have surprised you before reading this chapter. Apart from the use of the ? modifier causing confusion, you might have found it very odd that you could compare a DateTime? with null, or pass null as the argument for a DateTime? parameter.

Hopefully by now the meaning is intuitive—when we compare the death variable with null, we're asking whether its value is the null value or not. Likewise when we use null as a DateTime? instance, we're really creating the null value for the type by calling the default constructor. Indeed, you can see in the generated IL that the code the compiler spits out for listing 4.4 really does just call the death.HasValue property ❶, and creates a new instance of DateTime? ❹ using the default constructor (represented in IL as the initobj instruction). The date of Alan Turing's death ❸ is created by calling the normal DateTime constructor and then passing the result into the Nullable<DateTime> constructor, which takes a parameter.

I mention looking at the IL because that can be a useful way of finding out what your code is actually doing, particularly if something compiles when you don't expect it to. You can use the ildasm tool that comes with the .NET SDK, or for a rather better user interface you can use Reflector,[3] which has many other features (most notably decompilation to high-level languages such as C# as well as disassembly to IL).

We've seen how C# provides shorthand syntax for the concept of a null value, making the code more expressive once nullable types are understood in the first place. However, one part of listing 4.4 took a bit more work than we might have hoped—the subtraction at ❷. Why did we have to unwrap the value? Why could we not just return death-birth directly? What would we want that expression to mean in the case (excluded in our code by our earlier test for null, of course) where death had been null? These questions—and more—are answered in our next section.

---

[3] Available free of charge from http://www.aisto.com/roeder/dotnet/

4.3.3 *Nullable conversions and operators*

We've seen that we can compare instances of nullable types with `null`, but there are other comparisons that can be made and other operators that can be used in some cases. Likewise we've seen wrapping and unwrapping, but other conversions can be used with some types. This section explains what's available. I'm afraid it's pretty much impossible to make this kind of topic genuinely exciting, but carefully designed features like these are what make C# a pleasant language to work with in the long run. Don't worry if not all of it sinks in the first time: just remember that the details are here if you need to reference them in the middle of a coding session.

The "executive summary" is that if there is an operator or conversion available on a non-nullable value type, and that operator or conversion only involves other non-nullable value types, then the nullable value type also has the same operator or conversion available, usually converting the non-nullable value types into their nullable equivalents. To give a more concrete example, there's an implicit conversion from `int` to `long`, and that means there's also an implicit conversion from `int?` to `long?` that behaves in the obvious manner.

Unfortunately, although that broad description gives the right general idea, the exact rules are slightly more complicated. Each one is simple, but there are quite a few of them. It's worth knowing about them because otherwise you may well end up staring at a compiler error or warning for a while, wondering why it believes you're trying to make a conversion that you never intended in the first place. We'll start with the conversions, and then look at operators.

CONVERSIONS INVOLVING NULLABLE TYPES

For completeness, let's start with the conversions we already know about:

- An implicit conversion from the `null` literal to `T?`
- An implicit conversion from `T` to `T?`
- An explicit conversion from `T?` to `T`

Now consider the predefined and user-defined conversions available on types. For instance, there is a predefined conversion from `int` to `long`. For any conversion like this, from one non-nullable value type (`S`) to another (`T`), the following conversions are also available:

- `S?` to `T?` (explicit or implicit depending on original conversion)
- `S` to `T?` (explicit or implicit depending on original conversion)
- `S?` to `T` (always explicit)

To carry our example forward, this means that you can convert implicitly from `int?` to `long?` and from `int` to `long?` as well as explicitly from `int?` to `long`. The conversions behave in the natural way, with null values of `S?` converting to null values of `T?`, and non-null values using the original conversion. As before, the explicit conversion from `S?` to `T` will throw an `InvalidOperationException` when converting from a null value of `S?`. For user-defined conversions, these extra conversions involving nullable types are known as *lifted conversions*.

So far, so relatively simple. Now let's consider the operators, where things are slightly more tricky.

OPERATORS INVOLVING NULLABLE TYPES

C# allows the following operators to be overloaded:

- Unary: `+ ++ - -- ! ~ true false`
- Binary: `+ - * / % & | ^ << >>`
- Equality:[4] `== !=`
- Relational: `< > <= >=`

When these operators are overloaded for a non-nullable value type `T`, the nullable type `T?` has the same operators, with slightly different operand and result types. These are called *lifted operators* whether they're predefined operators like addition on numeric types, or user-defined operators like adding a `TimeSpan` to a `DateTime`. There are a few restrictions as to when they apply:

- The `true` and `false` operators are never lifted. They're incredibly rare in the first place, though, so it's no great loss.
- Only operators with non-nullable value types for the operands are lifted.
- For the unary and binary operators (other than equality and relational operators), the return type has to be a non-nullable value type.
- For the equality and relational operators, the return type has to be `bool`.
- The `&` and `|` operators on `bool?` have separately defined behavior, which we'll see in section 4.3.6.

For all the operators, the operand types become their nullable equivalents. For the unary and binary operators, the return type also becomes nullable, and a null value is returned if any of the operands is a null value. The equality and relational operators keep their non-nullable Boolean return types. For equality, two null values are considered equal, and a null value and any non-null value are considered different, which is consistent with the behavior we saw in section 4.2.3. The relational operators always return `false` if either operand is a null value. When none of the operands is a null value, the operator of the non-nullable type is invoked in the obvious way.

All these rules sound more complicated than they really are—for the most part, everything works as you probably expect it to. It's easiest to see what happens with a few examples, and as `int` has so many predefined operators (and integers can be so easily expressed), it's the natural demonstration type. Table 4.1 shows a number of expressions, the lifted operator signature, and the result. It is assumed that there are variables `four`, `five`, and `nullInt`, each with type `int?` and with the obvious values.

Possibly the most surprising line of the table is the bottom one—that a null value isn't deemed "less than or equal to" another null value, even though they *are* deemed

---

[4] The equality and relational operators are, of course, binary operators themselves, but we'll see that they behave slightly differently to the others, hence their separation here.

Table 4.1   Examples of lifted operators applied to nullable integers

Expression	Lifted operator	Result
`-nullInt`	`int? - (int? x)`	`null`
`-five`	`int? - (int? x)`	`-5`
`five + nullInt`	`int? + (int? x, int? y)`	`null`
`five + five`	`int? + (int? x, int? y)`	`10`
`nullInt == nullInt`	`bool == (int? x, int? y)`	`true`
`five == five`	`bool == (int? x, int? y)`	`true`
`five == nullInt`	`bool == (int? x, int? y)`	`false`
`five == four`	`bool == (int? x, int? y)`	`false`
`four < five`	`bool < (int? x, int? y)`	`true`
`nullInt < five`	`bool < (int? x, int? y)`	`false`
`five < nullInt`	`bool < (int? x, int? y)`	`false`
`nullInt < nullInt`	`bool < (int? x, int? y)`	`false`
`nullInt <= nullInt`	`bool <= (int? x, int? y)`	`false`

to be equal to each other (as per the fifth row)! Very odd—but unlikely to cause problems in real life, in my experience.

One aspect of lifted operators and nullable conversion that has caused some confusion is unintended comparisons with `null` when using a non-nullable value type. The code that follows is legal, but not useful:

```
int i = 5;
if (i == null)
{
    Console.WriteLine ("Never going to happen");
}
```

The C# compiler raises warnings on this code, but you may consider it surprising that it's allowed at all. What's happening is that the compiler sees the `int` expression on the left side of the `==`, sees `null` on the right side, and knows that there's an implicit conversion to `int?` from each of them. Because a comparison between two `int?` values is perfectly valid, the code doesn't generate an error—just the warning. As a further complication, this *isn't* allowed in the case where instead of `int`, we're dealing with a generic type parameter that has been constrained to be a value type—the rules on generics prohibit the comparison with `null` in that situation.

Either way, there'll be either an error or a warning, so as long as you look closely at warnings, you shouldn't end up with deficient code due to this quirk—and hopefully pointing it out to you now may save you from getting a headache trying to work out exactly what's going on.

Now we're able to answer the question at the end of the previous section—why we used death.Value-birth in listing 4.4 instead of just death-birth. Applying the previous rules, we *could* have used the latter expression, but the result would have been a TimeSpan? instead of a TimeSpan. This would have left us with the options of casting the result to TimeSpan, using its Value property, or changing the Age property to return a TimeSpan?—which just pushes the issue onto the caller. It's still a bit ugly, but we'll see a nicer implementation of the Age property in section 4.3.5.

In the list of restrictions regarding operator lifting, I mentioned that bool? works slightly differently than the other types. Our next section explains this and pulls back the lens to see the bigger picture of why all these operators work the way they do.

4.3.4 *Nullable logic*

I vividly remember my early electronics lessons at school. They always seemed to revolve around either working out the voltage across different parts of a circuit using the V=IR formula, or applying *truth tables*—the reference charts for explaining the difference between NAND gates and NOR gates and so on. The idea is simple—a truth table maps out every possible combination of inputs into whatever piece of logic you're interested in and tells you the output.

The truth tables we drew for simple, two-input logic gates always had four rows—each of the two inputs had two possible values, which means there were four possible combinations. Boolean logic is simple like that—but what should happen when you've got a tristate logical type? Well, bool? is just such a type—the value can be true, false, or null. That means that our truth tables now have to have nine rows for our binary operators, as there are nine combinations. The specification only highlights the logical AND and inclusive OR operators (& and |, respectively) because the other operators—unary logical negation (!) and exclusive OR (^)—follow the same rules as other lifted operators. There are no conditional logical operators (the short-circuiting && and || operators) defined for bool?, which makes life simpler.

For the sake of completeness, table 4.2 gives the truth tables for all four valid bool? operators.

Table 4.2 Truth table for the logical operators AND, inclusive OR, exclusive OR, and logical negation, applied to the bool? type

x	y	x & y	x | y	x ^ y	!x
true	true	true	true	false	false
true	false	false	true	true	false
true	null	null	true	null	false
false	true	false	true	true	true
false	false	false	false	false	true
false	null	false	null	null	true

Table 4.2   Truth table for the logical operators AND, inclusive OR, exclusive OR, and logical
negation, applied to the `bool?` type *(continued)*

x	y	x & y	x | y	x ^ y	!x
null	true	null	true	null	null
null	false	false	null	null	null
null	null	null	null	null	null

For those who find reasoning about rules easier to understand than looking up values
in tables, the idea is that a null `bool?` value is in some senses a "maybe." If you imagine
that each null entry in the input side of the table is a variable instead, then you will
always get a null value on the output side of the table if the result depends on the
value of that variable. For instance, looking at the third line of the table, the expression true `&` y will only be true if y is true, but the expression true `|` y will always be
true whatever the value of y is, so the nullable results are null and true, respectively.

When considering the lifted operators and particularly how nullable logic works, the
language designers had two slightly contradictory sets of existing behavior—C# 1 null
references and SQL NULL values. In many cases these don't conflict at all—C# 1 had no
concept of applying logical operators to null references, so there was no problem in
using the SQL-like results given earlier. The definitions we've seen may surprise some
SQL developers, however, when it comes to comparisons. In standard SQL, the result of
comparing two values (in terms of equality or greater than/less than) is always unknown
if either value is NULL. The result in C# 2 is *never* null, and in particular two null values
are considered to be equal to each other.

NOTE   *Reminder: this is C# specific!*   It's worth remembering that the lifted operators and conversions, along with the `bool?` logic described in this section,
are all provided by the C# compiler and *not* by the CLR or the framework
itself. If you use ildasm on code that evaluates any of these nullable operators, you'll find that the compiler has created all the appropriate IL to
test for null values and deal with them accordingly. This means that different languages can behave differently on these matters—definitely
something to look out for if you need to port code between different
.NET-based languages.

We now certainly know enough to use nullable types and predict how they'll behave,
but C# 2 has a sort of "bonus track" when it comes to syntax enhancements: the null
coalescing operator.

4.3.5   *The null coalescing operator*

Aside from the ? modifier, all of the rest of the C# compiler's tricks so far to do with
nullable types have worked with the existing syntax. However, C# 2 introduces a new
operator that can occasionally make code shorter and sweeter. It's called the *null coalescing operator* and appears in code as `??` between its two operands. It's a bit like the
conditional operator but specially tweaked for nulls.

It's a binary operator that evaluates first ?? second by going through the following steps (roughly speaking):

1 Evaluate first.

2 If the result is non-null, that's the result of the whole expression.

3 Otherwise, evaluate second; the result then becomes the result of the whole expression.

I say "roughly speaking" because the formal rules in the specification involve lots of situations where there are conversions involved between the types of first and second. As ever, these aren't important in most uses of the operator, and I don't intend to go through them—consult the specification if you need the details.

Importantly, if the type of the second operand is the underlying type of the first operand (and therefore non-nullable), then the overall result is that underlying type. Let's take a look at a practical use for this by revisiting the Age property of listing 4.4. As a reminder, here's how it was implemented back then, along with the relevant variable declarations:

```
DateTime birth;
DateTime? death;

public TimeSpan Age
{
    get
    {
        if (death==null)
        {
            return DateTime.Now-birth;
        }
        else
        {
            return death.Value-birth;
        }
    }
}
```

Note how both branches of the if statement subtract the value of birth from some non-null DateTime value. The value we're interested in is the latest time the person was alive—the time of the person's death if he or she has already died, or now otherwise. To make progress in little steps, let's try just using the normal conditional operator first:

```
DateTime lastAlive = (death==null ? DateTime.Now : death.Value);
return lastAlive-birth;
```

That's progress of a sort, but arguably the conditional operator has actually made it harder to read rather than easier, even though the new code is shorter. The conditional operator is often like that—how much you use it is a matter of personal preference, although it's worth consulting the rest of your team before using it extensively. Let's see how the null coalescing operator improves things. We want to use the value of death if it's non-null, and DateTime.Now otherwise. We can change the implementation to

```
DateTime lastAlive = death ?? DateTime.Now;
return lastAlive-birth;
```

Note how the type of the result is `DateTime` rather than `DateTime?` because we've used `DateTime.Now` as the second operand. We *could* shorten the whole thing to one expression:

```
return (death ?? DateTime.Now)-birth;
```

However, this is a bit more obscure—in particular, in the two-line version the name of the `lastAlive` variable helps the reader to see why we're applying the null coalescing operator. I hope you agree that the two-line version is simpler and more readable than either the original version using the `if` statement or the version using the normal conditional operator from C# 1. Of course, it relies on the reader understanding what the null coalescing operator does. In my experience, this is one of the least well-known aspects of C# 2, but it's useful enough to make it worth trying to enlighten your coworkers rather than avoiding it.

There are two further aspects that increase the operator's usefulness, too. First, it doesn't just apply to nullable types—reference types can also be used; you just can't use a non-nullable value type for the first operand as that would be pointless. Also, it's *right associative*, which means an expression of the form first `??` second `??` third is evaluated as first `??` (second `??` third)—and so it continues for more operands. You can have any number of expressions, and they'll be evaluated in order, stopping with the first non-null result. If all of the expressions evaluate to null, the result will be null too.

As a concrete example of this, suppose you have an online ordering system (and who doesn't these days?) with the concepts of a billing address, contact address, and shipping address. The business rules declare that any user *must* have a billing address, but the contact address is optional. The shipping address for a particular order is also optional, defaulting to the billing address. These "optional" addresses are easily represented as null references in the code. To work out who to contact in the case of a problem with a shipment, the code in C# 1 might look something like this:

```
Address contact = user.ContactAddress;
if (contact==null)
{
    contact = order.ShippingAddress;
    if (contact==null)
    {
        contact = user.BillingAddress;
    }
}
```

Using the conditional operator in this case is even more horrible. Using the null coalescing operator, however, makes the code very straightforward:

```
Address contact = user.ContactAddress ??
                  order.ShippingAddress ??
                  user.BillingAddress;
```

If the business rules changed to use the shipping address by default instead of the user's contact address, the change here would be extremely obvious. It wouldn't be *particularly* taxing with the if/else version, but I know I'd have to stop and think twice, and verify the code mentally. I'd also be relying on unit tests, so there'd be relatively little chance of me actually getting it wrong, but I'd prefer not to think about things like this unless I absolutely have to.

> **NOTE** *Everything in moderation*—Just in case you may be thinking that my code is littered with uses of the null coalescing operator, it's really not. I tend to consider it when I see defaulting mechanisms involving nulls and possibly the conditional operator, but it doesn't come up very often. When its use is natural, however, it can be a powerful tool in the battle for readability.

We've seen how nullable types can be used for "ordinary" properties of objects—cases where we just naturally might not have a value for some particular aspect that is still best expressed with a value type. Those are the more obvious uses for nullable types and indeed the most common ones. However, a few patterns aren't as obvious but can still be powerful when you're used to them. We'll explore two of these patterns in our next section. This is more for the sake of interest than as part of learning about the behavior of nullable types themselves—you now have all the tools you need to use them in your own code. If you're interested in quirky ideas and perhaps trying something new, however, read on...

4.4   *Novel uses of nullable types*

Before nullable types became a reality, I saw lots of people effectively asking for them, usually related to database access. That's not the only use they can be put to, however. The patterns presented in this section are slightly unconventional but can make code simpler. If you only ever stick to "normal" idioms of C#, that's absolutely fine—this section might not be for you, and I have a lot of sympathy with that point of view. I usually prefer simple code over code that is "clever"—but if a whole *pattern* provides benefits when it's known, that sometimes makes the pattern worth learning. Whether or not you use these techniques is of course entirely up to you—but you may find that they suggest other ideas to use elsewhere in your code. Without further ado, let's start with an alternative to the TryXXX pattern mentioned in section 3.3.3.

4.4.1   *Trying an operation without using output parameters*

The pattern of using a return value to say whether or not an operation worked, and an output parameter to return the real result, is becoming an increasingly common one in the .NET Framework. I have no issues with the aims—the idea that some methods are *likely* to fail to perform their primary purpose in nonexceptional circumstances is common sense. My one problem with it is that I'm just not a huge fan of output parameters. There's something slightly clumsy about the syntax of declaring a variable on one line, then immediately using it as an output parameter.

Methods returning reference types have often used a pattern of returning null on failure and non-null on success. It doesn't work so well when null is a valid return value in the success case. Hashtable is an example of both of these statements, in a slightly ambivalent way. You see, `null` is a theoretically valid value in a `Hashtable`, but in my experience most *uses* of `Hashtable` never use null values, which makes it perfectly acceptable to have code that assumes that a null value means a missing key. One common scenario is to have each value of the `Hashtable` as a list: the first time an item is added for a particular key, a new list is created and the item added to it. Thereafter, adding another item for the same key involves adding the item to the existing list. Here's the code in C# 1:

```
ArrayList list = hash[key];
if (list==null)
{
    list = new ArrayList();
    hash[key] = list;
}
list.Add(newItem);
```

Hopefully you'd use variable names more specific to your situation, but I'm sure you get the idea and may well have used the pattern yourself.[5] With nullable types, this pattern can be extended to value types—and in fact, it's *safer* with value types, because if the natural result type is a value type, then a null value could *only* be returned as a failure case. Nullable types add that extra Boolean piece of information in a nice generic way with language support—so why not use them?

To demonstrate this pattern in practice and in a context other than dictionary lookups, I'll use the classic example of the `TryXXX` pattern—parsing an integer. The implementation of the `TryParse` method in listing 4.5 shows the version of the pattern using an output parameter, but then we see the use of the version using nullable types in the main part at the bottom.

Listing 4.5 An alternative implementation of the `TryXXX` pattern

```
static int? TryParse (string data)
{
    int ret;
    if (int.TryParse(data, out ret))       Classic call with
    {                                       output parameter
        return ret;
    }
    else
    {
        return null;
    }
}
...                                         Nullable
int? parsed = TryParse("Not valid");   ◁─┘ call
if (parsed != null)
{
    Console.WriteLine ("Parsed to {0}", parsed.Value);
}
```

---

[5] Wouldn't it be great if `Hashtable` and `Dictionary<TKey,TValue>` could take a delegate to call whenever a new value was required due to looking up a missing key? Situations like this would be a lot simpler.

```
   else
   {
      Console.WriteLine ("Couldn't parse");
   }
```

You may well think there's very little to distinguish the two versions here—they're the same number of lines, after all. However, I believe there's a difference in emphasis. The nullable version encapsulates the natural return value and the success or failure into a single variable. It also separates the "doing" from the "testing," which puts the emphasis in the right place in my opinion. Usually, if I call a method in the condition part of an `if` statement, that method's primary purpose is to return a Boolean value. Here, the return value is in some ways less important than the output parameter. When you're reading code, it's easy to miss an output parameter in a method call and be left wondering what's actually doing all the work and magically giving the answer. With the nullable version, this is more explicit—the result of the method has all the information we're interested in. I've used this technique in a number of places (often with rather more method parameters, at which point output parameters become even harder to spot) and believe it has improved the general feel of the code. Of course, this only works for value types.

Another advantage of this pattern is that it can be used in conjunction with the null coalescing operator—you can try to understand several pieces of input, stopping at the first valid one. The normal `TryXXX` pattern allows this using the short-circuiting operators, but the meaning isn't nearly as clear when you use the same variable for two different output parameters in the same statement.

The next pattern is an answer to a specific pain point—the irritation and fluff that can be present when writing multitiered comparisons.

4.4.2   *Painless comparisons with the null coalescing operator*

I suspect you dislike writing the same code over and over again as much as I do. Refactoring can often get rid of duplication, but there are some cases that resist refactoring surprisingly effectively. Code for `Equals` and `Compare` often falls firmly into this category in my experience.

Suppose you are writing an e-commerce site and have a list of products. You may wish to sort them by popularity (descending), then price, then name—so that the five-star-rated products come first, but the cheapest within those come before the more expensive ones. If there are multiple products with the same price, products beginning with *A* are listed before products beginning with *B*. This isn't a problem specific to e-commerce sites—sorting data by multiple criteria is a fairly common requirement in computing.

Assuming we have a suitable `Product` type, we can write the comparison with code like this in C# 1:

```
public int Compare(Product first, Product second)
{
    // Reverse comparison of popularity to sort descending
    int ret = second.Popularity.CompareTo(first.Popularity);
```

```
    if (ret != 0)
    {
        return ret;
    }
    ret = first.Price.CompareTo(second.Price);
    if (ret != 0)
    {
        return ret;
    }
    return first.Name.CompareTo(second.Name);
}
```

This assumes that we won't be asked to compare null references, and that all of the properties will return non-null references too. We could use some up-front null comparisons and `Comparer<T>.Default` to handle those cases, but that would make the code even longer and more involved. The code could be shorter (and avoid returning from the middle of the method) by rearranging it slightly, but the fundamental "compare, check, compare, check" pattern would still be present, and it wouldn't be as obvious that once we've got a nonzero answer, we're done.

Ah… now, that last sentence is reminiscent of something else: the null coalescing operator. As we saw in section 4.3, if we have a lot of expressions separated by ?? then the operator will be repeatedly applied until it hits a non-null expression. Now all we've got to do is work out a way of returning null instead of zero from a comparison. This is easy to do in a separate method, and that can also encapsulate the use of the default comparer. We can even have an overload to use a specific comparer if we want. We'll also deal with the case where either of the `Product` references we're passed is null. First, let's look at the class implementing our helper methods, as shown in listing 4.6.

Listing 4.6   Helper class for providing "partial comparisons"

```
public static class PartialComparer
{
    public static int? Compare<T>(T first, T second)
    {
        return Compare(Comparer<T>.Default, first, second);
    }

    public static int? Compare<T>(IComparer<T> comparer,
                                  T first,
                                  T second)
    {
        int ret = comparer.Compare(first, second);
        if (ret == 0)
        {
            return null;
        }
        return ret;
    }

    public static int? ReferenceCompare<T>(T first, T second)
        where T : class
```

```
    {
        if (first==second)
        {
            return 0;
        }
        if (first==null)
        {
            return -1;
        }
        if (second==null)
        {
            return 1;
        }
        return null;
    }
}
```

The `Compare` methods in listing 4.6 are almost pathetically simple—when a comparer isn't specified, the default comparer for the type is used, and all that happens to the comparison's return value is that zero is translated to null. The `ReferenceCompare` method is longer but still very straightforward: it basically returns the correct comparison result (–1, 0, or 1) if it can tell the result just from the references, and `null` otherwise. Even though this class is simple, it's remarkably useful. We can now replace our previous product comparison with a neater implementation:

```
public int Compare(Product first, Product second)
{
    return PC.ReferenceCompare (first, second) ??
            // Reverse comparison of popularity to sort descending
            PC.Compare (second.Popularity, first.Popularity) ??
            PC.Compare (first.Price, second.Price) ??
            PC.Compare (first.Name, second.Name) ??
            0;
}
```

As you may have noticed, I've used `PC` rather than `PartialComparer`—this is solely for the sake of being able to fit the lines on the printed page. In real source I would use the full type name and have one comparison per line. Of course, if you wanted short lines for some reason, you could specify a using directive to make `PC` an alias for `PartialComparer`—I just wouldn't recommend it.

The final 0 is to indicate that if all of the earlier comparisons have passed, the two `Product` instances are equal. We *could* have just used `Comparer<string>.Default.Compare(first.Name, second.Name)` as the final comparison, but that would hurt the symmetry of the method.

This comparison plays nicely with nulls, is easy to modify, forms an easy pattern to use for other comparisons, and only compares as far as it needs to: if the prices are different, the names won't be compared.

You may be wondering whether the same technique could be applied to equality tests, which often have similar patterns. There's much less point in the case of equality, because after the nullity and reference equality tests, you can just use `&&` to provide the desired short-circuiting functionality for Booleans. A method returning a `bool?` can be used to obtain an initial *definitely equal, definitely not equal* or *unknown* result based on the references, however. The complete code of `PartialComparer` on this book's website contains the appropriate utility method and examples of its use.

4.5   *Summary*

When faced with a problem, developers tend to take the easiest short-term solution, even if it's not particularly elegant. That's often exactly the right decision—we don't want to be guilty of overengineering, after all. However, it's always nice when a *good* solution is also the *easiest* solution.

Nullable types solve a very specific problem that only had somewhat ugly solutions before C# 2. The features provided are just a better-supported version of a solution that was feasible but time-consuming in C# 1. The combination of generics (to avoid code duplication), CLR support (to provide suitable boxing and unboxing behavior), and language support (to provide concise syntax along with convenient conversions and operators) makes the solution far more compelling than it was previously.

It so happens that in providing nullable types, the C# and Framework designers have made some other patterns available that just weren't worth the effort before. We've looked at some of them in this chapter, and I wouldn't be at all surprised to see more of them appearing over time.

So far our two new features (generics and nullable types) have addressed areas where in C# 1 we occasionally had to hold our noses due to unpleasant code smells. This pattern continues in the next chapter, where we discuss the enhancements to delegates. These form an important part of the subtle change of direction of both the C# language and the .NET Framework, toward a slightly more functional viewpoint. This emphasis is made even clearer in C# 3, so while we're not looking at those features *quite* yet, the delegate enhancements in C# 2 act as a bridge between the familiarity of C# 1 and the potentially revolutionary style of C# 3.

Fast-tracked delegates

This chapter covers

- Longwinded C# 1 syntax
- Simplified delegate construction
- Covariance and contravariance
- Anonymous methods
- Captured variables

The journey of delegates in C# and .NET is an interesting one, showing remarkable foresight (or really good luck) on the part of the designers. The conventions suggested for event handlers in .NET 1.0/1.1 didn't make an awful lot of sense—until C# 2 showed up. Likewise, the effort put into delegates for C# 2 seems in some ways out of proportion to how widely used they are—until you see how pervasive they are in idiomatic C# 3 code. In other words, it's as if the language and platform designers had a vision of at least the rough direction they would be taking, years before the destination itself became clear.

Of course, C# 3 is not a "final destination" in itself, and we may be seeing further advances for delegates in the future—but the differences between C# 1 and C# 3 in this area are startling. (The primary change in C# 3 supporting delegates is in lambda expressions, which we'll meet in chapter 9.)

C# 2 is a sort of stepping stone in terms of delegates. Its new features pave the way for the even more dramatic changes of C# 3, keeping developers *reasonably* comfortable while still providing useful benefits. The extent to which this was a finely balanced act as opposed to intuition and a following wind is likely to stay unknown, but we can certainly reap the benefits.

Delegates play a more prominent part in .NET 2.0 than in earlier versions, although they're not as common as they are in .NET 3.5. In chapter 3 we saw how they can be used to convert from a list of one type to a list of another type, and way back in chapter 1 we sorted a list of products using the `Comparison` delegate instead of the `IComparer` interface. Although the framework and C# keep a respectful distance from each other where possible, I believe that the language and platform drove each other here: the inclusion of more delegate-based API calls supported the improved syntax available in C# 2, and vice versa.

In this chapter we'll see how C# 2 makes two small changes that make life easier when creating delegate instances from normal methods, and then we'll look at the biggest change: anonymous methods, which allow you to specify a delegate instance's action inline at the point of its creation. The largest section of the chapter is devoted to the most complicated part of anonymous methods, captured variables, which provide delegate instances with a richer environment to play in. We'll cover the topic in significant detail due to its importance and complexity.

First, though, let's remind ourselves of the pain points of C# 1's delegate facilities.

5.1   *Saying goodbye to awkward delegate syntax*

The syntax for delegates in C# 1 doesn't *sound* too bad—the language already has syntactic sugar around `Delegate.Combine`, `Delegate.Remove`, and the invocation of delegate instances. It makes sense to specify the delegate type when creating a delegate instance—it's the same syntax used to create instances of other types, after all.

This is all true, but for some reason it also sucks. It's hard to say exactly why the delegate creation expressions of C# 1 raise hackles, but they do—at least for me. When hooking up a bunch of event handlers, it just looks ugly to have to write "new `EventHandler`" (or whatever is required) all over the place, when the event itself has specified which delegate type it will use. Beauty is in the eye of the beholder, of course, and you could argue that there's less call for guesswork when reading event handler wiring code in the C# 1 style, but the extra text just gets in the way and distracts from the important part of the code: which method you want to handle the event.

Life becomes a bit more black and white when you consider covariance and contravariance as applied to delegates. Suppose you've got an event handling method that saves the current document, or just logs that it's been called, or any number of other actions that may well not need to know details of the event. The event itself shouldn't mind that your method is capable of working with only the information provided by the `EventHandler` signature, even though it is declared to pass in mouse event details. Unfortunately, in C# 1 you have to have a different method for each different event handler signature.

Likewise it's undeniably ugly to write methods that are so simple that their implementation is shorter than their signature, solely because delegates need to have code to execute and that code has to be in the form of a method. It adds an extra layer of indirection between the code creating the delegate instance and the code that should execute when the delegate instance is invoked. Often extra layers of indirection are welcome—and of course that option hasn't been removed in C# 2—but at the same time it often makes the code harder to read, and pollutes the class with a bunch of methods that are only used for delegates.

Unsurprisingly, all of these are improved greatly in C# 2. The syntax can still occasionally be wordier than we might like (which is where lambda expressions come into play in C# 3), but the difference is significant. To illustrate the pain, we'll start with some code in C# 1 and improve it in the next couple of sections. Listing 5.1 builds a (very) simple form with a button and subscribes to three of the button's events.

Listing 5.1   Subscribing to three of a button's events

```
static void LogPlainEvent(object sender, EventArgs e)
{
    Console.WriteLine ("LogPlain");
}

static void LogKeyEvent(object sender, KeyPressEventArgs e)
{
    Console.WriteLine ("LogKey");
}

static void LogMouseEvent(object sender, MouseEventArgs e)
{
    Console.WriteLine ("LogMouse");
}

...
Button button = new Button();
button.Text = "Click me";
button.Click      += new EventHandler(LogPlainEvent);
button.KeyPress   += new KeyPressEventHandler(LogKeyEvent);
button.MouseClick += new MouseEventHandler(LogMouseEvent);

Form form = new Form();
form.AutoSize=true;
form.Controls.Add(button);
Application.Run(form);
```

The output lines in the three event handling methods are there to prove that the code is working: if you press the spacebar with the button highlighted, you'll see that the `Click` and `KeyPress` events are both raised; pressing Enter just raises the `Click` event; clicking on the button raises the `Click` and `MouseClick` events. In the following sections we'll improve this code using some of the C# 2 features.

Let's start by asking the compiler to make a pretty obvious deduction—which delegate type we want to use when subscribing to an event.

5.2   *Method group conversions*

In C# 1, if you want to create a delegate instance you need to specify both the delegate type and the action. If you remember from chapter 2, we defined the *action* to be the method to call and (for instance methods) the target to call it on. So for example, in listing 5.1 when we needed to create a KeyPressEventHandler we used this expression:

```
new KeyPressEventHandler(LogKeyEvent)
```

As a stand-alone expression, it doesn't look too bad. Even used in a simple event subscription it's tolerable. It becomes a bit uglier when used as part of a longer expression. A common example of this is starting a new thread:

```
Thread t = new Thread (new ThreadStart(MyMethod));
```

What we want to do is start a new thread that will execute MyMethod as simply as possible. C# 2 allows you to do this by means of an implicit conversion from a *method group* to a compatible delegate type. A method group is simply the name of a method, optionally with a target—exactly the same kind of expression as we used in C# 1 to create delegate instances, in other words. (Indeed, the expression was called a method group back then—it's just that the conversion wasn't available.) If the method is generic, the method group may also specify type arguments. The new implicit conversion allows us to turn our event subscription into

```
button.KeyPress += LogKeyEvent;
```

Likewise the thread creation code becomes simply

```
Thread t = new Thread (MyMethod);
```

The readability differences between the original and the "streamlined" versions aren't huge for a single line, but in the context of a significant amount of code, they can reduce the clutter considerably. To make it look less like magic, let's take a brief look at what this conversion is doing.

First, let's consider the expressions LogKeyEvent and MyMethod as they appear in the examples. The reason they're classified as method *groups* is that more than one method may be available, due to overloading. The implicit conversions available will convert a method group to any delegate type with a compatible signature. So, if you had two method signatures as follows:

```
void MyMethod()
void MyMethod(object sender, EventArgs e)
```

you could use MyMethod as the method group in an assignment to either a ThreadStart or an EventHandler as follows:

```
ThreadStart x = MyMethod;
EventHandler y = MyMethod;
```

However, you *couldn't* use it as the parameter to a method that itself was overloaded to take either a ThreadStart or an EventHandler—the compiler would complain that the conversion was ambiguous. Likewise, you unfortunately can't use an implicit method group conversion to convert to the plain System.Delegate type since the compiler doesn't know which specific delegate type to create an instance of. This is a bit of a pain, but you *can* still be slightly briefer than in C# 1 by making the conversion explicit. For example:

```
Delegate invalid = SomeMethod;
Delegate valid = (ThreadStart)SomeMethod;
```

As with generics, the precise rules of conversion are slightly complicated, and the "just try it" rule works very well: if the compiler complains that it doesn't have enough information, just tell it what conversion to use and all should be well. If it doesn't complain, you should be fine. For the exact details, consult the language specification. Speaking of possible conversions, there may be more than you expect, as we'll see in our next section.

5.3   *Covariance and contravariance*

We've already talked quite a lot about the concepts of covariance and contravariance in different contexts, usually bemoaning their absence, but delegate construction is the one area in which they are actually available in C#. If you want to refresh yourself about the meaning of the terms at a relatively detailed level, refer back to section 2.2.2—but the gist of the topic with respect to delegates is that if it would be valid (in a static typing sense) to call a method and use its return value everywhere that you could invoke an instance of a particular delegate type and use *its* return value, then that method can be used to create an instance of that delegate type. That's all pretty wordy, but it's a lot simpler with examples.

Let's consider the event handlers we've got in our little Windows Forms application. The signatures[1] of the three delegate types involved are as follows:

```
void EventHandler (object sender, EventArgs e)
void KeyPressEventHandler (object sender, KeyPressEventArgs e)
void MouseEventHandler (object sender, MouseEventArgs e)
```

Now, consider that KeyPressEventArgs and MouseEventArgs both derive from Event-Args (as do a lot of other types—at the time of this writing, MSDN lists 386 types that derive directly from EventArgs). So, if you have a method that takes an EventArgs parameter, you could always call it with a KeyPressEventArgs argument instead. It therefore makes sense to be able to use a method with the same signature as EventHandler to create an instance of KeyPressEventHandler—and that's exactly what C# 2 does. This is an example of contravariance of parameter types.

To see that in action, let's think back to listing 5.1 and suppose that we don't need to know which event was firing—we just want to write out the fact that an event has happened. Using method group conversions and contravariance, our code becomes quite a lot simpler, as shown in listing 5.2.

---

[1] I've removed the **public delegate** part for reasons of space.

Listing 5.2   Demonstration of method group conversions and delegate contravariance

```
static void LogPlainEvent(object sender, EventArgs e)        ◁⊣  Handles
{                                                             ❶  all events
    Console.WriteLine ("An event occurred");
}
...
Button button = new Button();
button.Text = "Click me";                         ❷  Uses method
button.Click      += LogPlainEvent;      ◁            group conversion
button.KeyPress   += LogPlainEvent;
button.MouseClick += LogPlainEvent;      ◁        Uses conversion
                                              ❸  and contravariance
Form form = new Form();
form.AutoSize=true;
form.Controls.Add(button);
Application.Run(form);
```

We've managed to completely remove the two handler methods that dealt specifically with key and mouse events, using one event handling method ❶ for everything. Of course, this isn't terribly useful if you want to do different things for different types of events, but sometimes all you need to know is that an event occurred and, potentially, the source of the event. The subscription to the Click event ❷ only uses the implicit conversion we discussed in the previous section because it has a simple EventArgs parameter, but the other event subscriptions ❸ involve the conversion and contravariance due to their different parameter types.

I mentioned earlier that the .NET 1.0/1.1 event handler convention didn't make much sense when it was first introduced. This example shows exactly why the guidelines are more useful with C# 2. The convention dictates that event handlers should have a signature with two parameters, the first of which is of type object and is the origin of the event, and the second of which carries any extra information about the event in a type deriving from EventArgs. Before contravariance became available, this wasn't useful—there was no benefit to making the informational parameter derive from EventArgs, and sometimes there wasn't much use for the origin of the event. It was often more sensible just to pass the relevant information directly in the form of normal parameters, just like any other method. Now, however, you can use a method with the EventHandler signature as the action for *any* delegate type that honors the convention.

Demonstrating covariance of return types is a little harder as relatively few built-in delegates are declared with a nonvoid return type. There are some available, but it's easier to declare our own delegate type that uses Stream as its return type. For simplicity we'll make it parameterless:[2]

```
delegate Stream StreamFactory();
```

We can now use this with a method that is declared to return a specific type of stream, as shown in listing 5.3. We declare a method that always returns a MemoryStream with

---

[2] Return type covariance and parameter type contravariance can be used at the same time, although you're unlikely to come across situations where it would be useful.

some random data, and then use that method as the action for a `StreamFactory` delegate instance.

Listing 5.3   Demonstration of covariance of return types for delegates

```
delegate Stream StreamFactory();        ◁──❶ Declares delegate type returning Stream

static MemoryStream GenerateRandomData()    ◁──┐ Declares method
{                                              ❷ returning MemoryStream
    byte[] buffer = new byte[16];
    new Random().NextBytes(buffer);
    return new MemoryStream(buffer);
}
...                                         ❸ Converts method
StreamFactory factory = GenerateRandomData;  ◁──┘ group with covariance

Stream stream = factory();              ◁──┐ Invokes
int data;                                  ❹ delegate
while ( (data=stream.ReadByte()) != -1)
{
    Console.WriteLine(data);
}
```

The actual generation and display of the data in listing 5.3 is only present to give the code something to do. (In particular, the way of generating random data is pretty awful!) The important points are the annotated lines. We declare that the delegate type has a return type of `Stream` ❶, but the `GenerateRandomData` method ❷ has a return type of `MemoryStream`. The line creating the delegate instance ❸ performs the conversion we saw earlier and uses covariance of return types to allow `GenerateRandomData` to be used for the action for `StreamFactory`. By the time we invoke the delegate instance ❹, the compiler no longer knows that a `MemoryStream` will be returned—if we changed the type of the `stream` variable to `MemoryStream`, we'd get a compilation error.

Covariance and contravariance can also be used to construct one delegate instance from another. For instance, consider these two lines of code (which assume an appropriate `HandleEvent` method):

```
EventHandler general = new EventHandler(HandleEvent);
KeyPressEventHandler key = new KeyPressEventHandler(general);
```

The first line is valid in C#1, but the second isn't—in order to construct one delegate from another in C#1, the signatures of the two delegate types involved have to match. For instance, you could create a `MethodInvoker` from a `ThreadStart`—but you couldn't do what we're doing in the previous code. We're using contravariance to create a new delegate instance from an existing one with a *compatible* delegate type signature, where compatibility is defined in a less restrictive manner in C#2 than in C#1.

This new flexibility in C#2 causes one of the very few cases where existing valid C#1 code may produce different results when compiled under C#2: if a derived class overloads a method declared in its base class, a delegate creation expression that previously only matched the base class method could now match the derived class method due to covariance or contravariance. In this case the derived class method will take priority in C#2. Listing 5.4 gives an example of this.

Listing 5.4 Demonstration of breaking change between C# 1 and C# 2

```
delegate void SampleDelegate(string x);

public void CandidateAction(string x)
{
    Console.WriteLine("Snippet.CandidateAction");
}

public class Derived : Snippet
{
    public void CandidateAction(object o)
    {
        Console.WriteLine("Derived.CandidateAction");
    }
}
...
Derived x = new Derived();
SampleDelegate factory = new SampleDelegate(x.CandidateAction);
factory("test");
```

Remember that Snippy[3] will be generating all of this code within a class called Snippet which the nested type derives from. Under C#1, listing 5.4 would print `Snippet.CandidateAction` because the method taking an `object` parameter wasn't compatible with `SampleDelegate`. Under C#2, however, it *is* compatible and is the method chosen due to being declared in a more derived type—so the result is that `Derived.CandidateAction` is printed. Fortunately, the C#2 compiler knows that this is a breaking change and issues an appropriate warning.

Enough doom and gloom about potential breakage, however. We've still got to see the most important new feature regarding delegates: anonymous methods. They're a bit more complicated than the topics we've covered so far, but they're also *very* powerful—and a large step toward C#3.

5.4 *Inline delegate actions with anonymous methods*

Have you ever been writing C#1 and had to implement a delegate with a particular signature, even though you've already got a method that does what you want but doesn't happen to have quite the right parameters? Have you ever had to implement a delegate that only needs to do one teeny, tiny thing, and yet you need a whole extra method? Have you ever been frustrated at having to navigate away from an important bit of code in order to see what the delegate you're using does, only to find that the method used is only two lines long? This kind of thing happened to me quite regularly with C#1. The covariance and contravariance features we've just talked about can *sometimes* help with the first problem, but often they don't. *Anonymous methods*, which are also new in C#2, can pretty much *always* help with these issues.

Informally, anonymous methods allow you to specify the action for a delegate instance inline as part of the delegate instance creation expression. This means there's

---

[3]   In case you skipped the first chapter, Snippy is a tool I've used to create short but complete code samples. See section 1.4.2 for more details.

no need to "pollute" the rest of your class with an extra method containing a small piece of code that is only useful in one place and doesn't make sense elsewhere.

Anonymous methods also provide some far more powerful behavior in the form of *closures*, but we'll come to them in section 5.5. For the moment, let's stick with relatively simple stuff—as you may have noticed, a common theme in this book is that you can go a long way in C#2 without dealing with the more complex aspects of the language. Not only is this good in terms of learning the new features gradually, but if you only use the more complicated areas when they provide a lot of benefit, your code will be easier to understand as well. First we'll see examples of anonymous methods that take parameters but don't return any values; then we'll explore the syntax involved in providing return values and a shortcut available when we don't need to use the parameters passed to us.

5.4.1   *Starting simply: acting on a parameter*

In chapter 3 we saw the `Action<T>` delegate type. As a reminder, its signature is very simple (aside from the fact that it's generic):

```
public delegate void Action<T>(T obj)
```

In other words, an `Action<T>` does something with an instance of T. So an `Action<string>` could reverse the string and print it out, an `Action<int>` could print out the square root of the number passed to it, and an `Action<IList <double>>` could find the average of all the numbers given to it and print that out. By complete coincidence, these examples are all implemented using anonymous methods in listing 5.5.

Listing 5.5   Anonymous methods used with the `Action<T>` delegate type

```
Action<string> printReverse = delegate(string text)
    {
        char[] chars = text.ToCharArray();
        Array.Reverse(chars);
        Console.WriteLine(new string(chars));
    };

Action<int> printRoot = delegate(int number)
    {
        Console.WriteLine(Math.Sqrt(number));
    };

Action<IList<double>> printMean = delegate(IList<double> numbers)
    {
        double total = 0;
        foreach (double value in numbers)
        {
            total += value;
        }
        Console.WriteLine(total/numbers.Count);
    };

double[] samples = {1.5, 2.5, 3, 4.5};
```

❶ Uses anonymous method to create Action<string>

❷ Uses loop in anonymous method

```
printReverse("Hello world");
printRoot(2);
printMean(samples);
```

❸ Invokes delegates as normal

Anonymous methods just contain normal code

Listing 5.5 shows a few of the different features of anonymous methods. First, the syntax of anonymous methods: use the `delegate` keyword, followed by the parameters (if there are any), followed by the code for the action of the delegate instance, in a block. The string reversal code ❶ shows that the block can contain local variable declarations, and the "list averaging" code ❷ demonstrates looping within the block. Basically, anything you can do in a normal method body, you can do in an anonymous method.[4] Likewise, the result of an anonymous method is a delegate instance that can be used like any other one ❸. Be warned that contravariance doesn't apply to anonymous methods: you have to specify the parameter types that match the delegate type exactly.

In terms of implementation, we are still creating a method for each delegate instance: the compiler will generate a method within the class and use that as the action it uses to create the delegate instance, just as if it were a normal method. The CLR neither knows nor cares that an anonymous method was used. You can see the extra methods within the compiled code using ildasm or Reflector. (Reflector knows how to interpret the IL to display anonymous methods in the method that uses them, but the extra methods are still visible.)

It's worth pointing out at this stage that listing 5.5 is "exploded" compared with how you may well see anonymous methods in real code. You'll often see them used as parameters to another method (rather than assigned to a variable of the delegate type) and with very few line breaks—compactness is part of the reason for using them, after all. For example, we mentioned in chapter 3 that `List<T>` has a `ForEach` method that takes an `Action<T>` as a parameter and performs that action on each element. Listing 5.6 shows an extreme example of this, applying the same "square rooting" action we used in listing 5.5, but in a compact form.

Listing 5.6   Extreme example of code compactness. Warning: unreadable code ahead!

```
List<int> x = new List<int>();
x.Add(5);
x.Add(10);
x.Add(15);
x.Add(20);
x.Add(25);

x.ForEach(delegate(int n){Console.WriteLine(Math.Sqrt(n));});
```

That's pretty horrendous—especially when at first sight the last six characters appear to be ordered almost at random. There's a happy medium, of course. I tend to break my

---

[4]   One slight oddity is that if you're writing an anonymous method in a value type, you can't reference `this` from within it. There's no such restriction within a reference type.

usual "braces on a line on their own" rule for anonymous methods (as I do for trivial properties) but still allow a decent amount of whitespace. I'd usually write the last line of listing 5.6 as something like

```
x.ForEach(delegate(int n)
    { Console.WriteLine(Math.Sqrt(n)); }
);
```

The parentheses and braces are now less confusing, and the "what it does" part stands out appropriately. Of course, how you space out your code is entirely your own business, but I encourage you to actively think about where you want to strike the balance, and talk about it with your teammates to try to achieve some consistency. Consistency doesn't *always* lead to the most readable code, however—sometimes keeping everything on one line is the most straightforward format.

You should also consider how much code it makes sense to include in anonymous methods. The first two examples in listing 5.5 are reasonable , but printMean is probably doing enough work to make it worth having as a separate method. Again, it's a balancing act.

So far the only interaction we've had with the calling code is through parameters. What about return values?

5.4.2 *Returning values from anonymous methods*

The Action<T> delegate has a void return type, so we haven't had to return anything from our anonymous methods. To demonstrate how we can do so when we need to, we'll use the new Predicate<T> delegate type. We saw this briefly in chapter 3, but here's its signature just as a reminder:

```
public delegate bool Predicate<T>(T obj)
```

Listing 5.7 shows an anonymous method creating an instance of Predicate<T> to return whether the argument passed in is odd or even. Predicates are usually used in filtering and matching—you could use the code in listing 5.7 to filter a list to one containing just the even elements, for instance.

Listing 5.7   Returning a value from an anonymous method

```
Predicate<int> isEven = delegate(int x)
    { return x%2 == 0; };

Console.WriteLine(isEven(1));
Console.WriteLine(isEven(4));
```

The new syntax is almost certainly what you'd have expected—we just return the appropriate value as if the anonymous method were a normal method. You may have expected to see a return type declared near the parameter type, but there's no need. The compiler just checks that all the possible return values are compatible with the declared return type of the delegate type it's trying to convert the anonymous method into.

NOTE   *Just what are you returning from?*   When you return a value from an anonymous method it really *is* only returning from the anonymous method—
it's not returning from the method that is creating the delegate instance.
It's all too easy to look down some code, see the return keyword, and
think that it's an exit point from the current method.

Relatively few delegates in .NET 2.0 return values—in particular, few event handlers
do, partly because when the event is raised only the return value from the last action
to be called would be available. The Predicate<T> delegate type we've used so far
isn't used *very* widely in .NET 2.0, but it becomes important in .NET 3.5 where it's a key
part of LINQ. Another useful delegate type with a return value is Comparison<T>,
which can be used when sorting items. This works very well with anonymous methods.
Often you only need a particular sort order in one situation, so it makes sense to be
able to specify that order inline, rather than exposing it as a method within the rest of
the class. Listing 5.8 demonstrates this, printing out the files within the C:\ directory,
ordering them first by name and then (separately) by size.

Listing 5.8   Using anonymous methods to sort files simply

```
static void SortAndShowFiles(string title,
                             Comparison<FileInfo> sortOrder)
{
    FileInfo[] files = new DirectoryInfo(@"C:\").GetFiles();

    Array.Sort(files, sortOrder);

    Console.WriteLine(title);
    foreach (FileInfo file in files)
    {
        Console.WriteLine("  {0} ({1} bytes)",
                          file.Name, file.Length);
    }
}
...
SortAndShowFiles("Sorted by name:",
                 delegate(FileInfo first, FileInfo second)
    { return first.Name.CompareTo(second.Name); }
);

SortAndShowFiles("Sorted by length:",
                 delegate(FileInfo first, FileInfo second)
    { return first.Length.CompareTo(second.Length); }
);
```

If we weren't using anonymous methods, we'd have to have a separate method for
each of these sort orders. Instead, listing 5.8 makes it clear what we'll sort by in each
case right where we call SortAndShowFiles. (Sometimes you'll be calling Sort directly
at the point where the anonymous method is called for. In this case we're performing
the same fetch/sort/display sequence twice, just with different sort orders, so I encapsulated that sequence in its own method.)

There's one special syntactic shortcut that is sometimes available. If you don't care about the parameters of a delegate, you don't have to declare them at all. Let's see how that works.

5.4.3 Ignoring delegate parameters

Just occasionally, you want to implement a delegate that doesn't depend on its parameter values. You may wish to write an event handler whose behavior was only appropriate for one event and didn't depend on the event arguments: saving the user's work, for instance. Indeed, the event handlers from our original example in listing 5.1 fit this criterion perfectly. In this case, you can leave out the parameter list entirely, just using the delegate keyword and then the block of code to use as the action for the method. Listing 5.9 is equivalent to listing 5.1 but uses this syntax.

Listing 5.9   Subscribing to events with anonymous methods that ignore parameters

```
Button button = new Button();
button.Text = "Click me";
button.Click      += delegate { Console.WriteLine("LogPlain"); };
button.KeyPress   += delegate { Console.WriteLine("LogKey"); };
button.MouseClick += delegate { Console.WriteLine("LogMouse"); };

Form form = new Form();
form.AutoSize=true;
form.Controls.Add(button);
Application.Run(form);
```

Normally we'd have had to write each subscription as something like this:

```
button.Click += delegate (object sender, EventArgs e) { ... };
```

That wastes a lot of space for little reason—we don't need the values of the parameters, so the compiler lets us get away with not specifying them at all. Listing 5.9 also happens to be a perfect example of how consistency of formatting isn't *always* a good thing—I played around with a few ways of laying out the code and decided this was the clearest form.

I've found this shortcut most useful when it comes to implementing my own events. I get sick of having to perform a nullity check before raising an event. One way of getting around this is to make sure that the event starts off with a handler, which is then never removed. As long as the handler doesn't do anything, all you lose is a tiny bit of performance. Before C# 2, you had to explicitly create a method with the right signature, which usually wasn't worth the benefit. Now, however, you can do this:

```
public event EventHandler Click = delegate {};
```

From then on, you can just call Click without any tests to see whether there are any handlers subscribed to the event.

You should be aware of one trap about this "parameter wildcarding" feature—if the anonymous method could be converted to multiple delegate types (for example, to call different method overloads) then the compiler needs more help. To show you what I mean, let's look at how we start threads. There are four thread constructors in .NET 2.0:

```
public Thread (ParameterizedThreadStart start)
public Thread (ThreadStart start)
public Thread (ParameterizedThreadStart start, int maxStackSize)
public Thread (ThreadStart start, int maxStackSize)
```

The two delegate types involved are

```
public delegate void ThreadStart()
public delegate void ParameterizedThreadStart(object obj)
```

Now, consider the following three attempts to create a new thread:

```
new Thread(delegate()          { Console.WriteLine("t1"); } );

new Thread(delegate(object o) { Console.WriteLine("t2"); } );

new Thread(delegate          { Console.WriteLine("t3"); } );
```

The first and second lines contain parameter lists—the compiler knows that it can't convert the anonymous method in the first line into a `ParameterizedThreadStart`, or convert the anonymous method in the second line into a `ThreadStart`. Those lines compile, because there's only one applicable constructor overload in each case. The third line, however, is ambiguous—the anonymous method can be converted into either delegate type, so both of the constructor overloads taking just one parameter are applicable. In this situation, the compiler throws its hands up and issues an error. You can solve this either by specifying the parameter list explicitly or casting the anonymous method to the right delegate type.

Hopefully what you've seen of anonymous methods so far will have provoked some thought about your own code, and made you consider where you could use these techniques to good effect. Indeed, even if anonymous methods could *only* do what we've already seen, they'd still be very useful. However, there's more to anonymous methods than just avoiding the inclusion of an extra method in your code. Anonymous methods are C# 2's implementation of a feature known elsewhere as *closures* by way of *captured variables*. Our next section explains both of these terms and shows how anonymous methods can be extremely powerful—and confusing if you're not careful.

5.5   *Capturing variables in anonymous methods*

I don't like having to give warnings, but I think it makes sense to include one here: if this topic is new to you, then don't start this section until you're feeling reasonably awake and have a bit of time to spend on it. I don't want to alarm you unnecessarily, and you should feel confident that there's nothing so insanely complicated that you won't be able to understand it with a little effort. It's just that captured variables can be somewhat confusing to start with, partly because they overturn some of your existing knowledge and intuition.

Stick with it, though! The payback can be *massive* in terms of code simplicity and readability. This topic will also be crucial when we come to look at lambda expressions and LINQ in C#3, so it's worth the investment. Let's start off with a few definitions.

5.5.1 Defining closures and different types of variables

The concept of *closures* is a very old one, first implemented in Scheme, but it's been gaining more prominence in recent years as more mainstream languages have taken it on board. The basic idea is that a function[5] is able to interact with an environment beyond the parameters provided to it. That's all there is to it in abstract terms, but to understand how it applies to C#2, we need a couple more terms:

- An *outer variable* is a local variable or parameter[6] whose scope includes an anonymous method. The `this` reference also counts as an outer variable of any anonymous method where it can be used.
- A *captured outer variable* (usually shortened to just *"captured variable"*) is an outer variable that is used within an anonymous method. So to go back to closures, the function part is the anonymous method, and the environment it can interact with is the set of variables captured by it.

That's all very dry and may be hard to imagine, but the main thrust is that an anonymous method can use local variables defined in the same method that declares it. This may not sound like a big deal, but in many situations it's enormously handy—you can use contextual information that you have "on hand" rather than having to set up extra types just to store data you already know. We'll see some *useful* concrete examples soon, I promise—but first it's worth looking at some code to clarify these definitions. Listing 5.10 provides an example with a number of local variables. It's just a single method, so it can't be run on its own. I'm not going to explain how it would work or what it would do yet, but just explain how the different variables are classified.

Listing 5.10 Examples of different kinds of variables with respect to anonymous methods

```
void EnclosingMethod()                            ❶ Outer variable      ❷ Outer variable
{                                                    (uncaptured)           captured by
                                                                            anonymous
    int outerVariable = 5;                ◄─────────────┘                   method
    string capturedVariable = "captured";                      ◄───────────────┘

    if (DateTime.Now.Hour==23)
    {                                                                  ❸ Local variable of
        int normalLocalVariable = DateTime.Now.Minute;   ◄──────────┘    normal method
        Console.WriteLine(normalLocalVariable);
    }

    ThreadStart x = delegate()                                     ❹ Local variable
        {                                                             of anonymous
            string anonLocal="local to anonymous method";   ◄┘        method
```

---

[5] This is general computer science terminology, not C# terminology.

[6] Excluding `ref` and `out` parameters.

```
      Console.WriteLine(capturedVariable + anonLocal);
   };
x();
}
```
⑤ Capture of outer variable

Let's go through all the variables from the simplest to the most complicated:

- normalLocalVariable ❸ isn't an outer variable because there are no anonymous methods within its scope. It behaves exactly the way that local variables always have.
- anonLocal ❹ isn't an outer variable either, but it's local to the anonymous method, not to EnclosingMethod. It will only exist (in terms of being present in an executing stack frame) when the delegate instance is invoked.
- outerVariable ❶ is an outer variable because the anonymous method is declared within its scope. However, the anonymous method doesn't refer to it, so it's not captured.
- capturedVariable ❷ is an outer variable because the anonymous method is declared within its scope, and it's *captured* by virtue of being used at ❺.

Okay, so we now understand the terminology, but we're not a lot closer to seeing what captured variables do. I suspect you could guess the output if we ran the method from listing 5.10, but there are some other cases that would probably surprise you. We'll start off with a simple example and gradually build up to more complex ones.

5.5.2 *Examining the behavior of captured variables*

When a variable is captured, it really is the *variable* that's captured by the anonymous method, not its value at the time the delegate instance was created. We'll see later that this has far-reaching consequences, but first we'll make sure we understand what that means for a relatively straightforward situation. Listing 5.11 has a captured variable and an anonymous method that both prints out and changes the variable. We'll see that changes to the variable from outside the anonymous method are visible within the anonymous method, and vice versa. We're using the ThreadStart delegate type for simplicity as we don't need a return type or any parameters—no extra threads are actually created, though.

Listing 5.11 Accessing a variable both inside and outside an anonymous method

```
string captured = "before x is created";

ThreadStart x = delegate
   {
       Console.WriteLine(captured);
       captured = "changed by x";
   };

captured = "directly before x is invoked";
x();
```

```
Console.WriteLine (captured);

captured = "before second invocation";
x();
```

The output of listing 5.11 is as follows:

```
directly before x is invoked
changed by x
before second invocation
```

Let's look at how this happens. First, we declare the variable captured and set its value with a perfectly normal string literal. So far, there's nothing special about the variable. We then declare x and set its value using an anonymous method that captures captured. The delegate instance will always print out the current value of captured, and then set it to "changed by x".

Just to make it absolutely clear that just creating the delegate instance didn't read the variable and stash its value away somewhere, we now change the value of captured to "directly before x is invoked". We then invoke x for the first time. It reads the value of captured and prints it out—our first line of output. It sets the value of captured to "changed by x" and returns. When the delegate instance returns, the "normal" method continues in the usual way. It prints out the current value of captured, giving us our second line of output.

The normal method then changes the value of captured yet again (this time to before second invocation) and invokes x for the second time. The current value of captured is printed out, giving our last line of output. The delegate instance changes captured to changed by x and returns, at which point the normal method has run out of code and we're done.

That's a lot of detail about how a pretty short piece of code works, but there's really only one crucial idea in it: *the captured variable is the same one that the rest of the method uses.* For some people, that's hard to grasp; for others it comes naturally. Don't worry if it's tricky to start with—it'll get easier over time. Even if you've understood everything easily so far, you may be wondering why you'd want to do any of this. It's about time we had an example that was actually useful.

5.5.3   *What's the point of captured variables?*

To put it simply, captured variables get rid of the need for you to write extra classes just to store the information a delegate needs to act on, beyond what it's passed as parameters. Before ParameterizedThreadStart existed, if you wanted to start a new (non-threadpool) thread and give it some information—the URL of a page to fetch, for instance—you had to create an extra type to hold the URL and put the action of the ThreadStart delegate instance in that type. It was all a very ugly way of achieving something that should have been simple.

As another example, suppose you had a list of people and wanted to write a method that would return a second list containing all the people who were under a given age. We know about a method on List<T> that returns another list of everything matching a predicate: the FindAll method. Before anonymous methods and captured variables were around, it wouldn't have made much sense for List<T>.FindAll to exist, because of all the hoops you'd have to go through in order to create the right delegate to start with. It would have been simpler to do all the iteration and copying manually. With C#2, however, we can do it all very, very easily:

```
List<Person> FindAllYoungerThan(List<Person> people, int limit)
{
    return people.FindAll (delegate (Person person)
        { return person.Age < limit; }
    );
}
```

Here we're capturing the limit parameter within the delegate instance—if we'd had anonymous methods but not captured variables, we could have performed a test against a hard-coded limit, but not one that was passed into the method as a parameter. I hope you'll agree that this approach is very neat—it expresses exactly *what* we want to do with much less fuss about exactly *how* it should happen than you'd have seen in a C#1 version. (It's even neater in C#3, admittedly...[7]) It's relatively rare that you come across a situation where you need to *write* to a captured variable, but again that can certainly have its uses.

Still with me? Good. So far, we've only used the delegate instance within the method that creates it. That doesn't raise many questions about the lifetime of the captured variables—but what would happen if the delegate instance escaped into the big bad world? How would it cope after the method that created it had finished?

5.5.4   *The extended lifetime of captured variables*

The simplest way of tackling this topic is to state a rule, give an example, and then think about what would happen if the rule weren't in place. Here we go:

> *A captured variable lives for at least as long as any delegate instance referring to it.*

Don't worry if it doesn't make a lot of sense yet—that's what the example is for. Listing 5.12 shows a method that *returns* a delegate instance. That delegate instance is created using an anonymous method that captures an outer variable. So, what will happen when the delegate is invoked after the method has returned?

Listing 5.12   Demonstration of a captured variable having its lifetime extended

```
static ThreadStart CreateDelegateInstance()
{
    int counter = 5;

    ThreadStart ret = delegate
        {
            Console.WriteLine(counter);
            counter++;
        };
```

---

[7] In case you're wondering: return people.Where(person => person.Age < limit);

```
        ret();
        return ret;
    }
    ...
    ThreadStart x = CreateDelegateInstance();
    x();
    x();
```

The output of listing 5.12 consists of the numbers 5, 6, and 7 on separate lines. The first line of output comes from the invocation of the delegate instance within CreateDelegateInstance, so it makes sense that the value of counter is available at that point. But what about after the method has returned? Normally we would consider counter to be on the stack, so when the stack frame for CreateDelegate-Instance is destroyed we'd expect counter to effectively vanish... and yet subsequent invocations of the returned delegate instance seem to keep using it!

The secret is to challenge the assumption that counter is on the stack in the first place. It isn't. The compiler has *actually* created an extra class to hold the variable. The CreateDelegateInstance method has a reference to an instance of that class so it can use counter, and the delegate has a reference to the same instance—which lives on the heap in the normal way. That instance isn't eligible for garbage collection until the delegate is ready to be collected. Some aspects of anonymous methods are very compiler specific (in other words different compilers could achieve the same semantics in different ways), but it's hard to see how the specified behavior could be achieved *without* using an extra class to hold the captured variable. Note that if you only capture this, no extra types are required—the compiler just creates an instance method to act as the delegate's action.

OK, so local variables aren't always local anymore. You may well be wondering what I could possibly throw at you next—let's see now, how about multiple delegates capturing different instances of the same variable? It sounds crazy, so it's just the kind of thing you should be expecting by now.

5.5.5 *Local variable instantiations*

On a good day, captured variables act exactly the way I expect them to at a glance. On a bad day, I'm still surprised when I'm not taking a great deal of care. When there are problems, it's almost always due to forgetting just how many "instances" of local variables I'm actually creating. A local variable is said to be *instantiated* each time execution enters the scope where it's declared. Here's a simple example comparing two very similar bits of code:

```int single;```
```for (int i=0; i < 10; i++)```
```{```
```   single = 5;```
```   Console.WriteLine(single+i);```
```}```
	```for (int i=0; i < 10; i++)```
	```{```
	``` int multiple = 5;```
	``` Console.WriteLine(multiple+i);```
	```}```

In the good old days, it was reasonable to say that pieces of code like this were semantically identical. Indeed, they'd usually compile to the same IL. They still will, if there aren't any anonymous methods involved. All the space for local variables is allocated on the stack at the start of the method, so there's no cost to "redeclaring" the variable for each iteration of the loop. However, in our new terminology the `single` variable will be instantiated only once, but the `multiple` variable will be instantiated ten times—it's as if there are ten local variables, all called `multiple`, which are created one after another.

Variable instance is captured

I'm sure you can see where I'm going—when a variable is captured, it's the relevant "instance" of the variable that is captured. If we captured `multiple` inside the loop, the variable captured in the first iteration would be different from the variable captured the second time round, and so on. Listing 5.13 shows exactly this effect.

Listing 5.13   Capturing multiple variable instantiations with multiple delegates

```
List<ThreadStart> list = new List<ThreadStart>();

for (int index=0; index < 5; index++)
{
    int counter = index*10;        ◁——❶ Instantiates counter
    list.Add (delegate
        {
            Console.WriteLine(counter);    ❷ Prints and increments
            counter++;                        captured variable
        }
    );
}

foreach (ThreadStart t in list)
{                                  ❸ Executes all
    t();                              five delegate
}                                     instances

list[0]();
list[0]();      ❹ Executes first one
list[0]();         three more times

list[1]();      ◁——❺ Executes second one again
```

Listing 5.13 creates five different delegate instances ❷—one for each time we go around the loop. Invoking the delegate will print out the value of `counter` and then increment it. Now, because `counter` is declared *inside* the loop, it is instantiated for each iteration ❶, and so each delegate captures a different variable. So, when we go through and invoke each delegate ❸, we see the different values initially assigned to `counter`: 0, 10, 20, 30, 40. Just to hammer the point home, when we then go back to the first delegate instance and execute it three more times ❹, it keeps going from where that instance's `counter` variable had left off: 1, 2, 3. Finally we execute the second delegate instance ❺, and that keeps going from where *that* instance's `counter` variable had left off: 11.

So, each of the delegate instances has captured a different variable in this case. Before we leave this example, I should point out what would have happened if we'd captured index—the variable declared by the for loop—instead of counter. In this case, all the delegates would have shared the same variable. The output would have been the numbers 5 to 13; 5 first because the last assignment to index before the loop terminates would have set it to 5, and then incrementing the same variable regardless of which delegate was involved. We'd see the same behavior with a foreach loop: the variable declared by the initial part of the loop is only instantiated once. It's easy to get this wrong! If you want to capture the value of a loop variable for that particular iteration of the loop, introduce another variable within the loop, copy the loop variable's value into it, and capture that new variable—effectively what we've done in listing 5.13 with the counter variable.

For our final example, let's look at something really nasty—sharing some captured variables but not others.

5.5.6 *Mixtures of shared and distinct variables*

Let me just say before I show you this next example that it's *not* code I'd recommend. In fact, the whole point of presenting it is to show how if you try to use captured variables in too complicated a fashion, things can get tricky really fast. Listing 5.14 creates two delegate instances that each capture "the same" two variables. However, the story gets more convoluted when we look at what's actually captured.

Listing 5.14 Capturing variables in different scopes. Warning: nasty code ahead!

```
ThreadStart[] delegates = new ThreadStart[2];     ❶ Instantiates
                                                     variable once
int outside = 0;

for (int i=0; i < 2; i++)          ❷ Instantiates
{                                    variable
    int inside = 0;                  multiple times

    delegates[i] = delegate                     Captures variables
    {                                           with anonymous
        Console.WriteLine ("({0},{1})",      ❸ method
                            outside, inside);
        outside++;
        inside++;
    };
}

ThreadStart first = delegates[0];
ThreadStart second = delegates[1];

first();
first();
first();

second();
second();
```

How long would it take you to predict the output from listing 5.14 (even with the annotations)? Frankly it would take me a little while—longer than I like to spend understanding code. Just as an exercise, though, let's look at what happens.

First let's consider the outside variable **❶**. The scope it's declared in is only entered once, so it's a straightforward case—there's only ever one of it, effectively. The inside variable **❷** is a different matter—each loop iteration instantiates a new one. That means that when we create the delegate instance **❸** the outside variable is shared between the two delegate instances, but each of them has its own inside variable.

After the loop has ended, we call the first delegate instance we created three times. Because it's incrementing both of its captured variables each time, and we started off with them both as 0, we see (0,0), then (1,1), then (2,2). The difference between the two variables in terms of scope becomes apparent when we execute the second delegate instance. It has a different inside variable, so that still has its initial value of 0, but the outside variable is the one we've already incremented three times. The output from calling the second delegate twice is therefore (3,0), then (4,1).

NOTE   *How does this happen internally?*   Just for the sake of interest, let's think about how this is implemented—at least with Microsoft's C#2 compiler. What happens is that one extra class is generated to hold the outer variable, and another one is generated to hold an inner variable *and a reference to the first extra class*. Essentially, each scope that contains a captured variable gets its own type, with a reference to the next scope out that contains a captured variable. In our case, there were two instances of the type holding inner, and they both refer to the same instance of the type holding outer. Other implementations may vary, but this is the most obvious way of doing things.

Even after you understand this code fully, it's still quite a good template for experimenting with other elements of captured variables. As we noted earlier, certain elements of variable capture are implementation specific, and it's often useful to refer to the specification to see what's guaranteed—but it's also important to be able to just *play* with code to see what happens.

It's possible that there are situations where code like listing 5.14 would be the simplest and clearest way of expressing the desired behavior—but I'd have to see it to believe it, and I'd certainly want comments in the code to explain what would happen. So, when is it appropriate to use captured variables, and what do you need to look out for?

5.5.7   *Captured variable guidelines and summary*

Hopefully this section has convinced you to be *very* careful with captured variables. They make good logical sense (and any change to make them simpler would probably either make them less useful or less logical), but they make it quite easy to produce horribly complicated code.

Don't let that discourage you from using them sensibly, though—they can save you masses of tedious code, and when they're used appropriately they can be the most readable way of getting the job done. But what counts as "sensible"?

GUIDELINES FOR USING CAPTURED VARIABLES

The following is a list of suggestions for using captured variables:

- If code that doesn't use captured variables is just as simple as code that does, don't use them.
- Before capturing a variable declared by a for or foreach statement, consider whether your delegate is going to live beyond the loop iteration, and whether you want it to see the subsequent values of that variable. If not, create another variable inside the loop that just copies the value you *do* want.
- If you create multiple delegate instances (whether in a loop or explicitly) that capture variables, put thought into whether you want them to capture the same variable.
- If you capture a variable that doesn't actually change (either in the anonymous method or the enclosing method body), then you don't need to worry as much.
- If the delegate instances you create never "escape" from the method—in other words, they're never stored anywhere else, or returned, or used for starting threads—life is a lot simpler.
- Consider the extended lifetime of any captured variables in terms of garbage collection. This is normally not an issue, but if you capture an object that is expensive in terms of memory, it may be significant.

The first point is the golden rule. Simplicity is a good thing—so any time the use of a captured variable makes your code simpler (after you've factored in the additional inherent complexity of forcing your code's maintainers to understand what the captured variable does), use it. You need to include that extra complexity in your considerations, that's all—don't just go for minimal line count.

We've covered a lot of ground in this section, and I'm aware that it can be hard to take in. I've listed the most important things to remember next, so that if you need to come back to this section another time you can jog your memory without having to read through the whole thing again:

- The *variable* is captured—not its value at the point of delegate instance creation.
- Captured variables have lifetimes extended to at least that of the capturing delegate.
- Multiple delegates can capture the same variable…
- …but within loops, the same variable declaration can effectively refer to different variable "instances."
- for/foreach loop declarations create variables that live for the duration of the loop—they're not instantiated on each iteration.
- Captured variables aren't really local variables—extra types are created where necessary.
- Be careful! Simple is almost always better than clever.

We'll see more variables being captured when we look at C#3 and its lambda expressions, but for now you may be relieved to hear that we've finished our rundown of the new C#2 delegate features.

5.6   *Summary*

C# 2 has radically changed the ways in which delegates can be created, and in doing so it's opened up the framework to a more functional style of programming. There are more methods in .NET 2.0 that take delegates as parameters than there were in .NET 1.0/1.1, and this trend continues in .NET 3.5. The List<T> type is the best example of this, and is a good test-bed for checking your skills at using anonymous methods and captured variables. Programming in this way requires a slightly different mind-set—you must be able to take a step back and consider what the ultimate aim is, and whether it's best expressed in the traditional C# manner, or whether a functional approach makes things clearer.

All the changes to delegate handling are useful, but they do add complexity to the language, particularly when it comes to captured variables. Closures are always tricky in terms of quite how the available environment is shared, and C# is no different in this respect. The reason they've lasted so long as an idea, however, is that they can make code simpler to understand and more immediate. The balancing act between complexity and simplicity is always a difficult one, and it's worth not being too ambitious to start with. As anonymous methods and captured variables become more common, we should all expect to get better at working with them and understanding what they'll do. They're certainly not going away, and indeed LINQ encourages their use even further.

Anonymous methods aren't the only change in C# 2 that involves the compiler creating extra types behind the scenes, doing devious things with variables that appear to be local. We'll see a lot more of this in our next chapter, where the compiler effectively builds a whole state machine for us in order to make it easier for the developer to implement iterators.

Implementing iterators the easy way

This chapter covers

- Implementing iterators in C#1
- Iterator blocks in C#2
- A simple `Range` type
- Iterators as coroutines

The iterator pattern is an example of a *behavioral pattern*—a design pattern that simplifies communication between objects. It's one of the simplest patterns to understand, and incredibly easy to use. In essence, it allows you to access all the elements in a sequence of items without caring about what kind of sequence it is— an array, a list, a linked list, or none of the above. This can be very effective for building a *data pipeline*, where an item of data enters the pipeline and goes through a number of different transformations or filters before coming out at the other end. Indeed, this is one of the core patterns of LINQ, as we'll see in part 3.

In .NET, the iterator pattern is encapsulated by the IEnumerator and IEnumerable interfaces and their generic equivalents. (The naming is unfortunate—the pattern is normally called iteration rather than enumeration to avoid getting confused with other meanings of the word *enumeration*. I've used *iterator* and *iterable* throughout this chapter.) If a type implements IEnumerable, that means it can be iterated over; calling the GetEnumerator method will return the IEnumerator implementation, which is the iterator itself.

As a language, C# 1 has built-in support for consuming iterators using the foreach statement. This makes it incredibly easy to iterate over collections—easier than using a straight for loop—and is nicely expressive. The foreach statement compiles down to calls to the GetEnumerator and MoveNext methods and the Current property, with support for disposing the iterator afterwards if IDisposable has been implemented. It's a small but useful piece of syntactic sugar.

In C# 1, however, *implementing* an iterator is a relatively difficult task. The syntactic sugar provided by C# 2 makes this much simpler, which can sometimes lead to the iterator pattern being worth implementing in cases where otherwise it would have caused more work than it saved.

In this chapter we'll look at just what is required to implement an iterator and the support given by C# 2. As a complete example we'll create a useful Range class that can be used in numerous situations, and then we'll explore an exciting (if slightly off-the-wall) use of the iteration syntax in a new concurrency library from Microsoft.

As in other chapters, let's start off by looking at why this new feature was introduced. We'll implement an iterator the hard way.

6.1   *C# 1: the pain of handwritten iterators*

We've already seen one example of an iterator implementation in section 3.4.3 when we looked at what happens when you iterate over a generic collection. In some ways that was harder than a real C# 1 iterator implementation would have been, because we implemented the generic interfaces as well—but in some ways it was easier because it wasn't actually iterating over anything useful.

To put the C# 2 features into context, we'll first implement an iterator that is about as simple as it can be while still providing real, useful values. Suppose we had a new type of collection—which can happen, even though .NET provides most of the collections you'll want to use in normal applications. We'll implement IEnumerable so that users of our new class can easily iterate over all the values in the collection. We'll ignore the guts of the collection here and just concentrate on the iteration side. Our collection will store its values in an array (object[]—no generics here!), and the collection will have the interesting feature that you can set its logical "starting point"—so if the array had five elements, you could set the start point to 2, and expect elements 2, 3, 4, 0, and then 1 to be returned. (This constraint prevents us from implementing GetEnumerator by simply calling the same method on the array itself. That would defeat the purpose of the exercise.)

To make the class easy to demonstrate, we'll provide both the values and the starting point in the constructor. So, we should be able to write code such as listing 6.1 in order to iterate over the collection.

Listing 6.1 Code using the (as yet unimplemented) new collection type

```
object[] values = {"a", "b", "c", "d", "e"};
IterationSample collection = new IterationSample(values, 3);
foreach (object x in collection)
{
    Console.WriteLine (x);
}
```

Running listing 6.1 should (eventually) produce output of "d", "e", "a", "b", and finally "c" because we specified a starting point of 3. Now that we know what we need to achieve, let's look at the skeleton of the class as shown in listing 6.2.

Listing 6.2 Skeleton of the new collection type, with no iterator implementation

```
using System;
using System.Collections;

public class IterationSample : IEnumerable
{
    object[] values;
    int startingPoint;

    public IterationSample (object[] values, int startingPoint)
    {
        this.values = values;
        this.startingPoint = startingPoint;
    }

    public IEnumerator GetEnumerator()
    {
        throw new NotImplementedException();
    }
}
```

As you can see, we haven't implemented GetEnumerator yet, but the rest of the code is ready to go. So, how do we go about implementing GetEnumerator? The first thing to understand is that we need to store some *state* somewhere. One important aspect of the iterator pattern is that we don't return all of the data in one go—the client just asks for one element at a time. That means we need to keep track of how far we've already gone through our array.

So, where should this state live? Suppose we tried to put it in the IterationSample class itself, making that implement IEnumerator as well as IEnumerable. At first sight, this looks like a good plan—after all, the *data* is in the right place, including the starting point. Our GetEnumerator method could just return this. However, there's a big problem with this approach—if GetEnumerator is called several times, several independent iterators should be returned. For instance, we should be able to use two foreach statements, one inside another, to get all possible pairs of values. That suggests we need to create a new object each time GetEnumerator is called. We *could* still implement the functionality directly within IterationSample, but then we'd have a class that didn't have a clear single responsibility—it would be pretty confusing.

Instead, let's create another class to implement the iterator itself. We'll use the fact that in C# a nested type has access to its enclosing type's private members, which means we can just store a reference to the "parent" IterationSample, along with the state of how far we've gone so far. This is shown in listing 6.3.

Listing 6.3   Nested class implementing the collection's iterator

```
class IterationSampleIterator : IEnumerator       ❶ Refers to
{                                                      collection we're
    IterationSample parent;                            iterating over
    int position;
                                                  ❷ Indicates
    internal IterationSampleIterator(IterationSample parent)   how far we've
    {                                                 iterated
        this.parent = parent;
        position = -1;         ❸ Starts before
    }                            first element

    public bool MoveNext()
    {
        if (position != parent.values.Length)
        {                                        ❹ Increments
            position++;                            position if we're
        }                                          still going
        return position < parent.values.Length;
    }

    public object Current
    {
        get
        {
            if (position==-1 ||                  ❺ Prevents access before
                position==parent.values.Length)    first or after last element
            {
                throw new InvalidOperationException();
            }
            int index = (position+parent.startingPoint);   ❻ Implements
            index = index % parent.values.Length;            wraparound
            return parent.values[index];
        }
    }

    public void Reset()
    {                          ❼ Moves back to
        position = -1;           before first element
    }
}
```

What a lot of code to perform such a simple task! We remember the original collection of values we're iterating over ❶ and keep track of where we would be in a simple zero-based array ❷. To return an element we offset that index by the starting point ❻. In keeping with the interface, we consider our iterator to start logically before the first element ❸, so the client will have to call MoveNext before using the Current property for the first time. The conditional increment at ❹ makes the test at ❺ simple and correct even if MoveNext is called again after it's first reported that there's no more data available. To reset the iterator, we set our logical position back to "before the first element" ❼.

Most of the logic involved is fairly straightforward, although there's lots of room for off-by-one errors; indeed, my first implementation failed its unit tests for precisely that reason. The good news is that it works, and that we only need to implement IEnumerable in IterationSample to complete the example:

```
public IEnumerator GetEnumerator()
{
    return new IterationSampleIterator(this);
}
```

I won't reproduce the combined code here, but it's available on the book's website, including listing 6.1, which now has the expected output.

It's worth bearing in mind that this is a relatively simple example—there's not a lot of state to keep track of, and no attempt to check whether the collection has changed between iterations. With this large burden involved to implement a simple iterator, we shouldn't be surprised at the rarity of implementing the pattern in C#1. Developers have generally been happy to use foreach on the collections provided by the framework, but they use more direct (and collection-specific) access when it comes to their own collections.

So, 40 lines of code to implement the iterator in C#1, not including comments. Let's see if C#2 can do any better.

6.2   C#2: simple iterators with yield statements

I've always been the kind of person who likes to stay up until midnight on Christmas Eve in order to open a present as soon as Christmas Day arrives. In the same way, I think I'd find it almost impossible to wait any significant amount of time before showing you how neat the solution is in C#2.

6.2.1   Introducing iterator blocks and yield return

This chapter wouldn't exist if C#2 didn't have a powerful feature that cut down the amount of code you had to write to implement iterators. In some other topics the amount of code has only been reduced slightly, or has just made something more elegant. In this case, however, the amount of code required is reduced *massively*. Listing 6.4 shows the complete implementation of the GetEnumerator method in C#2.

> **Listing 6.4   Iterating through the sample collection with C#2 and `yield return`**

Much simpler, isn't it?

```
public IEnumerator GetEnumerator()
{
    for (int index=0; index < values.Length; index++)
    {
        yield return values[(index+startingPoint)%values.Length];
    }
}
```

Four lines of implementation, two of which are just braces. Just to make it clear, that replaces the whole of the `IterationSampleIterator` class. Completely. At least in the source code… Later on we'll see what the compiler has done behind our back, and some of the quirks of the implementation it's provided, but for the moment let's look at the source code we've used.

The method looks like a perfectly normal one until you see the use of `yield return`. That's what tells the C# compiler that this isn't a normal method but one implemented with an *iterator block*. The method is declared to return an `IEnumerator`, and you can only use iterator blocks to implement methods[1] that have a return type of `IEnumerable`, `IEnumerator`, or one of the generic equivalents. The *yield type* of the iterator block is `object` if the declared return type of the method is a nongeneric interface, or the type argument of the generic interface otherwise. For instance, a method declared to return `IEnumerable<string>` would have a yield type of `string`.

No normal `return` statements are allowed within iterator blocks—only `yield return`. All `yield return` statements in the block have to try to return a value compatible with the yield type of the block. To use our previous example, you couldn't write `yield return 1;` in a method declared to return `IEnumerable<string>`.

NOTE   *Restrictions on yield return*—There are a few further restrictions on yield statements. You can't use `yield return` inside a `try` block if it has any `catch` blocks, and you can't use either `yield return` or `yield break` (which we'll come to shortly) in a `finally` block. That doesn't mean you can't use `try/catch` or `try/finally` blocks inside iterators—it just restricts what you can do in them.

The big idea that you need to get your head around when it comes to iterator blocks is that although you've written a method that looks like it executes sequentially, what you've actually asked the compiler to do is create a *state machine* for you. This is necessary for exactly the same reason we had to put so much effort into implementing the iterator in C#1—the caller only wants to see one element at a time, so we need to keep track of what we were doing when we last returned a value.

In iterator blocks, the compiler creates a state machine (in the form of a nested type), which remembers exactly where we were within the block and what values the local variables (including parameters) had at that point. The compiler analyzes the iterator block and creates a class that is similar to the longhand implementation we wrote earlier, keeping all the necessary state as instance variables. Let's think about what this state machine has to do in order to implement the iterator:

- It has to have some initial state.
- Whenever `MoveNext` is called, it has to execute code from the `GetEnumerator` method until we're ready to provide the next value (in other words, until we hit a `yield return` statement).

---

[1]   Or properties, as we'll see later on. You can't use an iterator block in an anonymous method, though.

- When the Current property is used, it has to return the last value we yielded.
- It has to know when we've finished yielding values so that MoveNext can return false.

The second point in this list is the tricky one, because it always needs to "restart" the code from the point it had previously reached. Keeping track of the local variables (as they appear in the method) isn't too hard—they're just represented by instance variables in the state machine. The restarting aspect is trickier, but the good news is that unless you're writing a C# compiler yourself, you needn't care about how it's achieved: the result from a black box point of view is that it just works. You can write perfectly normal code within the iterator block and the compiler is responsible for making sure that the flow of execution is exactly as it would be in any other method; the difference is that a yield return statement appears to only "temporarily" exit the method—you could think of it as being paused, effectively.

Next we'll examine the flow of execution in more detail, and in a more visual way.

6.2.2 *Visualizing an iterator's workflow*

It may help to think about how iterators execute in terms of a sequence diagram.[2] Rather than drawing the diagram out by hand, let's write a program to print it out (listing 6.5). The iterator itself just provides a sequence of numbers (0, 1, 2, –1) and then finishes. The interesting part isn't the numbers provided so much as the *flow* of the code.

Listing 6.5 Showing the sequence of calls between an iterator and its caller

```
static readonly string Padding = new string(' ', 30);

static IEnumerable<int> GetEnumerable()
{
    Console.WriteLine ("{0}Start of GetEnumerator()", Padding);

    for (int i=0; i < 3; i++)
    {
        Console.WriteLine ("{0}About to yield {1}", Padding, i);
        yield return i;
        Console.WriteLine ("{0}After yield", Padding);
    }

    Console.WriteLine ("{0}Yielding final value", Padding);
    yield return -1;

    Console.WriteLine ("{0}End of GetEnumerator()", Padding);
}

...

IEnumerable<int> iterable = GetEnumerable();
IEnumerator<int> iterator = iterable.GetEnumerator();
```

---

[2] See http://en.wikipedia.org/wiki/Sequence_diagram if this is unfamiliar to you.

```
Console.WriteLine ("Starting to iterate");
while (true)
{
    Console.WriteLine ("Calling MoveNext()...");
    bool result = iterator.MoveNext();
    Console.WriteLine ("... MoveNext result={0}", result);
    if (!result)
    {
        break;
    }
    Console.WriteLine ("Fetching Current...");
    Console.WriteLine ("... Current result={0}", iterator.Current);
}
```

Listing 6.5 certainly isn't pretty, particularly around the iteration side of things. In the normal course of events we'd just use a foreach loop, but to show exactly what's happening when, I had to break the use of the iterator out into little pieces. This code broadly does what foreach does, although foreach also calls Dispose at the end, which is important for iterator blocks, as we'll see shortly. As you can see, there's no difference in the syntax within the method even though this time we're returning IEnumerable<int> instead of IEnumerator<int>. Here's the output from listing 6.5:

```
Starting to iterate
Calling MoveNext()...
                                        Start of GetEnumerator()
                                        About to yield 0

... MoveNext result=True
Fetching Current...
... Current result=0
Calling MoveNext()...
                                        After yield
                                        About to yield 1

... MoveNext result=True
Fetching Current...
... Current result=1
Calling MoveNext()...
                                        After yield
                                        About to yield 2

... MoveNext result=True
Fetching Current...
... Current result=2
Calling MoveNext()...
                                        After yield
                                        Yielding final value

... MoveNext result=True
Fetching Current...
... Current result=-1
Calling MoveNext()...
                                        End of GetEnumerator()
... MoveNext result=False
```

There are various important things to note from this output:

- None of the code we wrote in GetEnumerator is called until the first call to MoveNext.
- Calling MoveNext is the place all the work gets done; fetching Current doesn't run any of our code.
- The code stops executing at yield return and picks up again just afterwards at the next call to MoveNext.
- We can have multiple yield return statements in different places in the method.
- The code doesn't end at the last yield return—instead, the call to MoveNext that causes us to reach the end of the method is the one that returns false.

There are two things we haven't seen yet—an alternative way of halting the iteration, and how finally blocks work in this somewhat odd form of execution. Let's take a look at them now.

6.2.3 *Advanced iterator execution flow*

In normal methods, the return statement has two effects: First, it supplies the value the caller sees as the return value. Second, it terminates the execution of the method, executing any appropriate finally blocks on the way out. We've seen that the yield return statement temporarily exits the method, but only until MoveNext is called again, and we haven't examined the behavior of finally blocks at all yet. How can we *really* stop the method, and what happens to all of those finally blocks? We'll start with a fairly simple construct—the yield break statement.

ENDING AN ITERATOR WITH YIELD BREAK

You can always find a way to make a method have a single exit point, and many people work very hard to achieve this.[3] The same techniques can be applied in iterator blocks. However, should you wish to have an "early out," the yield break statement is your friend. This effectively terminates the iterator, making the current call to Move-Next return false.

Listing 6.6 demonstrates this by counting up to 100 but stopping early if it runs out of time. This also demonstrates the use of a method parameter in an iterator block,[4] and proves that the name of the method is irrelevant.

Listing 6.6   Demonstration of `yield break`

```
static IEnumerable<int> CountWithTimeLimit(DateTime limit)
{
    for (int i=1; i <= 100; i++)
    {
        if (DateTime.Now >= limit)
        {                              ⟵─────  Stops if our
            yield break;                        time is up
```

---

[3]   I personally find that the hoops you have to jump through to achieve this often make the code much harder to read than just having multiple return points, especially as try/finally is available for cleanup and you need to account for the possibility of exceptions occurring anyway. However, the point is that it can all be done.

[4]   Note that methods taking ref or out parameters can't be implemented with iterator blocks.

```
        }
        yield return i;
      }
   }
   ...

   DateTime stop = DateTime.Now.AddSeconds(2);
   foreach (int i in CountWithTimeLimit(stop))
   {
      Console.WriteLine ("Received {0}", i);
      Thread.Sleep(300);
   }
```

Typically when you run listing 6.6 you'll see about seven lines of output. The foreach loop terminates perfectly normally—as far as it's concerned, the iterator has just run out of elements to iterate over. The yield break statement behaves very much like a return statement in a normal method.

So far, so simple. There's one last aspect execution flow to explore: how and when finally blocks are executed.

EXECUTION OF FINALLY BLOCKS

We're used to finally blocks executing whenever we leave the relevant scope. Iterator blocks don't behave quite like normal methods, though—as we've seen, a yield return statement effectively pauses the method rather than exiting it. Following that logic, we wouldn't expect any finally blocks to be executed at that point—and indeed they aren't.

However, appropriate finally blocks *are* executed when a yield break statement is hit, just as you'd expect them to be when returning from a normal method.[5] Listing 6.7 shows this in action—it's the same code as listing 6.6, but with a finally block. The changes are shown in bold.

Listing 6.7   Demonstration of yield break working with try/finally

```
static IEnumerable<int> CountWithTimeLimit(DateTime limit)
{
   try
   {
      for (int i=1; i <= 100; i++)
      {
         if (DateTime.Now >= limit)
         {
            yield break;
         }
         yield return i;
      }
   }
   finally
   {
```

---

[5] They're also called when execution leaves the relevant scope without reaching either a yield return or a yield break statement. I'm only focusing on the behavior of the two yield statements here because that's where the flow of execution is new and different.

```
        Console.WriteLine ("Stopping!");          ◁──┐  Executes however
    }                                                 │  the loop ends
}
...

DateTime stop = DateTime.Now.AddSeconds(2);
foreach (int i in CountWithTimeLimit(stop))
{
    Console.WriteLine ("Received {0}", i);
    Thread.Sleep(300);
}
```

The `finally` block in listing 6.7 is executed whether the iterator block just finishes by counting to 100, or whether it has to stop due to the time limit being reached. (It would also execute if the code threw an exception.) However, there are other ways we might try to avoid the `finally` block from being called... let's try to be sneaky.

We've seen that code in the iterator block is only executed when `MoveNext` is called. So what happens if we never call `MoveNext`? Or if we call it a few times and then stop? Let's consider changing the "calling" part of listing 6.7 to this:

```
DateTime stop = DateTime.Now.AddSeconds(2);
foreach (int i in CountWithTimeLimit(stop))
{
    Console.WriteLine ("Received {0}", i);
    if (i > 3)
    {
        Console.WriteLine("Returning");
        return;
    }
    Thread.Sleep(300);
}
```

Here we're not stopping early in the iterator code—we're stopping early in the code *using* the iterator. The output is perhaps surprising:

```
Received 1
Received 2
Received 3
Received 4
Returning
Stopping!
```

Here, code is being executed after the `return` statement in the `foreach` loop. That doesn't normally happen unless there's a `finally` block involved—and in this case there are two! We already know about the `finally` block in the iterator method, but the question is what's causing it to be executed. I gave a hint to this earlier on— `foreach` calls `Dispose` on the `IEnumerator` it's provided with, in its own `finally` block (just like the `using` statement). When you call `Dispose` on an iterator created with an iterator block before it's finished iterating, the state machine executes any `finally` blocks that are in the scope of where the code is currently "paused."

We can prove very easily that it's the call to `Dispose` that triggers this by using the iterator manually:

```
DateTime stop = DateTime.Now.AddSeconds(2);
IEnumerable<int> iterable = CountWithTimeLimit(stop);
IEnumerator<int> iterator = iterable.GetEnumerator();

iterator.MoveNext();
Console.WriteLine ("Received {0}", iterator.Current);

iterator.MoveNext();
Console.WriteLine ("Received {0}", iterator.Current);
```

This time the "stopping" line is never printed. It's relatively rare that you'll want to terminate an iterator before it's finished, and it's relatively rare that you'll be iterating manually instead of using `foreach`, but if you *do*, remember to wrap the iterator in a `using` statement.

We've now covered most of the behavior of iterator blocks, but before we end this section it's worth considering a few oddities to do with the current Microsoft implementation.

6.2.4   *Quirks in the implementation*

If you compile iterator blocks with the Microsoft C#2 compiler and look at the resulting IL in either ildasm or Reflector, you'll see the nested type that the compiler has generated for us behind the scenes. In my case when compiling our (evolved) first iterator block example, it was called `IterationSample.<GetEnumerator>d__0` (where the angle brackets aren't indicating a generic type parameter, by the way). I won't go through exactly what's generated in detail here, but it's worth looking at it in Reflector to get a feel for what's going on, preferably with the language specification next to you: the specification defines different states the type can be in, and this description makes the generated code easier to follow.

Fortunately, as developers we don't need to care much about the hoops the compiler has to jump through. However, there are a few quirks about the implementation that are worth knowing about:

- Before `MoveNext` is called for the first time, the `Current` property will always return `null` (or the default value for the relevant type, for the generic interface).
- After `MoveNext` has returned `false`, the `Current` property will always return the last value returned.
- `Reset` always throws an exception instead of resetting like our manual implementation did. This is required behavior, laid down in the specification.
- The nested class always implements both the generic and nongeneric form of `IEnumerator` (and the generic and nongeneric `IEnumerable` where appropriate).

Failing to implement `Reset` is quite reasonable—the compiler can't reasonably work out what you'd need to do in order to reset the iterator, or even whether it's feasible. Arguably `Reset` shouldn't have been in the `IEnumerator` interface to start with, and I certainly can't remember the last time I called it.

Implementing extra interfaces does no harm either. It's interesting that if your method returns `IEnumerable` you end up with one class implementing five interfaces (including `IDisposable`). The language specification explains it in detail, but the upshot is that as a developer you don't need to worry.

The behavior of `Current` is odd—in particular, keeping hold of the last item after supposedly moving off it could keep it from being garbage collected. It's possible that this may be fixed in a later release of the C# compiler, though it's unlikely as it could break existing code.[6] Strictly speaking, it's correct from the C#2 language specification point of view—the behavior of the `Current` property is undefined. It would be nicer if it implemented the property in the way that the framework documentation suggests, however, throwing exceptions at appropriate times.

So, there are a few tiny drawbacks from using the autogenerated code, but *sensible* callers won't have any problems—and let's face it, we've saved a *lot* of code in order to come up with the implementation. This means it makes sense to use iterators more widely than we might have done in C#1. Our next section provides some sample code so you can check your understanding of iterator blocks and see how they're useful in real life rather than just in theoretical scenarios.

6.3 Real-life example: iterating over ranges

Have you ever written some code that is really simple in itself but makes your project *much* neater? It happens to me every so often, and it usually makes me happier than it probably ought to—enough to get strange looks from colleagues, anyway. That sort of slightly childish delight is particularly strong when it comes to using a new language feature in a way that is *clearly* nicer and not just doing it for the sake of playing with new toys.

6.3.1 Iterating over the dates in a timetable

While working on a project involving timetables, I came across a few loops, all of which started like this:

```
for (DateTime day = timetable.StartDate;
     day <= timetable.EndDate;
     day = day.AddDays(1))
```

I was working on this area of code quite a lot, and I always hated that loop, but it was only when I was reading the code out loud to another developer as pseudo-code that I realized I was missing a trick. I said something like, "For each day within the timetable." In retrospect, it's obvious that what I really wanted was a `foreach` loop. (This may well have been obvious to you from the start—apologies if this is the case. Fortunately I can't see you looking smug.) The loop is much nicer when rewritten as

```
foreach (DateTime day in timetable.DateRange)
```

In C#1, I might have looked at that as a fond dream but not bothered implementing it: we've seen how messy it is to implement an iterator by hand, and the end result

---

[6] The Microsoft C#3 compiler shipping with .NET 3.5 behaves in the same way.

only made a few `for` loops neater in this case. In C#2, however, it was easy. Within the class representing the timetable, I simply added a property:

```
public IEnumerable<DateTime> DateRange
{
   get
   {
      for (DateTime day = StartDate;
           day <= EndDate;
           day = day.AddDays(1))
      {
         yield return day;
      }
   }
}
```

Now this has clearly just moved the original loop into the timetable class, but that's OK—it's much nicer for it to be encapsulated there, in a property that *just* loops through the days, yielding them one at a time, than to be in business code that was dealing with those days. If I ever wanted to make it more complex (skipping weekends and public holidays, for instance), I could do it in one place and reap the rewards everywhere.

I thought for a while about making the timetable class implement `IEnumerable<DateTime>` itself, but shied away from it. Either way would have worked, but it so happened that the property led me toward the next step: why should the `DateRange` property just be iterable? Why isn't it a fully fledged object that can be iterated over, asked whether or not it contains a particular date, as well as for its start and end dates? While we're at it, what's so special about `DateTime`? The concept of a range that can be stepped through in a particular way is obvious and applies to many types, but it's still surprisingly absent from the Framework libraries.

For the rest of this section we'll look at implementing a simple `Range` class (and some useful classes derived from it). To keep things simple (and printable), we won't make it as feature-rich as we might want—there's a richer version in my open source miscellaneous utility library[7] that collects odds and ends as I occasionally write small pieces of useful code.

6.3.2   *Scoping the Range class*

First we'll decide (broadly) what we want the type to do, as well as what it *doesn't* need to be able to do. When developing the class, I applied test-driven development to work out what I wanted. However, the frequent iterative nature of test-driven development (TDD) doesn't work as well in a book as it does in reality, so I'll just lay down the requirements to start with:

- A range is defined by a start value and an end value (of the same type, the "element type").
- We must be able to compare one value of the element type with another.

[7] http://pobox.com/~skeet/csharp/miscutil

- We want to be able to find out whether a particular value is within the range.
- We want to be able to iterate through the range easily.

The last point is obviously the most important one for this chapter, but the others shape the fundamental decisions and ask further questions. In particular, it seems obvious that this should use generics, but should we allow *any* type to be used for the bounds of the range, using an appropriate IComparer, or should we only allow types that implement IComparable<T>, where T is the same type? When we're iterating, how do we move from one value to another? Should we *always* have to be able to iterate over a range, even if we're only interested in the other aspects? Should we be able to have a "reverse" range (in other words, one with a start that is greater than the end, and therefore counts down rather than up)? Should the start and end points be exclusive or inclusive?

All of these are important questions, and the normal answers would promote flexibility and usefulness of the type—but our overriding priority here is to keep things simple. So:

- We'll make comparisons simple by constraining the range's type parameter T to implement IComparable<T>.
- We'll make the class abstract and require a GetNextValue method to be implemented, which will be used during iteration.
- We won't worry about the idea of a range that can't be iterated over.
- We won't allow reverse ranges (so the end value must always be greater than or equal to the start value).
- Start and end points will both be inclusive (so both the start and end points are considered to be members of the range). One consequence of this is that we can't represent an empty range.

The decision to make it an abstract class isn't as limiting as it possibly sounds—it means we'll have derived classes like Int32Range and DateTimeRange that allow you to specify the "step" to use when iterating. If we ever wanted a more general range, we could always create a derived type that allows the step to be specified as a Converter delegate. For the moment, however, let's concentrate on the base type. With all the requirements specified,[8] we're ready to write the code.

6.3.3   *Implementation using iterator blocks*

With C#2, implementing this (fairly limited) Range type is remarkably easy. The hardest part (for me) is remembering how IComparable<T>.CompareTo works. The trick I usually use is to remember that if you compare the return value with 0, the result is the same as applying that comparison operator between the two values involved, in the order they're specified. So x.CompareTo(y) < 0 has the same meaning as x < y, for example.

---

[8] If only real life were as simple as this. We haven't had to get project approval and specification sign-off from a dozen different parties, nor have we had to create a project plan complete with resource requirements. Beautiful!

Listing 6.8 is the complete Range class, although we can't quite use it yet as it's still abstract.

Listing 6.8   The abstract Range class allowing flexible iteration over its values

```csharp
using System;
using System.Collections;
using System.Collections.Generic;

public abstract class Range<T> : IEnumerable<T>
    where T : IComparable<T>                                 ◁──────●❶ Ensures we can
{                                                                      compare values
    readonly T start;
    readonly T end;

    public Range(T start, T end)              ❷ Prevents
    {                                            "reversed"
        if (start.CompareTo(end) > 0)    ◁──┘   ranges
        {
            throw new ArgumentOutOfRangeException();
        }
        this.start = start;
        this.end = end;
    }

    public T Start
    {
        get { return start; }
    }

    public T End
    {
        get { return end; }
    }

    public bool Contains(T value)
    {
        return value.CompareTo(start) >= 0 &&
               value.CompareTo(end) <= 0;
    }

    public IEnumerator<T> GetEnumerator()    ◁──────── Implements
    {                                                  IEnumerable<T>
        T value = start;                         ❸    implicitly
        while (value.CompareTo(end) < 0)
        {
            yield return value;
            value = GetNextValue(value);
        }
        if (value.CompareTo(end) == 0)
        {
            yield return value;
        }
    }                                         ❹  Implements
                                                  IEnumerable
    IEnumerator IEnumerable.GetEnumerator()  ◁──┘  explicitly
    {
```

```
        return GetEnumerator();
    }
```

⑤ **"Steps" from
one value to
the next**

```
    protected abstract T GetNextValue(T current);    ◁─┘
}
```

The code is quite straightforward, due to C#2's iterator blocks. The type constraint on
T ❶ ensures that we'll be able to compare two values, and we perform an execution-
time check to prevent a range being constructed with a lower bound higher than the
upper bound ❷. We still need to work around the problem of implementing both
IEnumerable<T> and IEnumerable by using explicit interface implementation for the
nongeneric type ❹ and exposing the generic interface implementation in the more
usual, implicit way ❸. If you don't immediately see why this is necessary, look back to
the descriptions in sections 2.2.2 and 3.4.3.

The actual iteration merely starts with the lower end of the range, and repeatedly
fetches the next value by calling the abstract GetNextValue method ⑤ until we've
reached or exceeded the top of the range. If the last value found is in the range, we
yield that as well. Note that the GetNextValue method shouldn't need to keep any
state—given one value, it should merely return the next one in the range. This is useful as it means that we should be able to make most of the derived types immutable,
which is always nice. It's easy to derive from Range, and we'll implement the two
examples given earlier—a range for dates and times (DateTimeRange) and a range
for integers (Int32Range). They're very short and very similar—listing 6.9 shows both
of them together.

Listing 6.9 Two classes derived from Range, to iterate over dates/times and integers

```
using System;
public class DateTimeRange : Range<DateTime>
{
    readonly TimeSpan step;

    public DateTimeRange(DateTime start, DateTime end)       Uses
        : this (start, end, TimeSpan.FromDays(1))    ◁──┘  default
    { }                                                       step

    public DateTimeRange(DateTime start,         ◁─┐ Uses
                         DateTime end,              specified
                         TimeSpan step)             step
        : base(start, end)
    {
        this.step = step;
    }

    protected override DateTime GetNextValue(DateTime current)  ◁─┐
    {
        return current + step;                           Uses step to
    }                                                    find next value
}

public class Int32Range : Range<int>
{
    readonly int step;
```

```
    public Int32Range(int start, int end)
       : this (start, end, 1)
    { }

    public Int32Range(int start, int end, int step)
       : base(start, end)
    {
       this.step = step;
    }

    protected override int GetNextValue(int current)
    {
       return current + step;
    }
}
```

If we could have specified addition (potentially using another type) as a type parameter, we could have used a single type everywhere, which would have been neat. There are other obvious candidates, such as `SingleRange`, `DoubleRange`, and `DecimalRange`, which I haven't shown here. Even though we have to derive an extra class for each type we want to iterate over, the gain over C#1 is still tremendous. Without generics there would have been casts everywhere (and boxing for value types, which probably includes most types you want to use for ranges), and without iterator blocks the code for the separate iterator type we'd have needed would probably have been about as long as the base class itself. It's worth noting that when we use the step to find the next value we don't need to change anything within the instance—both of these types are immutable and so can be freely shared between threads, returned as properties, and used for all kinds of other operations without fear.

With the `DateTimeRange` type in place, I could replace the `DateRange` property in my timetable application, and remove the `StartDate` and `EndDate` properties entirely. The closely related values are now nicely encapsulated, the birds are singing, and all is right with the world. There's a lot more we *could* do to our `Range` type, but for the moment it's served its purpose well.

The `Range` type is just one example of a way in which iteration presents itself as a natural option in C#2 where it would have been significantly less elegant in C#1. I hope you'll consider it next time you find yourself writing a start/end pair of variables or properties. As examples go, however, it's pretty tame—iterating over a range isn't exactly a novel idea. To close the chapter, we'll look at a considerably less conventional use of iterator blocks—this time for the purpose of providing one side of a multithreaded conversation.

6.4 *Pseudo-synchronous code with the Concurrency and Coordination Runtime*

The *Concurrency and Coordination Runtime* (CCR) is a library developed by Microsoft to offer an alternative way of writing asynchronous code that is amenable to complex coordination. At the time of this writing, it's only available as part of the Microsoft Robotics Studio,[9] although hopefully that will change. We're not going to delve into the depths of it—fascinating as it is—but it has one very interesting feature that's relevant to this chapter. Rather than present real code that could compile and run (involving pages and pages of description of the library), we'll just look at some pseudo-code and the ideas behind it. The purpose of this section isn't to think too deeply about asynchronous code, but to show how by adding intelligence to the compiler, a different form of programming becomes feasible and reasonably elegant. The CCR uses iterator blocks in an interesting way that takes a certain amount of mental effort to start with. However, once you see the pattern it can lead to a radically different way of thinking about asynchronous execution.

Suppose we're writing a server that needs to handle lots of requests. As part of dealing with those requests, we need to first call a web service to fetch an authentication token, and then use that token to get data from two independent data sources (say a database and another web service). We then process that data and return the result. Each of the fetch stages could take a while—a second, say. The normal two options available are simply synchronous and asynchronous. The pseudo-code for the synchronous version might look something like this:

```
HoldingsValue ComputeTotalStockValue(string user, string password)
{
    Token token = AuthService.Check(user, password);
    Holdings stocks = DbService.GetStockHoldings(token);
    StockRates rates = StockService.GetRates(token);

    return ProcessStocks(stocks, rates);
}
```

That's very simple and easy to understand, but if each request takes a second, the whole operation will take three seconds and tie up a thread for the whole time it's running. If we want to scale up to hundreds of thousands of requests running in parallel, we're in trouble. Now let's consider a fairly simple asynchronous version, which avoids tying up a thread when nothing's happening[10] and uses parallel calls where possible:

```
void StartComputingTotalStockValue(string user, string password)
{
    AuthService.BeginCheck(user, password, AfterAuthCheck, null);
}

void AfterAuthCheck(IAsyncResult result)
{
    Token token = AuthService.EndCheck(result);
    IAsyncResult holdingsAsync = DbService.BeginGetStockHoldings
        (token, null, null);
    StockService.BeginGetRates
        (token, AfterGetRates, holdingsAsync);
}
```

---

[9] http://www.microsoft.com/robotics

[10] Well, mostly—in order to keep it relatively simple, it might still be inefficient as we'll see in a moment.

```
void AfterGetRates(IAsyncResult result)
{
    IAsyncResult holdingsAsync = (IAsyncResult)result.AsyncState;
    StockRates rates = StockService.EndGetRates(result);
    Holdings stocks = DbService.EndGetStockHoldings
        (holdingsAsync);

    OnRequestComplete(ProcessStocks(stocks, rates));
}
```

This is much harder to read and understand—and that's only a simple version! The coordination of the two parallel calls is only achievable in a simple way because we don't need to pass any other state around, and even so it's not ideal. (It will still block a thread waiting for the database call to complete if the second web service call completes first.) It's far from obvious what's going on, because the code is jumping around different methods so much.

By now you may well be asking yourself where iterators come into the picture. Well, the iterator blocks provided by C#2 effectively allow you to "pause" current execution at certain points of the flow through the block, and then come back to the same place, with the same state. The clever folks designing the CCR realized that that's exactly what's needed for something called a *continuation-passing style* of coding. We need to tell the system that there are certain operations we need to perform—including starting other operations asynchronously—but that we're then happy to wait until the asynchronous operations have finished before we continue. We do this by providing the CCR with an implementation of IEnumerator<ITask> (where ITask is an interface defined by the CCR). Here's pseudo-code for our request handling in this style:

```
IEnumerator<ITask> ComputeTotalStockValue(string user, string pass)
{
    Token token = null;

    yield return Ccr.ReceiveTask(
        AuthService.CcrCheck(user, pass)
            delegate(Token t) { token = t; }
    );

    Holdings stocks = null;
    StockRates rates = null;
    yield return Ccr.MultipleReceiveTask(
        DbService.CcrGetStockHoldings(token),
        StockService.CcrGetRates(token),
        delegate(Stocks s, StockRates sr)
            { stocks = s; rates = sr; }
    );

    OnRequestComplete(ProcessStocks(stocks, rates));
}
```

Confused? I certainly was when I first saw it—but now I'm somewhat in awe of how neat it is. The CCR will call into our code (with a call to MoveNext on the iterator), and we'll execute until and including the first yield return statement. The CcrCheck method within AuthService would kick off an asynchronous request, and the CCR would wait (without using a dedicated thread) until it had completed, calling the supplied delegate to handle the result. It would then call MoveNext again, and our method would continue. This time we kick off two requests in parallel, and the CCR to call another delegate with the results of both operations when they've *both* finished. After that, Move-Next is called for a final time and we get to complete the request processing.

Although it's obviously more complicated than the synchronous version, it's still all in one method, it will get executed in the order written, and the method itself can hold the state (in the local variables, which become state in the extra type generated by the compiler). It's fully asynchronous, using as few threads as it can get away with. I haven't shown any error handling, but that's also available in a sensible fashion that forces you to think about the issue at appropriate places.

It all takes a while to get your head around (at least unless you've seen continuation-passing style code before) but the potential benefits in terms of writing correct, scalable code are enormous—and it's only feasible in such a neat way due to C#2's syntactic sugar around iterators and anonymous methods. The CCR hasn't hit the mainstream at the time of writing, but it's possible that it will become another normal part of the development toolkit[11]—and that other novel uses for iterator blocks will be thought up over time. As I said earlier, the point of the section is to open your mind to possible uses of the work that the compiler can do for you beyond just simple iteration.

6.5   *Summary*

C# supports many patterns indirectly, in terms of it being feasible to implement them in C#. However, relatively few patterns are *directly* supported in terms of language features being specifically targeted at a particular pattern. In C#1, the iterator pattern was directly supported from the point of view of the calling code, but not from the perspective of the collection being iterated over. Writing a correct implementation of IEnumerable was time-consuming and error-prone, without being interesting. In C#2 the compiler does all the mundane work for you, building a state machine to cope with the "call-back" nature of iterators.

It should be noted that iterator blocks have one aspect in common with the anonymous methods we saw in chapter 5, even though the actual features are very different. In both cases, extra types may be generated, and a potentially complicated code transformation is applied to the original source. Compare this with C#1 where most of the transformations for syntactic sugar (lock, using, and foreach being the most obvious examples) were quite straightforward. We'll see this trend toward smarter compilation continuing with almost every aspect of C#3.

As well as seeing a real-life example of the use of iterators, we've taken a look at how one particular library has used them in a fairly radical way that has little to do with what comes to mind when we think about iteration over a collection. It's worth bearing in mind that different languages have also looked at this sort of problem

---

[11] Some aspects of the CCR may also become available as part of the Parallel Extensions library described in chapter 13.

before—in computer science the term *coroutine* is applied to concepts of this nature. Different languages have historically supported them to a greater or lesser extent, with tricks being applicable to simulate them sometimes—for example, Simon Tatham has an excellent article[12] on how even C can express coroutines if you're willing to bend coding standards somewhat. We've seen that C#2 makes coroutines easy to write and use.

Having seen some major and sometimes mind-warping language changes focused around a few key features, our next chapter is a change of pace. It describes a number of small changes that make C#2 more pleasant to work with than its predecessor, learning from the little niggles of the past to produce a language that has fewer rough edges, more scope for dealing with awkward backward-compatibility cases, and a better story around working with generated code. Each feature is relatively straightforward, but there are quite a few of them...

---

[12] http://www.chiark.greenend.org.uk/~sgtatham/coroutines.html

Concluding C#2: the final features

This chapter covers

- Partial types
- Static classes
- Separate getter/setter property access
- Namespace aliases
- Pragma directives
- Fixed-size buffers
- Friend assemblies

So far we've looked at the four biggest new features of C#2: generics, nullable types, delegate enhancements, and iterator blocks. Each of these addresses a fairly complex requirement, which is why we've gone into each of them in some depth. The remaining new features of C#2 are knocking a few rough edges off C#1. They're little niggles that the language designers decided to correct—either areas where the language needed a bit of improvement for its own sake, or where the experience of working with code generation and native code could be made more pleasant.

Over time, Microsoft has received a lot of feedback from the C# community (and its own developers, no doubt) about areas where C# hasn't gleamed quite as brightly as it might. Although it's impossible to please everyone—and in particular the value of each feature has to be weighed against the extra complexity it might bring to the language—several smaller changes made it into C#2 along with the larger ones.

None of the features in this chapter are particularly difficult, and we'll go through them fairly quickly. Don't underestimate how important they are, however—just because a topic can be explored in a few pages doesn't mean it's useless. You're likely to use some of these features on a fairly frequent basis. Here's a quick rundown of the features covered in this chapter, so you know what to expect:

- *Partial types*—The ability to write the code for a type in multiple source files; particularly handy for types where part of the code is autogenerated and the rest is written manually.
- *Static classes*—Tidying up utility classes so that the compiler can make it clearer when you're trying to use them inappropriately.
- *Separate getter/setter property access*—Finally, the ability to have a public getter and a private setter for properties! (That's not the only combination available, but it's the most common one.)
- *Namespace aliases*—Ways out of sticky situations where type names aren't unique.
- *Pragma directives*—Compiler-specific instructions for actions such as suppressing specific warnings for a particular section of code.
- *Fixed-size buffers*—More control over how structs handle arrays in unsafe code.
- *InternalsVisibleToAttribute (friend assemblies)*—A feature spanning library, framework, and runtime, this allows selected assemblies more access when required.

You may well be itching to get on to the sexy stuff from C#3 by this point, and I don't blame you. Nothing in this chapter is going to set the world on fire—but each of these features can make your life more pleasant, or dig you out of a hole in some cases. Having dampened your expectations somewhat, our first feature is actually pretty nifty.

7.1   *Partial types*

The first change we'll look at is due to the power struggle that was usually involved when using code generators with C#1. For Windows Forms, the designer in Visual Studio had to have its own regions of code that couldn't be touched by developers, within the same file that developers *had* to edit for user interface functionality. This was clearly a brittle situation.

In other cases, code generators create source that is compiled alongside manually written code. In C#1, adding extra functionality involved deriving new classes from the autogenerated ones, which is ugly. There are plenty of other scenarios where having an unnecessary link in the inheritance chain can cause problems or reduce encapsulation. For instance, if two different parts of your code want to call each other, you need virtual methods for the parent type to call the child, and protected methods for the reverse situation, where normally you'd just use two private nonvirtual methods.

900

C#2 allows more than one file to contribute to a type, and indeed IDEs can extend this notion so that some of the code that is used for a type may not even be visible as C# source code at all. Types built from multiple source files are called *partial types*.

In this section we'll also learn about *partial methods*, which are only relevant in partial types and allow a rich but efficient way of adding manually written hooks into autogenerated code. This is actually a C#3 feature (this time based on feedback about C#2), but it's far more logical to discuss it when we examine partial types than to wait until the next part of the book.

7.1.1   Creating a type with multiple files

Creating a partial type is a cinch—you just need to include the `partial` contextual keyword in the declaration for the type in each file it occurs in. A partial type can be declared within as many files as you like, although all the examples in this section use two.

The compiler effectively combines all the source files together before compiling. This means that code in one file can call code in another and vice versa, as shown in figure 7.1—there's no need for "forward references" or other tricks.

You can't write half of a member in one file and half of it in another—each individual member has to be complete within its own file.[1] There are a few obvious restrictions about the declarations of the type—the declarations have to be compatible. Any file can specify interfaces to be implemented (and they don't have to be implemented in that file); any file can specify the base type; any file can specify a type parameter constraint. However, if multiple files specify a base type, those base types have to be the same, and if multiple files specify type parameter constraints, the constraints have to be identical. Listing 7.1 gives an example of the flexibility afforded (while not doing anything even remotely useful).

Example1.cs   Example2.cs

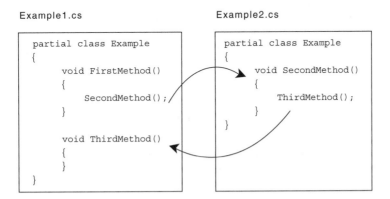

Figure 7.1   Code in partial types is able to "see" all of the members of the type, regardless of which file each member is in.

---

[1] There's an exception here: partial types can contain nested partial types spread across the same set of files.

Listing 7.1   Demonstration of mixing declarations of a partial type

```
// Example1.cs
using System;

partial class Example<TFirst,TSecond>        ❶ Specifies interface
    : IEquatable<string>                        and type parameter
    where TFirst : class                        constraint
{
    public bool Equals(string other))    ◁─┐  Implements
    {                                     ❷  IEquatable<string>
        return false;
    }
}

// Example2.cs
using System;

partial class Example<TFirst,TSecond>        ❸ Specifies base
    : EventArgs, IDisposable                    class and interface
{
    public void Dispose()    ◁─┐  Implements
    {                         ❹  IDisposable
    }
}
```

I stress that this listing is *solely* for the purpose of talking about what's legal in a declaration—the types involved were only picked for convenience and familiarity. We can see that both declarations (❶ and ❸) contribute to the list of interfaces that must be implemented. In this example, each file implements the interfaces it declares, and that's a common scenario, but it would be legal to move the implementation of IDisposable ❹ to Example1.cs and the implementation of IEquatable<string> ❷ to Example2.cs. Only ❶ specified any type constraints, and only ❸ specified a base class. If ❶ specified a base class, it would have to be EventArgs, and if ❸ specified any type constraints they'd have to be exactly as in ❶. In particular, we couldn't specify a type constraint for TSecond in ❸ even though it's not mentioned in ❶. Both types have to have the same access modifier, if any—we couldn't make one declaration internal and the other public, for example.

In "single file" types, initialization of member and static variables is guaranteed to occur in the order they appear in the file, but there's no guaranteed order when multiple files are involved. Relying on the order of declaration within the file is brittle to start with—it leaves your code wide open to subtle bugs if a developer decides to "harmlessly" move things around. So, it's worth avoiding this situation where you can anyway, but *particularly* avoid it with partial types.

Now that we know what we can and can't do, let's take a closer look at why we'd *want* to do it.

7.1.2   Uses of partial types

As I mentioned earlier, partial types are primarily useful in conjunction with designers and other code generators. If a code generator has to modify a file that is "owned" by a developer, there's always a risk of things going wrong. With the partial types model, a code generator can own the file where it will work, and completely overwrite the whole file every time it wants to.

Some code generators may even choose not to generate a C# file at all until the build is well under way. For instance, the Windows Presentation Foundation version of the Snippy application has Extensible Application Markup Language (XAML) files that describe the user interface. When the project is built, each XAML file is converted into a C# file in the obj directory (the filenames end with ".g.cs" to show they've been generated) and compiled along with the partial class providing extra code for that type (typically event handlers and extra construction code). This completely prevents developers from tweaking the generated code, at least without going to extreme lengths of hacking the build file.

I've been careful to use the phrase *code generator* instead of just *designer* because there are plenty of code generators around besides designers. For instance, in Visual Studio 2005 web service proxies are generated as partial classes, and you may well have your own tools that generate code based on other data sources. One reasonably common example of this is *Object Relational Mapping* (ORM)—some ORM tools use database entity descriptions from a configuration file (or straight from the database) and generate partial classes representing those entities.

This makes it very straightforward to add behavior to the type: overriding virtual methods of the base class, adding new members with business logic, and so forth. It's a great way of letting the developer and the tool work together, rather than constantly squabbling about who's in charge.

One scenario that is occasionally useful is for one file to be generated containing multiple partial types, and then some of those types are enhanced in other files, one manually generated file per type. To return to the ORM example, the tool could generate a single file containing all the entity definitions, and some of those entities could have extra code provided by the developer, using one file per entity. This keeps the number of automatically generated files low, but still provides good visibility of the manual code involved.

Figure 7.2 shows how the uses of partial types for XAML and entities are similar, but with slightly different timing involved when it comes to creating the autogenerated C# code.

A somewhat different use of partial types is as an aid to refactoring. Sometimes a type gets too big and assumes too many responsibilities. One first step to dividing the bloated type into smaller, more coherent ones can be to first split it into a partial type over two or more files. This can be done with no risk and in an experimental manner, moving methods between files until each file only addresses a particular concern. Although the next step of splitting the type up is still far from automatic at that stage, it should be a lot easier to see the end goal.

When partial types first appeared in C#2, no one knew exactly how they'd be used. One feature that was almost immediately requested was a way to provide optional "extra" code for generated methods to call. This need has been addressed by C#3 with *partial methods*.

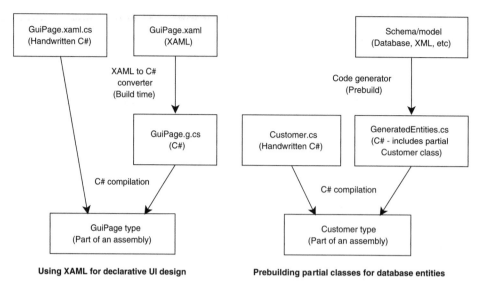

Figure 7.2   **Comparison between XAML precompilation and autogenerated entity classes**

7.1.3   *Partial methods—C#3 only!*

Just to reiterate my previous explanation, I realize that the rest of this part of the book has just been dealing with C#2 features—but partial methods don't fit with any of the other C#3 features and they *do* fit in very well when describing partial types. Apologies for any confusion this may cause.

Back to the feature: sometimes we want to be able to specify behavior in a manually created file and use that behavior from an automatically generated file. For instance, in a class that has lots of automatically generated properties, we might want to be able to specify code to be executed as validation of a new value for some of those properties. Another common scenario is for a code-generation tool to include constructors—manually written code often wants to hook into object construction to set default values, perform some logging, and so forth.

In C#2, these requirements could only be met either by using events that the manually generated code could subscribe to, or by making the automatically generated code *assume* that the handwritten code will include methods of a particular name—making the whole code fail to compile unless the relevant methods are provided. Alternatively, the generated code can provide a base class with virtual methods that do nothing by default. The manually generated code can then derive from the class and override some or all of the methods.

All of these solutions are somewhat messy. C#3's partial methods effectively provide *optional* hooks that have no cost whatsoever if they're not implemented—any calls to the unimplemented partial methods are removed by the compiler. It's easiest to understand this with an example. Listing 7.2 shows a partial type specified in two files, with the constructor in the automatically generated code calling two partial methods, one of which is implemented in the manually generated code.

```
Listing 7.2   A partial method called from a constructor

// Generated.cs
using System;
partial class PartialMethodDemo
{
    public PartialMethodDemo()
    {
        OnConstructorStart();
        Console.WriteLine("Generated constructor");
        OnConstructorEnd();
    }

    partial void OnConstructorStart();
    partial void OnConstructorEnd();
}
// Handwritten.cs
using System;
partial class PartialMethodDemo
{
    partial void OnConstructorEnd()
    {
        Console.WriteLine("Manual code");
    }
}
```

As shown in listing 7.2, partial methods are declared just like abstract methods: by providing the signature without any implementation but using the `partial` modifier. Similarly, the actual implementations just have the `partial` modifier but are otherwise like normal methods.

Calling the parameterless constructor of `PartialMethodDemo` would result in "Generated constructor" and then "Manual code" being printed out. Examining the IL for the constructor, you wouldn't see a call to `OnConstructorStart` because it no longer exists—there's no trace of it anywhere in the compiled type.

Because the method may not exist, partial methods must have a return type of `void` and can't take `out` parameters. They have to be private, but they can be static and/or generic. If the method isn't implemented in one of the files, the whole statement calling it is removed, *including any argument evaluations*. If evaluating any of the arguments has a side effect that you want to occur whether or not the partial method is implemented, you should perform the evaluation separately. For instance, suppose you have the following code:

```
LogEntity(LoadAndCache(id));
```

Here `LogEntity` is a partial method, and `LoadAndCache` loads an entity from the database and inserts it into the cache. You might want to use this instead:

```
MyEntity entity = LoadAndCache(id);
LogEntity(entity);
```

That way, the entity is loaded and cached regardless of whether an implementation has been provided for `LogEntity`. Of course, if the entity can be loaded equally cheaply later on, and may not even be required, you should leave the statement in the first form and avoid an unnecessary load in some cases.

To be honest, unless you're writing your own code generators, you're more likely to be implementing partial methods than declaring and calling them. If you're only implementing them, you don't need to worry about the argument evaluation side of things.

In summary, partial methods in C#3 allow generated code to interact with handwritten code in a rich manner without any performance penalties for situations where the interaction is unnecessary. This is a natural continuation of the C#2 partial types feature, which enables a much more productive relationship between code-generation tools and developers.

Our next feature is entirely different, and is just a way of telling the compiler more about the intended nature of a type so that it can perform more checking on both the type itself and any code using it.

7.2 Static classes

Our second new feature is in some ways completely unnecessary—it just makes things tidier and a bit more elegant when you write utility classes.

Everyone has utility classes. I haven't seen a significant project in either Java or C# that didn't have at least one class consisting solely of static methods. The classic example appearing in developer code is a type with string helper methods, doing anything from escaping, reversing, smart replacing—you name it. An example from the Framework is the `System.Math` class. The key features of a utility class are as follows:

- All members are static (except a private constructor).
- The class derives directly from `object`.
- Typically there's no state at all, unless there's some caching or a singleton involved.
- There are no visible constructors.
- The class is sealed if the developer remembers to do so.

The last two points are optional, and indeed if there are no visible constructors (including protected ones) then the class is *effectively* sealed anyway. Both of them help make the purpose of the class more obvious, however.

Listing 7.3 gives an example of a C#1 utility class—then we'll see how C#2 improves matters.

Listing 7.3 A typical C#1 utility class

```
using System;

public sealed class StringHelper          Seals class to
{                                          prevent derivation
    private StringHelper()              Prevents instantiation
    {                                ❶  from other code
    }
```

```
public static string Reverse(string input)          ◁─┐ All methods
{                                                      └ are static
    char[] chars = input.ToCharArray();
    Array.Reverse(chars);
    return new string(chars);
}
}
```

The private constructor ❶ may seem odd—why have it at all if it's private and never going to be used? The reason is that if you don't supply any constructors for a class, the C#1 compiler will always provide a *default constructor* that is public and parameterless. In this case, we don't want any visible constructors, so we have to provide a private one.

This pattern works reasonably well, but C#2 makes it explicit and actively prevents the type from being misused. First we'll see what changes are needed to turn listing 7.3 into a "proper" static class as defined in C#2. As you can see from listing 7.4, very little action is required.

Listing 7.4 The same utility class as in listing 7.3 but converted into a C#2 static class

```
using System;

public static class StringHelper
{
    public static string Reverse(string input)
    {
        char[] chars = input.ToCharArray();
        Array.Reverse(chars);
        return new string(chars);
    }
}
```

We've used the `static` modifier in the class declaration this time instead of `sealed`, and we haven't included a constructor at all—those are the only code differences. The C#2 compiler knows that a static class shouldn't have any constructors, so it doesn't provide a default one. In fact, the compiler enforces a number of constraints on the class definition:

- It can't be declared as `abstract` or `sealed`, although it's implicitly both.
- It can't specify any implemented interfaces.
- It can't specify a base type.
- It can't include any nonstatic members, including constructors.
- It can't include any operators.
- It can't include any `protected` or `protected internal` members.

It's worth noting that although all the members have to be static, you've got to *explicitly* make them static except for nested types and constants. Although nested types are implicitly static members of the enclosing class, the nested type itself can be a nonstatic type if that's required.

The compiler not only puts constraints on the definition of static classes, though—it also guards against their misuse. As it knows that there can never be any instances of the class, it prevents any use of it that would require one. For instance, all of the following are invalid when `StringHelper` is a static class:

```
StringHelper variable = null;
StringHelper[] array = null;
public void Method1(StringHelper x) {}
public StringHelper Method1() { return null; }
List<StringHelper> x = new List<StringHelper>();
```

None of these are prevented if the class just follows the C#1 pattern—but all of them are essentially useless. In short, static classes in C#2 don't allow you to do anything you couldn't do before—but they prevent you from doing things that you *shouldn't* have been doing anyway.

The next feature on our list is one with a more positive feel. It's aimed at a very specific—although widely encountered—situation, and allows a solution that is neither ugly nor breaks encapsulation, which was the choice available in C#1.

7.3   *Separate getter/setter property access*

I'll admit to being slightly bemused when I first saw that C#1 didn't allow you to have a public getter and a private setter for properties. This isn't the only combination of access modifiers that is prohibited by C#1, but it's the most commonly desired one. In fact, in C#1 both the getter and the setter have to have the same accessibility—it's declared as part of the property declaration rather than as part of the getter or setter.

There are perfectly good reasons to want different accessibility for the getter and the setter—often you may want some validation, logging, locking, or other code to be executed when changing a variable that backs the property but you don't want to make the property writable to code outside the class. In C#1 the alternatives were either to break encapsulation by making the property writable against your better judgment or to write a `SetXXX()` method in the class to do the setting, which frankly looks ugly when you're used to "real" properties.

C#2 fixes the problem by allowing either the getter or the setter to explicitly have a more restrictive access than that declared for the property itself. This is most easily seen with an example:

```
string name;

public string Name
{
   get { return name; }
   private set
   {
      // Validation, logging etc here
      name = value;
   }
}
```

In this case, the `Name` property is effectively read-only to all other types,[2] but we can use the familiar property syntax for setting the property within the type itself. The

---

[2] Except nested types, which always have access to private members of their enclosing types.

same syntax is also available for indexers as well as properties. You *could* make the setter more public than the getter (a protected getter and a public setter, for example) but that's a pretty rare situation, in the same way that write-only properties are few and far between compared with read-only properties.

NOTE *Trivia: The only place where "private" is required*—Everywhere else in C#, the default access modifier in any given situation is the most private one possible. In other words, if something *can* be declared to be private, then leaving out the access modifiers entirely will default it to being private. This is a nice element of language design, because it's hard to get it wrong accidentally: if you want something to be more public than it is, you'll notice when you try to use it. If, however, you accidentally make something "too public," then the compiler can't help you to spot the problem. For this reason, my personal convention is not to use any access modifiers unless I need to; that way, the code highlights (by way of an access modifier) when I've explicitly chosen to make something more public than it might be. Specifying the access of a property getter or setter is the one exception to this rule—if you don't specify anything, the default is to give the getter/setter the same access as the overall property itself.

Note that you can't declare the property itself to be private and make the getter public—you can only make a particular getter/setter *more* private than the property. Also, you can't specify an access modifier for both the getter and the setter—that would just be silly, as you could declare the property itself to be whichever is the more public of the two modifiers.

This aid to encapsulation is long overdue. There's still nothing in C#2 to stop other code in the same class from bypassing the property and going directly to whatever fields are backing it, unfortunately. As we'll see in the next chapter, C#3 fixes this in one particular case, but not in general. Maybe in C#4…

We move from a feature you may well want to use fairly regularly to one that you want to avoid most of the time—it allows your code to be absolutely explicit in terms of which types it's referring to, but at a significant cost to readability.

7.4 *Namespace aliases*

Namespaces are simply ways of keeping fully qualified names of types distinct even when the unqualified names may be the same. An example of this is the unqualified name `Button`. There are two classes with that name in the .NET 2.0 Framework: `System.Windows.Forms.Button` and `System.Web.UI.WebControls.Button`. Although they're both called `Button`, it's easy to tell them apart by their namespaces. This mirrors real life quite closely—you may know several people called Jon, but you're unlikely to know anyone else called Jon Skeet. If you're talking with friends in a particular context, you may well be able to just use the name Jon without specifying exactly which one you're talking about—but in other contexts you may need to provide more exact information.

The `using` directive of C#1 (not to be confused with the `using` statement that calls `Dispose` automatically) was available in two flavors—one created an *alias* for a namespace or type (for example, using Out = System.Console;) and the other just introduced a namespace into the list of contexts the compiler would search when looking for a type (for example, using System.IO;). By and large, this was adequate, but there are a few situations that the language simply couldn't cope with, and others where automatically generated code would have to go out of its way to make absolutely sure that the right namespaces and types were being used whatever happened.

C# 2 fixes these problems, bringing an additional robustness to the language. It's not that the code being generated is any more robust in terms of execution, but you can write code that is guaranteed to mean what you want it to regardless of which other types, assemblies, and namespaces are introduced. These extreme measures are rarely needed outside automatically generated code, but it's nice to know that they're there when you need them. In C# 2 there are three types of aliases: the namespace aliases of C# 1, the *global* namespace alias, and *extern* aliases. We'll start off with the one type of alias that was already present in C# 1, but we'll introduce a new way of using aliases to ensure that the compiler knows to treat it as an alias rather than checking to see whether it's the name of another namespace or type.

7.4.1   *Qualifying namespace aliases*

Even in C# 1, it was a good idea to avoid namespace aliases wherever possible. Every so often you might find that one type name clashed with another—as with our Button example earlier—and so you either had to specify the full name including the namespace every time you used them, or have an alias that distinguished the two, in some ways acting like a shortened form of the namespace. Listing 7.5 shows an example where the two types of Button are used, qualified by an alias.

Listing 7.5   Using aliases to distinguish between different Button types

```
using System;
using WinForms = System.Windows.Forms;
using WebForms = System.Web.UI.WebControls;

class Test
{
    static void Main()
    {
        Console.WriteLine (typeof (WinForms.Button));
        Console.WriteLine (typeof (WebForms.Button));
    }
}
```

Listing 7.5 compiles without any errors or warnings, although it's still not as pleasant as it would be if we only needed to deal with one kind of Button to start with. There's a problem, however—what if someone were to introduce a type or namespace called WinForms or WebForms? The compiler wouldn't know what WinForms.Button meant, and would use the type or namespace in preference to the alias. We want to be able to tell the compiler that we need it to treat WinForms as an alias, even though it's available elsewhere. C# 2 introduces the ::syntax to do this, as shown in listing 7.6.

Listing 7.6   Using : : to tell the compiler to use aliases

```csharp
using System;
using WinForms = System.Windows.Forms;
using WebForms = System.Web.UI.WebControls;

class WinForms
{
}

class Test
{
    static void Main()
    {
        Console.WriteLine (typeof (WinForms::Button));
        Console.WriteLine (typeof (WebForms::Button));
    }
}
```

Instead of WinForms.Button, listing 7.6 uses WinForms::Button, and the compiler is
happy. If you change the :: back to . you'll get a compilation error. So, if you use ::
everywhere you use an alias, you'll be fine, right? Well, not quite...

7.4.2   *The global namespace alias*

There's one part of the namespace hierarchy that you can't define your own alias for:
the root of it, or the *global* namespace. Suppose you have two classes, both named
Configuration; one is within a namespace of MyCompany and the other doesn't have
a namespace specified at all. Now, how can you refer to the "root" Configuration
class from within the MyCompany namespace? You can't use a normal alias, and if you
just specify Configuration the compiler will use MyCompany.Configuration.

   In C#1, there was simply no way of getting around this. Again, C#2 comes to the
rescue, allowing you to use global::Configuration to tell the compiler exactly what
you want. Listing 7.7 demonstrates both the problem and the solution.

Listing 7.7   Use of the global namespace alias to specify the desired type exactly

```csharp
using System;

class Configuration {}

namespace Chapter7
{
    class Configuration {}

    class Test
    {
        static void Main()
        {
            Console.WriteLine(typeof(Configuration));
            Console.WriteLine(typeof(global::Configuration));
            Console.WriteLine(typeof(global::Chapter7.Test));
        }
    }
}
```

Most of listing 7.7 is just setting up the situation—the three lines within `Main` are the interesting ones. The first line prints "Chapter7.Configuration" as the compiler resolves `Configuration` to that type before moving out to the namespace root. The second line indicates that the type has to be in the global namespace, and so simply prints "Configuration." I included the third line to demonstrate that using the global alias you can still refer to types within namespaces, but you have to specify the fully qualified name.

At this point we can get to any uniquely named type, using the global namespace alias if necessary—and indeed if you ever write a code generator where the code doesn't need to be readable, you may wish to use this feature liberally to make sure that you always refer to the correct type whatever other types are actually present by the time the code is compiled. What do we do if the type's name isn't unique even when we include its namespace? The plot thickens…

7.4.3   *Extern aliases*

At the start of this section, I referred to human names as examples of namespaces and contexts. I specifically said that you're unlikely to know more than one person called Jon Skeet. However, I know that there *is* more than one person with my name, and it's not beyond the realm of possibility to suppose that you might know two or more of us. In this case, in order to specify which one you mean you have to provide some more information beyond just the full name—the reason you know the particular person, or the country he lives in, or something similarly distinctive.

C# 2 lets you specify that extra information in the form of an *extern alias*—a name that exists not only in your source code, but also in the parameters you pass to the compiler. For the Microsoft C# compiler, this means specifying the assembly that contains the types in question. Let's suppose that two assemblies `First.dll` and `Second.dll` both contained a type called `Demo.Example`. We couldn't just use the fully qualified name to distinguish them, as they've both got the same fully qualified name. Instead, we can use extern aliases to specify which we mean. Listing 7.8 shows an example of the C# code involved, along with the command line needed to compile it.

Listing 7.8   Working with different types of the same type in different assemblies

```
// Compile with
// csc Test.cs /r:FirstAlias=First.dll /r:SecondAlias=Second.dll

extern alias FirstAlias;        Specifies two
extern alias SecondAlias;       extern aliases

using System;

using FD = FirstAlias::Demo;    ❶ Refers to extern alias
                                  with namespace alias
class Test
{
    static void Main()                          ❷ Uses
    {                                              namespace
        Console.WriteLine(typeof(FD.Example));     alias
```

```
        Console.WriteLine(typeof(SecondAlias::Demo.Example));
        Console.ReadLine();
    }
}
```

Uses
extern alias
❸ directly

The code in listing 7.8 is quite straightforward, and demonstrates that you can either use extern directives directly ❸ or via namespace aliases (❶ and ❷). In fact, a normal using directive without an alias (for example, using First-Alias::Demo;) would have allowed us to use the name Example without any further qualification at all. It's also worth noting that one extern alias can cover multiple assemblies, and several extern aliases can all refer to the same assembly. To specify an external alias in Visual Studio (2005 or 2008), just select the assembly reference within Solution Explorer and modify the Aliases value in the Properties window, as shown in figure 7.3.

Hopefully I don't need to persuade you to avoid this kind of situation wherever you possibly can. It can be necessary to work with assemblies from different third parties who happen to have used the same fully qualified type name. Where you have more control over the naming, however, make sure that your names never lead you into this territory in the first place.

Our next feature is almost a meta-feature. The exact purpose it serves depends on which compiler you're using, because its whole purpose is to enable control over compiler-specific features—but we'll concentrate on the Microsoft compiler.

Figure 7.3   Part of the Properties window of Visual Studio 2008, showing an extern alias of FirstAlias for the First.dll reference

7.5   Pragma directives

Describing *pragma directives* in general is extremely easy: a pragma directive is a pre-processing directive represented by a line beginning with #pragma. The rest of the line can contain any text at all. The result of a pragma directive cannot change the behavior of the program to contravene anything within the C# language specification, but it can do anything outside the scope of the specification. If the compiler doesn't understand a particular pragma directive, it can issue a warning but not an error.

That's basically everything the specification has to say on the subject. The Microsoft C# compiler understands two pragma directives: warnings and checksums.

7.5.1   Warning pragmas

Just occasionally, the C# compiler issues warnings that are justifiable but annoying. The correct response to a compiler warning is *almost always* to fix it—the code is rarely made worse by fixing the warning, and usually it's improved.

However, just occasionally there's a good reason to ignore a warning—and that's what warning pragmas are available for. As an example, we'll create a private field that is never read from or written to. It's almost always going to be useless... unless we happen to know that it will be used by reflection. Listing 7.9 is a complete class demonstrating this.

Listing 7.9   Class containing an unused field

```
public class FieldUsedOnlyByReflection
{
    int x;
}
```

If you try to compile listing 7.9, you'll get a warning message like this:

```
FieldUsedOnlyByReflection.cs(3,9): warning CS0169:
The private field 'FieldUsedOnlyByReflection.x' is never used
```

That's the output from the command-line compiler. In the Error List window of Visual Studio, you can see the same information (plus the project it's in) *except* that you don't get the warning number (CS0169). To find out the number, you need to either select the warning and bring up the help related to it, or look in the Output window, where the full text is shown. We need the number in order to make the code compile without warnings, as shown in listing 7.10.

Listing 7.10   Disabling (and restoring) warning CS0169

```
public class FieldUsedOnlyByReflection
{
#pragma warning disable 0169
    int x;
#pragma warning restore 0169
}
```

Listing 7.10 is self-explanatory—the first pragma disables the particular warning we're interested in, and the second one restores it. It's good practice to disable warnings for as short a space as you can, so that you don't miss any warnings you genuinely ought to fix. If you want to disable or restore multiple warnings in a single line, just use a comma-separated list of warning numbers. If you don't specify any warning numbers at all, the result is to disable or restore *all* warnings in one fell swoop—but that's a bad idea in almost every imaginable scenario.

7.5.2   Checksum pragmas

You're very unlikely to need the second form of pragma recognized by the Microsoft compiler. It supports the debugger by allowing it to check that it's found the right source file. Normally when a C# file is compiled, the compiler generates a checksum from the file and includes it in the debugging information. When the debugger needs to locate a source file and finds multiple potential matches, it can generate the checksum itself for each of the candidate files and see which is correct.

Now, when an ASP.NET page is converted into C#, the generated file is what the C# compiler sees. The generator calculates the checksum of the .aspx page, and uses a checksum pragma to tell the C# compiler to use *that* checksum instead of calculating one from the generated page.

The syntax of the checksum pragma is

```
#pragma checksum "filename" "{guid}" "checksum bytes"
```

The GUID indicates which hashing algorithm has been used to calculate the checksum. The documentation for the CodeChecksumPragma class gives GUIDs for SHA-1 and MD5, should you ever wish to implement your own dynamic compilation framework with debugger support.

It's possible that future versions of the C# compiler will include more pragma directives, and other compilers (such as the Mono compiler, mcs) could have their own support for different features. Consult your compiler documentation for the most up-to-date information.

The next feature is another one that you may well never use—but at the same time, if you ever do, it's likely to make your life somewhat simpler.

7.6   *Fixed-size buffers in unsafe code*

When calling into native code with P/Invoke, it's not particularly unusual to find yourself dealing with a structure that is defined to have a buffer of a particular length within it. Prior to C# 2, such structures were difficult to handle directly, even with unsafe code. Now, you can declare a buffer of the right size to be embedded directly with the rest of the data for the structure.

This capability isn't just available for calling native code, although that is its primary use. You could use it to easily populate a data structure directly corresponding to a file format, for instance. The syntax is simple, and once again we'll demonstrate it with an example. To create a field that embeds an array of 20 bytes within its enclosing structure, you would use

```
fixed byte data[20];
```

This would allow data to be used as if it were a byte* (a pointer to byte data), although the implementation used by the C# compiler is to create a new nested type within the declaring type and apply the new FixedBuffer attribute to the variable itself. The CLR then takes care of allocating the memory appropriately.

One downside of this feature is that it's only available within unsafe code: the enclosing structure has to be declared in an unsafe context, and you can only use the fixed-size buffer member within an unsafe context too. This limits the situations in which it's useful, but it can still be a nice trick to have up your sleeve at times. Also, fixed-size buffers are only applicable to primitive types, and can't be members of classes (only structures).

There are remarkably few Windows APIs where this feature is directly useful. There are numerous situations where a fixed array of characters is called for—the TIME_ ZONE_INFORMATION structure, for example—but unfortunately fixed-size buffers of characters appear to be handled poorly by P/Invoke, with the marshaler getting in the way.

As one example, however, listing 7.11 is a console application that displays the colors available in the current console window. It uses an API function GetConsoleScreen-BufferEx that is new to Vista and Windows Server 2008, and that retrieves extended console information. Listing 7.11 displays all 16 colors in hexadecimal format (bbggrr).

Listing 7.11 Demonstration of fixed-size buffers to obtain console color information

```csharp
using System;
using System.Runtime.InteropServices;

struct COORD
{
    public short X, Y;
}

struct SMALL_RECT
{
    public short Left, Top, Right, Bottom;
}

unsafe struct CONSOLE_SCREEN_BUFFER_INFOEX
{
    public int StructureSize;
    public COORD ConsoleSize, CursorPosition;
    public short Attributes;
    public SMALL_RECT DisplayWindow;
    public COORD MaximumWindowSize;
    public short PopupAttributes;
    public int FullScreenSupported;
    public fixed int ColorTable[16];
}

static class FixedSizeBufferDemo
{
    const int StdOutputHandle = -11;

    [DllImport("kernel32.dll")]
    static extern IntPtr GetStdHandle(int nStdHandle);

    [DllImport("kernel32.dll")]
    static extern bool GetConsoleScreenBufferInfoEx
        (IntPtr handle, ref CONSOLE_SCREEN_BUFFER_INFOEX info);

    unsafe static void Main()
    {
        IntPtr handle = GetStdHandle(StdOutputHandle);
        CONSOLE_SCREEN_BUFFER_INFOEX info;
        info = new CONSOLE_SCREEN_BUFFER_INFOEX();
        info.StructureSize = sizeof(CONSOLE_SCREEN_BUFFER_INFOEX);
        GetConsoleScreenBufferInfoEx(handle, ref info);

        for (int i=0; i < 16; i++)
        {
            Console.WriteLine ("{0:x6}", info.ColorTable[i]);
        }
    }
}
```

Listing 7.11 uses fixed-size buffers for the table of colors. Before fixed-size buffers, we could still have used the API either with a field for each color table entry or by marshaling a normal array as `UnmanagedType.ByValArray`. However, this would have created a separate array on the heap instead of keeping the information all within the structure. That's not a problem here, but in some high-performance situations it's nice to be able to keep "lumps" of data together. On a different performance note, if the buffer is part of a data structure on the managed heap, you have to pin it before accessing it. If you do this a lot, it can significantly affect the garbage collector. Stack-based structures don't have this problem, of course.

I'm not going to claim that fixed-size buffers are a hugely important feature in C# 2—at least, they're not important to most people. I've included them for completeness, however, and doubtless someone, somewhere will find them invaluable. Our final feature can barely be called a C# 2 *language* feature at all—but it *just* about counts, so I've included it for completeness.

7.7 *Exposing internal members to selected assemblies*

There are some features that are obviously in the language—iterator blocks, for example. There are some features that obviously belong to the runtime, such as JIT compiler optimizations. There are some that clearly sit in both camps, like generics. This last feature has a toe in each but is sufficiently odd that it doesn't merit a mention in *either* specification. In addition, it uses a term that has different meanings in C++ and VB.NET—adding a third meaning to the mix. To be fair, all the terms are used in the context of access permissions, but they have different effects.

7.7.1 *Friend assemblies in the simple case*

In .NET 1.1 it was entirely accurate to say that something defined to be *internal* (whether a type, a method, a property, a variable, or an event) could only be accessed within the same assembly in which it was declared.[3] In .NET 2.0 that's still *mostly* true, but there's a new attribute to let you bend the rules slightly: `Internals-VisibleToAttribute`, usually referred to as just `InternalsVisibleTo`. (When applying an attribute whose name ends with `Attribute`, the C# compiler will apply the suffix automatically.)

`InternalsVisibleTo` can only be applied to an assembly (not a specific member), and you can apply it multiple times to the same assembly. We will call the assembly containing the attribute the *source assembly*, although this is entirely unofficial terminology. When you apply the attribute, you have to specify another assembly, known as the *friend assembly*. The result is that the friend assembly can see all the internal members of the source assembly as if they were public. This may sound alarming, but it can be useful, as we'll see in a minute.

Listing 7.12 shows this with three classes in three different assemblies.

---

[3] Using reflection when running with suitable permissions doesn't count.

Listing 7.12   Demonstration of friend assemblies

```
// Compiled to Source.dll
using System.Runtime.CompilerServices;
[assembly:InternalsVisibleTo("FriendAssembly")]    ◁────┐ Grants
public class Source                                        additional access
{
    internal static void InternalMethod()
    {
    }

    public static void PublicMethod()
    {
    }
}

// Compiled to FriendAssembly.dll
public class Friend
{
    static void Main()                          Uses additional
    {                                           access within
        Source.InternalMethod();    ◁────       FriendAssembly
        Source.PublicMethod();
    }
}

// Compiled to EnemyAssembly.dll
public class Enemy
{
    static void Main()                       ❶ EnemyAssembly has
    {                                           no special access
        // Source.InternalMethod();  ◁────
        Source.PublicMethod();       ◁────── Accesses public
    }                                         method as normal
}
```

In listing 7.12 a special relationship exists between `FriendAssembly.dll` and `Source.dll`—although it only operates one way: `Source.dll` has no access to internal members of `FriendAssembly.dll`. If we were to uncomment the line at ❶, the `Enemy` class would fail to compile.

So, why on earth would we want to open up our well-designed assembly to certain assemblies to start with?

7.7.2   Why use InternalsVisibleTo?

I can't say I've ever used `InternalsVisibleTo` between two production assemblies. I'm not saying there aren't legitimate use cases for that, but I've not come across them. However, I *have* used the attribute when it comes to unit testing.

There are some who say you should only test the public interface to code. Personally I'm happy to test whatever I can in the simplest manner possible. Friend assemblies make that a lot easier: suddenly it's trivial to test code that only has internal access without taking the dubious step of making members public just for the sake of testing, or including the test code within the production assembly. (It does occasionally mean making members internal for the sake of testing where they might otherwise be private, but that's a less worrying step.)

The only downside to this is that the name of your test assembly lives on in your production assembly. In theory this could represent a security attack vector if your assemblies aren't signed, and if your code normally operates under a restricted set of permissions. (Anyone with full trust could use reflection to access the members in the first place. You could do that yourself for unit tests, but it's much nastier.) If this ever ends up as a genuine issue for anyone, I'll be very surprised. It does, however, bring the option of signing assemblies into the picture. Just when you thought this was a nice, simple little feature…

7.7.3   *InternalsVisibleTo and signed assemblies*

If a friend assembly is signed, the source assembly needs to specify the public key of the friend assembly, to make sure it's trusting the right code. Contrary to a lot of documentation, it isn't the public key *token* that is required but the public key itself. For instance, consider the following command line and output (rewrapped and modified slightly for formatting) used to discover the public key of a signed `FriendAssembly.dll`:

```
c:\Users\Jon\Test>sn -Tp FriendAssembly.dll

Microsoft (R) .NET Framework Strong Name Utility Version 3.5.21022.8
Copyright (c) Microsoft Corporation.  All rights reserved.

Public key is
00240000048000009400000006020000002400005253413100040000001
000100a51372c81ccfb8fba9c5fb84180c4129e50f0facdce932cf31fe
563d0fe3cb6b1d5129e28326060a3a539f287aaf59affc5aabc4d8f981
e1a82479ab795f410eab22e3266033c633400463ee7513378bb4ef41fc
0cae5fb03986d133677c82a865b278c48d99dc251201b9c43edd7bedef
d4b5306efd0dec7787ec6b664471c2

Public key token is 647b99330b7f792c
```

The source code for the `Source` class would now need to have this as the attribute:

```
[assembly:InternalsVisibleTo("FriendAssembly,PublicKey="+
"00240000048000009400000006020000002400005253413100040000001"+
"000100a51372c81ccfb8fba9c5fb84180c4129e50f0facdce932cf31fe"+
"563d0fe3cb6b1d5129e28326060a3a539f287aaf59affc5aabc4d8f981"+
"e1a82479ab795f410eab22e3266033c633400463ee7513378bb4ef41fc"+
"0cae5fb03986d133677c82a865b278c48d99dc251201b9c43edd7bedef"+
"d4b5306efd0dec7787ec6b664471c2")]
```

Unfortunately, you have to either have the public key on one line or use string concatenation—whitespace in the public key will cause a compilation failure. It would be a lot more pleasant to look at if we really *could* specify the token instead of the whole key, but fortunately this ugliness is usually confined to `AssemblyInfo.cs`, so you won't need to see it often.

In theory, it's possible to have an unsigned source assembly and a signed friend assembly. In practice, that's not terribly useful, as the friend assembly typically wants to have a reference to the source assembly—and you can't refer to an unsigned assembly from one that is signed! Likewise a signed assembly can't specify an unsigned friend assembly, so typically you end up with both assemblies being signed if either one of them is.

7.8   *Summary*

This completes our tour of the new features in C#2. The topics we've looked at in this chapter have broadly fallen into two categories: "nice to have" improvements that streamline development, and "hope you don't need it" features that can get you out of tricky situations when you need them. To make an analogy between C#2 and improvements to a house, the major features from our earlier chapters are comparable to full-scale additions. Some of the features we've seen in this chapter (such as partial types and static classes) are more like redecorating a bedroom, and features like namespace aliases are akin to fitting smoke alarms—you may never see a benefit, but it's nice to know they're there if you ever need them.

The range of features in C#2 is very broad—the designers tackled many of the areas where developers were feeling pain, without any one overarching goal. That's not to say the features don't work well together—nullable value types wouldn't be feasible without generics, for instance—but there's no one aim that every feature contributes to, unless you count general productivity.

Now that we've finished examining C#2, it's time to move on to C#3, where the picture is very different. Nearly every feature in C#3 (with the exception of partial methods, which we've covered in this chapter) forms part of the grand picture of LINQ, a conglomeration of technologies that could well change the way traditional programmers think—forever.

Part 3

C#3— revolutionizing how we code

There is no doubt that C#2 is a significant improvement over C#1. The benefits of generics in particular are fundamental to other changes, not just in C#2 but also in C#3. However, C#2 was in some sense a piecemeal collection of features. Don't get me wrong: they fit together nicely enough, but they address a set of individual issues. That was appropriate at that stage of C#'s development, but C#3 is different.

Almost every feature in C#3 enables one very specific technology: LINQ. Many of the features are useful outside this context, and you certainly shouldn't confine yourself to *only* using them when you happen to be writing a query expression, for example—but it would be equally silly not to recognise the complete picture created by the set of jigsaw puzzle pieces presented in the remaining chapters.

I'm writing this before C#3 and .NET 3.5 have been fully released, but I'd like to make a prediction: in a few years, we'll be collectively kicking ourselves for not using LINQ in a more widespread fashion in the early days of C#3. The buzz around LINQ—both within the community and in the messages from Microsoft—has been largely around database access and LINQ to SQL. Now databases are certainly important—but we manipulate data all the time, not just from databases but in memory, and from files, network resources, and other places. Why shouldn't other data sources get just as much benefit from LINQ as databases?

They do, of course—and that's the hidden jewel of LINQ. It's been in broad daylight, in public view—just not talked about very much. Even if you don't talk about it, I'd like you to keep it in the back of your mind while you read about the features of C#3. Look at your existing code in the light of the possibilities that LINQ has to offer. It's not suitable for all tasks, but where it *is* appropriate it can make a spectacular difference.

It's only been in the course of writing this book that I've become thoroughly convinced of the elegance and beauty of LINQ. The deeper you study the language, the more clearly you see the harmony between the various elements that have been introduced. Hopefully this will become apparent in the remainder of the book, but you're more likely to feel it gradually as you begin to see LINQ improving your own code. I don't wish to sound like a mindless and noncritical C# devotee, but I feel there's something special in C#3.

With that brief burst of abstract admiration out of the way, let's start looking at C#3 in a more concrete manner.

Cutting fluff
with a smart compiler

This chapter covers
- Automatically implemented properties
- Implicitly typed local variables
- Object and collection initializers
- Implicitly typed arrays
- Anonymous types

We start looking at C#3 in the same way that we finished looking at C#2—with a collection of relatively simple features. These are just the first small steps on the path to LINQ, however. Each of them can be used outside that context, but they're all pretty important for simplifying code to the extent that LINQ requires in order to be effective.

One important point to note is that while two of the biggest features of C#2—generics and nullable types—required CLR changes, there are no significant changes to the CLR that ships with .NET 3.5. There are some bug fixes, but nothing fundamental. The framework library has grown to support LINQ, along with introducing a few more features to the base class library, but that's a different matter. It's worth being quite clear in your mind which changes are only in the C# *language*, which are *library* changes, and which are *CLR* changes.

The fact that there are no CLR changes for .NET 3.5 means that almost all of the new features exposed in C#3 are due to the compiler being willing to do more work for you. We saw some evidence of this in C#2—particularly with anonymous methods and iterator blocks—and C#3 continues in the same vein. In this chapter, we'll meet the following features that are new to C#3:

- *Automatically implemented properties*—Removing the drudgery of writing simple properties backed directly by fields.
- *Implicitly typed local variables*—When you declare a variable and immediately assign a value to it, you no longer need to specify the type in the declaration.
- *Object and collection initializers*—Simple ways to initialize objects in single expressions.
- *Implicitly typed arrays*—Let the compiler work out the type of new arrays, based on their contents.
- *Anonymous types*—Primarily used in LINQ, these allow you to create new "ad hoc" types to contain simple properties.

As well as describing what the new features do, I'll make recommendations about their use. Many of the features of C#3 require a certain amount of discretion and restraint on the part of the developer. That's not to say they're not powerful and incredibly useful—quite the reverse—but the temptation to use the latest and greatest syntactic sugar shouldn't be allowed to overrule the drive toward clear and readable code.

The considerations I'll discuss in this chapter (and indeed in the rest of the book) will rarely be black and white. Perhaps more than ever before, readability is in the eye of the beholder—and as you become more comfortable with the new features, they're likely to become more readable to you. I should stress, however, that unless you have good reason to suppose you'll be the only one to ever read your code, you should consider the needs and views of your colleagues carefully.

Enough navel gazing for the moment. We'll start off with a feature that shouldn't cause any controversy—and that I always miss when coding in C#2. Simple but effective, automatically implemented properties just make life better.

8.1   *Automatically implemented properties*

Our first feature is probably the simplest in the whole of C#3. In fact, it's even simpler than any of the new features in C#2. Despite that—or possibly *because* of that—it's also immediately applicable in many, many situations. When you read about iterator blocks in chapter 6, you may not immediately have thought of any areas of your current codebase that could be improved by using them, but I'd be surprised to find any nontrivial C# program that couldn't be modified to use automatically implemented properties. This fabulously simple feature allows you to express trivial properties with less code than before.

What do I mean by a *trivial property*? I mean one that is read/write and that stores its value in a straightforward private variable without any validation or other custom code. In other words, it's a property like this:

```
string name;
public string Name
{
    get { return name; }
    set { name = value; }
}
```

Now, that's not an awful lot of code, but it's still five lines—and that's assuming your coding conventions allow you to get away with the "one line" forms of the getter and setter. If your coding conventions force you to keep member variables in one area of code and properties in another, it becomes a bit uglier—and then there's the question of whether to add XML documentation to the property, the variable, or both.

The C#3 version using an *automatically implemented property* is a single line:

```
public string Name { get; set; }
```

Where previously you *might* have been tempted to use a public variable (particularly for "throwaway code"—which we all know tends to live for longer than anticipated) just to make the code simple, there's now even less excuse for not following the best practice of using a property instead. The compiler generates a private variable that can't be referenced directly in the source, and fills in the property getter and setter with the simple code to read and write that variable.

NOTE *Terminology: Automatic property vs. automatically implemented property*—When automatically implemented properties were first discussed, long before the full C#3 specification was published, they were called *automatic properties*. Personally, I find this a lot less of a mouthful than the full name, and it's not like anything *other* than the implementation is going to be automatic. For the rest of this book I will use *automatic property* and *automatically implemented property* synonymously.

The feature of C#2 that allows you to specify different access for the getter and the setter is still available here, and you can also create static automatic properties. You need to be careful with static properties in terms of multithreading, however—although most types don't claim to have thread-safe instance members, publicly visible static members usually *should* be thread-safe, and the compiler doesn't do anything to help you in this respect. It's best to restrict automatic static properties to be private, and make sure you do any appropriate locking yourself. Listing 8.1 gives an example of this.

Listing 8.1 A `Person` class that counts created instances

```
public class Person
{
    public string Name { get; private set; }    Declares properties
    public int Age { get; private set; }         with public getters
```

```
    private static int InstanceCounter { get; set; }              Declares
    private static readonly object counterLock = new object();     private static
                                                                   property and
    public Person(string name, int age)                           lock
    {
        Name = name;
        Age = age;

        lock (counterLock)              Uses lock while
        {                               accessing static
            InstanceCounter++;          property
        }
    }
}
```

An alternative in this case is to use a simple static variable and rely on `Interlocked.Increment` to update the instance counter. You may decide that's simpler (and more efficient) code than using an explicit lock—it's a judgment call. Due to this sort of issue, static automatic properties are rarely useful: it's usually better to implement normal properties, allowing you more control. Note that you can't use automatic properties *and* use `Interlocked.Increment`: you no longer have access to the field, so you can't pass it by reference to the method.

The other automatic properties in listing 8.1, representing the name and age of the person, are real no-brainers. Where you've got properties that you would have implemented trivially in previous versions of C#, there's no benefit in *not* using automatic properties.

One slight wrinkle occurs if you use automatic properties when writing your own structs: all of your constructors need to explicitly call the parameterless constructor—`this()`—so that the compiler knows that all the fields have been definitely assigned. You can't set the fields directly because they're anonymous, and you can't use the properties until all the fields have been set. The only way of proceeding is to call the parameterless constructor, which will set the fields to their default values.

That's all there is to automatically implemented properties. There are no bells and whistles to them—for instance, there's no way of declaring them with initial default values, and no way of making them read-only. If all the C# 3 features were that simple, we could cover *everything* in a single chapter. Of course, that's not the case—but there are still some features that don't take *very* much explanation. Our next topic removes duplicate code in another common but specific situation—declaring local variables.

8.2   *Implicit typing of local variables*

In chapter 2, I discussed the nature of the C# 1 type system. In particular, I stated that it was static, explicit, and safe. That's still true in C# 2, and in C# 3 it's still *almost* completely true. The static and safe parts are still true (ignoring explicitly unsafe code, just as we did in chapter 2) and *most* of the time it's still explicitly typed—but you can ask the compiler to infer the types of local variables for you.

8.2.1 *Using var to declare a local variable*

In order to use implicit typing, all you need to do is replace the type part of a normal local variable declaration with var. Certain restrictions exist (we'll come to those in a moment), but essentially it's as easy as changing

```
MyType variableName = someInitialValue;
```

into

```
var variableName = someInitialValue;
```

The results of the two lines (in terms of compiled code) are *exactly the same*, assuming that the type of someInitialValue is MyType. The compiler simply takes the compile-time type of the initialization expression and makes the variable have that type too. The type can be any normal .NET type, including generics, delegates, and interfaces. The variable is still statically typed; it's just that you haven't written the name of the type in your code.

This is important to understand, as it goes to the heart of what a lot of developers initially fear when they see this feature—that C# has become dynamically or weakly typed. That's not true at all. The best way of explaining this is to show you some invalid code:

INVALID
```
var stringVariable = "Hello, world.";
stringVariable = 0;
```

That doesn't compile, because the type of stringVariable is System.String, and you can't assign the value 0 to a string variable. In many dynamic languages, the code *would* have compiled, leaving the variable with no particularly useful type as far as the compiler, IDE, or runtime environment is concerned. Using var is *not* like using a Variant type from COM or VB6. The variable is statically typed; it's just that the type has been inferred by the compiler. I apologize if I seem to be going on about this somewhat, but it's incredibly important.

In Visual Studio 2008, you can tell the type that the compiler has used for the variable by hovering over the var part of the declaration, as shown in figure 8.1. Note how the type parameters for the generic Dictionary type are also explained.

If this looks familiar, that's because it's *exactly* the same behavior you get when you declare local variables explicitly.

Tooltips aren't just available at the point of declaration, either. As you'd probably expect, the tooltip displayed when you hover over the variable name later on in the code indicates the type of the variable too. This is shown in figure 8.2, where the same declaration is used and then I've hovered over a *use* of the variable.

```
var namePeopleMap = new Dictionary<string, List<Person>>();
```
```
class System.Collections.Generic.Dictionary<TKey,TValue>
Represents a collection of keys and values.

TKey is System.String
TValue is List<Person>
```

Figure 8.1   Hovering over var in Visual Studio 2008 displays the type of the declared variable.

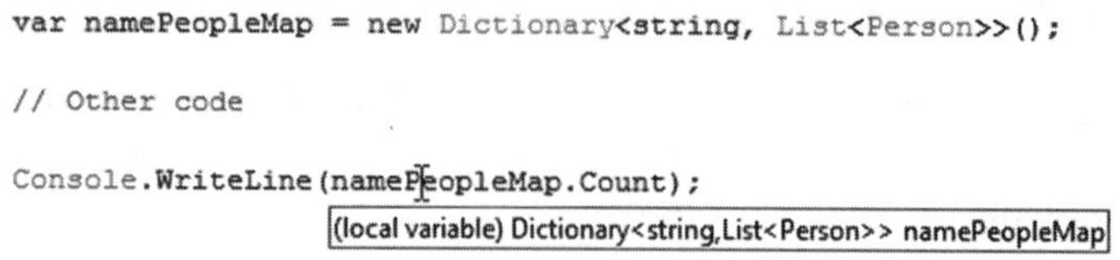

```
var namePeopleMap = new Dictionary<string, List<Person>>();

// Other code

Console.WriteLine(namePeopleMap.Count);
```
(local variable) Dictionary<string,List<Person>> namePeopleMap

Figure 8.2   Hovering over the use of an implicitly typed local variable displays its type.

Again, that's exactly the same behavior as a normal local variable declaration. Now, there are two reasons for bringing up Visual Studio 2008 in this context. The first is that it's more evidence of the static typing involved—the compiler clearly knows the type of the variable. The second is to point out that you can easily discover the type involved, even from deep within a method. This will be important when we talk about the pros and cons of using implicit typing in a minute. First, though, I ought to mention some limitations.

8.2.2   Restrictions on implicit typing

You can't use implicit typing for every variable in every situation. You can only use it when

- The variable being declared is a local variable.
- The variable is initialized as part of the declaration.
- The initialization expression isn't a method group or anonymous function[1] (without casting).
- The initialization expression isn't `null`.
- Only one variable is declared in the statement.
- The type you want the variable to have is the compile-time type of the initialization expression.

The third and fourth points are interesting. You can't write

INVALID
```
var starter = delegate() { Console.WriteLine(); }
```

This is because the compiler doesn't know what type to use. You *can* write

```
var starter = (ThreadStart) delegate() { Console.WriteLine(); }
```

but if you're going to do that you'd be better off explicitly declaring the variable in the first place. The same is true in the `null` case—you could cast the `null` appropriately, but there'd be no point. Note that you *can* use the result of method calls or properties as the initialization expression—you're not limited to constants and constructor calls. For instance, you could use

```
var args = Environment.GetCommandLineArgs();
```

In that case `args` would then be of type `string[]`. In fact, initializing a variable with the result of a method call is likely to be the most common situation where implicit

---

[1]   The term *anonymous function* covers both anonymous methods and lambda expressions, which we'll delve into in chapter 9.

typing is used, as part of LINQ. We'll see all that later on—just bear it in mind as the examples progress.

It's also worth noting that you *are* allowed to use implicit typing for the local variables declared in the first part of a using, for, or foreach statement. For example, the following are all valid (with appropriate bodies, of course):

```
for (var i = 0; i < 10; i++)
using (var x = File.OpenText("test.dat"))
foreach (var s in Environment.GetCommandLineArgs())
```

The variables in question would end up with types of int, StreamReader and string, respectively. Of course, just because you *can* do this doesn't mean you *should*. Let's have a look at the reasons for and against using implicit typing.

8.2.3 *Pros and cons of implicit typing*

The question of when it's a good idea to use implicit typing is the cause of an awful lot of community discussion. Views range from "everywhere" to "nowhere" with plenty of more balanced approaches between the two. We'll see in section 8.5 that in order to use another of C#3's features—anonymous types—you've often *got* to use implicit typing. You could avoid anonymous types as well, of course, but that's throwing the baby out with the bathwater.

The main reason *for* using implicit typing (leaving anonymous types aside for the moment) is that it reduces not only the number of keystrokes required to enter the code, but also the amount of code on the screen. In particular, when generics are involved the type names can get very long. Figures 8.1 and 8.2 used a type of Dictionary <string, List<Person>>, which is 33 characters. By the time you've got that twice on a line (once for the declaration and once for the initialization), you end up with a massive line just for declaring and initializing a single variable! An alternative is to use an alias, but that puts the "real" type involved a long way (conceptually at least) from the code that uses it.

When reading the code, there's no point in seeing the same long type name twice on the same line when it's obvious that they *should* be the same. If the declaration isn't visible on the screen, you're in the same boat whether implicit typing was used or not (all the ways you'd use to find out the variable type are still valid) and if it *is* visible, the expression used to initialize the variable tells you the type anyway.

All of this sounds good, so what are the arguments *against* implicit typing? Paradoxically enough, readability is the most important one, despite also being an argument in favor of implicit typing! By not being explicit about what type of variable you're declaring, you may be making it harder to work it out just by reading the code. It breaks the "state what are we declaring, then what value it will start off with" mindset that keeps the declaration and the initialization quite separate. To what extent that's an issue depends on both the reader and the initialization expression involved. If you're explicitly calling a constructor, it's always going to be pretty obvious what type you're creating. If you're calling a method or using a property, it depends on how obvious the return type is just from looking at the call. Integer literals are another example where guessing the inferred type is harder than one might suppose. How quickly can you work out the type of each of the variables declared here?

```
var a = 2147483647;
var b = 2147483648;
var c = 4294967295;
var d = 4294967296;
var e = 9223372036854775807;
var f = 9223372036854775808;
```

The answers are `int`, `uint`, `uint`, `long`, `long`, and `ulong`, respectively—the type used depends on the value of the expression. There's nothing new here in terms of the handling of literals—C# has always behaved like this—but implicit typing makes it easier to write obscure code in this case.

The argument that is rarely explicitly stated but that I believe is behind a lot of the concern over implicit typing is "It just doesn't feel right." If you've been writing in a C-like language for years and years, there is something unnerving about the whole business, however much you tell yourself that it's still static typing under the covers. This may not be a rational concern, but that doesn't make it any less real. If you're uncomfortable, you're likely to be less productive. If the advantages don't outweigh your negative feelings, that's fine. Depending on your personality, you may wish to try to push yourself to *become* more comfortable with implicit typing—but you certainly don't have to.

8.2.4   *Recommendations*

Here are some recommendations based on my experience with implicit typing. That's all they are—recommendations—and you should feel free to take them with a pinch of salt.

- Consult your teammates on the matter when embarking on a C#3 project.
- When in doubt, try a line both ways and go with your gut feelings.
- Unless there's a significant gain in code simplicity, use explicit typing. Note that numeric variables always fall into this category since you'd never gain more than a few characters anyway.
- If it's important that someone reading the code knows the type of the variable at a glance, use explicit typing.
- If the variable is directly initialized with a constructor and the type name is long (which often occurs with generics) consider using implicit typing.
- If the precise type of the variable isn't important, but its general nature is clear from the context, use implicit typing to deemphasize *how* the code achieves its aim and concentrate on the higher level of *what* it's achieving.

Effectively, my recommendation boils down to *not* using implicit typing either "because it's new" or for reasons of laziness, saving a few keystrokes. Where it keeps the code tidier, allowing you to concentrate on the most important elements of the code, go for it. I'll be using implicit typing extensively in the rest of the book, for the simple reason that code is harder to format in print than on a screen—there's not as much width available.

We'll come back to implicit typing when we see anonymous types, as they create situations where you are forced to ask the compiler to infer the types of some variables. Before that, let's have a look at how C#3 makes it easier to construct and populate a new object in one expression.

8.3 Simplified initialization

One would have thought that object-oriented languages would have streamlined object creation long ago. After all, before you start using an object, *something* has to create it, whether it's through your code directly or a factory method of some sort. And yet in C#2 very few language features are geared toward making life easier when it comes to initialization. If you can't do what you want using constructor arguments, you're basically out of luck—you need to create the object, then manually initialize it with property calls and the like.

This is particularly annoying when you want to create a whole bunch of objects in one go, such as in an array or other collection—without a "single expression" way of initializing an object, you're forced to either use local variables for temporary manipulation, or create a helper method that performs the appropriate initialization based on parameters.

C#3 comes to the rescue in a number of ways, as we'll see in this section.

8.3.1 Defining our sample types

The expressions we're going to be using in this section are called *object initializers*. These are just ways of specifying initialization that should occur after an object has been created. You can set properties, set properties of properties (don't worry, it's simpler than it sounds), and add to collections that are accessible via properties. To demonstrate all this, we'll use a `Person` class again. To start with, there's the name and age we've used before, exposed as writable properties. We'll provide both a parameterless constructor and one that accepts the name as a parameter. We'll also add a list of friends and the person's home location, both of which are accessible as read-only properties, but that can still be modified by manipulating the retrieved objects. A simple `Location` class provides `Country` and `Town` properties to represent the person's home. Listing 8.2 shows the complete code for the classes.

Listing 8.2 A fairly simple `Person` class used for further demonstrations

```
public class Person
{
    public int Age { get; set; }
    public string Name { get; set; }

    List<Person> friends = new List<Person>();
    public List<Person> Friends { get { return friends; } }

    Location home = new Location();
```

```
        public Location Home { get { return home; } }
        public Person() { }
        public Person(string name)
        {
            Name = name;
        }
    }
    public class Location
    {
        public string Country { get; set; }
        public string Town { get; set; }
    }
```

Listing 8.2 is straightforward, but it's worth noting that both the list of friends and the home location are created in a "blank" way when the person is created, rather than being left as just null references. That'll be important later on—but for the moment let's look at the properties representing the name and age of a person.

8.3.2   *Setting simple properties*

Now that we've got our Person type, we want to create some instances of it using the new features of C#3. In this section we'll look at setting the Name and Age properties—we'll come to the others later.

In fact, object initializers aren't restricted to using properties. All of the syntactic sugar here also applies to fields, but the vast majority of the time you'll be using properties. In a well-encapsulated system you're unlikely to have access to fields anyway, unless you're creating an instance of a type within that type's own code. It's worth knowing that you *can* use fields, of course—so for the rest of the section, just read *property and field* whenever the text says *property*.

With that out of the way, let's get down to business. Suppose we want to create a person called Tom, who is four years old. Prior to C#3, there are two ways this can be achieved:

```
Person tom1 = new Person();
tom1.Name = "Tom";
tom1.Age = 4;

Person tom2 = new Person("Tom");
tom2.Age = 4;
```

The first version simply uses the parameterless constructor and then sets both properties. The second version uses the constructor overload which sets the name, and then sets the age afterward. Both of these options are still available in C#3 of course, but there are other alternatives:

```
Person tom3 = new Person() { Name="Tom", Age=4 };

Person tom4 = new Person { Name="Tom", Age=4 };

Person tom5 = new Person("Tom") { Age = 4 };
```

The part in braces at the end of each line is the object initializer. Again, it's just compiler trickery. The IL used to initialize `tom3` and `tom4` is identical, and indeed it's very nearly[2] the same as we used for `tom1`. Predictably, the code for `tom5` is nearly the same as for `tom2`. Note how for `tom4` we omitted the parentheses for the constructor. You can use this shorthand for types with a parameterless constructor, which is what gets called in the compiled code.

After the constructor has been called, the specified properties are set in the obvious way. They're set in the order specified in the object initializer, and you can only specify any particular property at most once—you can't set the `Name` property twice, for example. (You could, however, call the constructor taking the name as a parameter, and then set the `Name` property. It would be pointless, but the compiler wouldn't stop you from doing it.) The expression used as the value for a property can be any expression that isn't itself an assignment—you can call methods, create new objects (potentially using another object initializer), pretty much anything.

You may well be wondering just how useful this is—we've saved one or two lines of code, but surely that's not a good enough reason to make the language more complicated, is it? There's a subtle point here, though: we've not just created an object in one *line*—we've created it in one *expression*. That difference can be very important. Suppose you want to create an array of type `Person[]` with some predefined data in it. Even without using the implicit array typing we'll see later, the code is neat and readable:

```
Person[] family = new Person[]
{
    new Person { Name="Holly", Age=31 },
    new Person { Name="Jon", Age=31 },
    new Person { Name="Tom", Age=4 },
    new Person { Name="William", Age=1 },
    new Person { Name="Robin", Age=1 }
};
```

Now, in a simple example like this we could have written a constructor taking both the name and age as parameters, and initialized the array in a similar way in C#1 or 2. However, appropriate constructors aren't always available—and if there are several constructor parameters, it's often not clear which one means what just from the position. By the time a constructor needs to take five or six parameters, I often find myself relying on IntelliSense more than I want to. Using the property names is a great boon to readability in such cases.

This form of object initializer is the one you'll probably use most often. However, there are two other forms—one for setting subproperties, and one for adding to collections. Let's look at subproperties—properties of properties—first.

---

[2] In fact, the variable's new value isn't assigned until all the properties have been set. A temporary local variable is used until then. This is very rarely noticeable, though, and where it is the code should probably be more straightforward anyway.

8.3.3   *Setting properties on embedded objects*

So far we've found it easy to set the Name and Age properties, but we can't set the Home property in the same way—it's read-only. However, we *can* set the town and the country of a person, by first fetching the Home property, and then setting properties on the result. The language specification refers to this as setting the properties of an *embedded object.* Just to make it clear, what we're talking about is the following C#1 code:

```
Person tom = new Person("Tom");
tom.Age = 4;
tom.Home.Country = "UK";
tom.Home.Town = "Reading";
```

When we're populating the home location, each statement is doing a get to retrieve the Location instance, and then a set on the relevant property on that instance. There's nothing new in that, but it's worth slowing your mind down to look at it carefully; otherwise, it's easy to miss what's going on behind the scenes.

C#3 allows all of this to be done in one expression, as shown here:

Looks like an assignment to Home, but it's not really!

```
Person tom = new Person("Tom")
{
    Age = 4,
    Home = { Country="UK", Town="Reading" }
};
```

The compiled code for these snippets is effectively the same. The compiler spots that to the right side of the = sign is another object initializer, and applies the properties to the embedded object appropriately. One point about the formatting I've used—just as in almost all C# features, it's whitespace independent: you can collapse the whitespace in the object initializer, putting it all on one line if you like. It's up to you to work out where the sweet spot is in balancing long lines against lots of lines.

The absence of the new keyword in the part initializing Home is significant. If you need to work out where the compiler is going to create new objects and where it's going to set properties on existing ones, look for occurrences of new in the initializer. Every time a new object is created, the new keyword appears *somewhere.*

We've dealt with the Home property—but what about Tom's friends? There are properties we can set on a List<Person>, but none of them will add entries to the list. It's time for the next feature—collection initializers.

8.3.4   *Collection initializers*

Creating a collection with some initial values is an extremely common task. Until C#3 arrived, the only language feature that gave any assistance was array creation—and even that was clumsy in many situations. C#3 has *collection initializers,* which allow you to use the same type of syntax as array initializers but with arbitrary collections and more flexibility.

CREATING NEW COLLECTIONS WITH COLLECTION INITIALIZERS

As a first example, let's use the now-familiar `List<T>` type. In C#2, you could populate a list either by passing in an existing collection, or by calling `Add` repeatedly after creating an empty list. Collection initializers in C#3 take the latter approach. Suppose we want to populate a list of strings with some names—here's the C#2 code (on the left) and the close equivalent in C#3 (on the right):

```
List<string> names = new List<string>();      var names = new List<string>
names.Add("Holly");                            {
names.Add("Jon");                                  "Holly", "Jon", "Tom",
names.Add("Tom");                                  "Robin", "William"
names.Add("Robin");                            };
names.Add("William");
```

Just as with object initializers, you can specify constructor parameters if you want, or use a parameterless constructor either explicitly or implicitly. Also as before, the decision about how much whitespace to use is entirely yours—in real code (where there's significantly more room than in a book), I might well have put the entire C#3 statement on one line. The use of implicit typing here was partly for space reasons—the names variable could equally well have been declared explicitly. Reducing the number of lines of code (without reducing readability) is nice, but there are two bigger benefits of collection initializers:

- The "create and initialize" part counts as a single expression.
- There's a lot less clutter in the code.

The first point becomes important when you want to use a collection as either an argument to a method or as one element in a larger collection. That happens *relatively* rarely (although often enough to still be useful)—but the second point is the real reason this is a killer feature in my view. If you look at the code on the right, you see the information you need, with each piece of information written only once. The variable name occurs once, the type being used occurs once, and each of the elements of the initialized collection appears once. It's all extremely simple, and much clearer than the C#2 code, which contains a lot of fluff around the *useful* bits.

Collection initializers aren't limited to just lists. You can use them with any type that implements `IEnumerable`, as long as it has an appropriate public `Add` method for each element in the initializer. You can use an `Add` method with more than one parameter by putting the values within another set of braces. The most common use for this is creating dictionaries. For example, if we wanted a dictionary mapping names to ages, we could use the following code:

```
Dictionary<string,int> nameAgeMap = new Dictionary<string,int>
{
    {"Holly", 31},
```

```
    {"Jon", 31},
    {"Tom", 4}
};
```

In this case, the `Add(string, int)` method would be called three times. If multiple `Add` overloads are available, different elements of the initializer can call different overloads. If no compatible overload is available for a specified element, the code will fail to compile. There are two interesting points about the design decision here:

- The fact that the type has to implement `IEnumerable` is never used by the compiler.
- The `Add` method is only found by name—there's no interface requirement specifying it.

These are both pragmatic decisions. Requiring `IEnumerable` to be implemented is a reasonable attempt to check that the type really is a collection of some sort, and using any public overload of the `Add` method (rather than requiring an exact signature) allows for simple initializations such as the earlier dictionary example. Nonpublic overloads, including those that explicitly implement an interface, are not used. This is a slightly different situation from object initializers setting properties, where internal properties are available too (within the same assembly, of course).

An early draft of the specification required `ICollection<T>` to be implemented instead, and the implementation of the single-parameter `Add` method (as specified by the interface) was called rather than allowing different overloads. This sounds more "pure," but there are far more types that implement `IEnumerable` than `ICollection<T>`—and using the single-parameter `Add` method would be inconvenient. For example, in our case it would have forced us to explicitly create an instance of a `KeyValuePair<string,int>` for each element of the initializer. Sacrificing a bit of academic purity has made the language far more useful in real life.

POPULATING COLLECTIONS WITHIN OTHER OBJECT INITIALIZERS

So far we've only seen collection initializers used in a stand-alone fashion to create whole new collections. They can also be combined with object initializers to populate embedded collections. To show this, we'll go back to our `Person` example. The `Friends` property is read-only, so we can't create a new collection and specify that as the collection of friends—but we *can* add to whatever collection is returned by the property's getter. The way we do this is similar to the syntax we've already seen for setting properties of embedded objects, but we just specify a collection initializer instead of a sequence of properties.

Let's see this in action by creating another `Person` instance for Tom, this time with friends (listing 8.3).

Listing 8.3 Building up a rich object using object and collection initializers

```
Person tom = new Person        ◁─────  Calls parameterless constructor
{
    Name = "Tom",                      │ Sets properties
    Age = 4,                           │ directly
```

```
       Home = { Town="Reading", Country="UK" },          ◁─────── Initializes
       Friends =                                                  embedded
       {                                                          object
          new Person { Name = "Phoebe" },
          new Person("Abi"),
          new Person { Name = "Ethan", Age = 4 },         Initializes collection
          new Person("Ben")                               with further object
          {                                               initializers
             Age = 4,
             Home = { Town = "Purley", Country="UK" }
          }
       }
    };
```

Listing 8.3 uses all the features of object and collection initializers we've come across. The main part of interest is the collection initializer, which itself uses all kinds of different forms of object initializers internally. Note that we're not specifying a type here as we did with the stand-alone collection creation: we're not creating a new collection, just adding to an existing one.

We could have gone further, specifying friends of friends, friends of friends of friends, and so forth. What we *couldn't* do with this syntax is specify that Tom is Ben's friend—while you're still initializing an object, you don't have access to it. This can be awkward in a few cases, but usually isn't a problem.

Collection initialization within object initializers works as a sort of cross between stand-alone collection initializers and setting embedded object properties. For each element in the collection initializer, the collection property getter (Friends in this case) is called, and then the appropriate Add method is called on the returned value. The collection isn't cleared in any way before elements are added. For example, if you were to decide that someone should always be their own friend, and added this to the list of friends within the Person constructor, using a collection initializer would only add extra friends.

As you can see, the combination of collection and object initializers can be used to populate whole trees of objects. But when and where is this likely to actually happen?

8.3.5 *Uses of initialization features*

Trying to pin down exactly where these features are useful is reminiscent of being in a Monty Python sketch about the Spanish Inquisition—every time you think you've got a reasonably complete list, another fairly common example pops up. I'll just mention three examples, which I hope will encourage you to consider where else *you* might use them.

"CONSTANT" COLLECTIONS

It's not uncommon for me to want some kind of collection (often a map) that is effectively constant. Of course, it can't be a constant as far as the C# language is concerned, but it *can* be declared static and read-only, with big warnings to say that it shouldn't be changed. (It's usually private, so that's good enough.) Typically, this involves creating a static constructor and often a helper method, just to populate the map. With C#3's collection initializers, it's easy to set the whole thing up inline.

SETTING UP UNIT TESTS

When writing unit tests, I frequently want to populate an object just for one test, often passing it in as a parameter to the method I'm trying to test at the time. This is particularly common with entity classes. Writing all of the initialization "long-hand" can be longwinded and also hides the essential structure of the object from the reader of the code, just as XML creation code can often obscure what the document would look like if you viewed it (appropriately formatted) in a text editor. With appropriate indentation of object initializers, the nested structure of the object hierarchy can become obvious in the very shape of the code, as well as make the values stand out more than they would otherwise.

PARAMETER ENCAPSULATION

Sometimes patterns occur in production code that can be aided by C#3's initialization features. For instance, rather than specifying several parameters to a single method, you can sometimes make code more straightforward by collecting the parameters together in an extra type. The framework `ProcessStartInfo` type is a good example of this—the designers *could* have overloaded `Process.Start` with many different sets of parameters, but using `ProcessStartInfo` makes everything clearer. C#3 allows you to create a `ProcessStartInfo` and fill in all the properties in a clearer manner—and you could even specify it inline in a call to `Process.Start`. In some ways, the method call would then act as if it had a lot of default parameters, with the properties providing the names of parameters you want to specify. It's worth considering this pattern when you find yourself using lots of parameters—it was always a useful technique to know about, but C#3 makes it that bit more elegant.

<INSERT YOUR FAVORITE USE HERE>

Of course, there are uses beyond these three in ordinary code, and I certainly don't want to put you off using the new features elsewhere. There's very little reason *not* to use them, other than possibly confusing developers who aren't familiar with C#3 yet. You may decide that using an object initializer just to set one property (as opposed to just explicitly setting it in a separate statement) is over the top—that's a matter of aesthetics, and I can't give you much guidance there. As with implicit typing, it's a good idea to try the code both ways, and learn to predict your own (and your team's) reading preferences.

So far we've looked at a fairly diverse range of features: implementing properties easily, simplifying local variable declarations, and populating objects in single expressions. In the remainder of this chapter we'll be gradually bringing these topics together, using more implicit typing and more object population, and creating whole *types* without giving any implementation details.

Our next topic appears to be quite similar to collection initializers when you look at code using it. I mentioned earlier that array initialization was a bit clumsy in C#1 and 2. I'm sure it won't surprise you to learn that it's been streamlined for C#3. Let's take a look.

8.4   *Implicitly typed arrays*

In C#1 and 2, initializing an array as part of a variable declaration and initialization statement was quite neat—but if you wanted to do it anywhere else, you had to specify the exact array type involved. So for example, this compiles without any problem:

```
string[] names = {"Holly", "Jon", "Tom", "Robin", "William"};
```

This doesn't work for parameters, though: suppose we want to make a call to MyMethod, declared as void MyMethod(string[] names). This code won't work:

INVALID
```
MyMethod({"Holly", "Jon", "Tom", "Robin", "William"});
```

Instead, you have to tell the compiler what type of array you want to initialize:

```
MyMethod(new string[] {"Holly", "Jon", "Tom", "Robin", "William"});
```

C#3 allows something in between:

```
MyMethod(new[] {"Holly", "Jon", "Tom", "Robin", "William"});
```

Clearly the compiler needs to work out what type of array to use. It starts by forming a set containing all the compile-time types of the expressions inside the braces. If there's exactly one type in that set that all the others can be implicitly converted to, that's the type of the array. Otherwise, (or if all the values are typeless expressions, such as constant null values or anonymous methods, with no casts) the code won't compile. Note that only the types of the expressions are considered as candidates for the overall array type. This means that occasionally you might have to explicitly cast a value to a *less* specific type. For instance, this won't compile:

INVALID
```
new[] { new MemoryStream(), new StringWriter() }
```

There's no conversion from MemoryStream to StringWriter, or vice versa. Both are implicitly convertible to object and IDisposable, but the compiler only considers types that are in the original set produced by the expressions themselves. If we change one of the expressions in this situation so that its type is either object or IDisposable, the code compiles:

```
new[] { (IDisposable) new MemoryStream(), new StringWriter() }
```

The type of this last expression is implicitly IDisposable[]. Of course, at that point you might as well explicitly state the type of the array just as you would in C#1 and 2, to make it clearer what you're trying to achieve.

Compared with the earlier features, implicitly typed arrays are a bit of an anticlimax. I find it hard to get particularly excited about them, even though they *do* make life that bit simpler in cases where an array is passed as a parameter. You could well argue that this feature doesn't prove itself in the "usefulness versus complexity" balance used by the language designers to decide what should be part of the language.

The designers haven't gone mad, however—there's one important situation in which this implicit typing is absolutely crucial. That's when you don't know (and indeed *can't* know) the name of the type of the elements of the array. How can you possibly get into this peculiar state? Read on...

8.5   Anonymous types

Implicit typing, object and collection initializers, and implicit array typing are all useful in their own right, to a greater or lesser extent. However, they all *really* serve a higher purpose—they make it possible to work with our final feature of the chapter, *anonymous types*. They, in turn, serve a higher purpose—LINQ.

8.5.1   First encounters of the anonymous kind

It's much easier to explain anonymous types when you've already got some idea of what they are through an example. I'm sorry to say that without the use of extension methods and lambda expressions, the examples in this section are likely to be a little contrived, but there's a distinct chicken-and-egg situation here: anonymous types are most useful within the context of the more advanced features, but we need to understand the building blocks before we can see much of the bigger picture. Stick with it—it *will* make sense in the long run, I promise.

Let's pretend we didn't have the `Person` class, and the only properties we cared about were the name and age. Listing 8.4 shows how we could still build objects with those properties, without ever declaring a type.

Listing 8.4   Creating objects of an anonymous type with `Name` and `Age` properties

```
var tom = new { Name = "Tom", Age = 4 };
var holly = new { Name = "Holly", Age = 31 };
var jon = new { Name = "Jon", Age = 31 };

Console.WriteLine("{0} is {1} years old", jon.Name, jon.Age);
```

As you can tell from listing 8.4, the syntax for initializing an anonymous type is similar to the object initializers we saw in section 8.3.2—it's just that the name of the type is missing between `new` and the opening brace. We're using implicitly typed local variables because that's all we *can* use—we don't have a type name to declare the variable with. As you can see from the last line, the type has properties for the `Name` and `Age`, both of which can be read and which will have the values specified in the *anonymous object initializer* used to create the instance—so in this case the output is "Jon is 31 years old." The properties have the same types as the expressions in the initializers—`string` for `Name`, and `int` for `Age`. Just as in normal object initializers, the expressions used in anonymous object initializers can call methods or constructors, fetch properties, perform calculations—whatever you need to do.

You may now be starting to see why implicitly typed arrays are important. Suppose we want to create an array containing the whole family, and then iterate through it to work out the total age. Listing 8.5 does just that—and demonstrates a few other interesting features of anonymous types at the same time.

Listing 8.5   Populating an array using anonymous types and then finding the total age

```
var family = new[]                      ◁——❶ Uses an implicitly typed array initializer
{
```

```
    new { Name = "Holly", Age = 31 },
    new { Name = "Jon", Age = 31 },              ❷  Uses same
    new { Name = "Tom", Age = 4 },                   anonymous type
    new { Name = "Robin", Age = 1 },                 five times
    new { Name = "William", Age = 1 }
};

int totalAge = 0;                            ❸  Uses implicit
foreach (var person in family)                   typing for person
{
    totalAge += person.Age;        ←——❹ Sums ages
}
Console.WriteLine("Total age: {0}", totalAge);
```

Putting together listing 8.5 and what we learned about implicitly typed arrays in section 8.4, we can deduce something very important: *all the people in the family are of the same type.* If each use of an anonymous object initializer in ❷ created a new type, there wouldn't be any appropriate type for the array declared at ❶. Within any given assembly, the compiler treats two anonymous object initializers as the same type if there are the same number of properties, with the same names and types, and they appear in the same order. In other words, if we swapped the Name and Age properties in one of the initializers, there'd be two different types involved—likewise if we introduced an extra property in one line, or used a long instead of an int for the age of one person, another anonymous type would have been introduced.

NOTE   *Implementation detail: how many types?*—If you ever decide to look at the IL (or decompiled C#) for an anonymous type, be aware that although two anonymous object initializers with the same property names in the same order but using different property types will produce two different types, they'll actually be generated from a single generic type. The generic type is parameterized, but the closed, constructed types will be different because they'll be given different type arguments for the different initializers.

Notice that we're able to use a foreach statement to iterate over the array just as we would any other collection. The type involved is inferred ❸, and the type of the person variable is the same anonymous type we've used in the array. Again, we can use the same variable for different instances because they're all of the same type.

Listing 8.5 also proves that the Age property really is strongly typed as an int—otherwise trying to sum the ages ❹ wouldn't compile. The compiler knows about the anonymous type, and Visual Studio 2008 is even willing to share the information via tooltips, just in case you're uncertain. Figure 8.3 shows the result of hovering over the person part of the person.Age expression from listing 8.5.

Now that we've seen anonymous types in action, let's go back and look at what the compiler is actually doing for us.

```
int totalAge = 0;
foreach (var person in family)
{
    totalAge += person.Age;
}                    ┌────────────────────────────────┐
                     │ (local variable) 'a person     │
                     │                                │
                     │ Anonymous Types:               │
                     │   'a is new { string Name, int Age }│
                     └────────────────────────────────┘
```

Figure 8.3   Hovering over a variable that is declared (implicitly) to be of an anonymous type shows the details of that anonymous type.

8.5.2   *Members of anonymous types*

Anonymous types are created by the compiler and included in the compiled assembly in the same way as the extra types for anonymous methods and iterator blocks. The CLR treats them as perfectly ordinary types, and so they are—if you later move from an anonymous type to a normal, manually coded type with the behavior described in this section, you shouldn't see anything change. Anonymous types contain the following members:

- A constructor taking all the initialization values. The parameters are in the same order as they were specified in the anonymous object initializer, and have the same names and types.
- Public read-only properties.
- Private read-only fields backing the properties.
- Overrides for `Equals`, `GetHashCode`, and `ToString`.

That's it—there are no implemented interfaces, no cloning or serialization capabilities—just a constructor, some properties and the normal methods from `object`.

The constructor and the properties do the obvious things. Equality between two instances of the same anonymous type is determined in the natural manner, comparing each property value in turn using the property type's `Equals` method. The hash code generation is similar, calling `GetHashCode` on each property value in turn and combining the results. The exact method for combining the various hash codes together to form one "composite" hash is unspecified, and you shouldn't write code that depends on it anyway—all you need to be confident in is that two equal instances will return the same hash, and two unequal instances will *probably* return different hashes. All of this only works if the `Equals` and `GetHashCode` implementations of all the different types involved as properties conform to the normal rules, of course.

Note that because the properties are read-only, all anonymous types are immutable so long as the types used for their properties are immutable. This provides you with all the normal benefits of immutability—being able to pass values to methods without fear of them changing, simple sharing of data across threads, and so forth.

We're almost done with anonymous types now. However, there's one slight wrinkle still to talk about—a shortcut for a situation that is fairly common in LINQ.

8.5.3   *Projection initializers*

The anonymous object initializers we've seen so far have all been lists of name/value pairs—`Name = "Jon"`, `Age=31` and the like. As it happens, I've always used constants because they make for smaller examples, but in real code you often want to copy properties from an existing object. Sometimes you'll want to manipulate the values in some way, but often a straight copy is enough.

Again, without LINQ it's hard to give convincing examples of this, but let's go back to our `Person` class, and just *suppose* we had a good reason to want to convert a collection of `Person` instances into a similar collection where each element has just a name, and a flag to say whether or not that person is an adult. Given an appropriate `person` variable, we could use something like this:

```
new { Name = person.Name, IsAdult = (person.Age >= 18) }
```

That certainly works, and for just a single property the syntax for setting the name (the part in bold) is not too clumsy—but if you were copying several properties it would get tiresome. C#3 provides a shortcut: if you don't specify the property name, but just the expression to evaluate for the value, it will use the last part of the expression as the name—provided it's a simple field or property. This is called a *projection initializer*. It means we can rewrite the previous code as

```
new { person.Name, IsAdult = (person.Age >= 18) }
```

It's quite common for all the bits of an anonymous object initializer to be projection initializers—it typically happens when you're taking some properties from one object and some properties from another, often as part of a join operation. Anyway, I'm getting ahead of myself. Listing 8.6 shows the previous code in action, using the `List.ConvertAll` method and an anonymous delegate.

Listing 8.6 Transformation from `Person` to a name and adulthood flag

```
List<Person> family = new List<Person>
{
    new Person {Name="Holly", Age=31},
    new Person {Name="Jon", Age=31},
    new Person {Name="Tom", Age=4},
    new Person {Name="Robin", Age=1},
    new Person {Name="William", Age=1}
};

var converted = family.ConvertAll(delegate(Person person)
    { return new { person.Name, IsAdult = (person.Age >= 18) }; }
);

foreach (var person in converted)
{
    Console.WriteLine("{0} is an adult? {1}",
                      person.Name, person.IsAdult);
}
```

In addition to the use of a projection initializer for the `Name` property, listing 8.6 shows the value of delegate type inference and anonymous methods. Without them, we couldn't have retained our strong typing of `converted`, as we wouldn't have been able to specify what the `TOutput` type parameter of `Converter` should be. As it is, we can iterate through the new list and access the `Name` and `IsAdult` properties as if we were using any other type.

Don't spend too long thinking about projection initializers at this point—the important thing is to be aware that they exist, so you won't get confused when you see them later. In fact, that advice applies to this entire section on anonymous types—so without going into details, let's look at why they're present at all.

8.5.4 What's the point?

I hope you're not feeling cheated at this point, but I sympathize if you do. Anonymous types are a fairly complex solution to a problem we haven't really encountered yet... except that I bet you *have* seen part of the problem before, really.

If you've ever done any real-life work involving databases, you'll know that you don't always want all of the data that's available on all the rows that match your query criteria. Often it's not a problem to fetch more than you need, but if you only need two columns out of the fifty in the table, you wouldn't bother to select all fifty, would you?

The same problem occurs in nondatabase code. Suppose we have a class that reads a log file and produces a sequence of log lines with many fields. Keeping all of the information might be far too memory intensive if we only care about a couple of fields from the log. LINQ lets you filter that information easily.

But what's the result of that filtering? How can we keep some data and discard the rest? How can we easily keep some *derived* data that isn't directly represented in the original form? How can we combine pieces of data that may not initially have been consciously associated, or that may only have a relationship in a particular situation? Effectively, we want a new data type—but manually creating such a type in every situation is tedious, particularly when you have tools such as LINQ available that make the rest of the process so simple. Figure 8.4 shows the three elements that make anonymous types a powerful feature.

If you find yourself creating a type that is only used in a single method, and that only contains fields and trivial properties, consider whether an anonymous type would be appropriate. Even if you're not developing in C# 3 yet, keep an eye out for places where it might be worth using an anonymous type when you upgrade. The more you think about this sort of feature, the easier the decisions about when to use it will become. I suspect that you'll find that most of the times when you find yourself leaning toward anonymous types, you could also use LINQ to help you—look out for that too.

If you find yourself using the same sequence of properties for the same purpose in several places, however, you might want to consider creating a normal type for the purpose, even if it still just contains trivial properties. Anonymous types naturally "infect" whatever code they're used in with implicit typing—which is often fine, but can be a nuisance at other times. As with the previous features, use anonymous types when they genuinely make the code simpler to work with, not just because they're new and cool.

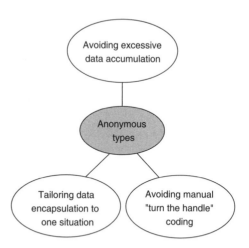

Figure 8.4 Anonymous types allow you to keep just the data you need for a particular situation, in a form that is tailored to that situation, without the tedium of writing a fresh type each time.

8.6 *Summary*

What a seemingly mixed bag of features! We've seen four features that are quite similar, at least in syntax: object initializers, collection initializers, implicitly typed arrays, and anonymous types. The other two features—automatic properties and implicitly typed local variables—are somewhat different. Likewise, most of the features would have been useful individually in C#2, whereas implicitly typed arrays and anonymous types only pay back the cost of learning about them when the rest of the C#3 features are brought into play.

So what do these features really have in common? *They all relieve the developer of tedious coding.* I'm sure you don't enjoy writing trivial properties any more than I do, or setting several properties, one at a time, using a local variable—particularly when you're trying to build up a collection of similar objects. Not only do the new features of C#3 make it easier to *write* the code, they also make it easier to *read* it too, at least when they're applied sensibly.

In our next chapter we'll look at a major new language feature, along with a framework feature it provides direct support for. If you thought anonymous methods made creating delegates easy, just wait until you see lambda expressions…

Lambda expressions
and expression trees

In chapter 5 we saw how C#2 made delegates much easier to use due to implicit conversions of method groups, anonymous methods, and return type and parameter covariance. This is enough to make event subscription significantly simpler and more readable, but delegates in C#2 are still too bulky to be used all the time: a page of code full of anonymous methods is quite painful to read, and you certainly wouldn't want to start putting multiple anonymous methods in a single statement on a regular basis.

One of the fundamental building blocks of LINQ is the ability to create pipelines of operations, along with any state required by those operations. These operations express all kinds of logic about data: how to filter it, how to order it, how to join different data sources together, and much more. When LINQ queries are executed "in process," those operations are usually represented by delegates.

Statements containing several delegates are common when manipulating data with LINQ to Objects,[1] and *lambda expressions* in C#3 make all of this possible without sacrificing readability. (While I'm mentioning readability, this chapter uses *lambda expression* and *lambda* interchangeably; as I need to refer to *normal* expressions quite a lot, it helps to use the short version in many cases.)

> **NOTE** *It's all Greek to me*—The term *lambda expression* comes from lambda calculus, also written as λ-calculus, where λ is the Greek letter lambda. This is an area of math and computer science dealing with defining and applying functions. It's been around for a long time and is the basis of functional languages such as ML. The good news is that you don't need to know lambda calculus to use lambda expressions in C#3.

Executing delegates is only part of the LINQ story. To use databases and other query engines efficiently, we need a different representation of the operations in the pipeline: a way of treating code as data that can be examined programmatically. The logic within the operations can then be transformed into a different form, such as a web service call, a SQL or LDAP query—whatever is appropriate.

Although it's possible to build up representations of queries in a particular API, it's usually tricky to read and sacrifices a lot of compiler support. This is where lambdas save the day again: not only can they be used to create delegate instances, but the C# compiler can also transform them into *expression trees*—data structures representing the logic of the lambda expressions so that other code can examine it. In short, lambda expressions are the idiomatic way of representing the operations in LINQ data pipelines—but we'll be taking things one step at a time, examining them in a fairly isolated way before we embrace the whole of LINQ.

In this chapter we'll look at both ways of using lambda expressions, although for the moment our coverage of expression trees will be relatively basic—we're not going to actually create any SQL just yet. However, with the theory under your belt you should be relatively comfortable with lambda expressions and expression trees by the time we hit the really impressive stuff in chapter 12.

In the final part of this chapter, we'll examine how type inference has changed for C#3, mostly due to lambdas with implicit parameter types. This is a bit like learning how to tie shoelaces: far from exciting, but without this ability you'll trip over yourself when you start running.

Let's begin by seeing what lambda expressions look like. We'll start with an anonymous method and gradually transform it into shorter and shorter forms.

---

[1] LINQ to Objects is the LINQ provider in .NET 3.5 that handles sequences of data within the same process. By contrast, providers such as LINQ to SQL offload the work to other "out of process" systems—databases, for example.

9.1   Lambda expressions as delegates

In many ways, lambda expressions can be seen as an evolution of anonymous methods from C#2. There's almost nothing that an anonymous method can do that can't be done using a lambda expression, and it's almost always more readable and compact using lambdas. In particular, the behavior of captured variables is exactly the same in lambda expressions as in anonymous methods. In their most explicit form, not much difference exists between the two—but lambda expressions have a lot of shortcuts available to make them compact in common situations. Like anonymous methods, lambda expressions have special conversion rules—the type of the expression isn't a delegate type in itself, but it can be converted into a delegate instance in various ways, both implicitly and explicitly. The term *anonymous function* covers anonymous methods and lambda expressions—in many cases the same conversion rules apply to both of them.

We're going to start with a very simple example, initially expressed as an anonymous method. We'll create a delegate instance that takes a `string` parameter and returns an `int` (which is the length of the string). First we need to choose a delegate type to use; fortunately, .NET 3.5 comes with a whole family of generic delegate types to help us out.

9.1.1   Preliminaries: introducing the Func<...> delegate types

There are five generic `Func` delegate types in the `System` namespace of .NET 3.5. There's nothing special about `Func`—it's just handy to have some predefined generic types that are capable of handling many situations. Each delegate signature takes between zero and four parameters, the types of which are specified as type parameters. The last type parameter is used for the return type in each case. Here are the signatures of all the `Func` delegate types:

```
public delegate TResult Func<TResult>()

public delegate TResult Func<T,TResult>(T arg)

public delegate TResult Func<T1,T2,TResult>(T1 arg1, T2 arg2)

public delegate TResult Func<T1,T2,T3,TResult>
    (T1 arg1, T2 arg2, T3 arg3)

public delegate TResult Func<T1,T2,T3,T4,TResult>
    (T1 arg1, T2 arg2, T3 arg3, T4 arg4)
```

For example, `Func<string,double,int>` is equivalent to a delegate type of the form

```
delegate int SomeDelegate(string arg1, double arg2)
```

The `Action<...>` set of delegates provide the equivalent functionality when you want a void return type. The single parameter form of `Action` existed in .NET 2.0, but the rest are new to .NET 3.5. For our example we need a type that takes a `string` parameter and returns an `int`, so we'll use `Func<string,int>`.

9.1.2   First transformation to a lambda expression

Now that we know the delegate type, we can use an anonymous method to create our delegate instance. Listing 9.1 shows this, along with executing the delegate instance afterward so we can see it working.

Listing 9.1 Using an anonymous method to create a delegate instance

```
Func<string,int> returnLength;
returnLength = delegate (string text) { return text.Length; };

Console.WriteLine (returnLength("Hello"));
```

Listing 9.1 prints "5," just as we'd expect it to. I've separated out the declaration of returnLength from the assignment to it so we can keep it on one line—it's easier to keep track of that way. The anonymous method expression is the part in bold, and that's the part we're going to convert into a lambda expression.

The most long-winded form of a lambda expression is this:

```
(explicitly-typed-parameter-list) => { statements }
```

The => part is new to C#3 and tells the compiler that we're using a lambda expression. Most of the time lambda expressions are used with a delegate type that has a nonvoid return type—the syntax is slightly less intuitive when there isn't a result. This is another indication of the changes in idiom between C#1 and C#3. In C#1, delegates were usually used for events and rarely returned anything. Although lambda expressions certainly *can* be used in this way (and we'll show an example of this later), much of their elegance comes from the shortcuts that are available when they need to return a value.

With the explicit parameters and statements in braces, this version looks very similar to an anonymous method. Listing 9.2 is equivalent to listing 9.1 but uses a lambda expression.

Listing 9.2 A long-winded first lambda expression, similar to an anonymous method

```
Func<string,int> returnLength;
returnLength = (string text) => { return text.Length; };

Console.WriteLine (returnLength("Hello"));
```

Again, I've used bold to indicate the expression used to create the delegate instance. When reading lambda expressions, it helps to think of the => part as "goes to"—so the example in listing 9.2 could be read as "text goes to text.Length." As this is the only part of the listing that is interesting for a while, I'll show it alone from now on. You can replace the bold text from listing 9.2 with any of the lambda expressions listed in this section and the result will be the same.

The same rules that govern return statements in anonymous methods apply to lambdas too: you can't try to return a value from a lambda expression with a void return type, whereas if there's a nonvoid return type every code path has to return a compatible value.[2] It's all pretty intuitive and rarely gets in the way.

So far, we haven't saved much space or made things particularly easy to read. Let's start applying the shortcuts.

---

[2] Code paths throwing exceptions don't need to return a value, of course, and neither do detectable infinite loops.

9.1.3   *Using a single expression as the body*

The form we've seen so far uses a full block of code to return the value. This is very flexible—you can have multiple statements, perform loops, return from different places in the block, and so on, just as with anonymous methods. Most of the time, however, you can easily express the whole of the body in a single expression, the value of which is the result of the lambda. In these cases, you can specify just that expression, without any braces, return statements, or semicolons. The format then is

```
(explicitly-typed-parameter-list) => expression
```

In our case, this means that the lambda expression becomes

```
(string text) => text.Length
```

That's starting to look simpler already. Now, what about that parameter type? The compiler already knows that instances of Func<string,int> take a single string parameter, so we should be able to just name that parameter...

9.1.4   *Implicitly typed parameter lists*

Most of the time, the compiler can guess the parameter types without you explicitly stating them. In these cases, you can write the lambda expression as

```
(implicitly-typed-parameter-list) => expression
```

An implicitly typed parameter list is just a comma-separated list of names, without the types. You can't mix and match for different parameters—either the whole list is explicitly typed, or it's all implicitly typed. Also, if any of the parameters are out or ref parameters, you are forced to use explicit typing. In our case, however, it's fine—so our lambda expression is now just

```
(text) => text.Length
```

That's getting pretty short now—there's not a lot more we could get rid of. The parentheses seem a bit redundant, though.

9.1.5   *Shortcut for a single parameter*

When the lambda expression only needs a single parameter, and that parameter can be implicitly typed, C#3 allows us to omit the parentheses, so it now has this form:

```
parameter-name => expression
```

The final form of our lambda expression is therefore

```
text => text.Length
```

You may be wondering why there are so many special cases with lambda expressions—none of the rest of the language cares whether a method has one parameter or more, for instance. Well, what sounds like a very particular case actually turns out to be *extremely* common, and the improvement in readability from removing the parentheses from the parameter list can be significant when there are many lambdas in a short piece of code.

It's worth noting that you can put parentheses around the whole lambda expression if you want to, just like other expressions. Sometimes this helps readability in the case where you're assigning the lambda to a variable or property—otherwise, the equals symbols can get confusing. Listing 9.3 shows this in the context of our original code.

Listing 9.3 A concise lambda expression, bracketed for clarity

```
Func<string,int> returnLength;
returnLength = (text => text.Length);

Console.WriteLine (returnLength("Hello"));
```

At first you may find listing 9.3 a bit confusing to read, in the same way that anonymous methods appear strange to many developers until they get used to them. When you *are* used to lambda expressions, however, you can appreciate how concise they are. It would be hard to imagine a shorter, clearer way of creating a delegate instance.[3] We could have changed the variable name text to something like x, and in full LINQ that's often useful, but longer names give a bit more information to the reader.

The decision of whether to use the short form for the body of the lambda expression, specifying just an expression instead of a whole block, is completely independent from the decision about whether to use explicit or implicit parameters. We happen to have gone down one route of shortening the lambda, but we could have started off by making the parameters implicit.

NOTE   *Higher-order functions*—The body of a lambda expression can itself contain a lambda expression—and it tends to be as confusing as it sounds. Alternatively, the parameter to a lambda expression can be another delegate, which is just as bad. Both of these are examples of *higher-order functions*. If you enjoy feeling dazed and confused, have a look at some of the sample code in the downloadable source. Although I'm being flippant, this approach is common in functional programming and can be very useful. It just takes a certain degree of perseverance to get into the right mind-set.

So far we've only dealt with a single lambda expression, just putting it into different forms. Let's take a look at a few examples to make things more concrete before we examine the details.

9.2 *Simple examples using List<T> and events*

When we look at extension methods in chapter 10, we'll use lambda expressions all the time. Until then, List<T> and event handlers give us the best examples. We'll start off with lists, using automatically implemented properties, implicitly typed local variables, and collection initializers for the sake of brevity. We'll then call methods that take delegate parameters—using lambda expressions to create the delegates, of course.

---

[3] That's not to say it's impossible, however. Some languages allow closures to be represented as simple blocks of code with a magic variable name to represent the common case of a single parameter.

9.2.1 *Filtering, sorting, and actions on lists*

If you remember the FindAll method on List<T>, it takes a Predicate<T> and returns a new list with all the elements from the original list that match the predicate. The Sort method takes a Comparison<T> and sorts the list accordingly. Finally, the ForEach method takes an Action<T> to perform on each element. Listing 9.4 uses lambda expressions to provide the delegate instance to each of these methods. The sample data in question is just the name and year of release for various films. We print out the original list, then create and print out a filtered list of only old films, then sort and print out the original list, ordered by name. (It's interesting to consider how much more code would have been required to do the same thing in C#1, by the way.)

Listing 9.4   Manipulating a list of films using lambda expressions

```
class Film
{
    public string Name { get; set; }
    public int Year { get; set; }
    public override string ToString()
    {
        return string.Format("Name={0}, Year={1}", Name, Year);
    }
}
...
var films = new List<Film>
{
    new Film {Name="Jaws", Year=1975},
    new Film {Name="Singing in the Rain", Year=1952},
    new Film {Name="Some Like It Hot", Year=1959},
    new Film {Name="The Wizard of Oz", Year=1939},
    new Film {Name="It's a Wonderful Life", Year=1946},
    new Film {Name="American Beauty", Year=1999},
    new Film {Name="High Fidelity", Year=2000},
    new Film {Name="The Usual Suspects", Year=1995}
};

Action<Film> print = film => Console.WriteLine(film);       ➊ Creates reusable list-printing delegate

films.ForEach(print);                      ➋ Prints original list

films.FindAll(film => film.Year < 1960)    ➌ Creates filtered list
     .ForEach(print);

films.Sort((f1, f2) => f1.Name.CompareTo(f2.Name));   ➍ Sorts original list
films.ForEach(print);
```

The first half of listing 9.4 involves just setting up the data. I would have used an anonymous type, but it's *relatively* tricky to create a generic list from a collection of anonymous type instances. (You can do it by creating a generic method that takes an array and converts it to a list of the same type, then pass an implicitly typed array into that method. An extension method in .NET 3.5 called ToList provides this functionality too, but that would be cheating as we haven't looked at extension methods yet!)

Before we use the newly created list, we create a delegate instance ❶, which we'll use to print out the items of the list. We use this delegate instance three times, which is why I've created a variable to hold it rather than using a separate lambda expression each time. It just prints a single element, but by passing it into List<T>.ForEach we can simply dump the whole list to the console.

The first list we print out ❷ is just the original one without any modifications. We then find all the films in our list that were made before 1960 and print those out ❸. This is done with another lambda expression, which is executed for each film in the list—it only has to determine whether or not a single film should be included in the filtered list. The source code uses the lambda expression as a method argument, but really the compiler has created a method like this:

```
private static bool SomeAutoGeneratedName(Film film)
{
    return film.Year < 1960;
}
```

The method call to FindAll is then effectively this:

```
films.FindAll(new Predicate<Film>(SomeAutoGeneratedName))
```

The lambda expression support here is just like the anonymous method support in C#2; it's all cleverness on the part of the compiler. (In fact, the Microsoft compiler is even smarter in this case—it realizes it can get away with reusing the delegate instance if the code is ever called again, so caches it.)

The sort ❹ is also performed using a lambda expression, which compares any two films using their names. I have to confess that explicitly calling CompareTo ourselves is a bit ugly. In the next chapter we'll see how the OrderBy extension method allows us to express ordering in a neater way.

Let's look at a different example, this time using lambda expressions with event handling.

9.2.2   Logging in an event handler

If you think back to chapter 5, in listing 5.9 we saw an easy way of using anonymous methods to log which events were occurring—but we were only able to get away with a compact syntax because we didn't mind losing the parameter information. What if we wanted to log both the nature of the event *and* information about its sender and arguments? Lambda expressions enable this in a very neat way, as shown in listing 9.5.

Listing 9.5   Logging events using lambda expressions

```
static void Log(string title, object sender, EventArgs e)
{
    Console.WriteLine("Event: {0}", title);
    Console.WriteLine("  Sender: {0}", sender);
    Console.WriteLine("  Arguments: {0}", e.GetType());
    foreach (PropertyDescriptor prop in
            TypeDescriptor.GetProperties(e))
```

```
    {
        string name = prop.DisplayName;
        object value = prop.GetValue(e);
        Console.WriteLine("    {0}={1}", name, value);
    }
}
...
Button button = new Button();
button.Text = "Click me";
button.Click       += (src, e) => Log("Click", src, e);
button.KeyPress    += (src, e) => Log("KeyPress", src, e);
button.MouseClick += (src, e) => Log("MouseClick", src, e);

Form form = new Form();
form.AutoSize=true;
form.Controls.Add(button);
Application.Run(form);
```

Listing 9.5 uses lambda expressions to pass the event name *and parameters* to the Log method, which logs details of the event. We don't log the details of the event source, beyond whatever its ToString override returns, because there's an overwhelming amount of information associated with controls. However, we use reflection over property descriptors to show the details of the EventArgs instance passed to us. Here's some sample output when you click the button:

```
Event: Click
  Sender: System.Windows.Forms.Button, Text: Click me
  Arguments: System.Windows.Forms.MouseEventArgs
    Button=Left
    Clicks=1
    X=53
    Y=17
    Delta=0
    Location={X=53,Y=17}
Event: MouseClick
  Sender: System.Windows.Forms.Button, Text: Click me
  Arguments: System.Windows.Forms.MouseEventArgs
    Button=Left
    Clicks=1
    X=53
    Y=17
    Delta=0
    Location={X=53,Y=17}
```

All of this is *possible* without lambda expressions, of course—but it's a lot neater than it would have been otherwise. Now that we've seen lambdas being converted into delegate instances, it's time to look at expression trees, which represent lambda expressions as data instead of code.

9.3   *Expression trees*

The idea of "code as data" is an old one, but it hasn't been used much in popular programming languages. You could argue that all .NET programs use the concept, because the IL code is treated as data by the JIT, which then converts it into native code to run on your CPU. That's quite deeply hidden, though, and while libraries exist to manipulate IL programmatically, they're not widely used.

Expression trees in .NET 3.5 provide an abstract way of representing some code as a tree of objects. It's like CodeDOM but operating at a slightly higher level, and only for expressions. The primary use of expression trees is in LINQ, and later in this section we'll see how crucial expression trees are to the whole LINQ story.

C# 3 provides built-in support for converting lambda expressions to expression trees, but before we cover that let's explore how they fit into the .NET Framework without using any compiler tricks.

9.3.1 *Building expression trees programmatically*

Expression trees aren't as mystical as they sound, although some of the uses they're put to look like magic. As the name suggests, they're trees of objects, where each node in the tree is an expression in itself. Different types of expressions represent the different operations that can be performed in code: binary operations, such as addition; unary operations, such as taking the length of an array; method calls; constructor calls; and so forth.

The `System.Linq.Expressions` namespace contains the various classes that represent expressions. All of them derive from the `Expression` class, which is abstract and mostly consists of static factory methods to create instances of other expression classes. It exposes two properties, however:

- The `Type` property represents the .NET type of the evaluated expression—you can think of it like a return type. The type of an expression that fetches the `Length` property of a string would be `int`, for example.
- The `NodeType` property returns the kind of expression represented, as a member of the `ExpressionType` enumeration, with values such as `LessThan`, `Multiply`, and `Invoke`. To use the same example, in `myString.Length` the property access part would have a node type of `MemberAccess`.

There are many classes derived from `Expression`, and some of them can have many different node types: `BinaryExpression`, for instance, represents any operation with two operands: arithmetic, logic, comparisons, array indexing, and the like. This is where the `NodeType` property is important, as it distinguishes between different kinds of expressions that are represented by the same class.

I don't intend to cover every expression class or node type—there are far too many, and MSDN does a perfectly good job of explaining them. Instead, we'll try to get a general feel for what you can do with expression trees.

Let's start off by creating one of the simplest possible expression trees, adding two constant integers together. Listing 9.6 creates an expression tree to represent 2+3.

Listing 9.6   A very simple expression tree, adding 2 and 3

```
Expression firstArg = Expression.Constant(2);
Expression secondArg = Expression.Constant(3);
Expression add = Expression.Add(firstArg, secondArg);

Console.WriteLine(add);
```

Running listing 9.6 will produce the output "(2 + 3)," which demonstrates that the various expression classes override ToString to produce human-readable output. Figure 9.1 depicts the tree generated by the code.

It's worth noting that the "leaf" expressions are created first in the code: you build expressions from the bottom up. This is enforced by the fact that expressions are immutable—once you've created an expression, it will never change, so you can cache and reuse expressions at will.

Now that we've built up an expression tree, let's try to actually execute it.

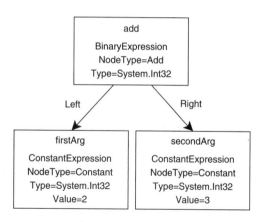

Figure 9.1   Graphical representation of the expression tree created by listing 9.6

9.3.2   *Compiling expression trees into delegates*

One of the types derived from Expression is LambdaExpression. The generic class Expression<TDelegate> then derives from LambdaExpression. It's all slightly confusing—figure 9.2 shows the type hierarchy to make things clearer.

The difference between Expression and Expression<TDelegate> is that the generic class is statically typed to indicate what kind of expression it is, in terms of return type and parameters. Fairly obviously, this is expressed by the TDelegate type parameter, which must be a delegate type. For instance, our simple addition expression is one that takes no parameters and returns an integer—this is matched by the signature of Func<int>, so we could use an Expression<Func<int>> to represent the expression in a statically typed manner. We do this using the Expression.Lambda method. This has a number of overloads—our examples use the generic method, which uses a type parameter to indicate the type of delegate we want to represent. See MSDN for alternatives.

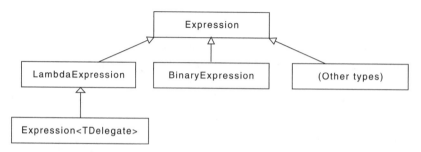

Figure 9.2   Type hierarchy from Expression<TDelegate> up to Expression

So, what's the point of doing this? Well, `LambdaExpression` has a `Compile` method that creates a delegate of the appropriate type. This delegate can now be executed in the normal manner, as if it had been created using a normal method or any other means. Listing 9.7 shows this in action, with the same expression as before.

Listing 9.7 Compiling and executing an expression tree

```
Expression firstArg = Expression.Constant(2);
Expression secondArg = Expression.Constant(3);
Expression add = Expression.Add(firstArg, secondArg);

Func<int> compiled = Expression.Lambda<Func<int>>(add).Compile();
Console.WriteLine(compiled());
```

Arguably listing 9.7 is one of the most convoluted ways of printing out "5" that you could ask for. At the same time, it's also rather impressive. We're programmatically creating some logical blocks and representing them as normal objects, and then asking the framework to compile the whole thing into "real" code that can be executed. You may never need to actually use expression trees this way, or even build them up programmatically at all, but it's useful background information that will help you understand how LINQ works.

As I said at the beginning of this section, expression trees are not too far removed from CodeDOM—Snippy compiles and executes C# code that has been entered as plain text, for instance. However, two significant differences exist between CodeDOM and expression trees.

First, expression trees are only able to represent single expressions. They're not designed for whole classes, methods, or even just statements. Second, C# supports expression trees directly in the language, through lambda expressions. Let's take a look at that now.

9.3.3 *Converting C# lambda expressions to expression trees*

As we've already seen, lambda expressions can be converted to appropriate delegate instances, either implicitly or explicitly. That's not the only conversion that is available, however. You can also ask the compiler to build an expression tree from your lambda expression, creating an instance of `Expression<TDelegate>` at execution time. For example, listing 9.8 shows a much shorter way of creating the "return 5" expression, compiling it and then invoking the resulting delegate.

Listing 9.8 Using lambda expressions to create expression trees

```
Expression<Func<int>> return5 = () => 5;
Func<int> compiled = return5.Compile();
Console.WriteLine(compiled());
```

In the first line of listing 9.8, the `()` `=>` `5` part is the lambda expression. In this case, putting it in an extra pair of parentheses around the whole thing makes it look worse rather than better. Notice that we don't need any casts because the compiler can verify everything as it goes. We could have written 2+3 instead of 5, but the compiler would have optimized the addition away for us. The important point to take away is that the lambda expression has been converted into an expression tree.

NOTE   *There* are *limitations*—Not *all* lambda expressions can be converted to expression trees. You can't convert a lambda with a block of statements (even just one return statement) into an expression tree—it has to be in the form that just evaluates a single expression. That expression can't contain assignments, as they can't be represented in expression trees. Although these are the most common restrictions, they're not the only ones—the full list is not worth describing here, as this issue comes up so rarely. If there's a problem with an attempted conversion, you'll find out at compile time.

Let's take a look at a more complicated example just to see how things work, particularly with respect to parameters. This time we'll write a predicate that takes two strings and checks to see if the first one begins with the second. The code is simple when written as a lambda expression, as shown in listing 9.9.

Listing 9.9   Demonstration of a more complicated expression tree

```
Expression<Func<string,string,bool>> expression =
    ( (x,y) => x.StartsWith(y) );

var compiled = expression.Compile();

Console.WriteLine(compiled("First", "Second"));
Console.WriteLine(compiled("First", "Fir"));
```

The expression tree itself is more complicated, especially by the time we've converted it into an instance of LambdaExpression. Listing 9.10 shows how it's built in code.

Listing 9.10   Building a method call expression tree in code

```
MethodInfo method = typeof(string).GetMethod
    ("StartsWith", new[] { typeof(string) });          ❶ Builds up
var target = Expression.Parameter(typeof(string), "x");    parts of
var methodArg = Expression.Parameter(typeof(string), "y"); method call
Expression[] methodArgs = new[] { methodArg };

Expression call = Expression.Call           ❷ Creates CallExpression
    (target, method, methodArgs);              from parts

var lambdaParameters = new[] { target, methodArg };  ❸ Converts call
var lambda = Expression.Lambda<Func<string,string,bool>>  into Lambda-
    (call, lambdaParameters);                            Expression

var compiled = lambda.Compile();

Console.WriteLine(compiled("First", "Second"));
Console.WriteLine(compiled("First", "Fir"));
```

As you can see, listing 9.10 is considerably more involved than the version with the C# lambda expression. However, it does make it more obvious exactly what is involved in the tree and how parameters are bound. We start off by working out everything we need to know about the method call that forms the body of the final expression ❶: the target of the method (in other words, the string we're calling `StartsWith` on); the method itself (as a `MethodInfo`); and the list of arguments (in this case, just the one). It so happens that our method target and argument will both be parameters passed into the expression, but they could be other types of expressions—constants, the results of other method calls, property evaluations, and so forth.

After building the method call as an expression ❷, we then need to convert it into a lambda expression ❸, binding the parameters as we go. We reuse the same `ParameterExpression` values we created as information for the method call: the order in which they're specified when creating the lambda expression is the order in which they'll be picked up when we eventually call the delegate.

Figure 9.3 shows the same final expression tree graphically. To be picky, even though it's still called an expression tree, the fact that we reuse the parameter expressions (and we have to—creating a new one with the same name and attempting to bind parameters that way causes an exception at execution time) means that it's not a tree anymore.

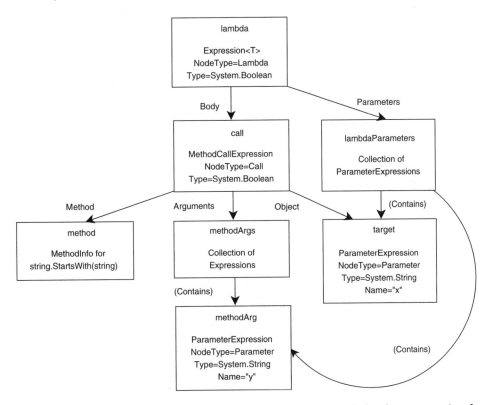

Figure 9.3 Graphical representation of expression tree that calls a method and uses parameters from a lambda expression

Glancing at the complexity of figure 9.3 and listing 9.10 without trying to look at the details, you'd be forgiven for thinking that we were doing something really complicated when in fact it's just a single method call. Imagine what the expression tree for a genuinely complex expression would look like—and then be grateful that C#3 can create expression trees from lambda expressions!

One small point to note is that although the C#3 compiler builds expression trees in the compiled code using code similar to listing 9.10, it has one shortcut up its sleeve: it doesn't need to use normal reflection to get the MethodInfo for string.StartsWith. Instead, it uses the method equivalent of the typeof operator. This is only available in IL, not in C# itself—and the same operator is also used to create delegate instances from method groups.

Now that we've seen how expression trees and lambda expressions are linked, let's take a brief look at why they're so useful.

9.3.4   *Expression trees at the heart of LINQ*

Without lambda expressions, expression trees would have relatively little value. They'd be an alternative to CodeDOM in cases where you only wanted to model a single expression instead of whole statements, methods, types and so forth—but the benefit would still be limited.

The reverse is also true to a limited extent: without expression trees, lambda expressions would certainly be *less* useful. Having a more compact way of creating delegate instances would still be welcome, and the shift toward a more functional mode of development would still be viable. Lambda expressions are particularly effective when combined with extension methods, as we'll see in the next chapter. However, with expression trees in the picture as well, things get a lot more interesting.

So what do we get by combining lambda expressions, expression trees, and extension methods? The answer is the language side of LINQ, pretty much. The extra syntax we'll see in chapter 11 is icing on the cake, but the story would still have been quite compelling with just those three ingredients. For a long time we've been able to *either* have nice compile-time checking *or* we've been able to tell another platform to run some code, usually expressed as text (SQL queries being the most obvious example). We haven't been able to do both at the same time.

By combining lambda expressions that provide compile-time checks and expression trees that abstract the execution model away from the desired logic, we can have the best of both worlds—within reason. At the heart of "out of process" LINQ providers is the idea that we can produce an expression tree from a familiar source language (C# in our case) and use the result as an intermediate format, which can then be converted into the native language of the target platform: SQL, for example. In some cases there may not be a simple native language so much as a native API—making different web service calls depending on what the expression represents, perhaps. Figure 9.4 shows the different paths of LINQ to Objects and LINQ to SQL.

In some cases the conversion may try to perform *all* the logic on the target platform, whereas other cases may use the compilation facilities of expression trees to execute

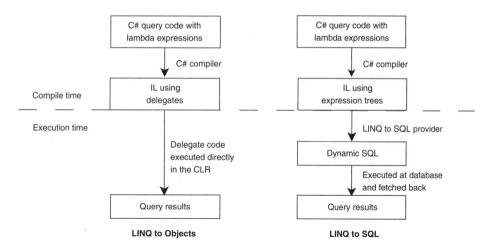

Figure 9.4   Both LINQ to Objects and LINQ to SQL start off with C# code, and end with query results. The ability to execute the code remotely comes through expression trees.

some of the expression locally and some elsewhere. We'll look at some of the details of this conversion step in chapter 12, but you should bear this end goal in mind as we explore extension methods and LINQ syntax in chapters 10 and 11.

> **NOTE** *Not all checking can be done by the compiler*—When expression trees are examined by some sort of converter, there are often cases that have to be rejected. For instance, although it's possible to convert a call to `string.StartsWith` into a similar SQL expression, a call to `string.IsInterned` doesn't make sense in a database environment. Expression trees allow a large amount of compile-time safety, but the compiler can only check that the lambda expression can be converted into a valid expression tree; it can't make sure that the expression tree will be suitable for its eventual use.

That finishes our direct coverage of lambda expressions and expression trees. Before we go any further, however, there are a few changes to C# that need some explanation, regarding type inference and how the compiler selects between overloaded methods.

9.4   *Changes to type inference and overload resolution*

The steps involved in type inference and overload resolution have been altered in C# 3 to accommodate lambda expressions and indeed to make anonymous methods more useful. This doesn't count as a new feature of C# as such, but it can be important to understand what the compiler is going to do. If you find details like this tedious and irrelevant, feel free to skip to the chapter summary—but remember that this section exists, so you can read it if you run across a compilation error related to this topic and can't understand why your code doesn't work. (Alternatively, you might want to come back to this section if you find your code *does* compile, but you don't think it should!)

Even within this section I'm not going to go into absolutely every nook and cranny—that's what the language specification is for. Instead, I'll give an overview of the new behavior, providing examples of common cases. The primary reason for changing the specification is to allow lambda expressions to work in a concise fashion, which is why I've included the topic in this particular chapter. Let's look a little deeper at what problems we'd have run into if the C# team had stuck with the old rules.

9.4.1   *Reasons for change: streamlining generic method calls*

Type inference occurs in a few situations. We've already seen it apply to implicitly typed arrays, and it's also required when you try to implicitly convert a method group to a delegate type as the parameter to a method—with overloading of the method being called, *and* overloading of methods within the method group, *and* the possibility of generic methods getting involved, the set of potential conversions can become quite overwhelming.

By far the most common situation for type inference is when you're calling a generic method without specifying the type arguments for that method. This happens all the time in LINQ—the way that query expressions work depends on this heavily. It's all handled so smoothly that it's easy to ignore how much the compiler has to work out on your behalf, all for the sake of making your code clearer and more concise.

The rules were *reasonably* straightforward in C# 2, although method groups and anonymous methods weren't always handled as well as we might have liked. The type inference process didn't deduce any information from them, leading to situations where the desired behavior was obvious to developers but not to the compiler. Life is more complicated in C# 3 due to lambda expressions—if you call a generic method using a lambda expression with an implicitly typed parameter list, the compiler needs to work out what types you're talking about, even before it can check the lambda expression's body.

This is much easier to see in code than in words. Listing 9.11 gives an example of the kind of issue we want to solve: calling a generic method using a lambda expression.

Listing 9.11   Example of code requiring the new type inference rules

```
static void PrintConvertedValue<TInput,TOutput>
    (TInput input, Converter<TInput,TOutput> converter)
{
    Console.WriteLine(converter(input));
}
...
PrintConvertedValue("I'm a string", x => x.Length);
```

The method `PrintConvertedValue` in listing 9.11 simply takes an input value and a delegate that can convert that value into a different type. It's completely generic—it makes no assumptions about the type parameters `TInput` and `TOutput`. Now, look at the types of the arguments we're calling it with in the bottom line of the listing. The first argument is clearly a string, but what about the second? It's a lambda expression, so we need to convert it into a `Converter<TInput,TOutput>`—and that means we need to know the types of `TInput` and `TOutput`.

If you remember, the type inference rules of C#2 were applied to each argument individually, with no way of using the types inferred from one argument to another. In our case, these rules would have stopped us from finding the types of TInput and TOutput for the second argument, so the code in listing 9.11 would have failed to compile.

Our eventual goal is to understand what makes listing 9.11 compile in C#3 (and it does, I promise you), but we'll start with something a bit more modest.

9.4.2 Inferred return types of anonymous functions

Listing 9.12 shows an example of some code that looks like it should compile but doesn't under the type inference rules of C#2.

Listing 9.12   Attempting to infer the return type of an anonymous method

```
delegate T MyFunc<T>();                              Declares Func<T>
                                                     that isn't in .NET 2.0
static void WriteResult<T> (MyFunc<T> function)
{
    Console.WriteLine(function());       Declares generic
                                         method with
}                                        delegate parameter
...
WriteResult(delegate { return 5; });                 Requires type
                                                     inference for T
```

Compiling listing 9.12 under C#2 gives an error

```
error CS0411: The type arguments for method
'Snippet.WriteResult<T>(Snippet.MyFunc<T>)' cannot be inferred from the
usage. Try specifying the type arguments explicitly.
```

We can fix the error in two ways—either specify the type argument explicitly (as suggested by the compiler) or cast the anonymous method to a concrete delegate type:

```
WriteResult<int>(delegate { return 5; });

WriteResult((MyFunc<int>)delegate { return 5; });
```

Both of these work, but they're slightly ugly. We'd *like* the compiler to perform the same kind of type inference as for nondelegate types, using the type of the returned expression to infer the type of T. That's exactly what C#3 does for both anonymous methods and lambda expressions—but there's one catch. Although in many cases only one return statement is involved, there can sometimes be more. Listing 9.13 is a slightly modified version of listing 9.12 where the anonymous method sometimes returns an integer and sometimes returns an object.

Listing 9.13   Code returning an integer or an object depending on the time of day

```
delegate T MyFunc<T>();

static void WriteResult<T> (MyFunc<T> function)
{
    Console.WriteLine(function());
}
...
```

```
WriteResult(delegate
{
    if (DateTime.Now.Hour < 12)
    {
        return 10;        ◁──┐ Return type
    }                        │ is int
    else
    {                           ┌── Return type
        return new object();  ◁─┘   is object
    }
});
```

The compiler uses the same logic to determine the return type in this situation as it does for implicitly typed arrays, as described in section 8.4. It forms a set of all the types from the return statements in the body of the anonymous function[4] (in this case int and object) and checks to see if exactly one of the types can be implicitly converted to from all the others. There's an implicit conversion from int to object (via boxing) but not from object to int, so the inference succeeds with object as the inferred return type. If there are no types matching that criterion, or more than one, no return type can be inferred and you'll get a compilation error.

So, now we know how to work out the *return* type of an anonymous function—but what about lambda expressions where the parameter types can be implicitly defined?

9.4.3 *Two-phase type inference*

The details of type inference in C# 3 are *much* more complicated than they are for C# 2. It's rare that you'll need to reference the specification for the exact behavior, but if you do I recommend you write down all the type parameters, arguments, and so forth on a piece of paper, and then follow the specification step by step, carefully noting down every action it requires. You'll end up with a sheet full of *fixed* and *unfixed* type variables, with a different set of *bounds* for each of them. A *fixed* type variable is one that the compiler has decided the value of; otherwise it is *unfixed*. A *bound* is a piece of information about a type variable. I suspect you'll get a headache, too.

I'm going to present a more "fuzzy" way of thinking about type inference—one that is likely to serve just as well as knowing the specification, and will be a lot easier to understand. The fact is, if the compiler doesn't perform type inference in exactly the way you want it to, it will almost certainly result in a compilation error rather than code that builds but doesn't behave properly. If your code doesn't build, try giving the compiler more information—it's as simple as that. However, here's *roughly* what's changed for C# 3.

The first big difference is that the method arguments work as a team in C# 3. In C# 2 every argument was used to try to pin down some type parameters *exactly*, and

---

[4] Returned expressions which don't have a type, such as null or another lambda expression, aren't included in this set. Their validity is checked later, once a return type has been determined, but they don't contribute to that decision.

the compiler would complain if any two arguments came up with different results for a particular type parameter, even if they were compatible. In C#3, arguments can contribute *pieces* of information—types that must be implicitly convertible to the final fixed value of a particular type parameter. The logic used to come up with that fixed value is the same as for inferred return types and implicitly typed arrays. Listing 9.14 shows an example of this—without using any lambda expressions or even anonymous methods.

Listing 9.14   Flexible type inference combining information from multiple arguments

```
static void PrintType<T> (T first, T second)
{
    Console.WriteLine(typeof(T));
}
...
PrintType(1, new object());
```

Although the code in listing 9.14 is *syntactically* valid in C#2, it wouldn't build: type inference would fail, because the `first` parameter would decide that `T` must be `int` and the second parameter would decide that `T` must be `object`. In C#3 the compiler determines that `T` should be `object` in exactly the same way that it did for the inferred return type in listing 9.13. In fact, the inferred return type rules are effectively one example of the more general process in C#3.

The second change is that type inference is now performed in two phases. The first phase deals with "normal" arguments where the types involved are known to begin with. This includes explicitly typed anonymous functions.

The second phase then kicks in, where implicitly typed lambda expressions and method groups have their types inferred. The idea is to see whether any of the information we've pieced together so far is enough to work out the parameter types of the lambda expression (or method group). If it is, the compiler is then able to examine the body of the lambda expression and work out the inferred return type—which is often another of the type parameters we're looking for. If the second phase gives some more information, we go through it again, repeating until either we run out of clues or we've worked out all the type parameters involved.

Let's look at two examples to show how it works. First we'll take the code we started the section with—listing 9.11.

```
static void PrintConvertedValue<TInput,TOutput>
    (TInput input, Converter<TInput,TOutput> converter)
{
    Console.WriteLine(converter(input));
}
...
PrintConvertedValue("I'm a string", x => x.Length);
```

The type parameters we need to work out in listing 9.11 are `TInput` and `TOutput`. The steps performed are as follows:

1   Phase 1 begins.

2   The first parameter is of type `TInput`, and the first argument is of type `string`. We infer that there must be an implicit conversion from `string` to `TInput`.

3   The second parameter is of type `Converter<TInput,TOutput>`, and the second argument is an implicitly typed lambda expression. No inference is performed—we don't have enough information.

4   Phase 2 begins.

5   `TInput` doesn't depend on any unfixed type parameters, so it's fixed to `string`.

6   The second argument now has a fixed *input* type, but an unfixed *output* type. We can consider it to be `(string x) => x.Length` and infer the return type as `int`. Therefore an implicit conversion must take place from `int` to `TOutput`.

7   Phase 2 repeats.

8   `TOutput` doesn't depend on anything unfixed, so it's fixed to `int`.

9   There are now no unfixed type parameters, so inference succeeds.

Complicated, eh? Still, it does the job—the result is what we'd want (`TInput=string`, `TOutput=int`) and everything compiles without any problems. The importance of phase 2 repeating is best shown with another example, however. Listing 9.15 shows *two* conversions being performed, with the output of the first one becoming the input of the second. Until we've worked out the output type of the first conversion, we don't know the input type of the second, so we can't infer its output type either.

Listing 9.15   Multistage type inference

```
static void ConvertTwice<TInput,TMiddle,TOutput>
    (TInput input,
     Converter<TInput,TMiddle> firstConversion,
     Converter<TMiddle,TOutput> secondConversion)
{
    TMiddle middle = firstConversion(input);
    TOutput output = secondConversion(middle);
    Console.WriteLine(output);
}
...
ConvertTwice("Another string",
            text => text.Length,
            length => Math.Sqrt(length));
```

The first thing to notice is that the method signature appears to be pretty horrific. It's not too bad when you stop being scared and just look at it carefully—and certainly the example usage makes it more obvious. We take a string, and perform a conversion on it: the same conversion as before, just a length calculation. We then take that length (an `int`) and find its square root (a `double`).

Phase 1 of type inference tells the compiler that there must be a conversion from `string` to `TInput`. The first time through phase 2, `TInput` is fixed to `string` and we infer that there must be a conversion from `int` to `TMiddle`. The second time through phase 2, TMiddle is fixed to int and we infer that there must be a conversion from double to TOutput. The third time through phase 2, TOutput is fixed to double and type inference succeeds. When type inference has finished, the compiler can look at the code within the lambda expression properly.

NOTE *Checking the body of a lambda expression*—The body of a lambda expression *cannot be checked* until the input parameter types are known. The lambda expression x => x.Length is valid if x is an array or a string, but invalid in many other cases. This isn't a problem when the parameter types are explicitly declared, but with an implicit parameter list the compiler needs to wait until it's performed the relevant type inference before it can try to work out what the lambda expression means.

These examples have shown only one change working at a time—in practice there can be several pieces of information about different type variables, potentially discovered in different iterations of the process. In an effort to save your sanity (and mine), I'm not going to present any more complicated examples—hopefully you understand the general mechanism, even if the exact details are hazy.

Although it may seem as if this kind of situation will occur so rarely that it's not worth having such complex rules to cover it, in fact it's quite common in C#3, particularly with LINQ. Indeed, you could easily use type inference extensively without even thinking about it—it's likely to become second nature to you. If it fails and you wonder why, however, you can always revisit this section and the language specification.

There's one more change we need to cover, but you'll be glad to hear it's easier than type inference: method overloading.

9.4.4 *Picking the right overloaded method*

Overloading occurs when there are multiple methods available with the same name but different signatures. Sometimes it's obvious which method is appropriate, because it's the only one with the right number of parameters, or it's the only one where all the arguments can be converted into the corresponding parameter types.

The tricky bit comes when there are multiple methods that *could* be the right one. The rules are quite complicated (yes, *again*)—but the key part is the way that each argument type is converted into the parameter type. For instance, consider these method signatures, as if they were both declared in the same type:

```
void Write(int x)
void Write(double y)
```

The meaning of a call to Write(1.5) is obvious, because there's no implicit conversion from double to int, but a call to Write(1) is trickier. There *is* an implicit conversion from int to double, so both methods are possible. At that point, the compiler considers the conversion from int to int, and from int to double. A conversion from any type to itself is defined to be *better than* any conversion to a different type, so the Write(int x) method is better than Write(double y) for this particular call.

When there are multiple parameters, the compiler has to make sure there is exactly one method that is *at least as good as* all the others for every parameter. As a simple example, suppose we had

```
void Write(int x, double y)
void Write(double x, int y)
```

A call to Write(1, 1) would be ambiguous, and the compiler would force you to add a cast to at least one of the parameters to make it clear which method you meant to call.

That logic still applies to C#3, but with one extra rule about anonymous functions, which never specify a return type. In this case, the inferred return type (as described in 9.4.2) is used in the "better conversion" rules.

Let's see an example of the kind of situation that needs the new rule. Listing 9.16 contains two methods with the name Execute, and a call using a lambda expression.

Listing 9.16   Sample of overloading choice influenced by delegate return type

```
static void Execute(Func<int> action)
{
    Console.WriteLine("action returns an int: "+action());
}

static void Execute(Func<double> action)
{
    Console.WriteLine("action returns a double: "+action());
}
...

Execute( () => 1 );
```

The call to Execute in listing 9.16 could have been written with an anonymous method or a method group instead—the same rules are applied whatever kind of conversion is involved. So, which Execute method should be called? The overloading rules say that when two methods are both applicable after performing conversions on the arguments, then those argument conversions are examined to see which one is "better." The conversions here aren't from a normal .NET type to the parameter type—they're from a lambda expression to two different delegate types. So, which conversion is better?

Surprisingly enough, the same situation in C#2 would result in a compilation error—there was no language rule covering this case. In C#3, however, the method with the Func<int> parameter would be chosen. The extra rule that has been added can be paraphrased to this:

> *If an anonymous function can be converted to two delegate types that have the same parameter list but different return types, then the delegate conversions are judged by the conversions from the inferred return type to the delegates' return types.*

That's pretty much gibberish without referring to an example. Let's look back at listing 9.16: we're converting from a lambda expression with no parameters and an inferred return type of int to either Func<int> or Func<double>. The parameter lists are the same (empty) for both delegate types, so the rule applies. We then just need to find the better conversion: `int` to `int`, or `int` to `double`. This puts us in more familiar territory—as we saw earlier, the `int` to `int` conversion is better. Listing 9.16 therefore prints out "action returns an int: 1."

9.4.5   *Wrapping up type inference and overload resolution*

This section has been pretty heavy. I would have loved to make it simpler—but it's a fundamentally complicated topic. The terminology involved doesn't make it any easier, especially as *parameter type* and *type parameter* mean completely different things! Congratulations if you made it through and actually understood it all. Don't worry if you didn't: hopefully next time you read through the section, it will shed a bit more light on the topic—particularly after you've run into situations where it's important in your own code. For the moment, here are the most important points:

- Anonymous functions (anonymous methods and lambda expressions) have inferred return types based on the types of all the return statements.
- Lambda expressions can only be understood by the compiler when the types of all the parameters are known.
- Type inference no longer requires that each argument independently comes to exactly the same conclusion about type parameters, as long as the results stay compatible.
- Type inference is now multistage: the inferred return type of one anonymous function may be used as a parameter type for another.
- Finding the "best" overloaded method when anonymous functions are involved takes the inferred return type into account.

9.5   *Summary*

In C#3, lambda expressions almost entirely replace anonymous methods. The *only* thing you can do with an anonymous method that you can't do with a lambda expression is say that you don't care about the parameters in the way that we saw in section 5.4.3. Of course, anonymous methods are supported for the sake of backward compatibility, but idiomatic, freshly written C#3 code will contain very few of them.

We've seen how lambda expressions are much more than just a more compact syntax for delegate creation, however. They can be converted into expression trees, which can then be processed by other code, possibly performing equivalent actions in different execution environments. This is arguably the most important part of the LINQ story.

Our discussion of type inference and overloading was a necessary evil to some extent: no one actually *enjoys* discussing the sort of rules which are required, but it's important to have at least a passing understanding of what's going on. Before we all feel too sorry for ourselves, spare a thought for the poor language designers who have to live and breathe this kind of thing, making sure the rules are consistent and don't fall apart in nasty situations. Then pity the testers who have to try to break the implementation!

That's it in terms of *describing* lambda expressions—but we'll be seeing a lot more of them in the rest of the book. For instance, our next chapter is all about *extension methods*. Superficially, they're completely separate from lambda expressions—but in reality the two features are often used together.

Extension methods 10

This chapter covers
- Writing extension methods
- Calling extension methods
- Method chaining
- Extension methods in .NET 3.5
- Other uses for extension methods

I'm not a fan of inheritance. Or rather, I'm not a fan of a number of places where inheritance has been used in code that I've maintained, or class libraries I've worked with. As with so many things, it's powerful when used properly, but it's got a design overhead to it that is often overlooked and can become painful over time. It's sometimes used as a way of adding extra behavior and functionality to a class, even when no real information is being added about the object—where nothing is being specialized.

Sometimes that's appropriate—if objects of the new type should carry around the details of the extra behavior—but often it's not. Indeed, often it's just not possible to use inheritance in this way in the first place—if you're working with a value type, a sealed class, or an interface. The alternative is usually to write a bunch of static methods, most of which take an instance of the type in question as at least

255

one of their parameters. This works fine, without the design penalty of inheritance, but does tend to make code look ugly.

C#3 introduces the idea of *extension methods*, which have the benefits of the static methods solution and also improve the readability of code that calls them. They let you call static methods as if they were instance methods of a completely different class. Don't panic—it's not as crazy or as arbitrary as it sounds.

In this chapter we'll first look at how to use extension methods and how to write them. We'll then examine a few of the extension methods provided by the .NET 3.5 Framework, and see how they can be chained together easily. This chaining ability is an important part of the reason for introducing extension methods to the language in the first place. Finally, we'll consider some of the pros and cons of using extension methods instead of "plain" static methods.

First, though, let's have a closer look at why extension methods are sometimes desirable compared with the plain old static methods available in C#1 and 2, particularly when you create utility classes.

10.1   *Life before extension methods*

You may be getting a sense of déjà vu at this point, because utility classes came up in chapter 7 when we looked at static classes. If you've written a lot of C#2 code by the time you start using C#3, you should look at your static classes—many of the methods in them may well be good candidates for turning into extension methods. That's not to say that all existing static classes are a good fit, but you may well recognize the following traits:

- You want to add some members to a type.
- You don't need to add any more data to the instances of the type.
- You can't change the type itself, because it's in someone else's code.

One slight variation on this is where you want to work with an interface instead of a class, adding useful behavior while only calling methods on the interface. A good example of this is IList<T>. Wouldn't it be nice to be able to sort any (mutable) implementation of IList<T>? It would be horrendous to force all implementations of the interface to implement sorting themselves, but it would be nice from the point of view of the *user* of the list.

The thing is, IList<T> provides all the building blocks for a completely generic sort routine (several, in fact), but you can't put that implementation in the interface. IList<T> could have been specified as an abstract class instead, and the sorting functionality included that way, but as C# and .NET have single inheritance of implementation, that would have placed a significant restriction on the types deriving from it. Extension methods would allow us to sort any IList<T> implementation, making it *appear* as if the list itself provided the functionality.

EXTRA
code available

We'll see later that a lot of the functionality of LINQ is built on extension methods over interfaces. For the moment, though, we'll use a different type for our examples:

`System.IO.Stream`. The `Stream` class is the bedrock of binary communications in .NET. `Stream` itself is an abstract class with several concrete derived classes, such as `Network-Stream`, `FileStream`, and `MemoryStream`. Unfortunately, there are a few pieces of functionality that would have been handy to include in `Stream` but that just aren't there.

The "missing features" I come across most often are the ability to read the whole of a stream into memory as a byte array, and the ability to copy[1] the contents of one stream into another. Both of these are frequently implemented badly, making assumptions about streams that just aren't valid (the most common is that `Stream.Read` will completely fill the given buffer if the data doesn't run out first).

It would be nice to have the functionality in a single place, rather than duplicating it in several projects. That's why I wrote the `StreamUtil` class in my miscellaneous utility library. The real code contains a fair amount of error checking and other functionality, but listing 10.1 shows a cut-down version that is more than adequate for our needs.

Listing 10.1 A simple utility class to provide extra functionality for streams

```
using System.IO;

public static class StreamUtil
{
    const int BufferSize = 8192;

    public static void Copy(Stream input,
                            Stream output)
    {
        byte[] buffer = new byte[BufferSize];
        int read;
        while ((read = input.Read(buffer, 0, buffer.Length)) > 0)
        {
            output.Write(buffer, 0, read);
        }
    }

    public static byte[] ReadFully(Stream input)
    {
        using (MemoryStream tempStream = new MemoryStream())
        {
            Copy(input, tempStream);
            return tempStream.ToArray();
        }
    }
}
```

The implementation details don't matter much, although it's worth noting that the `ReadFully` method calls the `Copy` method—that will be useful to demonstrate a point about extension methods later. The class is easy to use—listing 10.2 shows how we can write a web response to disk, for example.

---

[1] Due to the nature of streams, this "copying" doesn't necessarily *duplicate* the data—it just reads it from one stream and writes it to another. Although "copy" isn't a strictly accurate term in this sense, the difference is usually irrelevant.

Listing 10.2   Using `StreamUtil` to copy a web response stream to a file

```
WebRequest request = WebRequest.Create("http://manning.com");
using (WebResponse response = request.GetResponse())
using (Stream responseStream = response.GetResponseStream())
using (FileStream output = File.Create("response.dat"))
{
    StreamUtil.Copy(responseStream, output);
}
```

Listing 10.2 is quite compact, and the `StreamUtil` class has taken care of looping and asking the response stream for more data until it's all been received. It's done its job as a utility class perfectly reasonably. Even so, it doesn't feel very object-oriented. We'd really like to ask the response stream to copy itself to the output stream, just like the `MemoryStream` class has a `WriteTo` method. It's not a *big* problem, but it's just a little ugly as it is.

Inheritance wouldn't help us in this situation (we want this behavior to be available for all streams, not just ones we're responsible for) and we can't go changing the `Stream` class itself—so what can we do? With C#2, we were out of options—we had to stick with the static methods and live with the clumsiness. C#3 allows us to change our static class to expose its members as extension methods, so we can pretend that the methods have been part of `Stream` all along. Let's see what changes are required.

10.2   Extension method syntax

Extension methods are almost embarrassingly easy to create, and simple to use too. The considerations around when and how to use them are significantly deeper than the difficulties involved in learning how to write them in the first place. Let's start off by converting our `StreamUtil` class to have a couple of extension methods.

10.2.1   Declaring extension methods

You can't use just any method as an extension method—it has to have the following characteristics:

- It has to be in a non-nested, nongeneric static class (and therefore has to be a static method).
- It has to have at least one parameter.
- The first parameter has to be prefixed with the `this` keyword.
- The first parameter can't have any other modifiers (such as `out` or `ref`).
- The type of the first parameter must not be a pointer type.

That's it—the method can be generic, return a value, have `ref`/`out` parameters other than the first one, be implemented with an iterator block, be part of a partial class, use nullable types—anything, as long as the above constraints are met.

We will call the type of the first parameter the *extended type* of the method. It's not official specification terminology, but it's a useful piece of shorthand.

Not only does the previous list provide all the restrictions, but it also gives the details of what you need to do to turn a "normal" static method in a static class into an extension method—just add the `this` keyword. Listing 10.3 shows the same class as in listing 10.1, but this time with both methods as extension methods.

Listing 10.3   The `StreamUtil` class again, but this time with extension methods

```
public static class StreamUtil
{
    const int BufferSize = 8192;

    public static void CopyTo(this Stream input,
                                   Stream output)
    {
        byte[] buffer = new byte[BufferSize];
        int read;
        while ((read = input.Read(buffer, 0, buffer.Length)) > 0)
        {
            output.Write(buffer, 0, read);
        }
    }

    public static byte[] ReadFully(this Stream input)
    {
        using (MemoryStream tempStream = new MemoryStream())
        {
            CopyTo(input, tempStream);
            return tempStream.ToArray();
        }
    }
}
```

Yes, the only big change in listing 10.3 is the addition of the two modifiers, as shown in bold. I've also changed the name of the method from `Copy` to `CopyTo`. As we'll see in a minute, that will allow calling code to read more naturally, although it does look slightly strange in the `ReadFully` method at the moment.

Now, it's not much use *having* extension methods if we can't *use* them…

10.2.2 Calling extension methods

I've mentioned it in passing, but we haven't yet seen what an extension method actually *does*. Simply put, it pretends to be an instance method of another type—the type of the first parameter of the method.

The transformation of our example code that uses `StreamUtil` is as simple as the transformation of the utility class itself. This time, instead of adding something in we'll take it away. Listing 10.4 is a repeat performance of listing 10.2, but using the "new" syntax to call `CopyTo`. I say "new," but it's really not new at all—it's the same syntax we've always used for calling instance methods.

Listing 10.4   Copying a stream using an extension method

```
WebRequest request = WebRequest.Create("http://manning.com");
using (WebResponse response = request.GetResponse())
using (Stream responseStream = response.GetResponseStream())
```

```
using (FileStream output = File.Create("response.dat"))
{
    responseStream.CopyTo(output);
}
```

In listing 10.4 it at least *looks* like we're asking the response stream to do the copying. It's still `StreamUtil` doing the work behind the scenes, but the code reads in a more natural·way. In fact, the compiler has converted the `CopyTo` call into a normal static method call to `StreamUtil.CopyTo`, passing the value of `responseStream` as the first argument (followed by `output` as normal).

Now that you can see the code in question, I hope you can understand why I changed the method name from `Copy` to `CopyTo`. Some names work just as well for static methods as instance methods, but you'll find that others need tweaking to get the maximum readability benefit.

If we want to make the `StreamUtil` code slightly more pleasant, you can change the line of `ReadFully` that calls `CopyTo` like this:

```
input.CopyTo(tempStream);
```

At this point the name change is fully appropriate for all the uses—although there's nothing to stop you from using the extension method as a normal static method, which is useful when you're migrating a lot of code.

You may have noticed that there's nothing in these method calls to indicate that we're using an extension method instead of a regular instance method of `Stream`. This can be seen in two ways: it's a good thing if our aim is to make extension methods blend in as much as possible and cause very little alarm—but it's a bad thing if you want to be able to immediately see what's *really* going on. If you're using Visual Studio 2008, you can hover over a method call and get an indication in the tooltip when it's an extension method, as shown in figure 10.1.

IntelliSense also indicates when it's offering an extension method, in both the icon for the method and the tooltip when it's selected. Of course, you don't want to have to hover over every method call you make or be super-careful with IntelliSense, but most of the time it doesn't matter whether you're calling an instance or extension method.

There's one thing that's still rather strange about our calling code, though—it doesn't mention `StreamUtil` anywhere! How does the compiler know to use the extension method in the first place?

```
WebRequest request = WebRequest.Create("http://manning.com");
using (WebResponse response = request.GetResponse())
using (Stream responseStream = response.GetResponseStream())
using (FileStream output = File.Create("response.dat"))
{
    responseStream.CopyTo(output);
}
        (extension) void Stream.CopyTo(Stream output)
```

Figure 10.1 Hovering over a method call in Visual Studio 2008 reveals whether or not the method is actually an extension method.

10.2.3   *How extension methods are found*

It's important to know how to call extension methods—but it's also important to know how to *not* call them—how to *not* be presented with unwanted options. To achieve that, we need to know how the compiler decides which extension methods to use in the first place.

Extension methods are made available to the code in the same way that classes are made available without qualification—with `using` directives. When the compiler sees an expression that looks like it's trying to use an instance method but none of the instance methods are compatible with the method call (if there's no method with that name, for instance, or no overload matches the arguments given), it then looks for an appropriate extension method. It considers all the extension methods in all the imported namespaces and the current namespaces, and matches ones where there's an implicit conversion from the expression type to the extended type.

> **NOTE** *Implementation: How does the compiler spot an extension method in a library?*   To work out whether or not to use an extension method, the compiler has to be able to tell the difference between an extension method and other methods within a static class that happen to have an appropriate signature. It does this by checking whether `System.Runtime.CompilerServices.ExtensionAttribute` has been applied to the method. This attribute is new to .NET 3.5, but the compiler *doesn't* check which assembly the attribute comes from. This means that you can still use extension methods even if your project targets .NET 2.0—you just need to define your own attribute with the right name, in the right namespace.

If multiple applicable extension methods are available for different extended types (using implicit conversions), the most appropriate one is chosen with the "better conversion" rules used in overloading. For instance, if `IChild` inherits from `IParent`, and there's an extension method with the same name for both, then the `IChild` extension method is used in preference to the one on `IParent`. This is crucial to LINQ, as you'll see in section 12.2, where we meet the `IQueryable<T>` interface.

It's important to note that instance methods are always used before extension methods, but the compiler doesn't warn of an extension method that matches an existing instance method. If a new version of the framework were to introduce a `CopyTo` method in `Stream` that took the same parameters as our extension method, recompiling our code against the new framework would *silently* change the meaning of the method call. (Indeed, that's one reason for choosing `CopyTo` instead of `WriteTo`—we wouldn't want the meaning to change depending on whether the compile-time type was `Stream` or `MemoryStream`.)

One potential problem with the way that extension methods are made available to code is that it's very wide-ranging. If there are two classes in the same namespace containing methods with the same extended type, there's no way of only using the extension methods from one of the classes. Likewise, there's no way of importing a namespace for the sake of making types available using only their simple names, but without making the extension methods within that namespace available at the same time. I recommend using a namespace that solely contains static classes with extension methods to mitigate this problem.

There's one aspect of extension methods that can be quite surprising when you first encounter it but is also useful in some situations. It's all about null references—let's take a look.

10.2.4 *Calling a method on a null reference*

I'd be amazed if I ever encountered anyone who'd done a significant amount of .NET programming without seeing a `NullReferenceException` due to calling a method with a variable whose value turned out to be a null reference. You can't call instance methods on null references in C# (although IL itself supports it for nonvirtual calls)—but you *can* call extension methods with a null reference. This is demonstrated by listing 10.5. Note that this isn't a snippet since nested classes can't contain extension methods.

Listing 10.5   Extension method being called on a null reference

```
using System;
public static class NullUtil
{
    public static bool IsNull(this object x)
    {
        return x==null;
    }
}

public class Test
{
    static void Main()
    {
        object y = null;
        Console.WriteLine(y.IsNull());
        y = new object();
        Console.WriteLine(y.IsNull());
    }
}
```

The output of listing 10.5 is "True" then "False"—if `IsNull` had been a normal instance method, an exception would have been thrown in the second line of `Main`. Instead, `IsNull` was called with `null` as the argument. Prior to the advent of extension methods, C# had no way of letting you write the more readable `y.IsNull()` form safely, requiring `NullUtil.IsNull(y)` instead. There's one particularly obvious example in the framework where this could be useful: `string.IsNullOrEmpty`. C#3 allows you to write an extension method that has the same signature (other than the "extra" parameter for the extended type) as an existing static method on the extended type. To save you reading through that sentence several times, here's an example—even though the `string` class has a static, parameterless method `IsNullOrEmpty`, you can still create and use the following extension method:

```
public static bool IsNullOrEmpty(this string text)
{
    return string.IsNullOrEmpty(text);
}
```

At first it seems odd to be able to call `IsNullOrEmpty` on a variable that is null without an exception being thrown, particularly if you're familiar with it as a static method from .NET 2.0. In my view, code using the extension method is more easily understandable. For instance, if you read the expression `if (name.IsNullOrEmpty())` out loud, it says exactly what it's doing. As always, experiment to see what works for you—but be aware of the possibility of other people using this technique if you're debugging code. Don't be certain that an exception will be thrown on a method call unless you're sure it's not an extension method! Also note that you should think carefully before reusing an existing name for an extension method—the previous extension method could confuse readers who are only familiar with the static method from the framework.

Now that we know the syntax and behavior of extension methods, we can have a look at some examples of them, which are provided in .NET 3.5 as part of the framework.

10.3 Extension methods in .NET 3.5

The biggest use of extension methods in .NET 3.5 is in LINQ. Some LINQ providers have a few extension methods to help them along, but there are two classes that stand out, both of them appearing in the `System.Linq` namespace: `Enumerable` and `Queryable`. These contain many, many extension methods: most of the ones in `Enumerable` operate on `IEnumerable<T>` and most of those in `Queryable` operate on `IQueryable<T>`. We'll see the purpose of `IQueryable<T>` in chapter 12, but for the moment let's concentrate on `Enumerable`.

10.3.1 First steps with Enumerable

Even just looking at `Enumerable`, we're getting very close to LINQ now. Indeed, a lot of the time you don't need full-blown query expressions to solve a problem. `Enumerable` has a *lot* of methods in it, and the purpose of this section isn't to cover all of them but to give you enough of a feel for them to let you go off and experiment. It's a real joy to just play with everything available in `Enumerable`—although this time it's definitely worth firing up Visual Studio 2008 for your experiments (rather than using Snippy) as IntelliSense is handy for this kind of activity.

All the complete examples in this section deal with a simple situation: we start off with a collection of integers and transform it in various ways. Obviously real-life situations are likely to be somewhat more complicated, usually dealing with business-related types. At the end of this section, I'll present a couple of examples of just the transformation side of things applied to possible business situations, with full source code available on the book's website—but that's harder to play with than a straightforward collection of numbers. It's worth considering some recent projects you've been working on as we go, however—see if you can think of situations where you could have made your code simpler or more readable by using the kind of operations described here.

There are a few methods in `Enumerable` that aren't extension methods, and we'll use one of them in the examples for the rest of the chapter. The `Range` method takes two `int` parameters: a number to start with, and how many results to yield. The result is an `IEnumerable<int>`, which simply returns one number at a time in the obvious way. This isn't as flexible as the `Range<T>` type we built in chapter 6, but it's still handy for this sort of quick testing. If you've downloaded or typed in `Range<T>`, you can experiment with types other than `int`—all the extension methods presented here work with any `IEnumerable<T>`.

To demonstrate the `Range` method and give us a framework to play with, let's just print out the numbers 0 to 9, as shown in listing 10.6. To keep the examples short, I've stuck with the "snippet" format even though you'll probably want to play with this in Visual Studio.

Listing 10.6   Using `Enumerable.Range` to print out the numbers 0 to 9

```
var collection = Enumerable.Range(0, 10);

foreach (var element in collection)
{
    Console.WriteLine(element);
}
```

There are no extension methods called in listing 10.6, just a plain static method. And yes, it really does just print the numbers 0 to 9—I never claimed this code would set the world on fire.

NOTE   *Deferred execution*—The `Range` method doesn't build a list with the appropriate numbers—it just yields them at the appropriate time. In other words, constructing the enumerable instance doesn't do the bulk of the work—it just gets things ready, so that the data can be provided in a "just-in-time" fashion at the appropriate point. This is called *deferred execution* and is a crucial part of LINQ. We'll learn much more about this in the next chapter.

Pretty much the simplest thing we can do with a sequence of numbers (which is already in order) is to reverse it. Listing 10.7 uses the `Reverse` extension method to do this—it returns an `IEnumerable<T>` that yields the same elements as the original sequence but in the reverse order.

Listing 10.7   Reversing a collection with the `Reverse` method

```
var collection = Enumerable.Range(0, 10)
                           .Reverse();

foreach (var element in collection)
{
    Console.WriteLine(element);
}
```

Predictably enough, this prints out 9, then 8, then 7, and so on right down to 0. We've called Reverse (seemingly) on an `IEnumerable<int>` and the same type has been returned. This pattern of returning one enumerable based on another is pervasive in the `Enumerable` class.

NOTE *Efficiency: buffering vs. streaming*—The extension methods provided by the framework try very hard to "stream" or "pipe" data wherever possible—when an iterator is asked for its next element, it will often take an element off the iterator it's chained to, process that element, and then return something appropriate, preferably without using any more storage itself. Simple transformations and filters can do this very easily, and it's a really powerful way of efficiently processing data where it's possible—but some operations such as reversing the order, or sorting, require all the data to be available, so it's all loaded into memory for bulk processing. The difference between this buffered approach and piping is similar to the difference between reading data by loading a whole `DataSet` versus using a `DataReader` to process one record at a time. It's important to consider what's required when using LINQ—a single method call can have significant performance implications.

Let's do something a little more adventurous now—we'll use a lambda expression to remove the even numbers.

10.3.2 *Filtering with Where, and chaining method calls together*

The `Where` extension method is a simple but powerful way of filtering collections: it accepts a predicate, which it applies to each of the elements of the original collection. Again, it returns an `IEnumerable<T>`, and this time any element that matches the predicate is included in the resulting collection. Listing 10.8 demonstrates this, applying the odd/even filter to the collection of integers before reversing it. We don't *have* to use a lambda expression here—for instance, we could use a delegate we'd created earlier, or an anonymous method. In this case (and in many other real-life situations), it's simple to put the filtering logic inline, and lambda expressions keep the code concise.

Listing 10.8   Using the `Where` method with a lambda expression to keep odd numbers only

```
var collection = Enumerable.Range(0, 10)
                           .Where(x => x%2 != 0)
                           .Reverse();

foreach (var element in collection)
{
    Console.WriteLine(element);
}
```

Listing 10.8 prints out the numbers 9, 7, 5, 3, and 1. Hopefully you'll have noticed a pattern forming—we're chaining the method calls together. The chaining idea itself isn't new. For example, `StringBuilder.Append` always returns the instance you call it on, allowing code like this:

```
builder.Append(x).Append(y).Append(z)
```

That's fine for instance methods, but extension methods allow *static* method calls to be chained together. *This is one of the primary reasons for extension methods existing.* They're *useful* for other utility classes, but their true power is revealed in this ability to chain static methods in a natural way. That's why extension methods primarily show up in `Enumerable` and `Queryable` in .NET 3.5: LINQ is geared toward this approach to data processing, with information traveling through pipelines constructed of individual operations chained together.

> **NOTE** *Efficiency consideration: reordering method calls to avoid waste*—I'm certainly not a fan of micro-optimization without good cause, but it's worth looking at the ordering of the method calls in listing 10.8. We *could* have added the `Where` call after the `Reverse` call and achieved the same results. However, that would have wasted some effort—the `Reverse` call would have had to work out where the even numbers should come in the sequence even though they will be discarded from the final result. In this case it's not going to make much difference, but it *can* have a significant effect on performance: if you can reduce the amount of wasted work without compromising readability, that's a good thing. That doesn't mean you should always put filters at the start of the pipeline, however; you need to think carefully about any reordering to make sure you'll still get the correct results.

There are two obvious ways of writing the first part of listing 10.8 without using the fact that `Reverse` and `Where` are extension methods. One is to use a temporary variable, which keeps the structure intact:

```
var collection = Enumerable.Range(0, 10);
collection     = Enumerable.Where(collection, x => x%2 != 0)
collection     = Enumerable.Reverse(collection);
```

I hope you'll agree that the meaning of the code is far less clear here than in listing 10.8. It gets even worse with the other option, which is to keep the "single statement" style:

```
var collection = Enumerable.Reverse
             (Enumerable.Where
                (Enumerable.Range(0, 10),
                   x => x%2 != 0));
```

The method call order appears to be reversed, because the innermost method call (`Range`) will be performed first, then the others, with execution working its way outward.

Let's get back to our nice clean syntax but introduce another wrinkle—we'll transform (or *project*) each element in our original collection, creating an anonymous type for the result.

10.3.3 *Projections using the Select method and anonymous types*

The most important projection method in `Enumerable` is `Select`—it operates on an `IEnumerable<TSource>` and projects it into an `IEnumerable<TResult>` by way of a `Func<TSource, TResult>`, which is the transformation to use on each element, specified as a delegate. It's very like the `ConvertAll` method in `List<T>`, but operating on any enumerable collection and using deferred execution to perform the projection only as each element is requested.

When I introduced anonymous types, I said they were useful with lambda expressions and LINQ—well, here's an example of the kind of thing you can do with them. We've currently got the odd numbers between 0 and 9 (in reverse order)—let's create a type that encapsulates the square root of the number as well as the original number. Listing 10.9 shows both the projection and a slightly modified way of writing out the results. I've adjusted the whitespace solely for the sake of space on the printed page.

Listing 10.9 Projection using a lambda expression and an anonymous type

```
var collection = Enumerable.Range(0, 10)
    .Where(x => x%2 != 0)
    .Reverse()
    .Select(x => new { Original=x, SquareRoot=Math.Sqrt(x) } );

foreach (var element in collection)
{
    Console.WriteLine("sqrt({0})={1}",
                      element.Original,
                      element.SquareRoot);
}
```

This time the type of `collection` isn't `IEnumerable<int>`—it's `IEnumerable<Something>`, where `Something` is the anonymous type created by the compiler. We can't explicitly type the collection variable except as either the nongeneric `IEnumerable` type or `object`. Implicit typing is what allows us to use the `Original` and `SquareRoot` properties when writing out the results. The output of listing 10.9 is as follows:

```
sqrt(9)=3
sqrt(7)=2.64575131106459
sqrt(5)=2.23606797749979
sqrt(3)=1.73205080756888
sqrt(1)=1
```

Of course, a `Select` method doesn't *have* to use an anonymous type at all—we could have selected just the square root of the number, discarding the original. In that case the result would have been `IEnumerable<double>`. Alternatively, we could have manually written a type to encapsulate an integer and its square root—it was just easiest to use an anonymous type in this case.

Let's look at one last method to round off our coverage of `Enumerable` for the moment: `OrderBy`.

10.3.4 Sorting using the OrderBy method

Sorting data is a common requirement when processing data, and in LINQ this is usually performed using the `OrderBy` or `OrderByDescending` methods, sometimes followed by `ThenBy` or `ThenByDescending` if you need to sort by more than one property of the data. This ability to sort on multiple properties has always been available the hard way using a complicated comparison, but it's much clearer to be able to present a series of simple comparisons.

To demonstrate this, I'm going to change the operations we'll use a bit. We'll start off with the integers –5 to 5 (inclusive—11 elements in total), and then project to an anonymous type containing the original number and its square (rather than square root). Finally, we'll sort by the square and then the original number. Listing 10.10 shows all of this.

Listing 10.10   Ordering a sequence by two properties

```
var collection = Enumerable.Range(-5, 11)
      .Select(x => new { Original=x, Square=x*x })
      .OrderBy(x => x.Square)
      .ThenBy(x => x.Original);

foreach (var element in collection)
{
    Console.WriteLine(element);
}
```

Notice how aside from the call to `Enumerable.Range` (which isn't as clear as using our own `Range<T>` class) the code reads almost exactly like the textual description. This time I've decided to let the anonymous type's `ToString` implementation do the formatting, and here are the results:

```
{ Original = 0, Square = 0 }
{ Original = -1, Square = 1 }
{ Original = 1, Square = 1 }
{ Original = -2, Square = 4 }
{ Original = 2, Square = 4 }
{ Original = -3, Square = 9 }
{ Original = 3, Square = 9 }
{ Original = -4, Square = 16 }
{ Original = 4, Square = 16 }
{ Original = -5, Square = 25 }
{ Original = 5, Square = 25 }
```

As intended, the "main" sorting property is `Square`—but for two values that both have the same square, the negative original number is always sorted before the positive one. Writing a single comparison to do the same kind of thing (in a general case—there are mathematical tricks to cope with this particular example) would have been significantly more complicated, to the extent that you wouldn't want to include the code "inline" in the lambda expression.

We've seen just a few of the many extension methods available in `Enumerable`, but hopefully you can appreciate how neatly they can be chained together. In the next chapter we'll see how this can be expressed in a different way using extra syntax provided by C#3 (query expressions)—as well as some other operations we haven't covered here. It's worth remembering that you don't *have* to use query expressions, though—often it can be simpler to make a couple of calls to methods in `Enumerable`, using extension methods to chain operations together.

Now that we've seen how all these apply to our "collection of numbers" example, it's time for me to make good on the promise of some more business-related situations.

10.3.5 *Business examples involving chaining*

Much of what we do as developers involves moving data around. In fact, for many applications that's the *only* meaningful thing we do—the user interface, web services, database, and other components often exist solely to get data from one place to another, or from one form into another. It should be of no surprise that the extension methods we've looked at in this section are well suited to many business problems. I'll just give a couple of examples, as I'm sure you'll be able to take them as a springboard into thinking about *your* business requirements and how C# 3 and the `Enumerable` class can help you solve problems more expressively than before. For each example I'll only include a sample query—it should be enough to understand the purpose of the code, but without all the baggage. Full working code is on the book's website.

AGGREGATION: SUMMING SALARIES

The first example involves a company comprised of several departments. Each department has a number of employees, each of whom has a salary. Suppose we want to report on total salary cost by department, with the most expensive department first. The query is simply

```
company.Departments
       .Select(dept => new
               {
                  dept.Name,
                  Cost=dept.Employees.Sum (person => person.Salary)
               })
       .OrderByDescending (deptWithCost => deptWithCost.Cost);
```

This query uses an anonymous type to keep the department name (using a projection initializer) and the sum of the salaries of all the employees within that department. The salary summation uses a self-explanatory `Sum` extension method, again part of `Enumerable`. In the result, the department name and total salary can be retrieved as properties. If you wanted the original department reference, you'd just need to change the anonymous type used in the `Select` method.

GROUPING: COUNTING BUGS ASSIGNED TO DEVELOPERS

If you're a professional developer, I'm sure you've seen many project management tools giving you different metrics. If you have access to the raw data, LINQ can help you transform it in practically any way you choose. As a simple example, we could look at a list of developers and how many bugs they have assigned to them at the moment:

```
bugs.GroupBy(bug => bug.AssignedTo)
    .Select(list => new { Developer=list.Key, Count=list.Count() })
    .OrderByDescending (x => x.Count);
```

This query uses the `GroupBy` extension method, which groups the original collection by a projection (the developer assigned to fix the bug in this case), resulting in an

`IGrouping<TKey,TElement>`. There are many overloads of `GroupBy`, but I've used the simplest one here and then selected just the key (the name of the developer) and the number of bugs assigned to them. After that we've just ordered the result to show the developers with the most bugs first.

One of the problems when looking at the `Enumerable` class can be working out exactly what's going on—one of the overloads of `GroupBy` has four type parameters and five "normal" parameters (three of which are delegates), for instance. Don't panic, though—just follow the steps shown in chapter 3, assigning different types to different type parameters until you've got a concrete example of what the method would look like. That usually makes it a lot easier to understand what's going on.

We'll use the example of defect tracking as our sample data when we look at query expressions in the next chapter.

These examples aren't particularly involved ones, but I hope you can see the power of chaining method calls together, where each method takes an original collection and returns another one in some form or other, whether by filtering out some values, ordering them, transforming each element, aggregating some values, or many other options. In many cases, the resulting code can be read aloud and understood immediately—and in other situations it's still usually a lot simpler than the equivalent code would have been in previous versions of C#.

Now that we've seen some of the extension methods provided for us, we'll consider just how and when it makes sense for you to write them yourself.

10.4   *Usage ideas and guidelines*

Like implicit typing of local variables, extension methods are controversial. It would be hard to claim that they make the overall aim of the code harder to understand in many cases, but at the same time they *do* obscure the details of what method is getting called. In the words of one of the lecturers at my university, "I'm hiding the truth in order to show you a *bigger* truth"—if you believe that the most important aspect of the code is its result, extension methods are great. If the implementation is more important to you, then explicitly calling a static method is clearer. Effectively, it's the difference between the "what" and the "how."

We've already looked at using extension methods for utility classes and method chaining, but before we discuss the pros and cons further, it's worth calling out a couple of aspects of this that may not be obvious.

10.4.1 *"Extending the world" and making interfaces richer*

Wes Dyer, a former developer on the C# compiler team, has a fantastic blog[2] covering all kinds of subject matter. One of his posts about extension methods[3] particularly caught my attention. It's called "Extending the World," and it talks about how

2   http://blogs.msdn.com/wesdyer
3   http://blogs.msdn.com/wesdyer/archive/2007/03/09/extending-the-world.aspx

extension methods can make code easier to read by effectively adapting your environment to your needs:

> *Typically for a given problem, a programmer is accustomed to building up a solution until it finally meets the requirements. Now, it is possible to extend the world to meet the solution instead of solely just building up until we get to it. That library doesn't provide what you need, just extend the library to meet your needs.*

This has implications beyond situations where you'd use a utility class. Typically developers only start creating utility classes when they've seen the same kind of code reproduced in dozens of places—but extending a library is about clarity of expression as much as avoiding duplication. Extension methods can make the calling code feel like the library is richer than it really is.

We've already seen this with IEnumerable<T>, where even the simplest implementation *appears* to have a wide set of operations available, such as sorting, grouping, projection, and filtering. Of course, the benefits aren't limited to interfaces—you can also "extend the world" with enums, abstract classes, and so forth.

The .NET Framework also provides a good example of another use for extension methods: fluent interfaces.

10.4.2 *Fluent interfaces*

There used to be a television program in the United Kingdom called *Catchphrase*. The idea was that contestants would watch a screen where an animation would show some cryptic version of a phrase or saying, which they'd have to guess. The host would often try to help by instructing them: "Say what you see." That's pretty much the idea behind *fluent interfaces*—that if you read the code verbatim, its purpose will leap off the screen as if it were written in a natural human language. The term was originally coined by Martin Fowler[4] and Eric Evans. If you're familiar with *domain specific languages* (DSLs), you may be wondering what the differences are between a fluent interface and a DSL. A lot has been written on the subject, but the consensus seems to be that a DSL has more freedom to create its own syntax and grammar, whereas a fluent interface is constrained by the "host" language (C# in our case).

A good example of a fluent interface in the framework is the OrderBy and ThenBy methods: with a bit of interpretation of lambda expressions, the code explains exactly what it does. In the case of our numbers example earlier, we could read "order by the square, then by the original number" without much work. Statements end up reading as whole sentences rather than just individual noun-verb phrases.

Writing fluent interfaces can require a change of mind-set. Method names defy the normal "descriptive verb" form, with "And," "Then," and "If" sometimes being suitable methods in a fluent interface. The methods themselves often do little more than setting up context for future calls, often returning a type whose sole purpose is to act as a bridge between calls. Figure 10.2 gives an example of how this "bridging" works. It

---

[4] http://www.martinfowler.com/bliki/FluentInterface.html

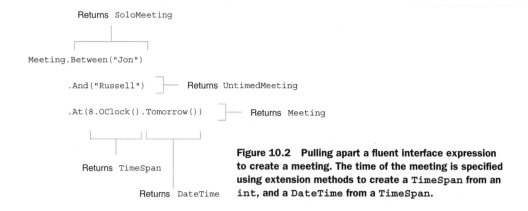

Figure 10.2   Pulling apart a fluent interface expression to create a meeting. The time of the meeting is specified using extension methods to create a `TimeSpan` from an `int`, and a `DateTime` from a `TimeSpan`.

only uses two extension methods (on `int` and `TimeSpan`), but they make all the difference to the readability.

The grammar of the example in figure 10.2 could have many different forms: you may be able to add additional attendees to an `UntimedMeeting`, or create an `UnattendedMeeting` at a particular time before specifying the attendees, for instance. Anders Norås has a full example on his blog[5] that can be a useful starting point when you're planning a fluent interface.

C#3 only supports extension *methods* rather than extension *properties*, which restricts fluent interfaces slightly—it means we can't have expressions such as `1.week.from.now` or `2.days + 10.hours` (which are both valid in Groovy with an appropriate package[6]) but with a few superfluous parentheses we can have achieve similar results. At first it looks odd to call a method on a number (such as `2.Dollars()` or `3.Meters ()`), but it's hard to deny that the meaning is clear. Without extension methods, this sort of clarity simply isn't possible when you need to act on types like numbers that aren't under your control.

At the time of this writing, the development community is still on the fence about fluent interfaces: they're relatively rare in most fields, although many mocking libraries used for unit testing have at least some fluent aspects. They're certainly not universally applicable, but in the right situations they can radically transform the readability of the calling code.

These aren't the only uses available for extension methods, of course—you may well discover something new and wonderful that makes the world a generally better place using extension methods. I constantly find it amazing how such a simple little feature can have such a profound impact on readability when used appropriately. The key word there is "appropriately."

10.4.3   *Using extension methods sensibly*

I'm in no position to dictate how you write your code. It may be possible to write tests to objectively measure readability for an "average" developer, but it only matters for

---

[5]   http://andersnoras.com/blogs/anoras/archive/2007/07/09/behind-the-scenes-of-the-planning-dsl.aspx
[6]   http://groovy.codehaus.org/Google+Data+Support

those who are going to use and maintain your code. So, you need to consult with the relevant people as far as you can: this depends on your type of project and its audience, of course, but it's nice to present different options and get appropriate feedback. Extension methods make this particularly easy in many cases, as you can demonstrate both options in working code simultaneously—turning a method into an extension method doesn't stop you from calling it explicitly in the same way as before.

The main question to ask is the one I referred to at the start of this section: is the "what does it do" of the code more important than the "how does it do it?" That varies by person and situation, but here are some guidelines to bear in mind:

- Everyone on the development team should be aware of extension methods and where they might be used. Where possible, avoid surprising code maintainers.
- By putting extensions in their own namespace, you make it hard to use them accidentally. Even if it's not obvious when *reading* the code, the developer *writing* it should at least be aware of what she's doing. Use a projectwide or companywide convention for naming the namespace. You may choose to take this one step further and use a single namespace for each extended type. For instance, you could create a `TypeExtensions` namespace for classes that extend `System.Type`.
- The decision to write an extension method should always be a conscious one. It shouldn't become habitual—certainly not every static method deserves to be an extension method.
- An extension method is reasonably valid if it's applicable to *all* instances of the extended type. If it's only appropriate in certain situations, I'd make it clear that the method is not part of the type by leaving it as a "normal" static method.
- Document whether or not the first parameter (the value your method appears to be called on) is allowed to be null—if it's not, check the value in the method and throw an exception if necessary.
- Be careful not to use a method name that already has a meaning in the extended type. If the extended type is a framework type or comes from a third-party library, check all your extended method names whenever you change versions of the library.
- Question your instincts, but acknowledge that they affect your productivity. Just like with implicit typing, there's little point in forcing yourself to use a feature you instinctively dislike.
- Try to group extension methods into static classes dealing with the same extended type. Sometimes related classes (such as `DateTime` and `TimeSpan`) can be sensibly grouped together, but avoid grouping extension methods targeting disparate types such as `Stream` and `string` within the same class.
- Think *really* carefully before adding extension methods with the same extended type and same name in two different namespaces, particularly if there are situations where the different methods may both be applicable (they have the same number of parameters). It's reasonable for adding or removing a `using` directive to make a program fail to build, but it's nasty if it still builds but changes the behavior.

Few of these guidelines are particularly clear-cut—to some extent you'll have to feel your own way to the best use or avoidance of extension methods. It's perfectly reasonable to never write your own extension methods at all but still use the LINQ-related ones for the readability gains available there. It's worth at least *thinking* about what's possible, though.

10.5   *Summary*

The mechanical aspect of extension methods is straightforward—it's a simple feature to describe and demonstrate. The benefits (and costs) of them are harder to talk about in a definitive manner—it's a touchy-feely topic, and different people are bound to have different views on the value provided.

In this chapter I've tried to show a bit of everything—early on we looked at what the feature achieves in the language, before we saw some of the capabilities available through the framework. In some ways, this was a relatively gentle introduction to LINQ: we'll be revisiting some of the extension methods we've seen so far when we delve into query expressions in the next chapter, as well as seeing some new ones.

A wide variety of methods are available within the `Enumerable` class, and we've only scratched the surface. An exhaustive description with examples of *all* the methods would take most of a book on its own, and it'd become rather dull. It's *much* more interesting to come up with a scenario of your own devising (whether hypothetical or in a real project) and browse through MSDN to see what's available to help you. I urge you to use a sandbox project of some description to play with the extension methods provided—it does feel like play rather than work, and you're unlikely to want to constrain yourself to just looking at what you need to achieve your most immediate goal. The appendix has a list of the standard query operators from LINQ, which covers many of the methods within `Enumerable`.

New patterns and practices keep emerging in software engineering, and ideas from some systems often cross-pollinate to others. That's one of the things that keeps development exciting. Extension methods allow code to be written in a way which was previously unavailable in C#, creating fluent interfaces and changing the environment to suit our code rather than the other way around. Those are just the techniques we've looked at in this chapter—there are bound to be interesting future developments using the new C# features, whether individually or combined.

The revolution obviously doesn't end here, however. For a few calls, extension methods are fine. In our next chapter we look at the real power tools: query expressions and full-blown LINQ.

Query expressions and LINQ to Objects

You may well be tired of all the hyperbole around LINQ by now. We've seen some examples in chapters 1 and 3, and you've almost certainly read some examples and articles on the Web. This is where we separate myth from reality:

- LINQ isn't going to turn the most complicated query into a one-liner.
- LINQ isn't going to mean you never need to look at raw SQL again.
- LINQ isn't going to magically imbue you with architectural genius.

Given all that, LINQ is still going to change how most of us think about code. It's not a silver bullet, but it's a *very* powerful tool to have in your development armory. We'll explore two distinct aspects of LINQ: the framework support, and the compiler translation of *query expressions*. The latter can look odd to start with, but I'm sure you'll learn to love them.

Query expressions are effectively "preprocessed" by the compiler into "normal" C# 3, which is then compiled in a perfectly ordinary way. This is a neat way of integrating queries into the language without changing its semantics all over the place: it's syntactic sugar in its purest form. Most of this chapter is a list of the preprocessing translations performed by the compiler, as well as the effects achieved when the result uses the `Enumerable` extension methods.

You won't see any SQL or XML here—all that awaits us in chapter 12. However, with this chapter as a foundation you should be able to understand what the more exciting LINQ providers do when we meet them. Call me a spoilsport, but I want to take away some of their magic. Even without the air of mystery, LINQ is still very cool.

First let's consider what LINQ is in the first place, and how we're going to explore it.

11.1 Introducing LINQ

A topic as large as LINQ needs a certain amount of background before we're ready to see it in action. In this section we'll look at what LINQ is (as far as we can discern it), a few of the core principles behind it, and the data model we're going to use for all the examples in this chapter and the next. I know you're likely to be itching to get into the code, so I'll keep it fairly brief. Let's start with an issue you'd think would be quite straightforward: what counts as LINQ?

11.1.1 What's in a name?

LINQ has suffered from the same problem that .NET had early in its life: it's a term that has never been precisely defined. We know what it stands for: **L**anguage **IN**tegrated **Q**uery—but that doesn't actually help much. LINQ is fundamentally about data manipulation: it's a means of accessing data from different sources in a unified manner. It allows you to express logic about that manipulation in the language of your choice—C# in our case—even when the logic needs to be *executed* in an entirely different environment. It also attempts to eliminate (or at least vastly reduce) the *impedance mismatch*[1]—the difficulties introduced when you need to integrate two environments with very different data models, such as the object-oriented model of .NET and the relational data model of SQL.

All of the C# 3 features we've seen so far (with the exception of partial methods and automatic properties) contribute to the LINQ story, so how many of these do you need to use before you can consider yourself to be using LINQ? Do you need to be using *query expressions*, which are the final genuine language feature in C# 3? If you use

---

[1] http://en.wikipedia.org/wiki/Object-Relational_impedance_mismatch explains this for the specific object-relational case, but impedance mismatches are present in other situations, such as XML representations and web services.

the extension methods of `Enumerable` but do it without query expressions, does that count? What about plain lambda expressions without any querying going on?

As a concrete example of this question, let's consider four slightly different ways of achieving the same goal. Suppose we have a `List<Person>` (where `Person` has properties `Name` and `Age` as in chapter 8) and we wish to apply a transformation so that we get a sequence of strings, just the names of the people in the list. Using *lambda expressions* in preference to *anonymous methods*, we can still use the standard `ConvertAll` method of `List<T>`, as follows:

```
var names = people.ConvertAll(p => p.Name);
```

Alternatively we can use the `Select` method of the `Enumerable` class, because `List<T>` implements `IEnumerable<T>`. The result of this will be an `IEnumerable<string>` rather than a `List<string>`, but in many cases that's fine. The code becomes

```
var names = Enumerable.Select(people, p => p.Name);
```

Knowing that `Select` is an extension method, we can simplify things a little bit:

```
var names = people.Select(p => p.Name);
```

Finally, we could use a query expression:

```
var names = from p in people select p.Name;
```

Four one-liners, all of which accomplish much the same goal.[2] Which of them count as LINQ? My *personal* answer is that the first isn't really using LINQ (even though it uses a lambda expression), but the rest are LINQ-based solutions. The second form certainly isn't idiomatic, but the last two are both perfectly respectable LINQ ways of achieving the same aim, and in fact all of the last three samples compile to the same IL.

In the end, there are no bonus points available for using LINQ, so the question is moot. However, it's worth being aware that when a fellow developer says they're using LINQ to solve a particular problem, that statement could have a variety of meanings.

The long and the short of it is that LINQ is a collection of technologies, including the language features of C# 3 (and VB9) along with the framework libraries provided as part of .NET 3.5. If your project targets .NET 3.5, you can use LINQ as much or as little as you like. You can use just the support for in-memory querying, otherwise known as *LINQ to Objects*, or providers that target XML documents, relational databases, or other data sources. The only provider we'll use in this chapter is LINQ to Objects, and in the next chapter we'll see how the same concepts apply to the other providers.

There are a few concepts that are vital to LINQ. We've seen them tangentially in chapter 10, but let's look at them a little more closely.

11.1.2 *Fundamental concepts in LINQ*

Most of this chapter is dedicated to exactly what the C# 3 compiler does with query expressions, but it won't make much sense until we have a better understanding of the

---

[2] There's actually a big difference between `ConvertAll` and `Select`, as we'll see in a minute, but in many cases either could be used.

ideas underlying LINQ as a whole. One of the problems with reducing the impedance mismatch between two data models is that it usually involves creating yet another model to act as the bridge. This section describes the LINQ model, beginning with its most important aspect: sequences.

SEQUENCES

You're almost certainly familiar with the concept of a sequence: it's encapsulated by the `IEnumerable` and `IEnumerable<T>` interfaces, and we've already looked at those fairly closely in chapter 6 when we studied iterators. Indeed, in many ways a sequence is just a slightly more abstract way of thinking of an iterator. A sequence is like a conveyor belt of items—you fetch them one at a time until either you're no longer interested or the sequence has run out of data. There are three other fairly obvious examples: a `Stream` represents a sequence of bytes, a `TextReader` represents a sequence of characters, and a `DataReader` represents a sequence of rows from a database.[3]

The key difference between a sequence and other collection data structures such as lists and arrays is that when you're reading from a sequence, you don't generally know how many more items are waiting, or have access to arbitrary items—just the current one. Indeed, some sequences could be never-ending: you could easily have an infinite sequence of random numbers, for example. Only one piece of data is provided at a time by the sequence, so you can implement an infinite sequence without having infinite storage. Lists and arrays can *act* as sequences, of course—just as `List<T>` implements `IEnumerable<T>`—but the reverse isn't always true. You can't have an infinite array or list, for example.

Think in sequences!

Sequences are the bread and butter of LINQ. When you read a query expression, it's *really* helpful to think of the sequences involved: there's always at least one sequence to start with, and it's usually transformed into other sequences along the way, possibly being joined with yet more sequences. We'll see examples of this as we go further into the chapter, but I can't emphasize enough how important it is. Examples of LINQ queries are frequently provided on the Web with very little explanation: when you take them apart by looking at the sequences involved, things make a lot more sense. As well as being an aid to *reading* code, it can also help a lot when *writing* it. Thinking in sequences can be tricky—it's a bit of a mental leap sometimes—but if you can get there, it will help you immeasurably when you're working with LINQ.

As a simple example, let's take another query expression running against a list of people. We'll apply the same transformation as before, but with a filter involved that keeps only adults in the resulting sequence:

```
var adultNames = from person in people
                 where person.Age >= 18
                 select person.Name;
```

---

[3] Interestingly, none of these actually implements `IEnumerable<T>`.

Figure 11.1 shows this query expression graphically, breaking it down into its individual steps. I've included a number of similar figures in this chapter, but unfortunately for complicated queries there is simply not enough room on the printed page to show as much data as we might like. More detailed diagrams are available on the book's website.

Each arrow represents a sequence— the description is on the left side, and some sample data is on the right. Each box is a transformation from our query expression. Initially, we have the whole family (as `Person` objects); then after filtering, the sequence only contains adults (again, as `Person` objects); and the final result has the names of those adults as strings. Each step simply takes one sequence and applies an operation

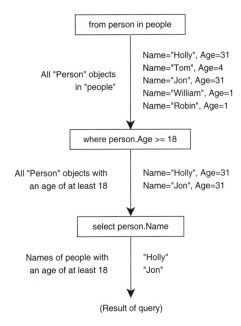

Figure 11.1   A simple query expression broken down into the sequences and transformations involved

to produce a new sequence. The result isn't the strings "Holly" and "Jon" —instead, it's an `IEnumerable<string>`, which, when asked for its elements one by one, will first yield "Holly" and then "Jon."

This example was straightforward to start with, but we'll apply the same technique later to more complicated query expressions in order to understand them more easily. Some advanced operations involve more than one sequence as input, but it's still a lot less to worry about than trying to understand the whole query in one go.

So, why are sequences so important? They're the basis for a streaming model for data handling—one that allows us to process data only when we need to.

DEFERRED EXECUTION AND STREAMING

When the query expression shown in figure 11.1 is created, no data is processed. The original list of people isn't accessed *at all.* Instead, a representation of the query is built up in memory. Delegate instances are used to represent the predicate testing for adulthood and the conversion from a person to that person's name. It's only when the resulting `IEnumerable<string>` is asked for its first element that the wheels start turning.

This aspect of LINQ is called *deferred execution.* When the first element of the result is requested, the `Select` transformation asks the `Where` transformation for its first element. The `Where` transformation asks the list for its first element, checks whether the predicate matches (which it does in this case), and returns that element back to `Select`. That in turn extracts the name and returns it as the result.

That's all a bit of a mouthful, but a sequence diagram makes it all much clearer. I'm going to collapse the calls to `MoveNext` and `Current` to a single fetch operation: it makes the diagram a lot simpler. Just remember that each time the fetch occurs, it's effectively checking for the end of the sequence as well. Figure 11.2 shows the first few stages of our sample query expression in operation, when we print out each element of the result using a `foreach` loop.

As you can see in figure 11.2, only one element of data is processed at a time. If we decided to stop printing output after writing "Holly," we would never execute any of the operations on the other elements of the original sequence. Although several stages are involved here, processing data in a *streaming* manner like this is efficient and

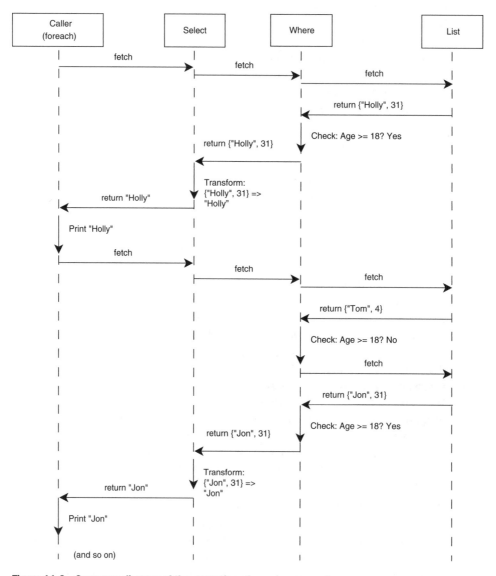

Figure 11.2   Sequence diagram of the execution of a query expression

flexible. In particular, regardless of how much source data there is, you don't need to know about more than one element of it at any one point in time. That's the difference between using `List.ConvertAll` and `Enumerable.Select`: the former creates a whole new in-memory list, whereas the latter just iterates through the original sequence, yielding a single converted element at a time.

This is a best-case scenario, however. There are times where in order to fetch the first result of a query, you have to evaluate *all* of the data from the source. We've already seen one example of this in the previous chapter: the `Enumerable.Reverse` method needs to fetch all the data available in order to return the last original element as the first element of the resulting sequence. This makes `Reverse` a *buffering* operation—which can have a huge effect on the efficiency (or even feasibility) of your overall operation. If you can't afford to have all the data in memory at one time, you can't use buffering operations.

Just as the streaming aspect depends on which operation you perform, some transformations take place as soon as you call them, rather than using deferred execution. This is called *immediate execution*. Generally speaking, operations that return another sequence (usually an `IEnumerable<T>` or `IQueryable<T>`) use deferred execution, whereas operations that return a single value use immediate execution.

The operations that are widely available in LINQ are known as the *standard query operators*—let's take a brief look at them now.

STANDARD QUERY OPERATORS

LINQ's *standard query operators* are a collection of transformations that have well-understood meanings. LINQ providers are encouraged to implement as many of these operators as possible, making the implementation obey the expected behavior. This is crucial in providing a consistent query framework across multiple data sources. Of course, some LINQ providers may expose more functionality, and some of the operators may not map appropriately to the target domain of the provider—but at least the opportunity for consistency is there.

C#3 has support for some of the standard query operators built into the language via query expressions, but they can always be called manually. You may be interested to know that VB9 has more of the operators present in the language: as ever, there's a trade-off between the added complexity of including a feature in the language and the benefits that feature brings. Personally I think the C# team has done an admirable job: I've always been a fan of a small language with a large library behind it.

We'll see some of these operators in our examples as we go through this chapter and the next, but I'm not aiming to give a comprehensive guide to them here: this book is primarily about C#, not the whole of LINQ. You don't need to know all of the operators in order to be productive in LINQ, but your experience is likely to grow over time. The appendix gives a brief description of each of the standard query operators, and MSDN gives more details of each specific overload. When you run into a problem, check the list: if it feels like there *ought* to be a built-in method to help you, there probably is!

Having mentioned examples, it's time to introduce the data model that most of the rest of the sample code in this chapter will use.

11.1.3 *Defining the sample data model*

In section 10.3.5 I gave a brief example of bug tracking as a real use for extension methods and lambda expressions. We'll use the same idea for almost all of the sample code in this chapter—it's a fairly simple model, but one that can be manipulated in many different ways to give useful information. It's also a domain that most professional developers are familiar with, while not involving frankly tedious relationships between customers and orders. You can find further examples using the same model in the downloadable source code, along with detailed comments. Some of these are more complicated than the ones presented in this chapter and provide good exercises for understanding larger query expressions.

Our fictional setting is SkeetySoft, a small software company with big ambition. The founders have decided to attempt to create an office suite, a media player, and an instant messaging application. After all, there are no big players in those markets, are there?

The development department of SkeetySoft consists of five people: two developers (Deborah and Darren), two testers (Tara and Tim), and a manager (Mary). The company currently has a single customer: Colin. The aforementioned products are Skeety-Office, SkeetyMediaPlayer, and SkeetyTalk, respectively. We're going to look at defects logged during August 2007, using the data model shown in figure 11.3.

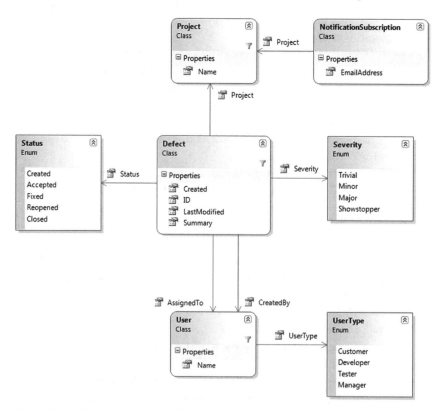

Figure 11.3   Class diagram of the SkeetySoft defect data model

As you can see, we're not recording an awful lot of data. In particular, there's no real history to the defects, but there's enough here to let us demonstrate the query expression features of C#3. For the purposes of this chapter, all the data is stored in memory. We have a class named `SampleData` with properties `AllDefects`, `AllUsers`, `AllProjects`, and `AllSubscriptions`, which each return an appropriate type of `IEnumerable<T>`. The `Start` and `End` properties return `DateTime` instances for the start and end of August respectively, and there are nested classes `Users` and `Projects` within `SampleData` to provide easy access to a particular user or project. The one type that may not be immediately obvious is `NotificationSubscription`: the idea behind this is to send an email to the specified address every time a defect is created or changed in the relevant project.

There are 41 defects in the sample data, created using C#3 object initializers. All of the code is available on the book's website, but I won't include the sample data itself in this chapter.

Now that the preliminaries are dealt with, let's get cracking with some queries!

11.2 Simple beginnings: selecting elements

Having brought up some general LINQ concepts beforehand, I'll introduce the concepts that are specific to C#3 as they arise in the course of the rest of the chapter. We're going to start with a simple query (even simpler than the ones we've seen so far in the chapter) and work up to some quite complicated ones, not only building up your expertise of what the C#3 compiler is doing, but also teaching you how to read LINQ code.

All of our examples will follow the pattern of defining a query, and then printing the results to the console. We're not interested in binding queries to data grids or anything like that—it's all important, but not directly relevant to learning C#3.

We can use a simple expression that just prints out all our users as the starting point for examining what the compiler is doing behind the scenes and learning about *range variables*.

11.2.1 Starting with a source and ending with a selection

Every query expression in C#3 starts off in the same way—stating the source of a sequence of data:

```
from element in source
```

The `element` part is just an identifier, with an optional type name before it. Most of the time you won't need the type name, and we won't have one for our first example. Lots of different things can happen after that first clause, but sooner or later you always end with a `select` clause or a `group` clause. We'll start off with a `select` clause to keep things nice and simple. The syntax for a `select` clause is also easy:

```
select expression
```

The `select` clause is known as a *projection*. Combining the two together and using the most trivial expression we can think of gives a simple (and practically useless) query, as shown in listing 11.1.

Listing 11.1   Trivial query to print the list of users

```
var query = from user in SampleData.AllUsers
            select user;

foreach (var user in query)
{
    Console.WriteLine(user);
}
```

The query expression is the part highlighted in bold. I've overridden ToString for each of the entities in the model, so the results of listing 11.1 are as follows:

```
User: Tim Trotter (Tester)
User: Tara Tutu (Tester)
User: Deborah Denton (Developer)
User: Darren Dahlia (Developer)
User: Mary Malcop (Manager)
User: Colin Carton (Customer)
```

You may be wondering how useful this is as an example: after all, we could have just used SampleData.AllUsers directly in our foreach statement. However, we'll use this query expression—however trivial—to introduce two new concepts. First we'll look at the general nature of the *translation* process the compiler uses when it encounters a query expression, and then we'll discuss *range variables*.

11.2.2 *Compiler translations as the basis of query expressions*

The C#3 query expression support is based on the compiler translating query expressions into "normal" C# code. It does this in a mechanical manner that doesn't try to understand the code, apply type inference, check the validity of method calls, or any of the normal business of a compiler. That's all done later, after the translation. In many ways, this first phase can be regarded as a preprocessor step. The compiler translates listing 11.1 into listing 11.2. before doing the *real* compilation.

Listing 11.2   The query expression of listing 11.1 translated into a method call

```
var query = SampleData.AllUsers.Select(user => user);

foreach (var user in query)
{
    Console.WriteLine(user);
}
```

The C#3 compiler translates the query expression into *exactly* that code before properly compiling it further. In particular, it doesn't assume that it should use Enumerable. Select, or that List<T> will contain a method called Select. It merely translates the code and then lets the next phase of compilation deal with finding an appropriate method—whether as a straightforward member or as an extension method. The parameter can be a suitable delegate type or an Expression<T> for an appropriate type T.

This is where it's important that lambda expressions can be converted into both delegate instances and expression trees. All the examples in this chapter will use delegates, but we'll see how expression trees are used when we look at the other LINQ providers in chapter 12. When I present the signatures for some of the methods called by the compiler later on, remember that these are just the ones called in LINQ to Objects—whenever the parameter is a delegate type (which most of them are), the compiler will use a lambda expression as the argument, and then try to find a method with a suitable signature.

It's also important to remember that wherever a normal variable (such as a local variable within the method) appears within a lambda expression after translation has been performed, it will become a captured variable in the same way that we saw back in chapter 5. This is just normal lambda expression behavior—but unless you understand which variables will be captured, you could easily be confused by the results of your queries.

The language specification gives details of the *query expression pattern*, which must be implemented for all query expressions to work, but this isn't defined as an interface as you might expect. It makes a lot of sense, however: it allows LINQ to be applied to interfaces such as IEnumerable<T> using extension methods. This chapter tackles each element of the query expression pattern, one at a time.

Listing 11.3 proves how the compiler translation works: it provides a dummy implementation of both Select and Where, with Select being a normal instance method and Where being an extension method. Our original simple query expression only contained a select clause, but I've included the where clause to show both kinds of methods in use. Unfortunately, because it requires a top-level class to contain the extension method it can't be represented as a snippet but only as a full listing.

Listing 11.3 Compiler translation calling methods on a dummy LINQ implementation

```
using System;

static class Extensions
{
    public static Dummy<T> Where<T>(this Dummy<T> dummy,           ⟵┐ Declares
                                    Func<T,bool> predicate)          │ Where
    {                                                                │ extension
        Console.WriteLine ("Where called");                         │ method
        return dummy;
    }
}

public class Dummy<T>
{
    public Dummy<U> Select<U>(Func<T,U> selector)       ⟵┐ Declares Select
    {                                                     │ instance method
        Console.WriteLine ("Select called");
        return new Dummy<U>();
    }
}

public class TranslationExample
{
```

```
static void Main()
{                                                    Creates source
    var source = new Dummy<string>();          ◁──── to be queried

    var query = from dummy in source
                where dummy.ToString()=="Ignored"     Calls methods via a
                select "Anything";                    query expression
}
}
```

Running listing 11.3 prints "Where called" and then "Select called" just as we'd expect, because the query expression has been translated into this code:

```
var query = source.Where(dummy => dummy.ToString()=="Ignored")
                .Select(dummy => "Anything");
```

Of course, we're not doing any querying or transformation here, but it shows how the compiler is translating our query expression. If you're puzzled as to why we've selected `"Anything"` instead of just `dummy`, it's because a projection of just `dummy` (which is a "do nothing" projection) would be removed by the compiler in this particular case. We'll look at that later in section 11.3.2, but for the moment the important idea is the overall type of translation involved. We only need to learn what translations the C# compiler will use, and then we can take any query expression, convert it into the form that doesn't use query expressions, and then look at what it's doing from that point of view.

Notice how we don't implement `IEnumerable<T>` at all in `Dummy<T>`. The translation from query expressions to "normal" code doesn't depend on it, but in practice almost all LINQ providers will expose data either as `IEnumerable<T>` or `IQueryable<T>` (which we'll look at in chapter 12). The fact that the translation doesn't depend on any particular types but merely on the method names and parameters is a sort of compile-time form of duck typing. This is similar to the same way that the collection initializers presented in chapter 8 find a public method called `Add` using normal overload resolution rather than using an interface containing an `Add` method with a particular signature. Query expressions take this idea one step further—the translation occurs early in the compilation process in order to allow the compiler to pick either instance methods or extension methods. You could even consider the translation to be the work of a separate preprocessing engine.

NOTE   *Why* from ... where ... select *instead of select ... from ... where?*   Many developers find the order of the clauses in query expressions confusing to start with. It looks just like SQL—except back to front. If you look back to the translation into methods, you'll see the main reason behind it. The query expression is processed in the same order that it's written: we start with a source in the `from` clause, then filter it in the `where` clause, then project it in the `select` clause. Another way of looking at it is to consider the diagrams throughout this chapter. The data flows from top to bottom, and the boxes appear in the diagram in the same order as their corresponding clauses appear in the query expression. Once you get over any initial discomfort due to unfamiliarity, you may well find this approach appealing—I certainly do.

So, we know that a source level translation is involved—but there's another crucial concept to understand before we move on any further.

11.2.3 *Range variables and nontrivial projections*

Let's look back at our original query expression in a bit more depth. We haven't examined the identifier in the `from` clause or the expression in the `select` clause. Figure 11.4 shows the query expression again, with each part labeled to explain its purpose.

The contextual keywords are easy to explain—they specify to the compiler what we want to do with the data. Likewise the source expression is just a normal C# expression— a property in this case, but it could just as easily have been a method call, or a variable.

The tricky bits are the *range variable* declaration and the projection expression. Range variables aren't like any other type of variable. In some ways they're not variables at all! They're only available in query expressions, and they're effectively present to propagate context from one expression to another. They represent one element of a particular sequence, and they're used in the compiler translation to allow other expressions to be turned into lambda expressions easily.

We've already seen that our original query expression was turned into

```
SampleData.AllUsers.Select(user => user)
```

The left side of the lambda expression—the part that provides the parameter name— comes from the range variable declaration. The right side comes from the `select` clause. The translation is as simple as that (in this case). It all works out OK because we've used the same name on both sides. Suppose we'd written the query expression like this:

```
from user in SampleData.AllUsers
select person
```

In that case, the translated version would have been

```
SampleData.AllUsers.Select(user => person)
```

At that point the compiler would have complained because it wouldn't have known what `person` referred to. Now that we know how simple the process is, however, it

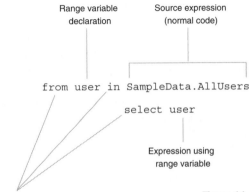

Figure 11.4 A simple query expression broken down into its constituent parts

becomes easier to understand a query expression that has a slightly more complicated projection. Listing 11.4 prints out just the names of our users.

Listing 11.4   Query selecting just the names of the users

```
var query = from user in SampleData.AllUsers
            select user.Name;

foreach (string name in query)
{
    Console.WriteLine(name);
}
```

This time we're using user.Name as the projection, and we can see that the result is a sequence of strings, not of User objects. The translation of the query expression follows the same rules as before, and becomes

```
SampleData.AllUsers.Select(user => user.Name)
```

The compiler allows this, because the Select extension method as applied to AllUsers *effectively* has this signature, acting as if it were a member of IEnumerable<T>:

```
IEnumerable<TResult> Select<TResult> (Func<T,TResult> selector)
```

NOTE   *Extension methods pretending to be instance methods*—Just to be clear, Select *isn't* a member of IEnumerable<T> itself, and the real signature has an IEnumerable<T> parameter at the start. However, the translation process doesn't care whether the result is a call to a normal instance method or an extension method. I find it easier to pretend it's a normal method just for the sake of working out the query translation. I've used the same convention for the remainder of the chapter.

The type inference described in chapter 9 kicks in, converting the lambda expression into a Func<User,TResult> by deciding that the user parameter must be of type User, and then inferring that the return type (and thus TResult) should be string. This is why lambda expressions allow implicitly typed parameters, and why there are such complicated type inference rules: these are the gears and pistons of the LINQ engine.

NOTE   *Why do you need to know all this?*   You can almost ignore what's going on with range variables for a lot of the time. You may well have seen many, many queries and understood what they achieve without ever knowing about what's going on behind the scenes. That's fine for when things are working (as they tend to with examples in tutorials), but it's when things go wrong that it pays to know about the details. If you have a query expression that won't compile because the compiler is complaining that it doesn't know about a particular identifier, you should look at the range variables involved.

So far we've only seen implicitly typed range variables. What happens when we include a type in the declaration? The answer lies in the Cast and OfType standard query operators.

11.2.4 *Cast, OfType, and explicitly typed range variables*

Most of the time, range variables can be implicitly typed; in .NET 3.5, you're likely to be working with generic collections where the specified type is all you need. What if that weren't the case, though? What if we had an `ArrayList`, or perhaps an `object[]` that we wanted to perform a query on? It would be a pity if LINQ couldn't be applied in those situations. Fortunately, there are two standard query operators that come to the rescue: `Cast` and `OfType`. Only `Cast` is supported directly by the query expression syntax, but we'll look at both in this section.

The two operators are similar: both take an arbitrary untyped sequence and return a strongly typed sequence. `Cast` does this by casting each element to the target type (and failing on any element that isn't of the right type) and `OfType` does a test first, skipping any elements of the wrong type.

Listing 11.5 demonstrates both of these operators, used as simple extension methods from `Enumerable`. Just for a change, we won't be using our SkeetySoft defect system for our sample data—after all, that's all strongly typed! Instead, we'll just use two `ArrayList` objects.

> **Listing 11.5   Using `Cast` and `OfType` to work with weakly typed collections**

```
ArrayList list = new ArrayList { "First", "Second", "Third"};
IEnumerable<string> strings = list.Cast<string>();
foreach (string item in strings)
{
    Console.WriteLine(item);
}
list = new ArrayList { 1, "not an int", 2, 3};
IEnumerable<int> ints = list.OfType<int>();
foreach (int item in ints)
{
    Console.WriteLine(item);
}
```

The first list has only strings in it, so we're safe to use `Cast<string>` to obtain a sequence of strings. The second list has mixed content, so in order to fetch just the integers from it we use `OfType<int>`. If we'd used `Cast<int>` on the second list, an exception would have been thrown when we tried to cast "not an int" to int. Note that this would only have happened *after* we'd printed "1"—both operators stream their data, converting elements as they fetch them.

When you introduce a range variable with an explicit type, the compiler uses a call to `Cast` to make sure the sequence used by the rest of the query expression is of the appropriate type. Listing 11.6 shows this, with a projection using the `Substring` method to prove that the sequence generated by the `from` clause is a sequence of strings.

> **Listing 11.6   Using an explicitly typed range variable to automatically call `Cast`**

```
ArrayList list = new ArrayList { "First", "Second", "Third"};
var strings = from string entry in list
              select entry.Substring(0, 3);
```

```
foreach (string start in strings)
{
    Console.WriteLine(start);
}
```

The output of listing 11.6 is "Fir," "Sec," "Thi"—but what's more interesting is the translated query expression, which is

```
list.Cast<string>().Select(entry => entry.Substring(0,3));
```

Without the cast, we wouldn't be able to call `Select` at all, because the extension method is only defined for `IEnumerable<T>` rather than `IEnumerable`. Even when you're using a strongly typed collection, you might still want to use an explicitly typed range variable, though. For instance, you could have a collection that is defined to be a `List<ISomeInterface>` but you know that all the elements are instances of `MyImplementation`. Using a range variable with an explicit type of `MyImplementation` allows you to access all the members of `MyImplementation` without manually inserting casts all over the code.

We've covered a lot of important conceptual ground so far, even though we haven't achieved any impressive results. To recap the most important points briefly:

- LINQ is based on sequences of data, which are streamed wherever possible.
- Creating a query doesn't immediately execute it: most operations use deferred execution.
- Query expressions in C# 3 involve a preprocessing phase that converts the expression into normal C#, which is then compiled properly with all the normal rules of type inference, overloading, lambda expressions, and so forth.
- The variables declared in query expressions don't act like anything else: they are range variables, which allow you to refer to data consistently within the query expression.

I know that there's a lot of somewhat abstract information to take in. Don't worry if you're beginning to wonder if LINQ is worth all this trouble. I promise you that it is. With a lot of the groundwork out of the way, we can start doing genuinely useful things—like filtering our data, and then ordering it.

11.3   *Filtering and ordering a sequence*

You may be surprised to learn that these two operations are some of the simplest to explain in terms of compiler translations. The reason is that they always return a sequence of the same type as their input, which means we don't need to worry about any new range variables being introduced. It also helps that we've seen the corresponding extension methods in chapter 10.

11.3.1   *Filtering using a where clause*

It's remarkably easy to understand the where clause. The format is just

```
where filter-expression
```

The compiler translates this into a call to the Where method with a lambda expression, which uses the appropriate range variable as the parameter and the filter expression as the body. The filter expression is applied as a predicate to each element of the incoming stream of data, and only those that return true are present in the resulting sequence. Using multiple where clauses results in multiple chained Where calls—only elements that match *all* of the predicates are part of the resulting sequence. Listing 11.7 demonstrates a query expression that finds all open defects assigned to Tim.

Listing 11.7 Query expression using multiple where clauses

```
User tim = SampleData.Users.TesterTim;

var query = from bug in SampleData.AllDefects
            where bug.Status != Status.Closed
            where bug.AssignedTo == tim
            select bug.Summary;

foreach (var summary in query)
{
    Console.WriteLine(summary);
}
```

The query expression in listing 11.7 is translated into

```
SampleData.AllDefects.Where (bug => bug.Status != Status.Closed)
            .Where (bug => bug.AssignedTo == tim)
            .Select(bug => bug.Summary)
```

The output of listing 11.7 is as follows:

```
Installation is slow
Subtitles only work in Welsh
Play button points the wrong way
Webcam makes me look bald
Network is saturated when playing WAV file
```

Of course, we could write a single where clause that combined the two conditions as an alternative to using multiple where clauses. In some cases this may improve performance, but it's worth bearing the readability of the query expression in mind, too. Once more, this is likely to be a fairly subjective matter. My personal inclination is to combine conditions that are logically related but keep others separate. In this case, both parts of the expression deal directly with a defect (as that's all our sequence contains), so it would be reasonable to combine them. As before, it's worth trying both forms to see which is clearer.

In a moment, we'll start trying to apply some ordering rules to our query, but first we should look at a small detail to do with the select clause.

11.3.2 Degenerate query expressions

While we've got a fairly simple translation to work with, let's revisit a point I glossed over earlier in section 11.2.2 when I first introduced the compiler translations. So far, all our translated query expressions have included a call to `Select`. What happens if our select clause does nothing, effectively returning the same sequence as it's given? The answer is that the compiler removes that call to `Select`—but only if there are other operations being performed within the query expression. For example, the following query expression just selects all the defects in the system:

```
from defect in SampleData.AllDefects
select defect
```

This is known as a *degenerate query expression*. The compiler deliberately generates a call to `Select` even though it seems to do nothing:

```
SampleData.AllDefects.Select (defect => defect)
```

There's a big difference between this and the simple expression `SampleData.AllDefects`, however. The items returned by the two sequences are the same, but the result of the `Select` method is *just* the sequence of items, not the source itself. The result of a query expression is never the same object as the source data, unless the LINQ provider has been poorly coded. This can be important from a data integrity point of view—a provider can return a mutable result object, knowing that changes to the returned data set won't affect the "master" even in the face of a degenerate query.

When other operations are involved, there's no need for the compiler to keep "no-op" select clauses. For example, suppose we change the query expression in listing 11.7 to select the whole defect rather than just the name:

```
from bug in SampleData.AllDefects
where bug.Status != Status.Closed
where bug.AssignedTo == SampleData.Users.TesterTim
select bug
```

We now don't need the final call to `Select`, so the translated code is just this:

```
SampleData.AllDefects.Where (bug => bug.Status != Status.Closed)
                .Where (bug => bug.AssignedTo == tim)
```

These rules rarely get in the way when you're writing query expressions, but they can cause confusion if you decompile the code with a tool such as Reflector—it can be surprising to see the `Select` call go missing for no apparent reason.

With that knowledge in hand, let's improve our query so that we know what Tim should work on next.

11.3.3 *Ordering using an orderby clause*

It's not uncommon for developers and testers to be asked to work on the most critical defects before they tackle more trivial ones. We can use a simple query to tell Tim the order in which he should tackle the open defects assigned to him. Listing 11.8 does exactly this using an `orderby` clause, printing out all the details of the bugs, in descending order of priority.

Listing 11.8 Sorting by the severity of a bug, from high to low priority

```
User tim = SampleData.Users.TesterTim;

var query = from bug in SampleData.AllDefects
            where bug.Status != Status.Closed
            where bug.AssignedTo == tim
            orderby bug.Severity descending
            select bug;

foreach (var bug in query)
{
    Console.WriteLine("{0}: {1}", bug.Severity, bug.Summary);
}
```

The output of listing 11.8 shows that we've sorted the results appropriately:

```
Showstopper: Webcam makes me look bald
Major: Subtitles only work in Welsh
Major: Play button points the wrong way
Minor: Network is saturated when playing WAV file
Trivial: Installation is slow
```

However, you can see that we've got two major defects. Which order should those be tackled in? Currently no clear ordering is involved. Let's change the query so that after sorting by severity in descending order, we sort by "last modified time" in *ascending* order. This means that Tim will test the bugs that have been fixed a long time ago before the ones that were fixed recently. This just requires an extra expression in the orderby clause, as shown in listing 11.9.

Listing 11.9 Ordering by severity and then last modified time

```
User tim = SampleData.Users.TesterTim;

var query = from bug in SampleData.AllDefects
            where bug.Status != Status.Closed
            where bug.AssignedTo == tim
            orderby bug.Severity descending, bug.LastModified
            select bug;

foreach (var bug in query)
{
    Console.WriteLine("{0}: {1} ({2:d})",
                      bug.Severity, bug.Summary, bug.LastModified);
}
```

The results of listing 11.9 are shown here. Note how the order of the two major defects has been reversed.

```
Showstopper: Webcam makes me look bald (08/27/2007)
Major: Play button points the wrong way (08/17/2007)
Major: Subtitles only work in Welsh (08/23/2007)
Minor: Network is saturated when playing WAV file (08/31/2007)
Trivial: Installation is slow (08/15/2007)
```

So, that's what the query expression looks like—but what does the compiler do? It simply calls the `OrderBy` and `ThenBy` methods (or `OrderByDescending`/`ThenBy-Descending` for descending orders). Our query expression is translated into

```
SampleData.AllDefects.Where (bug => bug.Status != Status.Closed)
                    .Where (bug => bug.AssignedTo == tim)
                    .OrderByDescending (bug => bug.Severity)
                    .ThenBy (bug => bug.LastModified)
```

Now that we've seen an example, let's look at the general syntax of orderby clauses. They're basically the contextual keyword orderby followed by one or more orderings. An *ordering* is just an expression (which can use range variables) optionally followed by descending, which has the obvious meaning. The translation for the first ordering is a call to `OrderBy` or `OrderByDescending`, and any other orderings are translated using a call to `ThenBy` or `ThenByDescending`, as shown in our example.

The difference between `OrderBy` and `ThenBy` is quite simple: `OrderBy` assumes it has primary control over the ordering, whereas `ThenBy` understands that it's subservient to one or more previous orderings. For LINQ to Objects, `ThenBy` is only defined as an extension method for `IOrderedEnumerable<T>`, which is the type returned by `OrderBy` (and by `ThenBy` itself, to allow further chaining).

Warning: only use one orderby clause!

It's very important to note that although you can use multiple orderby clauses, each one will start with its own `OrderBy` or `OrderByDescending` clause, which means the last one will effectively "win." There may be *some* reason for including multiple orderby clauses, but it would be very unusual. You should almost always use a single clause containing multiple orderings instead.

As noted in chapter 10, applying an ordering requires all the data to be loaded (at least for LINQ to Objects)—you can't order an infinite sequence, for example. Hopefully the reason for this is obvious—you don't know whether you'll see something that should come at the start of the resulting sequence until you've seen all the elements, for example.

We're about halfway through learning about query expressions, and you may be surprised that we haven't seen any *joins* yet. Obviously they're important in LINQ just as they're important in SQL, but they're also complicated. I promise we'll get to them in due course, but in order to introduce just one new concept at a time, we'll detour via let clauses first. That way we can learn about *transparent identifiers* before we hit joins.

11.4   *Let clauses and transparent identifiers*

Most of the rest of the operators we still need to look at involve *transparent identifiers*. Just like range variables, you can get along perfectly well without understanding transparent identifiers, if you only want to have a fairly shallow grasp of query expressions. If you've bought this book, I hope you want to know C# 3 at a deeper level, which will (among other things) enable you to look compilation errors in the face and know what they're talking about.

You don't need to know *everything* about transparent identifiers, but I'll teach you enough so that if you see one in the language specification you won't feel like running and hiding. You'll also understand why they're needed at all—and that's where an example will come in handy. The `let` clause is the simplest transformation available that uses transparent identifiers.

11.4.1 Introducing an intermediate computation with let

A `let` clause simply introduces a new range variable with a value that can be based on other range variables. The syntax is as easy as pie:

```
let identifier = expression
```

To explain this operator in terms that don't use any other complicated operators, I'm going to resort to a very artificial example. Suspend your disbelief, and imagine that finding the length of a string is a costly operation. Now imagine that we had a completely bizarre system requirement to order our users by the lengths of their names, and then display the name and its length. Yes, I know it's somewhat unlikely. Listing 11.10 shows one way of doing this without a `let` clause.

Listing 11.10 Sorting by the lengths of user names without a `let` clause

```
var query = from user in SampleData.AllUsers
            orderby user.Name.Length
            select user.Name;

foreach (var name in query)
{
    Console.WriteLine("{0}: {1}", name.Length, name);
}
```

That works fine, but it uses the dreaded Length property twice—once to sort the users, and once in the display side. Surely not even the fastest supercomputer could cope with finding the lengths of six strings *twice*! No, we need to avoid that redundant computation. We can do so with the `let` clause, which evaluates an expression and introduces it as a new range variable. Listing 11.11 achieves the same result as listing 11.10, but only uses the Length property once per user.

Listing 11.11 Using a `let` clause to remove redundant calculations

```
var query = from user in SampleData.AllUsers
            let length = user.Name.Length
            orderby length
            select new { Name = user.Name, Length = length };

foreach (var entry in query)
{
    Console.WriteLine("{0}: {1}", entry.Length, entry.Name);
}
```

Listing 11.11 introduces a new range variable called length, which contains the length of the user's name (for the current user in the original sequence). We then use that new range variable for both sorting and the projection at the end. Have you spotted the problem yet? We need to use two range variables, but the lambda expression passed to `Select` only takes one parameter! This is where transparent identifiers come on the scene.

11.4.2 *Transparent identifiers*

In listing 11.11, we've got *two* range variables involved in the final projection, but the `Select` method only acts on a single sequence. How can we combine the range variables? The answer is to create an anonymous type that contains both variables but apply a clever translation to make it *look* as if we've actually got two parameters for the `select` and `orderby` clauses. Figure 11.5 shows the sequences involved.

The `let` clause achieves its objectives by using another call to `Select`, creating an anonymous type for the resulting sequence, and effectively creating a new range variable whose name can never be seen or used in source code. Our query expression from listing 11.11 is translated into something like this:

```
SampleData.AllUsers.Select(user => new { user,
                                         length=user.Name.Length })
              .OrderBy(z => z.length)
              .Select(z => new { Name=z.user.Name,
                                 Length=z.length })
```

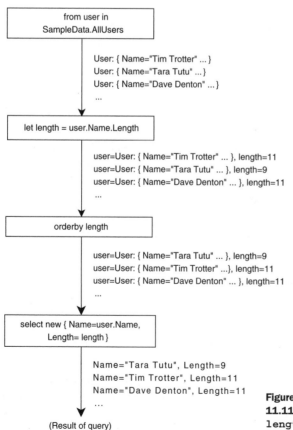

Figure 11.5 Sequences involved in listing 11.11, where a `let` clause introduces the `length` range variable

Each part of the query has been adjusted appropriately: where the original query expression referenced `user` or `length` directly, if the reference occurs after the `let` clause, it's replaced by `z.user` or `z.length`. The choice of `z` as the name here is arbitrary—it's all hidden by the compiler.

If you read the C#3 language specification on `let` clauses, you'll see that the translation it describes is from one query expression to another. It uses an asterisk (*) to represent the transparent identifier introduced. The transparent identifier is then *erased* as a final step in translation. I won't use that notation in this chapter, as it's hard to come to grips with and unnecessary at the level of detail we're going into. Hopefully with this background, the specification won't be quite as impenetrable as it might be otherwise, should you need to refer to it.

The good news is that we can now take a look at the rest of the translations making up C#3's query expression support. I won't go into the details of every transparent identifier introduced, but I'll mention the situations in which they occur. Let's look at the support for joins first.

11.5 Joins

If you've ever read *anything* about SQL, you probably have an idea what a database join is. It takes two tables and creates a result by matching one set of rows against another set of rows. A LINQ join is similar, except it works on sequences. Three types of joins are available, although not all of them use the `join` keyword in the query expression. We'll start with the join that is closest to a SQL inner join.

11.5.1 Inner joins using join clauses

Inner joins involve two sequences. One *key selector* expression is applied to each element of the first sequence and another key selector (which may be totally different) is applied to each element of the second sequence. The result of the join is a sequence of all the pairs of elements where the key from the first element is the same as the key from the second element.

NOTE *Terminology clash! Inner and outer sequences*—The MSDN documentation for the `Join` method used to evaluate inner joins unhelpfully calls the sequences involved *inner* and *outer*. This has nothing to do with inner joins and outer joins—it's just a way of differentiating between the sequences. You can think of them as first and second, left and right, Bert and Ernie—anything you like that helps you. I'll use *left* and *right* for this chapter. Aside from anything else, it makes it obvious which sequence is which in diagram form.

The two sequences can be anything you like: the right sequence can even be the same as the left sequence, if that's useful. (Imagine finding pairs of people who were born on the same day, for example.) The only thing that matters is that the two key selector expressions must result in the same type of key[4]. You can't join a sequence of people

---

[4] It is also valid for there to be two key types involved, with an implicit conversion from one to the other. One of the types must be a better choice than the other, in the same way that the compiler infers the type of an implicitly typed array. In my experience you rarely need to consciously consider this detail.

to a sequence of cities by saying that the birth date of the person is the same as the population of the city—it doesn't make any sense.

The syntax for an inner join looks more complicated than it is:

```
[query selecting the left sequence]
join right-range-variable in right-sequence
on left-key-selector equals right-key-selector
```

Seeing `equals` as a contextual keyword rather than using symbols can be slightly disconcerting, but it makes it easier to distinguish the left key selector from the right key selector. Often (but not always) at least one of the key selectors is a trivial one that just selects the exact element from that sequence.

Let's look at an example from our defect system. Suppose we had just added the notification feature, and wanted to send the first batch of emails for all the existing defects. We need to join the list of notifications against the list of defects, where their projects match. Listing 11.12 performs just such a join.

Listing 11.12   Joining the defects and notification subscriptions based on project

```
var query = from defect in SampleData.AllDefects
            join subscription in SampleData.AllSubscriptions
              on defect.Project equals subscription.Project
            select new { defect.Summary, subscription.EmailAddress };

foreach (var entry in query)
{
    Console.WriteLine("{0}: {1}", entry.EmailAddress, entry.Summary);
}
```

Listing 11.12 will show each of the media player bugs twice—once for "mediabugs@skeetysoft.com" and once for "theboss@skeetysoft.com" (because the boss really cares about the media player project).

In this particular case we could easily have made the join the other way round, reversing the left and right sequences. The result would have been the same entries but in a different order. The implementation in LINQ to Objects returns entries so that all the pairs using the first element of the left sequence are returned (in the order of the right sequence), then all the pairs using the second element of the left sequence, and so on. The right sequence is buffered, but the left sequence is streamed—so if you want to join a massive sequence to a tiny one, it's worth using the tiny one as the right sequence if you can.

One error that might trip you up is putting the key selectors the wrong way round. In the left key selector, only the left sequence range variable is in scope; in the right key selector only the right range variable is in scope. If you reverse the left and right sequences, you have to reverse the left and right key selectors too. Fortunately the compiler knows that it's a common mistake and suggests the appropriate course of action.

Just to make it more obvious what's going on, figure 11.6 shows the sequences as they're processed.

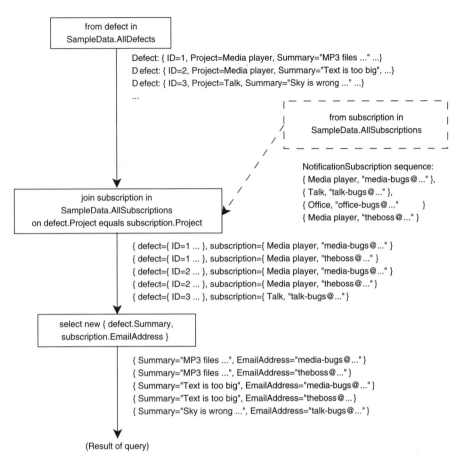

Figure 11.6   The join from listing 11.12 in graphical form, showing two different sequences (defects and subscriptions) used as data sources

Often you want to filter the sequence, and filtering before the join occurs is more efficient than filtering it afterward. At this stage the query expression is simpler if the left sequence is the one requiring filtering. For instance, if we wanted to show only defects that are closed, we could use this query expression:

```
from defect in SampleData.AllDefects
where defect.Status == Status.Closed
join subscription in SampleData.AllSubscriptions
   on defect.Project equals subscription.Project
select new { defect.Summary, subscription.EmailAddress }
```

We *can* perform the same query with the sequences reversed, but it's messier:

```
from subscription in SampleData.AllSubscriptions
join defect in (from defect in SampleData.AllDefects
                where defect.Status == Status.Closed
                select defect)
   on subscription.Project equals defect.Project
select new { defect.Summary, subscription.EmailAddress }
```

Notice how you can use one query expression inside another—indeed, the language specification describes many of the compiler translations in these terms. Nested query expressions are useful but hurt readability as well: it's often worth looking for an alternative, or using a variable for the right-hand sequence in order to make the code clearer.

NOTE   *Are inner joins useful in LINQ to Objects?*   Inner joins are used all the time in SQL. They are effectively the way that we navigate from one entity to a related one, usually joining a foreign key in one table to the primary key on another. In the object-oriented model, we tend to navigate from one object to another via references. For instance, retrieving the summary of a defect and the name of the user assigned to work on it would require a join in SQL—in C# we just use a chain of properties. If we'd had a reverse association from `Project` to the list of `NotificationSubscription` objects associated with it in our model, we wouldn't have needed the join to achieve the goal of this example, either. That's not to say that inner joins aren't useful sometimes even within object-oriented models—but they don't naturally occur nearly as often as in relational models.

Inner joins are translated by the compiler into calls to the `Join` method. The signature of the overload used for LINQ to Objects is as follows (when imagining it to be an instance method of `IEnumerable<TOuter>`):

```
IEnumerable<TResult> Join<TInner,TKey,TResult> (
    IEnumerable<TInner> inner,
    Func<TOuter,TKey> outerKeySelector,
    Func<TInner,TKey> innerKeySelector,
    Func<TOuter,TInner,TResult> resultSelector
)
```

The first three parameters are self-explanatory when you've remembered to treat *inner* and *outer* as *right* and *left*, respectively, but the last one is slightly more interesting. It's a projection from two elements (one from the left sequence and one from the right sequence) into a single element of the resulting sequence. When the join is followed by anything other than a `select` clause, the C#3 compiler introduces a transparent identifier in order to make the range variables used in both sequences available for later clauses, and creates an anonymous type and simple mapping to use for the `resultSelector` parameter.

However, if the next part of the query expression is a `select` clause, the projection from the `select` clause is used directly as the `resultSelector` parameter—there's no point in creating a pair and then calling `Select` when you can do the transformation in one step. You can still *think* about it as a "join" step followed by a "select" step despite the two being squished into a single method call. This leads to a more consistent mental model in my view, and one that is easier to reason about. Unless you're looking at the generated code, just ignore the optimization the compiler is performing for you.

The good news is that having learned about inner joins, our next type of join is much easier to approach.

11.5.2 Group joins with join ... into clauses

Result contains embedded subsequences

We've seen that the result sequence from a normal `join` clause consists of pairs of elements, one from each of the input sequences. A *group join* looks similar in terms of the query expression but has a significantly different outcome. Each element of a group join result consists of an element from the left sequence (using its original range variable), and also a *sequence* of all the matching elements of the right sequence, exposed as a new range variable specified by the identifier coming after `into` in the `join` clause.

Let's change our previous example to use a group join. Listing 11.13 again shows all the defects and the notifications required for each one, but breaks them out in a per-defect manner. Pay particular attention to how we're displaying the results, and to the nested `foreach` loop.

> **Listing 11.13   Joining defects and subscriptions with a group join**

```
var query = from defect in SampleData.AllDefects
            join subscription in SampleData.AllSubscriptions
               on defect.Project equals subscription.Project
            into groupedSubscriptions
            select new { Defect=defect,
                         Subscriptions=groupedSubscriptions };

foreach (var entry in query)
{
   Console.WriteLine(entry.Defect.Summary);
   foreach (var subscription in entry.Subscriptions)
   {
      Console.WriteLine (" {0}", subscription.EmailAddress);
   }
}
```

The `Subscriptions` property of each entry is the embedded sequence of subscriptions matching that entry's defect. Figure 11.7 shows how the two initial sequences are combined.

One important difference between an inner join and a group join—and indeed between a group join and normal grouping—is that for a group join there's a one-to-one correspondence between the left sequence and the result sequence, even if some of the elements in the left sequence don't match any elements of the right sequence. This can be very important, and is sometimes used to simulate a *left outer join* from SQL. The embedded sequence is empty when the left element doesn't match any right elements. As with an inner join, a group join buffers the right sequence but streams the left one.

Listing 11.14 shows an example of this, counting the number of bugs created on each day in August. It uses a `DateTimeRange` (as described in chapter 6) as the left sequence, and a projection that calls `Count` on the embedded sequence in the result of the group join.

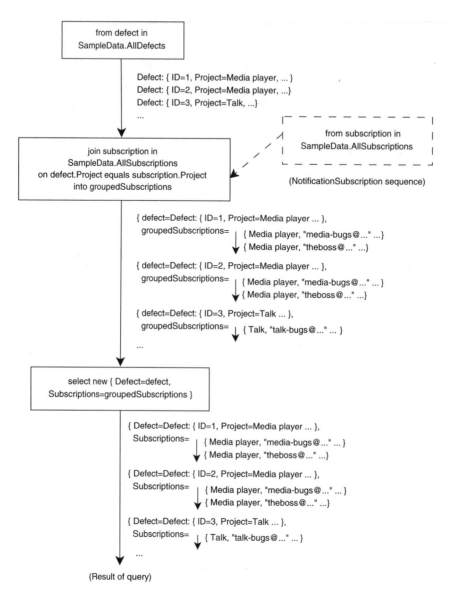

Figure 11.7   Sequences involved in the group join from listing 11.13. The short arrows indicate embedded sequences within the result entries. In the output, some entries contain multiple email addresses for the same bug.

Listing 11.14   Counting the number of bugs raised on each day in August

```
var dates = new DateTimeRange(SampleData.Start, SampleData.End);

var query = from date in dates
            join defect in SampleData.AllDefects
                on date equals defect.Created.Date
            into joined
            select new { Date=date, Count=joined.Count() };
```

```
foreach (var grouped in query)
{
    Console.WriteLine("{0:d}: {1}", grouped.Date, grouped.Count);
}
```

Count itself uses *immediate execution*, iterating through all the elements of the sequence it's called on—but we're only calling it in the projection part of the query expression, so it becomes part of a lambda expression. This means we still have deferred execution: nothing is evaluated until we start the foreach loop.

Here is the first part of the results of listing 11.14, showing the number of bugs created each day in the first week of August:

```
08/01/2007: 1
08/02/2007: 0
08/03/2007: 2
08/04/2007: 1
08/05/2007: 0
08/06/2007: 1
08/07/2007: 1
```

The compiler translation involved for a group join is simply a call to the GroupJoin method, which has the following signature:

```
IEnumerable<TResult> GroupJoin<TInner,TKey,TResult> (
    IEnumerable<TInner> inner,
    Func<TOuter,TKey> outerKeySelector,
    Func<TInner,TKey> innerKeySelector,
    Func<TOuter,IEnumerable<TInner>,TResult> resultSelector
)
```

The signature is exactly the same as for inner joins, except that the resultSelector parameter has to work with a sequence of right-hand elements, not just a single one. As with inner joins, if a group join is followed by a select clause the projection is used as the result selector of the GroupJoin call; otherwise, a transparent identifier is introduced. In this case we have a select clause immediately after the group join, so the translated query looks like this:

```
dates.GroupJoin(SampleData.AllDefects,
                date => date,
                defect => defect.Created.Date,
                (date, joined) => new { Date=date,
                                        Count=joined.Count() })
```

Our final type of join is known as a *cross join*—but it's not quite as straightforward as it might seem at first.

11.5.3 *Cross joins using multiple from clauses*

So far all our joins have been *equijoins*—a match has been performed between elements of the left and right sequences. Cross joins don't perform any matching between the sequences: the result contains every possible pair of elements. They're achieved by simply using two (or more) from clauses. For the sake of sanity we'll only consider two from clauses for the moment—when there are more, just mentally perform a cross join on the first two `from` clauses, then cross join the resulting sequence with the next `from` clause, and so on. Each extra `from` clause adds its own range variable.

Listing 11.15 shows a simple (but useless) cross join in action, producing a sequence where each entry consists of a user and a project. I've deliberately picked two completely unrelated initial sequences to show that no matching is performed.

Listing 11.15   Cross joining users against projects

```
var query = from user in SampleData.AllUsers
            from project in SampleData.AllProjects
            select new { User=user, Project=project };

foreach (var pair in query)
{
    Console.WriteLine("{0}/{1}",
                    pair.User.Name,
                    pair.Project.Name);
}
```

The output of listing 11.15 begins like this:

```
Tim Trotter/Skeety Media Player
Tim Trotter/Skeety Talk
Tim Trotter/Skeety Office
Tara Tutu/Skeety Media Player
Tara Tutu/Skeety Talk
Tara Tutu/Skeety Office
```

Figure 11.8 shows the sequences involved to get this result.

If you're familiar with SQL, you're probably quite comfortable so far—it looks just like a Cartesian product obtained from a query specifying multiple tables. Indeed, most of the time that's exactly how cross joins are used. However, there's more power available when you want it: the right sequence used at any particular point in time can depend on the "current" value of the left sequence. When this is the case, it's not a cross join in the normal sense of the term. The query expression translation is the same whether or not we're using a true cross join, so we need to understand the more complicated scenario in order to understand the translation process.

Before we dive into the details, let's see the effect it produces. Listing 11.16 shows a simple example, using sequences of integers.

Listing 11.16   Cross join where the right sequence depends on the left element

```
var query = from left in Enumerable.Range(1, 4)
            from right in Enumerable.Range(11, left)
            select new { Left=left, Right=right };

foreach (var pair in query)
{
    Console.WriteLine("Left={0}; Right={1}",
                    pair.Left, pair.Right);
}
```

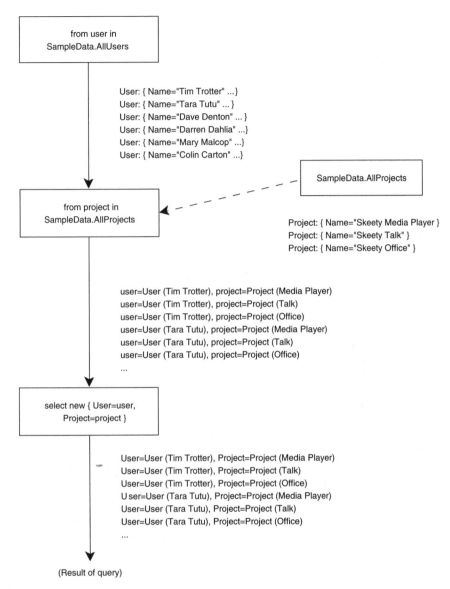

Figure 11.8 Sequences from listing 11.15, cross joining users and projects. All possible combinations are returned in the results.

Listing 11.16 starts with a simple range of integers, 1 to 4. For each of those integers, we create another range, beginning at 11 and having as many elements as the original integer. By using multiple from clauses, the left sequence is joined with each of the generated right sequences, resulting in this output:

```
Left=1; Right=11
Left=2; Right=11
Left=2; Right=12
```

```
Left=3; Right=11
Left=3; Right=12
Left=3; Right=13
Left=4; Right=11
Left=4; Right=12
Left=4; Right=13
Left=4; Right=14
```

The method the compiler calls to generate this sequence is `SelectMany`. It takes a single input sequence (the *left* sequence in our terminology), a delegate to *generate* another sequence from any element of the left sequence, and a delegate to generate a result element given an element of each of the sequences. Here's the signature of the method, again written as if it were an instance method on `IEnumerable<TSource>`:

```
public IEnumerable<TResult> SelectMany<TCollection, TResult> (
    Func<TSource, IEnumerable<TCollection>> collectionSelector,
    Func<TSource, TCollection, TResult> resultSelector
)
```

As with the other joins, if the part of the query expression following the join is a `select` clause, that projection is used as the final argument; otherwise, a transparent identifier is introduced to make both the left and right sequences' range variables available.

Just to make this all a bit more concrete, here's the query expression of listing 11.16, as the translated source code:

```
Enumerable.Range(1, 4)
          .SelectMany (left => Enumerable.Range(11, left),
                       (left, right) => new {Left=left,
                                             Right=right})
```

One interesting feature of `SelectMany` is that the execution is completely streamed—it only needs to process one element of each sequence at a time, because it uses a freshly generated right sequence for each different element of the left sequence. Compare this with inner joins and group joins: they both load the right sequence completely before starting to return any results. You should bear in mind the expected size of sequence, and how expensive it might be to evaluate it multiple times, when considering which type of join to use and which sequence to use as the left and which as the right.

This behavior of flattening a sequence of sequences, one produced from each element in an original sequence, can be very useful. Consider a situation where you might want to process a lot of log files, a line at a time. We can process a seamless sequence of lines, with barely any work. The following pseudo-code is filled in more thoroughly in the downloadable source code, but the overall meaning and usefulness should be clear:

```
var query = from file in Directory.GetFiles(logDirectory, "*.log")
            from line in new FileLineReader(file)
            let entry = new LogEntry(line)
            where entry.Type == EntryType.Error
            select entry;
```

In just five lines of code we have retrieved, parsed, and filtered a whole collection of log files, returning a sequence of entries representing errors. Crucially, we *haven't* had to load even a single full log file into memory all in one go, let alone all of the files— all the data is streamed.

Having tackled joins, the last items we need to look at are slightly easier to understand. We're going to look at grouping elements by a key, and continuing a query expression after a `group ... by` or `select` clause.

11.6 Groupings and continuations

One common requirement is to group a sequence of elements by one of its properties. LINQ makes this easy with the `group ... by` clause. As well as describing this final type of clause, we'll also revisit our earliest one (`select`) to see a feature called *query continuations* that can be applied to both groupings and projections. Let's start with a simple grouping.

11.6.1 Grouping with the group ... by clause

Grouping is largely intuitive, and LINQ makes it simple. To group a sequence in a query expression, all you need to do is use the `group ... by` clause, with this syntax:

```
group projection by grouping
```

This clause comes at the end of a query expression in the same way a `select` clause does. The similarities between these clauses don't end there: the *projection* expression is the same kind of projection a `select` clause uses. The outcome is somewhat different, however.

The *grouping* expression determines what the sequence is grouped by—the *key* of the grouping. The overall result is a sequence where each element is itself a sequence of projected elements, and also has a `Key` property, which is the key for that group; this combination is encapsulated in the `IGrouping<TKey,TElement>` interface, which extends `IEnumerable<TElement>`.

Let's have a look at a simple example from the SkeetySoft defect system: grouping defects by their current assignee. Listing 11.17 does this with the simplest form of projection, so that the resulting sequence has the assignee as the key, and a sequence of defects embedded in each entry.

Listing 11.17 Grouping defects by assignee—trivial projection

```
var query = from defect in SampleData.AllDefects          ❶ Filters out
            where defect.AssignedTo != null                  unassigned defects
            group defect by defect.AssignedTo;            ❷ Groups by
foreach (var entry in query)        Uses key of each  ❸     assignee
{                                   entry: the assignee
    Console.WriteLine(entry.Key.Name);
    foreach (var defect in entry)                      Iterates over entry's
    {                                                ❹ subsequence
        Console.WriteLine("  ({0}) {1}",
```

```
                        defect.Severity,
                        defect.Summary);
     }
    Console.WriteLine();
  }
```

Listing 11.17 might be useful in a daily build report, to quickly see what defects each person needs to look at. We've filtered out all the defects that don't need any more attention ❶ and then grouped using the `AssignedTo` property. Although this time we're just using a property, the grouping expression can be anything you like—it's just applied to each entry in the incoming sequence, and the sequence is grouped based on the result of the expression. Note that grouping cannot stream the results, although it streams the input, applying the key selection and projection to each element and buffering the grouped sequences of projected elements.

The projection we've applied in the grouping ❷ is trivial—it just selects the original element. As we go through the resulting sequence, each entry has a `Key` property, which is of type `User` ❸, and each entry also implements `IEnumerable<Defect>`, which is the sequence of defects assigned to that user ❹.

The results of listing 11.17 start like this:

```
Darren Dahlia
  (Showstopper) MP3 files crash system
  (Major) Can't play files more than 200 bytes long
  (Major) DivX is choppy on Pentium 100
  (Trivial) User interface should be more caramelly
```

After all of Darren's defects have been printed out, we see Tara's, then Tim's, and so on. The implementation effectively keeps a list of the assignees it's seen so far, and adds a new one every time it needs to. Figure 11.9 shows the sequences generated throughout the query expression, which may make this ordering clearer.

Within each entry's subsequence, the order of the defects is the same as the order of the original defect sequence. If you actively care about the ordering, consider explicitly stating it in the query expression, to make it more readable.

If you run listing 11.17, you'll see that Mary Malcop doesn't appear in the output at all, because she doesn't have any defects assigned to her. If you wanted to produce a full list of users and defects assigned to each of them, you'd need to use a group join like the one used in listing 11.14.

The compiler always uses a method called `GroupBy` for grouping clauses. When the projection in a grouping clause is trivial—in other words, when each entry in the original sequence maps directly to the exact same object in a subsequence—the compiler uses a simple method call, which just needs the grouping expression, so it knows how to map each element to a key. For instance, the query expression in listing 11.17 is translated into this nonquery expression:

```
SampleData.AllDefects.Where(defect => defect.AssignedTo != null)
                     .GroupBy(defect => defect.AssignedTo)
```

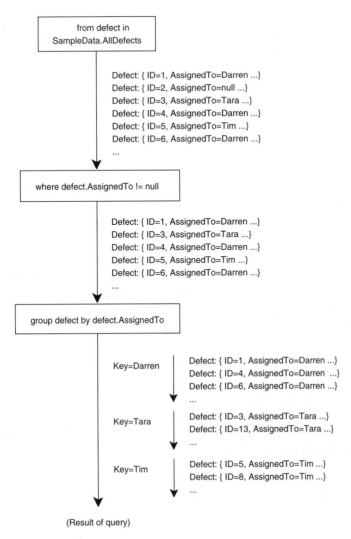

Figure 11.9 Sequences used when grouping defects by assignee. Each entry of the result has a `Key` property and is also a sequence of defect entries.

When the projection is nontrivial, a slightly more complicated version is used. Listing 11.18 gives an example of a projection so that we only capture the summary of each defect rather than the `Defect` object itself.

Listing 11.18 Grouping defects by assignee—projection retains just the summary

```
var query = from defect in SampleData.AllDefects
            where defect.AssignedTo != null
            group defect.Summary by defect.AssignedTo;

foreach (var entry in query)
```

```
{
    Console.WriteLine(entry.Key.Name);
    foreach (var summary in entry)
    {
        Console.WriteLine("  {0}", summary);
    }
    Console.WriteLine();
}
```

I've highlighted the differences between listing 11.18 and listing 11.17 in bold. Having projected a defect to just its summary, the embedded sequence in each entry is just an IEnumerable<string>. In this case, the compiler uses an overload of GroupBy with another parameter to represent the projection. The query expression in listing 11.18 is translated into the following expression:

```
SampleData.AllDefects.Where(defect => defect.AssignedTo != null)
          .GroupBy(defect => defect.AssignedTo,
                   defect => defect.Summary)
```

There are more complex overloads of GroupBy available as extension methods on IEnumerable<T>, but they aren't used by the C#3 compiler when translating query expressions. You can call them manually, of course—if you find you want more powerful grouping behavior than query expressions provide natively, then they're worth looking into.

Grouping clauses are relatively simple but very useful. Even in our defect-tracking system, you could easily imagine wanting to group defects by project, creator, severity, or status, as well as the assignee we've used for these examples.

So far, we've ended each query expression with a select or group ... by clause, and that's been the end of the expression. There are times, however, when you want to do more with the results—and that's where *query continuations* are used.

11.6.2 *Query continuations*

Query continuations provide a way of using the result of one query expression as the initial sequence of another. They apply to both group ... by and select clauses, and the syntax is the same for both—you simply use the contextual keyword into and then provide the name of a new range variable. That range variable can then be used in the next part of the query expression.

The C#3 specification explains this in terms of a translation from one query expression to another, changing

```
first-query into identifier
second-query-body
```

into

```
from identifier in (first-query)
second-query-body
```

An example will make this a lot clearer. Let's go back to our grouping of defects by assignee, but this time imagine we only want the count of the defects assigned to each person. We can't do that with the projection in the grouping clause, because that only applies to each individual defect. We want to project an assignee and the sequence of their defects into the assignee and the count from that sequence, which is achieved using the code in listing 11.19.

Listing 11.19 Continuing a grouping with another projection

```
var query = from defect in SampleData.AllDefects
            where defect.AssignedTo != null
            group defect by defect.AssignedTo into grouped
            select new { Assignee=grouped.Key,
                         Count=grouped.Count() };

foreach (var entry in query)
{
   Console.WriteLine("{0}: {1}",
                     entry.Assignee.Name,
                     entry.Count);
}
```

The changes to the query expression are highlighted in bold. We can use the grouped range variable in the second part of the query, but the defect range variable is no longer available—you can think of it as being out of scope. Our projection simply creates an anonymous type with Assignee and Count properties, using the key of each group as the assignee, and counting the sequence of defects associated with each group. The results of listing 11.19 are as follows:

```
Darren Dahlia: 14
Tara Tutu: 5
Tim Trotter: 5
Deborah Denton: 9
Colin Carton: 2
```

Following the specification, the query expression from listing 11.19 is translated into this one:

```
from grouped in (from defect in SampleData.AllDefects
                 where defect.AssignedTo != null
                 group defect by defect.AssignedTo)
select new { Assignee=grouped.Key, Count=grouped.Count() }
```

The rest of the translations are then performed, resulting in the following code:

```
SampleData.AllDefects
        .Where (defect => defect.AssignedTo != null)
        .GroupBy(defect => defect.AssignedTo)
        .Select(grouped => new { Assignee=grouped.Key,
                                 Count=grouped.Count() })
```

An alternative way of understanding continuations is to think of two separate statements. This isn't as accurate in terms of the actual compiler translation, but I find it makes it easier to see what's going on. In this case, the query expression (and assignment to the query variable) can be thought of as the following two statements:

```
var tmp = from defect in SampleData.AllDefects
          where defect.AssignedTo != null
          group defect by defect.AssignedTo;

var query = from grouped in tmp
            select new { Assignee=grouped.Key,
                         Count=grouped.Count() };
```

Of course, if you find this easier to read there's nothing to stop you from breaking up
the original expression into this form in your source code. Nothing will be evaluated
until you start trying to step through the query results anyway, due to deferred execution.

Let's extend this example to see how multiple continuations can be used. Our
results are currently unordered—let's change that so we can see who's got the most
defects assigned to them first. We could use a let clause after the first continuation, but listing 11.20 shows an alternative with a second continuation after our current expression.

> **Listing 11.20   Query expression continuations from group and select**

```
var query = from defect in SampleData.AllDefects
            where defect.AssignedTo != null
            group defect by defect.AssignedTo into grouped
            select new { Assignee=grouped.Key,
                         Count=grouped.Count() } into result
            orderby result.Count descending
            select result;

foreach (var entry in query)
{
   Console.WriteLine("{0}: {1}",
                     entry.Assignee.Name,
                     entry.Count);
}
```

The changes between listing 11.19 and 11.20 are highlighted in bold. We haven't had
to change any of the output code as we've got the same type of sequence—we've just
applied an ordering to it. This time the translated query expression is as follows:

```
SampleData.AllDefects
          .Where (defect => defect.AssignedTo != null)
          .GroupBy(defect => defect.AssignedTo)
          .Select(grouped => new { Assignee=grouped.Key,
                                   Count=grouped.Count() })
          .OrderByDescending(result => result.Count);
```

By pure coincidence, this is remarkably similar to the first defect tracking query we
came across, in section 10.3.5. Our final select clause effectively does nothing, so the
C# compiler ignores it. It's required in the query expression, however, as all query
expressions have to end with either a select or a group ... by clause. There's nothing
to stop you from using a different projection or performing other operations with the
continued query—joins, further groupings, and so forth. Just keep an eye on the readability of the query expression as it grows.

11.7 *Summary*

In this chapter, we've looked at how LINQ to Objects and C# 3 interact, focusing on the way that query expressions are first translated into code that *doesn't* involve query expressions, then compiled in the usual way. We've seen how all query expressions form a series of sequences, applying a transformation of some description at each step. In many cases these sequences are evaluated using deferred execution, fetching data only when it is first required.

Compared with all the other features of C# 3, query expressions look somewhat alien—more like SQL than the C# we're used to. One of the reasons they look so odd is that they're *declarative* instead of *imperative*—a query talks about the features of the end result rather than the exact steps required to achieve it. This goes hand in hand with a more functional way of thinking. It can take a while to click, and it's certainly not suitable for every situation, but where declarative syntax is appropriate it can vastly improve readability, as well as making code easier to test and also easier to parallelize.

Don't be fooled into thinking that LINQ should only be used with databases: plain in-memory manipulation of collections is common, and as we've seen it's supported very well by query expressions and the extension methods in Enumerable.

In a very real sense, you've seen all the new features of C# 3 now! Although we haven't looked at any other LINQ providers yet, we now have a clearer understanding of what the compiler will do for us when we ask it to handle XML and SQL. The compiler itself doesn't know the difference between LINQ to Objects, LINQ to SQL, or any of the other providers: it just follows the same rules blindly. In the next chapter we'll see how these rules form the final piece of the LINQ jigsaw puzzle when they convert lambda expressions into the expression trees so that the various clauses of query expressions can be executed on different platforms.

LINQ beyond collections

In the previous chapter, we saw how LINQ to Objects works, with the C#3 compiler translating query expressions into normal C# code, which for LINQ to Objects just happens to call the extension methods present in the `Enumerable` class. Even without any other features, query expressions would have been useful for manipulating data in memory. It probably wouldn't have been worth the extra complexity in the language, though. In reality, LINQ to Objects is just one aspect of the big picture.

In this chapter we'll take a whirlwind tour of other LINQ providers and APIs. First we'll look at LINQ to SQL, an Object Relational Mapping (ORM) solution from Microsoft that ships as part of .NET 3.5. After we've seen it working as if by magic, we'll take a look at what's happening behind the scenes, and how query expressions written in C# end up executing as SQL on the database.

LINQ to DataSet and LINQ to XML are both frameworks that tackle existing problems (manipulating datasets and XML respectively) but do so in a LINQ-friendly fashion. Both of them use LINQ to Objects for the underlying query support, but the APIs have been designed so that query expressions can be used to access data in a painless and consistent manner.

Having covered the LINQ APIs shipped with .NET 3.5, we'll take a peek at some other providers. Microsoft developers aren't the only ones writing LINQ providers, and I'll show a few third-party examples, before revealing what Microsoft has in store for us with the ADO.NET Entity Framework and Parallel LINQ.

This chapter is *not* meant to provide you with a comprehensive knowledge of using LINQ by any means: it's a truly massive topic, and I'm only going to scratch the surface of each provider here. The purpose of the chapter is to give you a broad idea of what LINQ is capable of, and how much easier it can make development. Hopefully there'll be enough of a "wow" factor that you'll want to study some or all of the providers further. To this end, there are great online resources, particularly blog posts from the various LINQ teams (see this book's website for a list of links), but I also thoroughly recommend *LINQ in Action* (Manning 2008).

As well as understanding LINQ itself, by the end of this chapter you should see how the different pieces of the C#3 feature set all fit together, and why they're all present in the first place. Just as a reminder, you shouldn't expect to see any *new* features of C# at this point—we've covered them all in the previous chapters—but they may well make more sense when you see how they help to provide unified querying over multiple data sources.

The change in pace, from the detail of the previous chapters to the sprint through features in this one, may be slightly alarming at first. Just relax and enjoy the ride, remembering that the big picture is the important thing here. There won't be a test afterward, I promise. There's a lot to cover, so let's get cracking with the most impressive LINQ provider in .NET 3.5: LINQ to SQL.

12.1 LINQ to SQL

I'm sure by now you've absorbed the message that LINQ to SQL converts query expressions into SQL, which is then executed on the database. There's more to it than that, however—it's a full ORM solution. In this section we'll move our defect system into a SQL Server 2005 database, populate it with the sample defects, query it, and update it. We won't look at the details of *how* the queries are converted into SQL until the next section, though: it's easier to understand the mechanics once you've seen the end result. Let's start off by getting our database and entities up and running.

12.1.1 Creating the defect database and entities

To use LINQ to SQL, you need a database (obviously) and some classes representing the entities. The classes have metadata associated with them to tell LINQ to SQL how they map to database tables. This metadata can be built directly into the classes using attributes, or specified with an XML file. To keep things simple, we're going to use attributes—and by using the designer built into Visual Studio 2008, we won't even need to specify the attributes ourselves. First, though, we need a database. It's possible to generate the database schema from the entities, but my personal preference is to work "database first."

CREATING THE SQL SERVER 2005 DATABASE SCHEMA

The mapping from the classes we had before to SQL Server 2005 database tables is straightforward. Each table has an autoincrementing integer ID column, with an appropriate name: `ProjectID`, `DefectID`, and so forth. The references between tables simply use the same name, so the `Defect` table has a `ProjectID` column, for instance, with a foreign key constraint. There are a few exceptions to this simple set of rules:

- `User` is a reserved word in T-SQL, so the `User` class is mapped to the `DefectUser` table.
- The enumerations (status, severity, and user type) don't have tables: their values are simply mapped to `tinyint` columns in the `Defect` and `DefectUser` tables.
- The `Defect` table has two links to the `DefectUser` table, one for the user who created the defect and one for the current assignee. These are represented with the `CreatedByUserId` and `AssignedToUserId` columns, respectively.

The database is available as part of the downloadable source code so that you can use it with SQL Server 2005 Express yourself. If you leave the files in the same directory structure that they come in, you won't even need to change the connection string when you use the sample code.

CREATING THE ENTITY CLASSES

Once our tables are created, creating the entity classes from Visual Studio 2008 is easy. Simply open Server Explorer (View, Server Explorer) and add a data source to the SkeetySoftDefects database (right-click on Data Connections and select Add Connection). You should be able to see four tables: Defect, DefectUser, Project, and NotificationSubscription.

In a C# project targeting .NET 3.5, you should then be able to add a new item of type "LINQ to SQL classes." When choosing a name for the item, bear in mind that among the classes it will create for you, there will be one with the selected name followed by `DataContext`—this is going to be an important class, so choose the name carefully. Visual Studio 2008 doesn't make it terribly easy to refactor this after you've created it, unfortunately. I chose `DefectModel`—so the data context class is called `DefectModelDataContext`.

The designer will open when you've created the new item. You can then drag the four tables from Server Explorer into the designer, and it will figure out all the associations. After that, you can rearrange the diagram, and adjust various properties of the entities. Here's a list of what I changed:

- I renamed the `DefectID` property to `ID` to match our previous model.
- I renamed `DefectUser` to `User` (so although the table is still called `DefectUser`, we'll generate a class called `User`, just like before).

- I changed the type of the `Severity`, `Status`, and `UserType` properties to their enum equivalents (having copied those enumerations into the project).
- I renamed the parent and child properties used for the associations between `Defect` and `DefectUser`—the designer guessed suitable names for the other associations, but had trouble here because there were two associations between the same pair of tables. I named the relationships `AssignedTo/AssignedDefects` and `CreatedBy/CreatedDefects`.

Figure 12.1 shows the designer diagram after all of these changes.

As you can see, the model in figure 12.1 is exactly the same as the code model shown in figure 11.3, except without the enumerations. The public interface is so similar that we can create instances of our entities with the same sample data code. If you look in the C# code generated by the designer (`DefectModel.designer.cs`), you'll find five partial classes: one for each of the entities, and the `DefectModelDataContext` class I mentioned earlier. The fact that they're partial classes is important when it comes to making the sample data creation code work seamlessly. I had created a constructor for `User`, which took the name and user type as parameters. By creating another file containing a partial `User` class, we can add that constructor to our model again, as shown in listing 12.1.

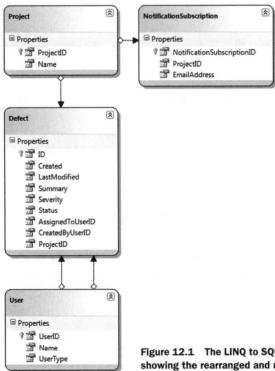

Figure 12.1   The LINQ to SQL classes designer showing the rearranged and modified entities

```
public partial class User
{
    public User (string name, UserType userType)
        : this()
    {
        Name = name;
        UserType = userType;
    }
}
```

It's important to call the parameterless constructor from our new one—the generated
code initializes some members there. In the same way as we added a constructor, we
can override `ToString` in all the entities, so that the results will be exactly as they were
in chapter 11. The generated code contains many partial method declarations, so you
can easily react to various events occurring on particular instances.

At this point, we can simply copy over the `SampleData.cs` file from chapter 11 and
build the project. Now for the tricky bit—copying the sample data into the database
from the in-memory version.

12.1.2 *Populating the database with sample data*

OK, I lied. Populating the database is ludicrously easy. Listing 12.2 shows just how simple it is.

```
using (var context = new DefectModelDataContext())              ◁──────┐  Creates
{                                                                        context to
    context.Log = Console.Out;     ◁──❷ Enables console logging   ❶    work in

    context.Users.InsertAllOnSubmit(SampleData.AllUsers);
    context.Projects.InsertAllOnSubmit(SampleData.AllProjects);
    context.Defects.InsertAllOnSubmit(SampleData.AllDefects);
    context.NotificationSubscriptions.InsertAllOnSubmit
        (SampleData.AllSubscriptions);
                                                          Populates ❸
                                                          entities
    context.SubmitChanges();     ◁──┐ Flushes changes
}                                ❹  to database
```

I'm sure you'll agree that's not a lot of code—but all of it is new. Let's take it one step
at a time. First we create a new *data context* to work with ❶. Data contexts are pretty
multifunctional, taking responsibility for connection and transaction management,
query translation, tracking changes in entities, and dealing with identity. For the purposes of this chapter, we can regard a data context as our point of contact with the
database. We won't be looking at the more advanced features here, but there's one
useful capability we'll take advantage of: at ❷ we tell the data context to write out all
the SQL commands it executes to the console.

The four statements at ❸ add the sample entities to the context. The four properties of the context (`Users`, `Projects`, `Defects`, and `NotificationSubscriptions`) are

each of type `Table<T>` for the corresponding type T (`User`, `Project`, and so on). We access particular entities via these tables—in this case, we're adding our sample data to the tables.

At this point nothing has actually been sent "across the wire" to the database—it's just in the context, in memory. All the associations in our model have been generated bi-directionally (a user entity knows all the defects currently assigned to it, as well as the defect knowing the user it's assigned to, for example), which means that we could have just called `InsertAllOnSubmit` once, with any of the entity types, and everything else would have cascaded. However, I've explicitly added all the entities here for clarity. The data context makes sure that everything is inserted once, only once, and in an appropriate order to avoid constraint violations.

Statement ❹ is where the SQL is actually executed—it's only here that we see any log entries in the console, too. `SubmitChanges` is the equivalent of `DataAdapter.Update` from ADO.NET 1.0—it calls all the necessary INSERT, DELETE, and UPDATE commands on the actual database.

Running listing 12.2 multiple times will insert the data multiple times too. There are many ways of cleaning up the database before we start populating it. We could ask the data context to delete the database and re-create it, assuming we have enough security permissions: the metadata captured by the designer contains all the information required for simple cases like ours.

Alternatively, we can delete the existing data. This can either be done with a bulk delete statement, or by fetching all the existing entities and asking LINQ to SQL to delete them individually. Clearly deleting in bulk is more efficient, but LINQ to SQL doesn't provide any mechanism to do this without resorting to a direct SQL command. The `ExecuteCommand` on `DataContext` makes this easy to accomplish without worrying about connection management, but it certainly sidesteps many of the benefits of using an ORM solution to start with. It's nice to be able to execute arbitrary SQL where necessary, but you should only do so when there's a compelling reason.

We won't examine the code for any of these methods of wiping the database clean, but they're all available as part of the source code you can download from the website.

So far, we've seen nothing that isn't available in a normal ORM system. What makes LINQ to SQL different is the querying…

12.1.3 *Accessing the database with query expressions*

I'm sure you've guessed what's coming, but hopefully that won't make it any less impressive. We're going to execute query expressions against our data source, watching LINQ to SQL convert the query into SQL on the fly. For the sake of familiarity, we'll use some of the same queries we saw executing against our in-memory collections in chapter 11.

FIRST QUERY: FINDING DEFECTS ASSIGNED TO TIM

I'll skip over the trivial examples from early in the chapter, starting instead with the query from listing 11.7 that checks for open defects assigned to Tim. Here's the query part of listing 11.7, for the sake of comparison:

```
User tim = SampleData.Users.TesterTim;

var query = from defect in SampleData.AllDefects
            where defect.Status != Status.Closed
            where defect.AssignedTo == tim
            select defect.Summary;
```

The LINQ to SQL equivalent is shown in listing 12.3.

Listing 12.3   Querying the database to find all Tim's open defects

```
using (var context = new DefectModelDataContext())        ◁──┐ Creates context
{                                                              │ to work with
    context.Log = Console.Out;

    User tim = (from user in context.Users                    Queries database
                where user.Name=="Tim Trotter"                to find Tim
                select user).Single();

    var query = from defect in context.Defects               Queries database
                where defect.Status != Status.Closed         to find Tim's open
                where defect.AssignedTo == tim                defects
                select defect.Summary;

    foreach (var summary in query)
    {
        Console.WriteLine(summary);
    }
}
```

We can't use `SampleData.Users.TesterTim` in the main query because that object doesn't know the ID of Tim's row in the `DefectUser` table. Instead, we use one query to load Tim's user entity, and then a second query to find the open defects. The `Single` method call at the end of the query expression just returns a single result from a sequence, throwing an exception if there isn't exactly one element. In a real-life situation, you may well have the entity as a product of other operations such as logging in—and if you don't have the full entity, you may well have its ID, which can be used equally well within the main query.

Within the second query expression, the only difference between the in-memory query and the LINQ to SQL query is the data source—instead of using `Sample-Data.Defects`, we use `context.Defects`. The final results are the same (although the ordering isn't guaranteed), but the work has been done on the database. The console output shows both of the queries executed on the database, along with the query parameter values:[1]

```
SELECT [t0].[UserID], [t0].[Name], [t0].[UserType]
FROM [dbo].[DefectUser] AS [t0]
WHERE [t0].[Name] = @p0
-- @p0: Input String (Size = 11; Prec = 0; Scale = 0) [Tim Trotter]

SELECT [t0].[Summary]
```

---

[1] Additional log output is generated showing some details of the data context, which I've cut to avoid distracting from the SQL.

```
FROM [dbo].[Defect] AS [t0]
WHERE ([t0].[AssignedToUserID] = @p0) AND ([t0].[Status] <> @p1)
-- @p0: Input Int32 (Size = 0; Prec = 0; Scale = 0) [2]
-- @p1: Input Int32 (Size = 0; Prec = 0; Scale = 0) [4]
```

Notice how the first query fetches all of the properties of the user because we're populating a whole entity—but the second query only fetches the summary as that's all we need. LINQ to SQL has also converted our two separate where clauses in the second query into a single filter on the database.

NOTE *An alternative to console logging: the debug visualizer*—For a more interactive view into LINQ to SQL queries, you can use the debug visualizer, which Scott Guthrie has made available. This shows the SQL corresponding to the query, and allows you to execute and even edit it manually within the debugger. It's free, and includes source code: http://weblogs.asp.net/scottgu/archive/2007/07/31/linq-to-sql-debug-visualizer.aspx

LINQ to SQL is capable of translating a wide range of expressions. Let's look at some more examples from chapter 11, just to see what SQL is generated.

SQL GENERATION FOR A MORE COMPLEX QUERY: A LET CLAUSE

Our next query shows what happens when we introduce a sort of "temporary variable" with a let clause. In chapter 11 we considered quite a bizarre situation, if you remember—pretending that calculating the length of a string took a long time. Again, the query expression is exactly the same as in listing 11.11, with the exception of the data source. Listing 12.4 shows the LINQ to SQL code.

Listing 12.4   Using a `let` clause in LINQ to SQL

```
using (var context = new DefectModelDataContext())
{
    context.Log = Console.Out;

    var query = from user in context.Users
                let length = user.Name.Length
                orderby length
                select new { Name = user.Name, Length = length };

    foreach (var entry in query)
    {
        Console.WriteLine("{0}: {1}", entry.Length, entry.Name);
    }
}
```

The generated SQL is very close to the spirit of the sequences we saw in figure 11.5—the innermost sequence (the first one in the diagram) is the list of users; that's transformed into a sequence of name/length pairs (as the nested select), and then the no-op projection is applied, with an ordering by length:

```
SELECT [t1].[Name], [t1].[value]
FROM (
    SELECT LEN([t0].[Name]) AS [value], [t0].[Name]
```

```
    FROM [dbo].[DefectUser] AS [t0]
    ) AS [t1]
ORDER BY [t1].[value]
```

This is a good example of where the generated SQL is wordier than it needs to be. Although we couldn't reference the elements of the final output sequence when performing an ordering on the query expression, you can in SQL. This simpler query would have worked fine:

```
SELECT LEN([t0].[Name]) AS [value], [t0].[Name]
FROM [dbo].[DefectUser] AS [t0]
ORDER BY [value]
```

Of course, what's important is what the query optimizer does on the database—the execution plan displayed in SQL Server Management Studio Express is the same for both queries, so it doesn't look like we're losing out.

Next we'll have a look at a couple of the joins we used in chapter 11.

EXPLICIT JOINS: MATCHING DEFECTS WITH NOTIFICATION SUBSCRIPTIONS

We'll try both inner joins and group joins, using the examples of joining notification subscriptions against projects. I suspect you're used to the drill now—the pattern of the code is the same for each query, so from here on I'll just show the query expression and the generated SQL unless something else is going on.

```
// Query expression (modified from listing 11.12)
from defect in context.Defects
join subscription in context.NotificationSubscriptions
    on defect.Project equals subscription.Project
select new { defect.Summary, subscription.EmailAddress }

-- Generated SQL
SELECT [t0].[Summary], [t1].[EmailAddress]
FROM [dbo].[Defect] AS [t0]
INNER JOIN [dbo].[NotificationSubscription] AS [t1]
ON [t0].[ProjectID] = [t1].[ProjectID]
```

Unsurprisingly, it uses an inner join in SQL. It would be easy to guess at the generated SQL in this case. How about a group join, though? Well, this is where things get slightly more hectic:

```
// Query expression (modified from listing 11.13)
from defect in context.Defects
join subscription in context.NotificationSubscriptions
    on defect.Project equals subscription.Project
    into groupedSubscriptions
select new { Defect = defect, Subscriptions = groupedSubscriptions }

-- Generated SQL
SELECT [t0].[DefectID] AS [ID], [t0].[Created],
[t0].[LastModified], [t0].[Summary], [t0].[Severity],
[t0].[Status], [t0].[AssignedToUserID],
[t0].[CreatedByUserID], [t0].[ProjectID],
[t1].[NotificationSubscriptionID],
[t1].[ProjectID] AS [ProjectID2], [t1].[EmailAddress],
    (SELECT COUNT(*)
```

```
      FROM [dbo].[NotificationSubscription] AS [t2]
      WHERE [t0].[ProjectID] = [t2].[ProjectID]) AS [count]
   FROM [dbo].[Defect] AS [t0]
   LEFT OUTER JOIN [dbo].[NotificationSubscription] AS [t1]
   ON [t0].[ProjectID] = [t1].[ProjectID]
   ORDER BY [t0].[DefectID], [t1].[NotificationSubscriptionID]
```

That's a pretty major change in the amount of SQL generated! There are two important things to notice. First, it uses a *left outer join* instead of an inner join, so we would
still see a defect even if it didn't have anyone subscribing to its project. If you want a
left outer join but without the grouping, the conventional way of expressing this is to
use a group join and then an extra `from` clause using the `DefaultIfEmpty` extension
method on the embedded sequence. It looks quite odd, but it works well. See the sample source code for this chapter on the book's website for more details.

   The second odd thing about the previous query is that it calculates the count for
each group within the database. This is effectively a trick performed by LINQ to SQL to
make sure that all the processing can be done on the server. A naive implementation
would have to perform the grouping in memory, after fetching all the results. In some
cases the provider could do tricks to avoid needing the count, simply spotting when
the grouping ID changes, but there are issues with this approach for some queries. It's
possible that a later implementation of LINQ to SQL will be able to switch courses of
action depending on the exact query.

   You don't need to explicitly write a join in the query expression to see one in the
SQL, however. We're able to express our query in an object-oriented way, even though
it will be converted into SQL. Let's see this in action.

IMPLICIT JOINS: SHOWING DEFECT SUMMARIES AND PROJECT NAMES

Let's take a simple example. Suppose we want to list each defect, showing its summary and the name of the project it's part of. The query expression is just a matter
of a projection:

```
// Query expression
from defect in context.Defects
select new { defect.Summary, ProjectName=defect.Project.Name }

-- Generated SQL
SELECT [t0].[Summary], [t1].[Name]
FROM [dbo].[Defect] AS [t0]
INNER JOIN [dbo].[Project] AS [t1]
ON [t1].[ProjectID] = [t0].[ProjectID]
```

Notice how we've navigated from the defect to the project via a property—LINQ to
SQL has converted that navigation into an inner join. It's able to use an inner join
here because the schema has a non-nullable constraint on the `ProjectID` column of
the `Defect` table—every defect has a project. Not every defect has an assignee, however—the `AssignedToUserID` field is nullable, so if we use the assignee in a projection
instead, a left outer join is generated:

```
// Query expression
from defect in context.Defects
select new { defect.Summary, Assignee=defect.AssignedTo.Name }
```

```
-- Generated SQL
SELECT [t0].[Summary], [t1].[Name]
FROM [dbo].[Defect] AS [t0]
LEFT OUTER JOIN [dbo].[DefectUser] AS [t1]
ON [t1].[UserID] = [t0].[AssignedToUserID]
```

Of course, if you navigate via more properties, the joins get more and more complicated. I'm not going into the details here—the important thing is that LINQ to SQL has to do a lot of analysis of the query expression to work out what SQL is required.

Before we leave LINQ to SQL, I ought to show you one more feature. It's part of what you'd expect from any decent ORM system, but leaving it out would just feel wrong. Let's update some values in our database.

12.1.4 Updating the database

Although insertions are straightforward, updates can be handled in a variety of ways, depending on how concurrency is configured. If you've done any serious database work you'll know that handling conflicts in updates from different users at the same time is quite hairy—and I'm not going to open that particular can of worms here. I'll just show you how easy it is to persist a changed entity when there are no conflicts.

Let's change the status of one of our defects, and its assignee, and that person's name, all in one go. As it happens, I know that the defect with an ID of 1 (as created on a clean system) is a bug that was created by Tim, and is currently in an "accepted" state, assigned to Darren. We'll imagine that Darren has now fixed the bug, and assigned it back to Tim. At the same time, Tim has decided he wants to be a bit more formal, so we'll change his name to Timothy. Oh, and we should remember to update the "last modified" field of the defect too. (In a real system, we'd probably handle that with a trigger—in LINQ to SQL we could implement partial methods to set the last modified time when any of the other fields changed. For the sake of simplicity here, we'll do it manually.)

Listing 12.5 accomplishes all of this and shows the result—loading it in a fresh DataContext to show that it has gone back to the database.

> **Listing 12.5 Updating a defect and showing the new details**

```
using (var context = new DefectModelDataContext())
{
    context.Log = Console.Out;

    Defect defect = context.Defects
                        .Where(d => d.ID==1)      ❶ Finds defect with
                        .Single();                   extension methods

    User tim = defect.CreatedBy;

    defect.AssignedTo = tim;
    tim.Name = "Timothy Trotter";                 ❷ Updates
    defect.Status = Status.Fixed;                    entity details
    defect.LastModified = SampleData.August(31);

    context.SubmitChanges();         ◁———— ❸ Submits changes to database
}
```

```
using (var context = new DefectModelDataContext())
{
    Defect d = (from defect in context.Defects
                where defect.ID==1
                select defect).Single();

    Console.WriteLine (d);
}
```

❹ Finds defect with query expression

Listing 12.5 is easy enough to follow—we open up a context and fetch the first defect ❶. After changing the defect and the entity representing Tim Trotter ❷, we ask LINQ to SQL to save the changes to the database ❸. Finally, we fetch the defect ❹ again in a new context and write the details to the console. Just for a bit of variety, I've shown two different ways of fetching the defect—they're absolutely equivalent, because the compiler translates the query expression form into the "method call" form anyway.

That's all the LINQ to SQL we're going to see—hopefully it's shown you enough of the capabilities to understand how it's a normal ORM system, but one that has good support for query expressions and the LINQ standard query operators.

12.1.5 *LINQ to SQL summary*

There are lots of ORMs out there, and many of them allow you to build up queries programmatically in a way that can look like LINQ to SQL—if you ignore compile-time checking. It's the combination of lambda expressions, expression trees, extension methods, and query expressions that make LINQ special, giving these advantages:

- We've been able to use familiar syntax to write the query (at least, familiar when you know LINQ to Objects!).
- The compiler has been able to do a lot of validation for us.
- Visual Studio 2008 is able to help us build the query with IntelliSense.
- If we need a mixture of client-side and server-side processing, we can do both in a consistent manner.
- We're still using the database to do the hard work.

Of course, this comes at a cost. As with any ORM system, you want to keep an eye on what SQL queries are being executed for a particular query expression. That's where the logging is invaluable—but don't forget to turn it off for production! In particular, you will need to be careful of the infamous "N+1 selects" issue, where an initial query pulls back results from a single table, but using each result transparently executes another query to lazily load associated entities. Sometimes you'll be able to find an elegant query expression that results in exactly the SQL you want to use; other times you'll need to bend the query expression out of shape somewhat. Occasionally you'll need to write the SQL manually or use a stored procedure instead—as is often the case with ORMs.

I find it interesting just to take query expressions that you already know work in LINQ to Objects and see what SQL is generated when you run them against a database.

Sometimes you can predict how things will work, but sometimes there's more going on than you might expect. There's sample code on the book's website for various queries, but query expressions are pretty easy to write, and I'd strongly encourage you to write your own for fun. The SkeetySoft defects model is quite a simple one to query, of course—but you've seen how Visual Studio 2008 makes it easy to generate entities, so give it a try with a schema from a *real* system. I can't emphasize enough that this brief look at LINQ to SQL should *not* be taken as sufficient information to start building production code. It should be enough to let you experiment, but please read more detailed documentation before embarking on a real application!

I've deliberately not gone into how query expressions are converted into SQL in this section. I wanted you to get a feel for the capabilities of LINQ to SQL before starting to pick it apart.

12.2   Translations using IQueryable and IQueryProvider

In this section we're going to find out the basics of how LINQ to SQL manages to convert our query expressions into SQL. This is the starting point for implementing your own LINQ provider, should you wish to. This is the most theoretical section in the chapter, but it's useful to have some insight as to how LINQ is able to decide whether to use in-memory processing, a database, or some other query engine.

In all the query expressions we've seen in LINQ to SQL, the source has been a `Table<T>`. However, if you look at `Table<T>`, you'll see it doesn't have a `Where` method, or `Select`, or `Join`, or any of the other standard query operators. Instead, it uses the same trick that LINQ to Objects does—just as the source in LINQ to Objects always implements `IEnumerable<T>` (possibly after a call to `Cast` or `OfType`) and then uses the extension methods in `Enumerable`, so `Table<T>` implements `IQueryable<T>` and then uses the extension methods in `Queryable`. We'll see how LINQ builds up an expression tree and then allows a provider to execute it at the appropriate time. Let's start off by looking at what `IQueryable<T>` consists of.

12.2.1   Introducing IQueryable<T> and related interfaces

If you look up `IQueryable<T>` in the documentation and see what members it contains directly (rather than inheriting), you may be disappointed. There aren't any. Instead, it inherits from `IEnumerable<T>` and the nongeneric `IQueryable.IQueryable` in turn inherits from the nongeneric `IEnumerable`. So, `IQueryable` is where the new and exciting members are, right? Well, nearly. In fact, `IQueryable` just has three properties: `QueryProvider`, `ElementType`, and `Expression`. The `QueryProvider` property is of type `IQueryProvider`—yet another new interface to consider.

Lost? Perhaps figure 12.2 will help out—a class diagram of all the interfaces directly involved.

The easiest way of thinking of `IQueryable` is that it represents a query that, when executed, will yield a sequence of results. The details of the query in LINQ terms are held in an expression tree, as returned by the `Expression` property of the `IQueryable`. Executing a query is performed by beginning to iterate through an `IQueryable` (in other

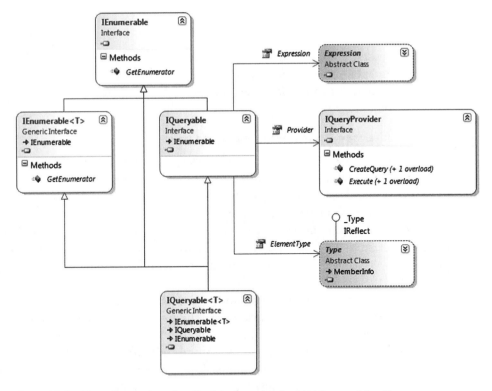

Figure 12.2   Class diagram based on the interfaces involved in `IQueryable<T>`

words, calling the `GetEnumerator` method) or by a call to the `Execute` method on an `IQueryProvider`, passing in an expression tree.

So, with at least some grasp of what `IQueryable` is for, what is `IQueryProvider`? Well, we can do more than execute a query—we can also build a bigger query from it, which is the purpose of the standard query operators in LINQ.[2] To build up a query, we need to use the `CreateQuery` method on the relevant `IQueryProvider`.[3]

Think of a data source as a simple query (`SELECT * FROM SomeTable` in SQL, for instance)—calling `Where`, `Select`, `OrderBy`, and similar methods results in a different query, based on the first one. Given any `IQueryable` query, you can create a new query by performing the following steps:

1. Ask the existing query for its query expression tree (using the `Expression` property).
2. Build a new expression tree that contains the original expression and the extra functionality you want (a filter, projection, or ordering, for instance).

---

[2] Well, the ones that keep deferring execution, such as `Where` and `Join`. We'll see what happens with the aggregations such as `Count` in a little while.

[3] Both `Execute` and `CreateQuery` have generic and nongeneric overloads. The nongeneric versions make it easier to create queries dynamically in code. Compile-time query expressions use the generic version.

3 Ask the existing query for its query provider (using the `Provider` property).

4 Call `CreateQuery` on the provider, passing in the new expression tree.

Of those steps, the only tricky one is creating the new expression tree. Fortunately, there's a whole bunch of extension methods on the static `Queryable` class that do all that for us. Enough theory—let's start implementing the interfaces so we can see all this in action.

12.2.2 *Faking it: interface implementations to log calls*

Before you get too excited, we're not going to build our own fully fledged query provider in this chapter. However, if you understand everything in this section, you'll be in a much better position to build one if you ever need to—and possibly more importantly, you'll understand what's going on when you issue LINQ to SQL queries. Most of the hard work of query providers goes on at the point of execution, where they need to parse an expression tree and convert it into the appropriate form for the target platform. We're concentrating on the work that happens before that—how LINQ *prepares* to execute a query.

We'll write our own implementations of `IQueryable` and `IQueryProvider`, and then try to run a few queries against them. The interesting part isn't the results—we won't be doing anything useful with the queries when we execute them—but the series of calls made up to the point of execution. We'll write types `FakeQueryProvider` and `FakeQuery`. The implementation of each interface method writes out the current expression involved, using a simple logging method (not shown here). Let's look first at `FakeQuery`, as shown in listing 12.6.

> **Listing 12.6 A simple implementation of `IQueryable` that logs method calls**

```
class FakeQuery<T> : IQueryable<T>
{
    public Expression Expression { get; private set; }      ❶ Declares simple
    public IQueryProvider Provider { get; private set; }        automatic
    public Type ElementType { get; private set; }              properties

    internal FakeQuery(IQueryProvider provider,
                       Expression expression)
    {
        Expression = expression;
        Provider = provider;
        ElementType = typeof(T);
    }

    internal FakeQuery()
        : this(new FakeQueryProvider(), null)
    {                                                          ❷ Uses this query as
        Expression = Expression.Constant(this);                  initial expression
    }

    public IEnumerator<T> GetEnumerator()
    {
        Logger.Log(this, Expression);
```

```
            return Enumerable.Empty<T>().GetEnumerator();
    }
```
◁─┐ **Returns empty**
❸   **result sequence**

```
    IEnumerator IEnumerable.GetEnumerator()
    {
        Logger.Log(this, Expression);
        return Enumerable.Empty<object>().GetEnumerator();
    }

    public override string ToString()
    {
        return "FakeQuery";
    }
}
```
◁─┐ **Overrides for**
❹   **sake of logging**

The property members of `IQueryable` are implemented in `FakeQuery` with automatic properties ❶, which are set by the constructors. There are two constructors: a parameterless one that is used by our main program to create a plain "source" for the query, and one that is called by `FakeQueryProvider` with the current query expression.

The use of `Expression.Constant(this)` as the initial source expression ❷ is just a way of showing that the query initially represents the original object. (Imagine an implementation representing a table, for example—until you apply any query operators, the query would just return the whole table.) When the constant expression is logged, it uses the overridden `ToString` method, which is why we've given a short, constant description ❹. This makes the final expression much cleaner than it would have been without the override. When we are asked to iterate over the results of the query, we always just return an empty sequence ❸ to make life easy. Production implementations would parse the expression here, or (more likely) call `Execute` on their query provider and just return the result.

As you can see, there's not a lot going on in `FakeQuery`, and listing 12.7 shows that `FakeQueryProvider` is equally simple.

Listing 12.7   An implementation of `IQueryProvider` that uses `FakeQuery`

```
class FakeQueryProvider : IQueryProvider
{
    public IQueryable<T> CreateQuery<T>(Expression expression)
    {
        Logger.Log(this, expression);
        return new FakeQuery<T>(this, expression);
    }

    public IQueryable CreateQuery(Expression expression)
    {
        Logger.Log(this, expression);
        return new FakeQuery<object>(this, expression);
    }

    public T Execute<T>(Expression expression)
    {
        Logger.Log(this, expression);
        return default(T);
    }
```

```
    }

    public object Execute(Expression expression)
    {
        Logger.Log(this, expression);
        return null;
    }
}
```

There's even less to talk about in terms of the implementation of `FakeQueryProvider` than there was for `FakeQuery`. The `CreateQuery` methods do no real processing but act as factory methods for `FakeQuery`. The `Execute` method overloads just return empty results after logging the call. This is where a lot of analysis would *normally* be done, along with the actual call to the web service, database, or whatever the target platform is.

Even though we've done no real work, when we start to use `FakeQuery` as the source in a query expression interesting things start to happen. I've already let slip how we are able to write query expressions without explicitly writing methods to handle the standard query operators: it's all about extension methods, this time the ones in the `Queryable` class.

12.2.3 *Gluing expressions together: the Queryable extension methods*

Just as the `Enumerable` type contains extension methods on `IEnumerable<T>` to implement the LINQ standard query operators, the `Queryable` type contains extension methods on `IQueryable<T>`. There are two big differences between the implementations in `Enumerable` and those in `Queryable`.

First, the `Enumerable` methods all use delegates as their parameters—the `Select` method takes a `Func<TSource,TResult>`, for example. That's fine for in-memory manipulation, but for LINQ providers that execute the query elsewhere, we need a format we can examine more closely—expression trees. For example, the corresponding overload of `Select` in `Queryable` takes a parameter of type `Expression<Func<TSource,TResult>>`. The compiler doesn't mind at all—after query translation, it has a lambda expression that it needs to pass as a parameter to the method, and lambda expressions can be converted to either delegate instances or expression trees.

This is the reason that LINQ to SQL is able to work so seamlessly. The four key elements involved are all new features of C#3: lambda expressions, the translation of query expressions into "normal" expressions that *use* lambda expressions, extension methods, and expression trees. Without all four, there would be problems. If query expressions were always translated into delegates, for instance, they couldn't be used with a provider such as LINQ to SQL, which requires expression trees. Figure 12.3 shows the two paths taken by query expressions; they differ only in what interfaces their data source implements.

Notice how in figure 12.3 the early parts of the compilation process are independent of the data source. The same query expression is used, and it's translated in exactly the same way. It's only when the compiler looks at the translated query to find the appropriate `Select` and `Where` methods to use that the data source is truly important. At that

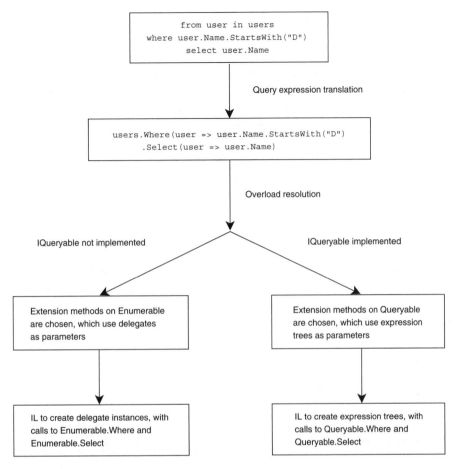

Figure 12.3 A query taking two paths, depending on whether the data source implements `IQueryable` or only `IEnumerable`

point, the lambda expressions can be converted to either delegate instances or expression trees, potentially giving radically different implementations: typically in-memory for the left path, and SQL executing against a database in the right path.

The second big difference between `Enumerable` and `Queryable` is that the `Enumerable` extension methods do the actual work associated with the corresponding query operator. There is code in `Enumerable.Where` to execute the specified filter and only yield appropriate elements as the result sequence, for example. By contrast, the query operator "implementations" in `Queryable` do very little: they just create a new query based on the parameters or call `Execute` on the query provider, as described at the end of section 12.2.1. In other words, they are only used to build up queries and request that they be executed—they don't contain the logic behind the operators. This means they're suitable for any LINQ provider that uses expression trees.

With the `Queryable` extension methods available and making use of our `IQueryable` and `IQueryProvider` implementations, it's finally time to see what happens when we use a query expression with our custom provider.

12.2.4 The fake query provider in action

Listing 12.8 shows a simple query expression, which (supposedly) finds all the strings in our fake source beginning with "abc" and projects the results into a sequence of the lengths of the matching strings. We iterate through the results, but don't do anything with them, as we know already that they'll be empty. Of course, we have no source data, and we haven't written any code to do any real filtering—we're just logging which calls are made by LINQ in the course of creating the query expression and iterating through the results.

```
var query = from x in new FakeQuery<string>()
            where x.StartsWith("abc")
            select x.Length;

foreach (int i in query) { }
```

What would you expect the results of running listing 12.8 to be? In particular, what would you like to be logged *last*, at the point where we'd normally expect to do some real work with the expression tree? Here are the results of listing 12.8, reformatted slightly for clarity:

```
FakeQueryProvider.CreateQuery
Expression=FakeQuery.Where(x => x.StartsWith("abc"))

FakeQueryProvider.CreateQuery
Expression=FakeQuery.Where(x => x.StartsWith("abc"))
                .Select(x => x.Length)

FakeQuery<Int32>.GetEnumerator
Expression=FakeQuery.Where(x => x.StartsWith("abc"))
                .Select(x => x.Length)
```

The two important things to note are that GetEnumerator is only called at the end, not on any intermediate queries, and that by the time GetEnumerator is called we have all the information present in the original query expression. We haven't manually had to keep track of earlier parts of the expression in each step—a single expression tree captures all the information "so far" at any point in time.

Don't be fooled by the concise output, by the way—the actual expression tree is quite deep and complicated, particularly due to the where clause including an extra method call. This expression tree is what LINQ to SQL would be examining to work out what query to execute. LINQ providers *could* build up their own queries (in whatever form they may need) as calls to CreateQuery are made, but usually looking at the final tree when GetEnumerator is called is simpler, as all the necessary information is available in one place.

The final call logged by listing 12.8 was to FakeQuery.GetEnumerator, and you may be wondering why we *also* need an Execute method on IQueryProvider. Well, not all query expressions generate sequences—if you use an aggregation operator such as Sum,

`Count`, or `Average`, we're no longer really creating a "source"—we're evaluating a result immediately. That's when `Execute` is called, as shown by listing 12.9 and its output.

Listing 12.9   `IQueryProvider.Execute`

```
var query = from x in new FakeQuery<string>()
            where x.StartsWith("abc")
            select x.Length;

double mean = query.Average();

// Output
FakeQueryProvider.CreateQuery
Expression=FakeQuery.Where(x => x.StartsWith("abc"))

FakeQueryProvider.CreateQuery
Expression=FakeQuery.Where(x => x.StartsWith("abc"))
                    .Select(x => x.Length)

FakeQueryProvider.Execute
Expression=FakeQuery.Where(x => x.StartsWith("abc"))
                    .Select(x => x.Length)
                    .Average()
```

The `FakeQueryProvider` can be quite useful when it comes to understanding what the C# compiler is doing behind the scenes with query expressions. It will show the transparent identifiers introduced within a query expression, along with the translated calls to `SelectMany`, `GroupJoin`, and the like.

12.2.5 *Wrapping up IQueryable*

We haven't written any of the significant code that a real query provider would need in order to get useful work done, but hopefully our fake provider has given you insight into how LINQ providers are given the information from query expressions. It's all built up by the `Queryable` extension methods, given an appropriate implementation of `IQueryable` and `IQueryProvider`.

We've gone into a bit more detail in this section than we will for the rest of the chapter, as it's involved the foundations that underpin the LINQ to SQL code we saw earlier. You're unlikely to want to write your own query provider—it takes a lot of work to produce a really good one—but this section has been important in terms of conceptual understanding. The steps involved in taking a C# query expression and (at execution time) running some SQL on a database are quite profound and lie at the heart of the big features of C# 3. Understanding why C# has gained these features will help keep you more in tune with the language.

In fact, LINQ to SQL is the only provider built into the framework that actually uses `IQueryable`—the other "providers" are just APIs that play nicely with LINQ to Objects. I don't wish to diminish their importance—they're still useful. However, it does mean that you can relax a bit now—the hardest part of the chapter is behind you. We're still staying with database-related access for our next section, though, which looks at LINQ to DataSet.

12.3   LINQ to DataSet

Seeing all the neat stuff that LINQ to SQL can achieve is all very well, but most developers are likely to be improving an existing application rather than creating a new one from the ground up. Rather than ripping out the entire persistence layer and replacing it with LINQ to SQL, it would be nice to be able to gain some of the advantages of LINQ while using existing technology. Many ADO.NET applications use datasets, whether *typed* or *untyped*[4]—and LINQ to DataSet gives you access to a lot of the benefits of LINQ with little change to your current code.

The query expressions used within LINQ to DataSet are just LINQ to Objects queries—there's no translation into a call to `DataTable.Select`, for example. Instead, data rows are filtered and ordered with normal delegate instances that operate on those rows.

Unsurprisingly, you'll get a better experience using typed datasets, but a set of extension methods on `DataTable` and `DataRow` make it at least *possible* to work with untyped datasets too. In this section we'll look at both kinds of datasets, starting with untyped ones.

12.3.1   *Working with untyped datasets*

Untyped datasets have two problems as far as LINQ is concerned. First, we don't have access to the fields within the tables as typed properties; second, the tables themselves aren't enumerable. To some extent both are merely a matter of convenience—we *could* use direct casts in all the queries, handle DBNull explicitly and so forth, as well as enumerate the rows in a table using `dataTable.Rows.Cast<DataRow>`. These workarounds are quite ugly, which is why the `DataTableExtensions` and `DataRowExtensions` classes exist.

Code using untyped datasets is never going to be pretty, but using LINQ is far nicer than filtering and sorting using `DataTable.Select`. No more escaping, worrying about date and time formatting, and similar nastiness.

Listing 12.10 gives a simple example. It just fills a single defect table and prints the summaries of all the defects that don't have a status of "closed."

Listing 12.10   Displaying the summaries of open defects from an untyped `DataTable`

```
DataTable dataTable = new DataTable();

using (var connection = new SqlConnection
    (Settings.Default.SkeetySoftDefectsConnectionString))      ❶ Fills table
{                                                                  from
    string sql = "SELECT Summary, Status FROM Defect";            database
    new SqlDataAdapter(sql, connection).Fill(dataTable);
}
                                                                ❷ Makes table
var query = from defect in dataTable.AsEnumerable()               enumerable
```

---

[4]   An untyped dataset is one that has no static information about the contents of its tables. Typed datasets, usually generated in the Visual Studio designer, know the tables which can be present in the dataset, and the columns within the rows in those tables.

```
           where defect.Field<Status>("Status") != Status.Closed    ◄─────┐
           select defect.Field<string>("Summary");    ◄─────┐             │
                                                             │    Accesses │
foreach (string summary in query)             Selects       │    Status   │
{                                          Summary field  ❹  field ❸
    Console.WriteLine (summary);
}
```

Coming so soon after the nice, clean world of LINQ to SQL, listing 12.10 makes me feel somewhat dirty. There's hard-coded SQL, column names, and casts all over the place. However, we'll see that things are better when we have a typed dataset—and this code *does* get the job done. If you're using both LINQ to SQL *and* LINQ to DataSet, you can fill a DataTable using the DataTableExtensions.CopyToDataTable extension method, but I wanted to keep to just one new technology at a time for this example.

The first part ❶ is "old-fashioned" ADO.NET code to fill the data table. I haven't used an actual dataset for this example because we're only interested in a single table—putting it in a dataset would have made things slightly more complicated for no benefit. It's only when we reach the query expression (❷ ❸ and ❹) that LINQ starts coming in.

The source of a query expression has to be enumerable in some form—and the DataTable type doesn't even implement IEnumerable, let alone IEnumerable<T>. The DataTableExtensions class provides the AsEnumerable extension method (❷), which merely returns an IEnumerable<DataRow> that iterates over the rows in the table.

Accessing fields within a row is made slightly easier in LINQ to DataSet using the Field<T> extension method on DataRow. This not only removes the need to cast results, but it also deals with null values for you—it converts DBNull to a null reference for you, or the null value of a nullable type.

I won't give any further examples of untyped datasets here, although there are a couple more queries in the book's sample code. Hopefully you'll find yourself in the situation where you can use a typed dataset instead.

12.3.2 *Working with typed datasets*

Although typed datasets aren't as rich as using LINQ to SQL directly, they provide much more static type information, which lets your code stay cleaner. There's a bit of work to start with: we have to create a typed dataset for our defect-tracking system before we can begin using it.

CREATING THE TYPED DATASET WITH VISUAL STUDIO

The process for generating a typed dataset in Visual Studio 2008 is almost *exactly* the same as it is to generate LINQ to SQL entities. Again, you add a new item to the project (this time selecting DataSet in the list of options), and again you can drag and drop tables from the Server Explorer window onto the designer surface.

There aren't quite as many options available in the property panes for typed datasets, but we can still rename the DefectUser table, the DefectID field, along with the associations. Likewise, we can still tell the Status, Summary, and UserType properties to use the enumeration types from the model. Figure 12.4 shows the designer after a bit of editing and rearranging.

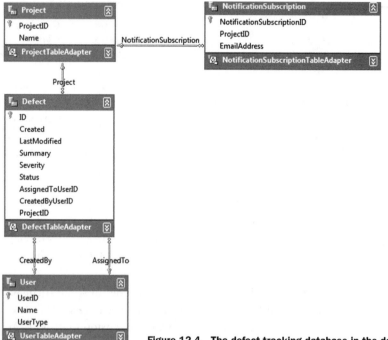

Figure 12.4   The defect-tracking database in the dataset designer

Each table in the dataset has its own types for the table, rows, notification event handlers, notification event arguments, and adapters. The adapters are placed into a separate namespace, based on the name of the dataset.

Once you've created the dataset, using it is easy.

POPULATING AND QUERYING TYPED DATASETS

As in previous versions of ADO.NET, typed datasets are populated using *adapters*. The adapters generated by the designer already use the connection string of the server originally used to create the dataset: this can be changed in the application settings. This means that in many cases, you can fill the tables with barely any code. Listing 12.11 achieves the same results as the query on the untyped dataset, but in a considerably cleaner fashion.

Listing 12.11   Displaying the summaries of open defects from a typed dataset

```
DefectDataSet dataSet = new DefectDataSet();
new DefectTableAdapter().Fill(dataSet.Defect);

var query = from defect in dataSet.Defect
            where defect.Status != Status.Closed
            select defect.Summary;

foreach (string summary in query)
{
    Console.WriteLine(summary);
}
```

Creating and populating the dataset is now a breeze—and even though we use only one table, it's as easy to do that using a complete dataset as it would have been if we'd only created a single data table. Of course, we're pulling more data down this time because we haven't specified a SQL projection, but you can access the "raw" adapter of a typed data adapter and modify the query yourself if you need to.

The query expression in listing 12.11 looks like it could have come straight from LINQ to SQL or LINQ to Objects, other than using `dataSet` instead of `context` or `SampleData.AllDefects`. The `DefectDataSet.Defect` property returns a `DefectData-Table`, which implements `IEnumerable<DefectDataRow>` already (via its base class, `TypedTableBase<DefectDataRow>`) so we don't need any extension methods, and each row is strongly typed.

For me, one of the most compelling aspects of LINQ is this consistency between different data access mechanisms. Even if you only query a single data source, LINQ is useful—but being able to query multiple data sources with the same syntax is phenomenal. You still need to be aware of the consequences of querying against the different technologies, but the fundamental grammar of query expressions remains constant.

Using associations between different tables is also simple with typed datasets. In listing 12.12 we group the open defects according to their status, and display the defect ID, the name of the project, and the name of the user assigned to work on it.

Listing 12.12 Using associations in a typed dataset

```
DefectDataSet dataSet = new DefectDataSet();

var query = from defect in dataSet.Defect                    ❶ Defines
            where defect.Status != Status.Closed                query
            group defect by defect.Status;

new DefectTableAdapter().Fill(dataSet.Defect);               ❷ Populates
new UserTableAdapter().Fill(dataSet.User);                      dataset
new ProjectTableAdapter().Fill(dataSet.Project);

foreach (var group in query)
{
    Console.WriteLine(group.Key);
    foreach (var defect in group)                            ❸ Displays
    {                                                           results
        Console.WriteLine("  {0}: {1}/{2}",
                    defect.ID,
                    defect.ProjectRow.Name,
                    defect.UserRowByAssignedTo.Name);
    }
}
```

Unlike in LINQ to SQL (which can lazily load entities), we have to load all the data we're interested in before we execute the query. Just for fun, this time I've populated the dataset ❷ *after* we've defined the query ❶ but *before* we've executed it ❸. Apart from anything else, this proves that LINQ is still working in a deferred execution mode—it doesn't try to look at the list of defects until we iterate through them.

When we display the results ❸, the associations (`ProjectRow`, `UserRowBy-AssignedTo`) aren't *quite* as neat as they are in LINQ to SQL, because the dataset designer doesn't give us as much control over those names as the entity model designer does. It's still a lot nicer than the equivalent code for untyped datasets, however.

As you can see, Microsoft has made LINQ work nicely with databases and associated technologies. That's not the only form of data access we can use, though—in a world where XML is so frequently used for storing and exchanging data, LINQ makes processing documents that much simpler.

12.4   LINQ to XML

Whereas LINQ to DataSet is really just some extensions to the existing dataset capabilities (along with a new base class for typed data tables), LINQ to XML is a completely new XML API. If your immediate reaction to hearing about *yet another* XML API is to ask whether or not we need one, you're not alone. However, LINQ to XML simplifies document manipulation considerably, and is designed to play well with LINQ to Objects. It doesn't have much extra querying functionality in itself, and it doesn't perform any query translations in the way that LINQ to SQL does, but the integration with LINQ via iterators makes it a pleasure to work with.

It's not just about querying, though—one of the major benefits of LINQ to XML over the existing APIs is its "developer friendliness" when it comes to creating and transforming and XML documents too. We'll see that in a moment, when we create an XML document containing all our sample data, ready for querying. Of course, this won't be a comprehensive guide to LINQ to XML, but the deeper topics that we won't cover here (such as XML namespace handling) have been well thought out to make development easier.

Let's start by looking at two of the most important classes of LINQ to XML.

12.4.1   XElement and XAttribute

The bulk of LINQ to XML consists of a set of classes in the `System.Xml.Linq` namespace, most of which are prefixed with X: `XName`, `XDocument`, `XComment`, and so forth. Even though lots of classes are available, for our purposes we only need to know about `XElement` and `XAttribute`, which obviously represent XML elements and attributes, respectively.

We'll also be using `XName` indirectly, which is used for names of elements and attributes, and can contain namespace information. The reason we only need to use it indirectly is that there's an implicit conversion from `string` to `XName`, so every time we create an element or attribute by passing the name as a string, it's converting it into an `XName`. I mention this only so that you won't get confused about what's being called if you look at the available methods and constructors in MSDN.

One of the great things about LINQ to XML is how easy it is to construct elements and attributes. In DOM, to create a simple document with a nested element you'd have to go through lots of hoops:

- Create a document.
- Create a root element from the document.
- Add the root element to the document.
- Create a child element from the document.
- Add the child element to the root element.

Adding attributes was relatively painful, too. None of this would be naturally nested in the code to give an at-a-glance indication of the final markup. LINQ to XML makes life easier in the following ways:

- You don't need an XDocument unless you want one—you can create elements and attributes separately.
- You can specify the contents of an element (or document) in the constructor.

These don't immediately sound important, but seeing the API in action makes things clearer. Listing 12.13 creates and prints out an XML element with attributes and a nested element containing some text.

Listing 12.13   Creating a simple piece of XML

```
var root = new XElement("root",
                        new XAttribute ("attr", "value"),
                        new XElement("child",
                                     "text")
                       );

Console.WriteLine (root);
```

Choosing how you format LINQ to XML creation code is a personal decision, in terms of where to use whitespace and how much to use, where to place parentheses, and so forth. However, the important point to note from listing 12.13 is how it's quite clear that the element "root" contains two nodes: an attribute and a child element. The child element then has a text node ("text"). In other words, the structure of the result is apparent from the structure of the code. The output from listing 12.13 is the XML we'd hope for:

```
<root attr="value">
  <child>text</child>
</root>
```

The equivalent code in DOM would have been much nastier. If we'd *wanted* to include an XML declaration (<xml version="1.0" encoding="utf-8">, for instance), it would have been easy to do so with XDocument—but I'm trying to keep things as simple as possible for this brief tour. Likewise, you can modify XElements after creating them in a DOM-like manner, but we don't need to go down that particular path here.

The constructor for XElement accepts any number of objects using a params parameter, but importantly it will also then recurse into any enumerable arguments that are passed to it. This is absolutely crucial when using LINQ queries within XML creation expressions. Speaking of which, let's start building some XML with our familiar defect data.

12.4.2 *Converting sample defect data into XML*

We've currently got our sample data available in three different forms—in memory as objects, in the database, and in a typed dataset. Of course, the typed dataset can write XML directly, but let's convert our original in-memory version for simplicity. To start with, we'll just generate a list of the users. Listing 12.14 creates a list of `user` elements within a `users` element, and then writes it out; the output is shown beneath the listing.

Listing 12.14   Creating an element from the sample users

```
var users = new XElement("users",
    from user in SampleData.AllUsers
    select new XElement("user",
                        new XAttribute("name", user.Name),
                        new XAttribute("type", user.UserType))
);

Console.WriteLine (users);

// Output
<users>
  <user name="Tim Trotter" type="Tester" />
  <user name="Tara Tutu" type="Tester" />
  <user name="Deborah Denton" type="Developer" />
  <user name="Darren Dahlia" type="Developer" />
  <user name="Mary Malcop" type="Manager" />
  <user name="Colin Carton" type="Customer" />
</users>
```

I hope you'll agree that listing 12.14 is simple, once you've got your head around the idea that the contents of the top-level element depend on the result of the embedded query expression. It's possible to make it even simpler, however. I've written a small extension method on `object` that generates an `IEnumerable<XAttribute>` based on the properties of the object it's called on, which are discovered with reflection. This is ideal for anonymous types—listing 12.15 creates the same output, but without the explicit `XAttribute` constructor calls. With only two attributes, there isn't much difference in the code, but for more complicated elements it's a real boon.

Listing 12.15   Using object properties to generate `XAttributes` with reflection

```
var users = new XElement("users",
    from user in SampleData.AllUsers
    select new XElement("user",
                        new { name=user.Name, type=user.UserType }
                            .AsXAttributes()
                        )
);

Console.WriteLine (users);
```

For the rest of the chapter I'll use the "vanilla" LINQ to XML calls, but it's worth being aware of the possibilities available with a bit of reusable code. (The source for the extension method is available as part of the code for the book.)

You can nest query expressions and do all kinds of other clever things with them. Listing 12.16 generates an element containing the project information: the notification subscriptions for a project are embedded within the project element by using a nested query. The results are shown beneath the listing.

Listing 12.16 Generating projects with nested subscription elements

```
var projects = new XElement("projects",
    from project in SampleData.AllProjects
    select new XElement("project",
        new XAttribute("name", project.Name),
        new XAttribute("id", project.ProjectID),
        from subscription in SampleData.AllSubscriptions
        where subscription.Project == project
        select new XElement("subscription",
            new XAttribute("email", subscription.EmailAddress)
        )
    )
);

Console.WriteLine (projects);

// Output
<projects>
  <project name="Skeety Media Player" id="1">
    <subscription email="media-bugs@skeetysoft.com" />
    <subscription email="theboss@skeetysoft.com" />
  </project>
  <project name="Skeety Talk" id="2">
    <subscription email="talk-bugs@skeetysoft.com" />
  </project>
  <project name="Skeety Office" id="3">
    <subscription email="office-bugs@skeetysoft.com" />
  </project>
</projects>
```

The two queries are highlighted in bold. There are alternative ways of generating the same output, of course—you could use a single query that groups the subscriptions by project, for instance. The code in listing 12.16 was just the first way I thought of tackling the problem—and in cases where the performance isn't terribly important it doesn't matter that we'll be running the nested query multiple times. In production code you'd want to consider possible performance issues more carefully, of course!

I won't show you all the code to generate all the elements—even with LINQ to XML, it's quite tedious just because there are so many attributes to set. I've placed it all in a single `XmlSampleData.GetElement()` method that returns a root `XElement`. We'll use this method as the starting point for the examples in our final avenue of investigation: querying.

12.4.3 Queries in LINQ to XML

You may well be expecting me to reveal that `XElement` implements `IEnumerable` and that LINQ queries come for free. Well, it's not *quite* that simple, because there are so many different things that an `XElement` could iterate through. `XElement` contains a number of *axis methods* that are used as query sources. If you're familiar with XPath, the idea of an axis will no doubt be familiar to you. Here are the axis methods used directly for querying, each of which returns an appropriate `IEnumerable<T>`:

- `Ancestors`
- `AncestorsAndSelf`
- `Annotations`
- `Attributes`
- `Descendants`
- `DescendantsAndSelf`
- `DescendantNodes`
- `DescendantNodesAndSelf`
- `Elements`
- `ElementsAfterSelf`
- `ElementsBeforeSelf`

All of these are fairly self-explanatory (and the MSDN documentation provides more details). There are useful overloads to retrieve only nodes with an appropriate name: calling `Descendants("user")` on an `XElement` will return all `user` elements underneath the element you call it on, for instance. A number of extension methods also make these axes available to whole sequences of nodes: the result is a concatenated sequence as if the method has been called on each node in turn.

As well as these calls returning sequences, there are some methods that return a single result—`Attribute` and `Element` are the most important, returning the named attribute and the first descendant element with the specified name, respectively.

One aspect of `XAttribute` that is particularly relevant to querying is the set of the explicit conversions from an `XAttribute` to any number of other types, such as `int`, `string`, and `DateTime`. These are important for both filtering and projecting results.

Enough talk! Let's see some code. We'll start off simply, just displaying the users within our XML structure, as shown in listing 12.17.

Listing 12.17 Displaying the users within an XML structure

```
XElement root = XmlSampleData.GetElement();

var query = from user in root.Element("users").Elements()
            select new { Name=(string)user.Attribute("name"),
                         UserType=(string)user.Attribute("type") };

foreach (var user in query)
{
    Console.WriteLine ("{0}: {1}", user.Name, user.UserType);
}
```

After creating the data at the start, we navigate down to the users element, and ask it for its direct child elements. This two-step fetch could be shortened to just `root.Descendants("user")`, but it's good to see the more rigid navigation so you can use it where necessary. It's also more robust in the face of changes to the document structure, such as another (unrelated) user element being added elsewhere in the document.

The rest of the query expression is merely a projection of an `XElement` into an anonymous type. I'll admit that we're cheating slightly with the user type: we've kept it as a string instead of calling `Enum.Parse` to convert it into a proper `UserType` value. The latter approach works perfectly well—but it's quite longwinded when you only need the string form, and the code becomes hard to format sensibly within the strict limits of the printed page.

Listing 12.17 isn't doing anything particularly impressive, of course. In particular, it would be easy to achieve a similar effect with a single XPath expression. Joins, however, are harder to express in XPath. They work, but they're somewhat messy. With LINQ to XML, we can use our familiar query expression syntax. Listing 12.18 demonstrates this, showing each open defect's ID with its assignee and project.

Listing 12.18   Two joins and a filter within a LINQ to XML query

```
XElement root = XmlSampleData.GetElement();

var query = from defect in root.Descendants("defect")
            join user in root.Descendants("user")
              on (int?)defect.Attribute("assigned-to") equals
                 (int)user.Attribute("id")
            join project in root.Descendants("project")
              on (int)defect.Attribute("project") equals
                 (int)project.Attribute("id")
            where (string)defect.Attribute("status") != "Closed"
            select new { ID=(int)defect.Attribute("id"),
                         Project=(string)project.Attribute("name"),
                         Assignee=(string)user.Attribute("name") };

foreach (var defect in query)
{
    Console.WriteLine ("{0}: {1}/{2}",
                       defect.ID,
                       defect.Project,
                       defect.Assignee);
}
```

I'm not going to pretend that listing 12.18 is particularly pleasant. It has lots of string literals (which could easily be turned into constants) and it's generally pretty wordy. On the other hand, it's doing quite a lot of work, including coping with the possibility of a defect not being assigned to a user (the int? conversion in the join of defect to assignee). Consider how horrible the corresponding XPath expression would have to be, or how much manual code you'd have to write to perform the same query in direct code. The other standard query operators are available, too: once you've got a query source, LINQ to XML itself takes a back seat and lets LINQ to Objects do most of the work. We'll stop there, however—you may have seen enough query expressions to make you dizzy by now, and if you want to experiment further it's easy enough to do so.

12.4.4   *LINQ to XML summary*

Like the other topics in this chapter, we've barely scratched the surface of the LINQ to XML API. I haven't touched the integration with the previous technologies such as DOM and XPath, nor have I given details of the other node types—not even XDocument!

Even if I were to go through all of the features, that wouldn't come close to explaining all the possible *uses* of it. Practically everywhere you currently deal with XML, I expect LINQ to XML will make your life easier. To reiterate a cliché, the only limit is your imagination.

Just as an example, remember how we created our XML from LINQ queries? Well, there's nothing to stop the sources involved in those queries being LINQ to XML in the first place: lo and behold, a new (and powerful) way of transforming one form of XML to another is born.

Even though we've been so brief, I hope that I've opened the door for you—given you an inkling of the kind of XML processing that can be achieved *relatively* simply using LINQ to XML. You'll need to learn a lot more before you master the API, but my aim was to whet your appetite and show you how LINQ query expressions have a consistency between providers that easily surpasses previous query techniques and technologies.

We've now seen all of the LINQ providers that are built into the .NET 3.5 Framework. That's not the same thing as saying that you've seen all the LINQ providers you'll ever use, however.

12.5   *LINQ beyond .NET 3.5*

Even before .NET 3.5 was finally released, developers outside Microsoft were hard at work writing their own providers, and Microsoft isn't resting on its laurels either. We'll round this chapter off with a quick look at what else is available now, and some of what's still to come. In this section we're moving even faster than before, covering providers in even less depth. We don't need to know much about them, but their variety is important to demonstrate LINQ's flexibility.

12.5.1   *Third-party LINQ*

From the start, LINQ was designed to be general purpose. It would be hard to deny its SQL-like feel, but at the same time LINQ to Objects proves that you don't need to be working with a database in order to benefit from it.

A number of third-party providers have started popping up, and although at the time of this writing most are "proof of concept" more than production code—ways of exploring LINQ as much as anything else—they give a good indication of the wide range of potential uses for LINQ. We'll only look at three examples, but providers for other data sources (SharePoint and Flickr, for example) are emerging, and the list will only get longer. Let's start off with a slightly closer look at the example we first saw in chapter 1.

LINQ TO AMAZON

One of the flagship e-commerce sites, Amazon has always tried to drive technology forward, and it has a number of web services available for applications to talk to. Some cost money—but fortunately searching for a list of books is free. Simply visit http://aws.amazon.com, sign up to the scheme, and you'll receive an access ID by email. You'll need this if you want to run the example for yourself.

As part of Manning's *LINQ in Action* book, Fabrice Marguerie implemented a LINQ provider to make requests to the Amazon web service.[5] Listing 12.19 shows an example of using the provider to query Amazon's list of books with "LINQ" in the title.

---

[5] See http://linqinaction.net for more information and updates.

Listing 12.19   Querying Amazon's web service with LINQ

```
AmazonBookSearch source = new AmazonBookSearch(<Id>);     ➊ Creates provider
                                                            with your access ID
var webQuery = from book in source
               where book.Title.Contains("LINQ")         ➋ Creates query
               select book;                                 for web service

var query = from book in webQuery.AsEnumerable()
            orderby book.Year, book.Title                ➌ Performs more
            select book;                                    operations in memory

foreach (AmazonBook book in query)                       ➍ Executes
{                                                           query,
    Console.WriteLine ("{0}: {1}", book.Year, book.Title);  displays
}                                                           results
```

I've taken Fabrice's provider and tweaked it slightly so that we can pass our own Amazon Access ID into the provider's constructor ➊. The source is part of the Visual Studio 2008 solution containing the examples for this chapter.

You may be slightly surprised to see two query expressions in listing 12.19. As a proof of concept, the LINQ to Amazon provider only allows a limited number of operations, not including ordering. We use the web query ➋ as the source for an in-memory LINQ to Objects query expression ➌. The web service call still only takes place when we start executing the query ➍, due to the deferred execution approach taken by LINQ.

The output at the time of this writing is included here. By the time you read this, I expect the list may be considerably longer.

```
1998: A linq between nonwovens and wovens. (...)
2007: Introducing Microsoft  LINQ
2007: LINQ for VB 2005
2007: LINQ for Visual C# 2005
2007: Pro LINQ: Language Integrated Query in C# 2008
2008: Beginning ASP.NET 3.5 Data Access with LINQ , C# (...)
2008: Beginning ASP.NET 3.5 Data Access with LINQ, VB (...)
2008: LINQ in Action
2008: Professional LINQ
```

Even though LINQ to Amazon is primitive, it demonstrates an important point: LINQ is capable of more than just database and in-memory queries. Our next provider proves that even when it's talking to databases, there's more to LINQ than just LINQ to SQL.

LINQ TO NHIBERNATE

NHibernate is an open source ORM framework for .NET, based on the Hibernate project for Java. It supports textual queries in its own query language (HQL) and also a more programmatic way of building up queries—the *Criteria* API.

Prolific blogger and NHibernate contributor Ayende[6] has initiated a LINQ to NHibernate provider that converts LINQ queries not into SQL but into NHibernate Criteria queries, taking advantage of the SQL translation code in the rest of the project. Aside

---

[6] www.ayende.com/Blog/

from anything else, this means that the feature of RDBMS independence comes for free. The same LINQ queries can be run against SQL Server, Oracle, or Postgres, for example: any system that NHibernate knows about, with SQL tailored for that particular implementation.

Before writing this book, I hadn't used NHibernate (although I am reasonably experienced with its cousin in the Java world), and it's a testament to the project that within about an hour I was up and running with the SkeetySoft defect database, using nothing but the online tutorial. Listing 12.20 shows the same query we used against LINQ to SQL in listing 12.3 to list all of Tim's open defects.

Listing 12.20   LINQ to NHibernate query to list defects assigned to Tim Trotter

```
ISessionFactory sessionFactory =
    new Configuration().Configure().BuildSessionFactory();

using (ISession session = sessionFactory.OpenSession())
{
    using (ITransaction tx = session.BeginTransaction())
    {
        User tim = (from user in session.Linq<User>()
                    where user.Name == "Tim Trotter"
                    select user).Single();

        var query = from defect in session.Linq<Defect>()
                    where defect.Status != Status.Closed
                    where defect.AssignedTo == tim
                    select defect.Summary;

        foreach (var summary in query)
        {
            Console.WriteLine(summary);
        }
        tx.Commit();
    }
}
```

As you can see, once the session and transaction have been set up, the code is similar to that used in LINQ to SQL. The generated SQL is different, although it executes the same *sort* of queries. In other cases, identical query expressions can generate different SQL, mostly due to decisions regarding the lazy or eager loading of entities. This is an example of a *leaky abstraction*[7]—where in theory the abstraction layer of LINQ might be considered to isolate the developer from the implementation performing the actual query, but in practice the implementation details leak through. Don't fall for the abstraction: it takes nothing away from the value of LINQ, but you *do* need to be aware of what you're coding against, and keep an eye on what queries are being executed for you.

So, we've seen LINQ working against both web services and multiple databases. There's another piece of infrastructure that is commonly queried, though: an enterprise directory.

---

[7] www.joelonsoftware.com/articles/LeakyAbstractions.html

LINQ TO ACTIVE DIRECTORY

Almost all companies running their IT infrastructure on Windows use Active Directory to manage users, computers, settings, and more. Active Directory is a directory server that implements LDAP as one query protocol, but other LDAP servers are available, including the free OpenLDAP platform.[8]

Bart De Smet[9] (who now works for Microsoft) implemented a prototype LINQ to Active Directory provider as a tutorial on how LINQ providers work—but it has also proved to be a valuable reminder of how broadly LINQ is targeted. Despite the name, it is capable of querying non-Microsoft servers. He has also repeated the feat with a LINQ to SharePoint provider, which we won't cover here, but which is a more complete provider implementation.

If you're not familiar with directories, you can think of them as a sort of cross between file system directory trees and databases. They form hierarchies rather than tables, but each node in the tree is an entity with properties and an associated schema. (For those of you who *are* familiar with directories, please forgive this gross oversimplification.)

Installing and populating a directory is a bit of an effort, so for the sample code I've connected to a public server. If you happen to have access to an internal server, you'll probably find the results more meaningful if you connect to that.

Listing 12.21 connects to an LDAP server and lists all the users whose first name begins with K. The `Person` type is described elsewhere in the sample source code, complete with attributes to describe to LINQ to Active Directory how the properties within the object map to attributes within the directory.

> **Listing 12.21 LINQ to Active Directory sample, querying users by first name**

```
string url = "LDAP://ldap.andrew.cmu.edu/dc=cmu,dc=edu";
DirectoryEntry root = new DirectoryEntry(url);
root.AuthenticationType = AuthenticationTypes.None;

var users = new DirectorySource<Person>(root, SearchScope.Subtree);
users.Log = Console.Out;

var query = from user in users
            where user.FirstName.StartsWith("K")
            select user;

foreach (Person person in query)
{
   Console.WriteLine (person.DisplayName);
   foreach (string title in person.Titles)
   {
      Console.WriteLine(" {0}", title);
   }
}
```

Are you getting a sense of déjà vu yet? Listing 12.21 shows yet another query expression, which just happens to target LDAP. If you didn't have the first part, which sets the

---

[8] www.openldap.org
[9] http://blogs.bartdesmet.net/bart

scene, you wouldn't know that LDAP was involved at all. As we've already noted, you should be aware of the data source particularly with regard to the limitations of any one provider—but I'm sure you understood the query expression despite not knowing LDAP. The plain text version is `(&(objectClass=person)(givenName=K*))`, which isn't horrific but isn't nearly as familiar as the query expression should be by now.

The third-party examples we've seen are all "early adoption" code, largely written for the sake of investigating what's possible rather than creating production code. I predict that 2008 and 2009 will see a number of more feature-complete and high-quality providers emerging. At least two of these are likely to come from Microsoft.

12.5.2 *Future Microsoft LINQ technologies*

LINQ providers can work in very different ways. As we've already seen, LINQ to XML and LINQ to DataSet are just APIs that offer easy integration with LINQ to Objects, whereas LINQ to SQL is a more fully fledged provider, offering translation of queries to SQL. There are more providers being developed by Microsoft at the time of this writing, however—another ORM system, and an intriguing project to provide "no cost" parallelism where appropriate.

THE ADO.NET ENTITY FRAMEWORK

While LINQ to SQL is far from a toy, it doesn't have all the features that many developers expect from a modern ORM solution. For example, fetching strategies can be set on a per-context basis, but they can't be set for individual queries. Likewise, the entity inheritance strategies of LINQ to SQL are somewhat limited. Also, LINQ to SQL only supports SQL Server, which will obviously rule out its use for many projects that have already chosen a different RDBMS.

The "ADO.NET Entity Framework" forms the basis of Microsoft's "Data Access Strategy" and will ship with SQL Server 2008. The entity framework is a much more powerful solution than LINQ to SQL, including its own text-based query language (*Entity SQL*, also known as eSQL) and allowing a flexible mapping between the *conceptual model* (which is what the business layer of your code will use) and the *logical model* (which is what the database sees). An *Object Services* aspect of the entity framework deals with object identity and update management, and an *Entity Client* layer is responsible for all queries. The LINQ part of the entity framework is known as *LINQ to Entities.*

As with so many aspects of software development, flexibility comes with the burden of complexity—the two models and the mapping between them require their own XML files, for example. Microsoft will release an update to Visual Studio 2008 when the entity framework is released, with designers to help lighten the load of the various mapping tasks. The framework itself is still more complicated than LINQ to SQL, however, and will take longer to master.

Rather than provide yet another ORM query against the SkeetySoft defect database—and one that would look nearly identical to those we've already seen—I've just included some examples in the downloadable source code.[10]

---

[10] I will update these when the entity framework is released, if necessary.

All of the LINQ providers we've seen so far have acted on a particular data source, and performed the appropriate transformations. Our next topic is slightly different—but it's one I'm particularly excited about.

PARALLEL LINQ (PLINQ)

Ten years ago, the idea of even fairly low-to-middling laptops having dual-processor cores would have seemed ridiculous. Today, that's taken for granted—and if the chip manufacturers' plans are anything to go by, that's only the start. Of course, it's only useful to have more than one processor core if you've got tasks you can run in parallel.

Parallel LINQ, or PLINQ for short, is a project with one "simple" goal: to execute LINQ to Objects queries in parallel, realizing the benefits of multithreading with as few headaches as possible. At the time of this writing, PLINQ is targeted to be released as part of *Parallel Extensions,* the next generation of .NET concurrency support. The sample I describe is based on the December 2007 Community Technology Preview (CTP).

Using PLINQ is simple, if (and only if) you have to perform the same task on each element in a sequence, and those tasks are independent. If you need the result of one calculation step in order to find the next, PLINQ is not for you—but many CPU-intensive tasks can in fact be done in parallel. To tell the compiler to use PLINQ, you just need to call `AsParallel` (an extension method on `IEnumerable<T>`) on your data source, and let PLINQ handle the threading. As with `IQueryable`, the magic is just normal compiler method resolution: `AsParallel` returns an `IParallelEnumerable`, and the `ParallelEnumerable` class provides static methods to handle the standard query operators.

Listing 12.22 demonstrates PLINQ in an entirely artificial way, putting threads to sleep for random periods instead of actually hitting the processor hard.

Listing 12.22   Executing a LINQ query on multiple threads with Parallel LINQ

```
static int ObtainLengthSlowly(string name)
{
    Thread.Sleep(StaticRandom.Next(10000));
    return name.Length;
}
...

string[] names = {"Jon", "Holly", "Tom", "Robin", "William"};

var query = from name in names.AsParallel(3)
            select ObtainLengthSlowly(name);

foreach (int length in query)
{
    Console.WriteLine(length);
}
```

Listing 12.22 will print out the length of each name. We're using a random[11] sleep to simulate doing some real work within the call to `ObtainLengthSlowly`. Without the

---

[11] The `StaticRandom` class used for this is merely a thread-safe wrapper of static methods around a normal `Random` class. It's part of my miscellaneous utility library.

AsParallel call, we would only use a single thread, but AsParallel and the resulting calls to the ParallelEnumerable extension methods means that the work is split into up to three threads.[12]

One caveat about this: unless you specify that you want the results in the same order as the strings in the original sequence, PLINQ will assume you don't mind getting results as soon as they're available, even if results from earlier elements haven't been returned yet. You can prevent this by passing QueryOptions.PreserveOrdering as a parameter to AsParallel.

There are other subtleties to using PLINQ, such as handling the possibility of multiple exceptions occurring instead of the whole process stopping on the first problematic element—consult the documentation for further details when Parallel Extensions is fully released. More examples of PLINQ are included in the downloadable source code.

As you can see, PLINQ isn't a "data source"—it's a kind of meta-provider, altering *how* a query is executed. Many developers will never need it—but I'm sure that those who do will be eternally grateful for the coordination it performs for them behind the scenes.

These won't be the only new providers Microsoft comes up with—we should expect new APIs to be built with LINQ in mind, and that should include your own code as well. I confidently expect to see some weird and wonderful uses of LINQ in the future.

12.6   *Summary*

Phew! This chapter has been the exact opposite of most of the rest of the book. Instead of focusing on a single topic in great detail, we've covered a vast array of LINQ providers, but at a shallow level.

I wouldn't expect you to feel particularly familiar with any one of the specific technologies we've looked at here, but I hope you've got a deeper understanding of why LINQ is important. It's not about XML, or in-memory queries, or even SQL queries—it's about consistency of expression, and giving the C# compiler the opportunity to validate your queries to at least some extent, regardless of their final execution platform.

You should now appreciate why expression trees are so important that they are among the few *framework* elements that the C# compiler has direct intimate knowledge of (along with strings, IDisposable, IEnumerable<T>, and Nullable<T>, for example). They are passports for behavior, allowing it to cross the border of the local machine, expressing logic in whatever foreign tongue is catered for by a LINQ provider.

It's not just expression trees—we've also relied on the query expression translation employed by the compiler, and the way that lambda expressions can be converted to both delegates and expression trees. Extension methods are also important, as without them each provider would have to give implementations of all the relevant methods. If

---

[12] I've explicitly specified the number of threads in this example to force parallelism even on a single-core system. If the number of threads isn't specified, the system acts as it sees fit, depending on the number of cores available and how much other work they have.

you look back at all the new features of C#, you'll find few that don't contribute significantly to LINQ in some way or other. That is part of the reason for this chapter's existence: to show the connections between all the features.

I shouldn't wax lyrical for too long, though—as well as the upsides of LINQ, we've seen a few "gotchas." LINQ will not always allow us to express everything we need in a query, nor does it hide *all* the details of the underlying data source. The impedance mismatches that have caused developers so much trouble in the past are still with us: we can reduce their impact with ORM systems and the like, but without a proper understanding of the query being executed on your behalf, you are likely to run into significant issues. In particular, don't think of LINQ as a way of removing your need to understand SQL—just think of it as a way of hiding the SQL when you're not interested in the details.

Despite the limitations, LINQ is undoubtedly going to play a major part in future .NET development. In the final chapter, I will look at some of the ways development is likely to change in the next few years, and the part I believe C#3 will play in that evolution.

13

Elegant code in the new era

This chapter covers
- Reasons for language evolution
- Changes of emphasis for C#3
- Readability: "what" over "how"
- Effects of parallel computing

You've now seen all the features that C#3 has to offer, and you've had a taste of some of the flavors of LINQ available now and in the near future. Hopefully I've given you a feeling for the directions C#3 might guide you in when coding, and this chapter puts those directions into the context of software development in general.

There's a certain amount of speculation in this chapter. Take everything with a grain of salt—I don't have a crystal ball, after all, and technology is notoriously difficult to predict. However, the themes are fairly common ones and I am confident that they'll *broadly* hit the mark, even if the details are completely off.

Life is all about learning from our mistakes—and occasionally failing to do so. The software industry has been both innovative and shockingly backward at times. There are elegant new technologies such as C#3 and LINQ, frameworks that do more than we might have dreamed about ten years ago, and tools that hold our hands throughout the development processes… and yet we know that a large proportion of software projects fail. Often this is due to management failures or even customer failures, but sometimes developers need to take at least some of the blame.

Many, many books have been written about why this is the case, and I won't pretend to be an expert, but I believe that ultimately it comes down to human nature. The vast majority of us are sloppy—and I certainly include myself in that category. Even when we *know* that best practices such as unit testing and layered designs will help us in the long run, we sometimes go for quick fixes that eventually come back to haunt us.

There's only so much a language or a platform can do to counter this. The only way to appeal to laziness is to make the *right* thing to do also the *easiest* one. Some areas make that difficult—it will always seem easier in some ways to not write unit tests than to write them. Quite often breaking our design layers ("just for this one little thing, honest") really *is* easier than doing the job properly—temporarily.

On the bright side, C#3 and LINQ allow many ideas and goals to be expressed much more easily than before, improving readability while simultaneously speeding up development. If you have the opportunity to use C#3 for pleasure before putting it in a business context, you may well find yourself being frustrated at the shackles imposed when you have to go back to C#2 (or, heaven forbid, C#1). There are so many shortcuts that you may often find yourself surprised at just how easy it is to achieve what might previously have been a time-consuming goal.

Some of the improvements are simply obvious: automatic properties replace several lines of code with a single one, at no cost. There's no need to change the way you think or how you approach design and development—it's just a common scenario that is now more streamlined.

What I find more interesting are the features that *do* ask us to take a step back. They suggest to us that while we haven't been doing things "wrong," there may be a better way of looking at the world. In a few years' time, we may look back at old code and be amazed at the way we used to develop. Whenever a language evolves, it's worth asking what the changes mean in this larger sense. I'll try to answer that question now, for C#3.

13.1 The changing nature of language preferences

The changes in C#3 haven't just added more features. They've altered the idiom of the language, the natural way of expressing certain ideas and implementing behavior. These shifts in emphasis aren't limited to C#, however—they're part of what's happening within our industry as a whole.

13.1.1 A more functional emphasis

It would be hard to deny that C# has become more functional in the move from version 2 to version 3. Delegates have been part of C#1 since the first version, but they have become increasingly convenient to specify and increasingly widely used in the framework libraries.

The most extreme example of this is LINQ, of course, which has delegates at its very core. While LINQ queries can be written quite readably without using query expressions, if you take away lambda expressions and extension methods they become frankly hideous. Even a simple query expression requires extra methods to be written so that they can be used as delegate actions. The creation of those delegates is ugly, and the way that the calls are chained together is unintuitive. Consider this fairly simple query expression:

```
from user in SampleData.AllUsers
where user.UserType == UserType.Developer
orderby user.Name
select user.Name.ToUpper();
```

That is translated into the equally reasonable set of extension method calls:

```
SampleData.AllUsers
          .Where(user => user.UserType == UserType.Developer)
          .OrderBy(user => user.Name)
          .Select(user => user.Name.ToUpper());
```

It's not quite as pretty, but it's still clear. To express that in a single expression without any extra local variables and without using any C#2 or 3 features beyond generics requires something along these lines:

```
Enumerable.Select
    (Enumerable.OrderBy
        (Enumerable.Where(SampleData.AllUsers,
                          new Func<User,bool>(AcceptDevelopers)),
         new Func<User, string>(OrderByName)),
     new Func<User, string>(ProjectToUpperName));
```

Oh, and the `AcceptDevelopers`, `OrderByName`, and `ProjectToUpperName` methods all need to be defined, of course. It's an abomination. LINQ is just not designed to be useful without a concise way of specifying delegates. Where previously functional languages have been *relatively* obscure in the business world, some of their benefits are now being reaped in C#.

At the same time as mainstream languages are becoming more functional, functional languages are becoming more mainstream. The Microsoft Research "F#" language[1] is in the ML family, but executing on the CLR: it's gained enough interest to now have a dedicated team within the nonresearch side of Microsoft bringing it into production so that it can be a truly integrated language in the .NET family.

The differences aren't just about being more functional, though. Is C# becoming a dynamic language?

13.1.2 *Static, dynamic, implicit, explicit, or a mixture?*

As I've emphasized a number of times in this book, C#3 is still a statically typed language. It has *no* truly dynamic aspects to it. However, many of the features in C#2 and 3 are those

---

[1] http://research.microsoft.com/projects/cambridge/fsharp/fsharp.aspx

associated with dynamic languages. In particular, the implicitly typed local variables and arrays, extra type inference capabilities for generic methods, extension methods, and better initialization structures are all things that in some ways look like they belong in dynamic languages.

While C# itself is currently statically typed, the Dynamic Language Runtime (DLR) will bring dynamic languages to .NET. Integration between static languages and dynamic ones such as IronRuby and IronPython should therefore be relatively straightforward—this will allow projects to pick which areas they want to write dynamically, and which are better kept statically typed.

Should C# become dynamic in the future? Given recent blog posts from the C# team, it seems likely that C#4 will allow dynamic lookup in clearly marked sections of code. *Calling* code dynamically isn't the same as *responding* to calls dynamically, however—and it's possible that C# will remain statically typed at that level. That doesn't mean there can't be a language that is *like* C# in many ways but dynamic, in the same way that Groovy is like Java in many ways but with some extra features and dynamic execution. It should be noted that Visual Basic already allows for optionally dynamic lookups, just by turning `Option Strict` on and off. In the meantime, we should be grateful for the influence of dynamic languages in making C#3 a lot more expressive, allowing us to state our intentions without as much fluff surrounding the really *useful* bits of code.

The changes to C# don't just affect how our source code looks in plain text terms, however. They should also make us reconsider the structure of our programs, allowing designs to make much greater use of delegates without fear of forcing thousands of one-line methods on users.

13.2   *Delegation as the new inheritance*

There are many situations where inheritance is currently used to alter the behavior of a component in just one or two ways—and they're often ways that aren't so much inherent in the component itself as in how it interacts with the world around it.

Take a data grid, for example. A grid may use inheritance (possibly of a type related to a specific row or column) to determine how data should be formatted. In many ways, this is absolutely right—you can build up a flexible design that allows for all kinds of different values to be displayed, possibly including images, buttons, embedded tables, and the like. The vast majority of read-only data is likely to consist of some plain text, however. Now, we could have a `TextDataColumn` type with an abstract `FormatData` method, and derive from that in order to format dates, plain strings, numbers, and all kinds of other data in whatever way we want.

Alternatively, we could allow the user to specify the formatting by way of a delegate, which simply converts the appropriate data type to a string. With C#3's lambda expressions, this makes it easy to provide a custom display of the data. Of course, you may well want to provide easy ways of handling common cases—but delegates are immutable in .NET, so simple "constant" delegates for frequently used types can fill this need neatly.

This works well when a single, isolated aspect of the component needs to be specialized. It's certainly not a complete replacement of inheritance, nor would I want it to be (the title of this section notwithstanding)—but it allows a more direct approach to be used in many situations. Using interfaces with a small set of methods has often been another way of providing custom behavior, and delegates can be regarded as an extreme case of this approach.

Of course, this is similar to the point made earlier about a more functional bias, but it's applied to the specific area of inheritance and interface implementation. It's not entirely new to C#3, either: List<T> made a start in .NET 2.0 even when only C#2 was available, with methods such as Sort and FindAll. Sort allows both an interface-based comparison (with IComparer) and a delegate-based comparison (with Comparison), whereas FindAll is purely delegate based. Anonymous methods made these calls *relatively* simple and lambda expressions add even more readability.

In short, when a type or method needs a single aspect of specialized behavior, it's worth at least *considering* the ability to specify that behavior in terms of a delegate instead of via inheritance or an interface.

All of this contributes to our next big goal: readable code.

13.3   *Readability of results over implementation*

The word *readability* is bandied around quite casually as if it can only mean one thing and can somehow be measured objectively. In real life, different developers find different things readable, and in different ways. There are two kinds of readability I'd like to separate—while acknowledging that many more categorizations are possible.

First, there is the ease with which a reader can understand exactly what your code is doing at every step. For instance, making every conversion explicit even if there's an implicit one available makes it clear that a conversion is indeed taking place. This sort of detail can be useful if you're maintaining code and have already isolated the problem to a few lines of code. However, it tends to be longwinded, making it harder to browse large sections of source. I think of this as "readability of implementation."

When it comes to getting the broad sweep of code, what is required is "readability of results"—I want to know what the code does, but I don't care how it does it right now. Much of this has traditionally been down to refactoring, careful naming, and other best practices. For example, a method that needs to perform several steps can often be refactored into a method that simply calls other (reasonably short) methods to do the actual work. Declarative languages tend to emphasize readability of results.

C#3 and LINQ combine to improve readability of results quite significantly—at the cost of readability of implementation. Almost all the cleverness shown by the C#3 compiler adds to this: extension methods make the intention of the code clearer, but at the cost of the visibility of the extra static class involved, for example.

This isn't just a language issue, though; it's also part of the framework support. Consider how you might have implemented our earlier user query in .NET 1.1. The essential ingredients are filtering, sorting, and projecting:

```
ArrayList filteredUsers = new ArrayList();
foreach (User user in SampleData.AllUsers)
{
    if (user.UserType==UserType.Developer)
    {
        filteredUsers.Add(user);
    }
}

filteredUsers.Sort(new UserNameComparer());

ArrayList upperCasedNames = new ArrayList();
foreach (User user in filteredUsers)
{
    upperCasedNames.Add(user.Name.ToUpper());
}
```

Each step is clear, but it's relatively hard to understand exactly what's going on! The version we saw earlier with the explicit calls to Enumerable was shorter, but the evaluation order still made it difficult to read. C#3 hides exactly how and where the filtering, sorting, and projection is taking place—even after translating the query expression into method calls—but the overall purpose of the code is much more obvious.

Usually this type of readability is a good thing, but it does mean you need to keep your wits about you. For instance, capturing local variables makes it a lot easier to write query expressions—but you need to understand that if you change the values of those local variables after creating the query expression, those changes will apply when you execute the query expression.

One of the aims of this book has been to make you sufficiently comfortable with the *mechanics* of C#3 that you can make use of the magic without finding it hard to understand what's going on when you need to dig into it—as well as warning you of some of the potential hazards you might run into.

So far these have all been somewhat inward-looking aspects of development—changes that could have happened at any time. The next point is very much due to what a biologist might call an "external stimulus."

13.4 *Life in a parallel universe*

In chapter 12 we looked briefly at Parallel LINQ, and I mentioned that it is part of a wider project called Parallel Extensions. This is Microsoft's next attempt to make concurrency easier. I don't expect it to be the final word on such a daunting topic, but it's exciting nonetheless.

As I write this, most computers still have just a few cores. Some servers have eight or possibly even 16 (within the x86/x64 space—other architectures already support far more than this). Given how everything in the industry is progressing, it may not be long before that looks like small fry, with genuine *massively* parallel chips becoming part of everyday life. Concurrency is at the tipping point between "nice to have" and "must have" as a developer skill.

We've already seen how the functional aspects of C#3 and LINQ enable some concurrency scenarios—parallelism is often a matter of breaking down a big task into lots of smaller ones that can run at the same time, after all, and delegates are nice building blocks for that. The support for delegates in the form of lambda expressions—and even expression trees to express logic in a more data-like manner—will certainly help parallelization efforts in the future.

There will be more advances to come. Some improvements may come through new frameworks such as Parallel Extensions, while others may come through future language features. Some of the frameworks may use existing language features in novel ways, just as the Concurrency and Coordination Runtime uses iterator blocks as we saw in chapter 6.

One area we may well see becoming more prominent is *provability*. Concurrency is a murky area full of hidden pitfalls, and it's also *very* hard to test properly. Testing every possibility is effectively impossible—but in some cases source code can be analyzed for concurrency correctness automatically. Making this applicable to business software at a level that is usable by "normal" developers such as ourselves is likely to be challenging, but we may see progress as it becomes increasingly important to use the large number of cores becoming available to us.

There are clearly dozens of areas I could have picked that could become crucial in the next decade—mobile computing, service-oriented architectures (SOA), human computer interfaces, rich Internet applications, system interoperability, and so forth. These are all likely to be transformed significantly—but parallel computing is likely to be at the heart of many of them. If you don't know much about threading, I strongly advise you to start learning right now.

13.5   *Farewell*

So, that's C#—for now. I doubt that it will stay at version 3 forever, although I would personally like Microsoft to give us at least a few years of exploring and becoming comfortable with C#3 before moving the world on again. I don't know about you, but I could do with a bit of time to use what we've got instead of learning the next version. If we need a bit more variety and spice, there are always other languages to be studied...

In the meantime, there will *certainly* be new libraries and architectures to come to grips with. Developers can never afford to stand still—but hopefully this book has given you a rock-solid foundation in C#, enabling you to learn new technologies without worrying about what the language is doing.

There's more to life than learning about the new tools available, and while you *may* have bought this book purely out of intellectual curiosity, it's more likely that you just want to get the most out of C#3. After all, there's relatively little point in acquiring a skill if you're not going to use it. C#3 is a wonderful language, and .NET 3.5 is a great platform—but on their own they mean very little. They need to be *used* to provide value.

I've tried to give you a thorough understanding of C#3, but that doesn't mean that you've seen all that it can do, any more than playing each note on a piano in turn means you've heard every possible tune. I've put the features in context and given some examples of where you might find them helpful. I can't tell you exactly what ground-breaking use *you* might find for C#3—but I wish you the very best of luck.

appendix:
LINQ standard
query operators

There are many standard query operators in LINQ, only some of which are supported directly in C# query expressions—the others have to be called "manually" as normal methods. Some of the standard query operators are demonstrated in the main text of the book, but they're all listed in this appendix. For the examples, I've defined two sample sequences:

```
string[] words = {"zero", "one", "two", "three", "four"};
int[] numbers = {0, 1, 2, 3, 4};
```

For completeness I've included the operators we've already seen, although in most cases chapter 11 contains more detail on them than I've provided here. For each operator, I've specified whether it uses deferred or immediate execution.

A.1 Aggregation

The aggregation operators (see table A.1) all result in a single value rather than a sequence. Average and Sum all operate either on a sequence of numbers (any of the built-in numeric types) or on a sequence of elements with a delegate to convert from each element to one of the built-in numeric types. Min and Max have overloads for numeric types, but can also operate on any sequence either using the default comparer for the element type or using a conversion delegate. Count and LongCount are equivalent to each other, just with different return types. Both of these have two overloads—one that just counts the length of the sequence, and one that takes a predicate: only elements matching the predicate are counted.

The most generalized aggregation operator is just called Aggregate. All the other aggregation operators could be expressed as calls to Aggregate, although it would be relatively painful to do so. The basic idea is that there's always a "result so far," starting with an initial seed. An aggregation delegate is applied for each element of the input sequence: the delegate takes the result so far and the input element, and produces the next result. As a final optional step, a conversion is applied from the aggregation result to the return value of the method. This conversion may result in a different type, if necessary. It's not quite as complicated as it sounds, but you're still unlikely to use it very often.

All of the aggregation operators use immediate execution.

Table A.1   Examples of aggregation operators

Expression	Result
`numbers.Sum()`	`10`
`numbers.Count()`	`5`
`numbers.Average()`	`2`
`numbers.LongCount(x => x%2 == 0)`	`3` (as a `long`; there are three even numbers)
`words.Min(word => word.Length)`	`3` (`"one"` and `"two"`)
`words.Max(word => word.Length)`	`5` (`"three"`)

`numbers.Aggregate("seed",`
`  (soFar, elt) => soFar+elt.ToString(),`
`  result => result.ToUpper())`
	`SEED01234`

A.2   Concatenation

There is a single concatenation operator: `Concat` (see table A.2). As you might expect, this operates on two sequences, and returns a single sequence consisting of all the elements of the first sequence followed by all the elements of the second. The two input sequences must be of the same type, and execution is deferred.

Table A.2   `Concat` example

Expression	Result
`numbers.Concat(new[] {2, 3, 4, 5, 6})`	`0, 1, 2, 3, 4, 2, 3, 4, 5, 6`

A.3   Conversion

The conversion operators (see table A.3) cover a fair range of uses, but they all come in pairs. `AsEnumerable` and `AsQueryable` allow a sequence to be treated as `IEnumerable<T>` or `IQueryable` respectively, forcing further calls to convert lambda expressions into delegate instances or expression trees respectively, and use the appropriate extension methods. These operators use deferred execution.

`ToArray` and `ToList` are fairly self-explanatory: they read the whole sequence into memory, returning it either as an array or as a `List<T>`. Both use immediate execution.

Cast and OfType convert an untyped sequence into a typed one, either throwing an exception (for Cast) or ignoring (for OfType) elements of the input sequence that aren't implicitly convertible to the output sequence element type. This may also be used to convert typed sequences into more specifically typed sequences, such as converting IEnumerable<object> to IEnumerable<string>. The conversions are performed in a streaming manner with deferred execution.

ToDictionary and ToLookup both take delegates to obtain the key for any particular element; ToDictionary returns a dictionary mapping the key to the element type, whereas ToLookup returns an appropriately typed ILookup<,>. A lookup is like a dictionary where the value associated with a key isn't one element but a sequence of elements. Lookups are generally used when duplicate keys are expected as part of normal operation, whereas a duplicate key will cause ToDictionary to throw an exception. More complicated overloads of both methods allow a custom IEqualityComparer<T> to be used to compare keys, and a conversion delegate to be applied to each element before it is put into the dictionary or lookup.

The examples in table A.3 use two additional sequences to demonstrate Cast and OfType:

```
object[] allStrings = {"These", "are", "all", "strings"};
object[] notAllStrings = {"Number", "at", "the", "end", 5};
```

Table A.3 Conversion examples

Expression	Result
allStrings.Cast<string>()	"These", "are", "all", "strings" (as IEnumerable<string>)
allStrings.OfType<string>()	"These", "are", "all", "strings" (as IEnumerable<string>)
notAllStrings.Cast<string>()	Exception is thrown while iterating, at point of failing conversion
notAllStrings.OfType<string>()	"Number", "at", "the", "end" (as IEnumerable<string>)
numbers.ToArray()	0, 1, 2, 3, 4 (as int[])
numbers.ToList()	0, 1, 2, 3, 4 (as List<int>)
words.ToDictionary(word => word.Substring(0, 2))	Dictionary contents: "ze": "zero" "on": "one" "tw": "two" "th": "three" "fo": "four"

Table A.3   Conversion examples *(continued)*

Expression	Result

`// Key is first character of word`
`words.ToLookup(word => word[0])`
	Lookup contents:
	`'z'`: `"zero"`
	`'o'`: `"one"`
	`'t'`: `"two"`, `"three"`
	`'f'`: `"four"`

`words.ToDictionary(word => word[0])`	Exception: Can only have one entry per key, so fails on `'t'`

I haven't provided examples for `AsEnumerable` or `AsQueryable` because they don't affect the results in an immediately obvious way. Instead, they affect the manner in which the query is executed. `Queryable.AsQueryable` is an extension method on `IEnumerable` that returns an `IQueryable` (both types being generic or nongeneric, depending on which overload you pick). If the `IEnumerable` you call it on is already an `IQueryable`, it just returns the same reference—otherwise it creates a wrapper around the original sequence. The wrapper allows you to use all the normal `Queryable` extension methods, passing in expression trees, but when the query is executed the expression tree is compiled into normal IL and executed directly, using the `LambdaExpression.Compile` method shown in section 9.3.2.

`Enumerable.AsEnumerable` is an extension method on `IEnumerable<T>` and has a trivial implementation, simply returning the reference it was called on. No wrappers are involved—it just returns the same reference. This forces the `Enumerable` extension methods to be used in subsequent LINQ operators. Consider the following query expressions:

```
// Filter the users in the database with LIKE
from user in context.Users
where user.Name.StartsWith("Tim")
select user;

// Filter the users in memory
from user in context.Users.AsEnumerable()
where user.Name.StartsWith("Tim")
select user;
```

The second query expression forces the compile-time type of the source to be `IEnumerable<User>` instead of `IQueryable<User>`, so all the processing is done in memory instead of at the database. The compiler will use the `Enumerable` extension methods (taking delegate parameters) instead of the `Queryable` extension methods (taking expression tree parameters). Normally you want to do as much processing as possible in SQL, but when there are transformations that require "local" code, you sometimes have to force LINQ to use the appropriate `Enumerable` extension methods.

A.4 Element operations

This is another selection of query operators that are grouped in pairs (see table A.4). This time, the pairs all work the same way. There's a simple version that picks a single element if it can or throws an exception if the specified element doesn't exist, and a version with OrDefault at the end of the name. The OrDefault version is exactly the same except that it returns the default value for the result type instead of throwing an exception if it can't find the element you've asked for. All of these operators use immediate execution.

The operator names are easily understood: First and Last return the first and last elements of the sequence respectively (only defaulting if there are no elements), Single returns the only element in a sequence (defaulting if there isn't exactly one element), and ElementAt returns a specific element by index (the fifth element, for example). In addition, there's an overload for all of the operators other than ElementAt to filter the sequence first—for example, First can return the first element that matches a given condition.

Table A.4 Single element selection examples

Expression	Result
words.ElementAt(2)	"two"
words.ElementAtOrDefault(10)	null
words.First()	"zero"
words.First(word => word.Length==3)	"one"
words.First(word => word.Length==10)	Exception: No matching elements
words.FirstOrDefault (word => word.Length==10)	null
words.Last()	"four"
words.Single()	Exception: More than one element
words.SingleOrDefault()	null
words.Single(word => word.Length==5)	"three"
words.Single(word => word.Length==10)	Exception: No matching elements

A.5 Equality operations

There's only one equality operation: SequenceEqual (see table A.5). This just compares two sequences for element-by-element equality, including order. For instance, the sequence 0, 1, 2, 3, 4 is not equal to 4, 3, 2, 1, 0. An overload allows a specific IEqualityComparer<T> to be used when comparing elements. The return value is just a Boolean, and is computed with immediate execution.

Table A.5   Sequence equality examples

Expression	Result

words.SequenceEqual
  (new[]{"zero","one",
      "two","three","four"})
	True

words.SequenceEqual
  (new[]{"ZERO","ONE",
      "TWO","THREE","FOUR"})
	False

words.SequenceEqual
  (new[]{"ZERO","ONE",
      "TWO","THREE","FOUR"},
  StringComparer.OrdinalIgnoreCase)
	True

A.6   *Generation*

Out of all the generation operators (see table A.6), only one acts on an existing sequence: DefaultIfEmpty. This returns either the original sequence if it's not empty, or a sequence with a single element otherwise. The element is normally the default value for the sequence type, but an overload allows you to specify which value to use.

There are three other generation operators that are just static methods in Enumerable:

- Range generates a sequence of integers, with the parameters specifying the first value and how many values to generate.
- Repeat generates a sequence of any type by repeating a specified single value for a specified number of times.
- Empty generates an empty sequence of any type.

All of the generation operators use deferred execution.

Table A.6   Generation examples

Expression	Result
numbers.DefaultIfEmpty()	0, 1, 2, 3, 4
new int[0].DefaultIfEmpty()	0 (within an IEnumerable<int>)
new int[0].DefaultIfEmpty(10)	10 (within an IEnumerable<int>)
Enumerable.Range(15, 2)	15, 16
Enumerable.Repeat(25, 2)	25, 25
Enumerable.Empty<int>()	An empty IEnumerable<int>

A.7 Grouping

There are two grouping operators, but one of them is ToLookup (which we've already seen in A.3 as a conversion operator). That just leaves GroupBy, which we saw in section 11.6.1 when discussing the group ... by clause in query expressions. It uses deferred execution, but buffers results.

The result of GroupBy is a sequence of appropriately typed IGrouping elements. Each element has a key and a sequence of elements that match that key. In many ways, this is just a different way of looking at a lookup—instead of having random access to the groups by key, the groups are enumerated in turn. The order in which the groups are returned is the order in which their respective keys are discovered. Within a group, the order is the same as in the original sequence.

GroupBy (see table A.7) has a daunting number of overloads, allowing you to specify not only how a key is derived from an element (which is always required) but also optionally the following:

- How to compare keys.
- A projection from original element to the element within a group.
- A projection from a key and an enumeration of elements to a result type. If this is specified, the result is just a sequence of elements of this result type.

Frankly the last option is very confusing. I'd recommend avoiding it unless it definitely makes the code simpler for some reason.

Table A.7 GroupBy examples

Expression	Result
words.GroupBy(word => word.Length)	Key: 4; Sequence: "zero", "four" Key: 3; Sequence: "one", "two" Key: 5; Sequence: "three"

words.GroupBy
  (word => word.Length, // Key
   word => word.ToUpper() // Group element
)
	Key: 4; Sequence: "ZERO", "FOUR"
	Key: 3; Sequence: "ONE", "TWO"
	Key: 5; Sequence: "THREE"

A.8 Joins

Two operators are specified as join operators: Join and GroupJoin, both of which we saw in section 11.5 using join and join ... into query expression clauses respectively. Each method takes several parameters: two sequences, a key selector for each sequence, a projection to apply to each matching pair of elements, and optionally a key comparison.

For Join the projection takes one element from each sequence and produces a result; for GroupJoin the projection takes an element from the left sequence (in the chapter 11 terminology—the first one specified, usually as the sequence the extension method appears to be called on) and a sequence of matching elements from the right sequence. Both use deferred execution, and stream the left sequence but buffer the right sequence.

Table A.8 Join examples

Expression	Result
| ```
names.Join // Left sequence
  (colors, // Right sequence
   name => name[0], // Left key selector
   color => color[0], // Right key selector
   // Projection for result pairs
   (name, color) => name+" - "+color
  )
``` | "Robin - Red",<br>"Ruth - Red",<br>"Bob - Blue",<br>"Bob - Beige" |
| ```
names.GroupJoin
  (colors,
   name => name[0],
   color => color[0],
   // Projection for key/sequence pairs
   (name, matches) => name+": "+
      string.Join("/", matches.ToArray())
  )
``` | "Robin: Red",<br>"Ruth: Red",<br>"Bob: Blue/Beige",<br>"Emma: " |

For the join examples in table A.8, we'll match a sequence of names (Robin, Ruth, Bob, Emma) against a sequence of colors (Red, Blue, Beige, Green) by looking at the first character of both the name and the color, so Robin will join with Red and Bob will join with both Blue and Beige, for example.

Note that Emma doesn't match any of the colors—the name doesn't appear at all in the results of the first example, but it *does* appear in the second, with an empty sequence of colors.

A.9 *Partitioning*

The partitioning operators either *skip* an initial part of the sequence, returning only the rest, or *take* only the initial part of a sequence, ignoring the rest. In each case you can either specify how many elements are in the first part of the sequence, or specify a condition—the first part of the sequence continues until the condition fails. After the condition fails for the first time, it isn't tested again—it doesn't matter whether later elements in the sequence match or not. All of the partitioning operators (see table A.9) use deferred execution.

Table A.9 Partitioning examples

Expression	Result
`words.Take(3)`	"zero", "one", "two"
`words.Skip(3)`	"three", "four"

Table A.9 Partitioning examples *(continued)*

Expression	Result
words.TakeWhile(word => word[0] > 'k')	"zero", "one", "two", "three"
words.SkipWhile(word => word[0] > 'k')	"four"

A.10 Projection

We've seen both projection operators (Select and SelectMany) in chapter 11. Select is a simple one-to-one projection from element to result. SelectMany is used when there are multiple from clauses in a query expression: each element in the original sequence is used to generate a new sequence. Both projection operators (see table A.10) use deferred execution.

There are overloads we didn't see in chapter 11. Both methods have overloads that allow the index within the original sequence to be used within the projection, and SelectMany either flattens all of the generated sequences into a single sequence without including the original element at all, or uses a projection to generate a result element for each pair of elements. Multiple from clauses always use the overload that takes a projection. (Examples of this are quite long-winded, and not included here. See chapter 11 for more details.)

Table A.10 Projection examples

Expression	Result
words.Select(word => word.Length)	4, 3, 3, 5, 4

words.Select
  ((word, index) =>
    index.ToString()+": "+word)
	"0: zero", "1: one", "2: two",
	"3: three", "4: four"

words.SelectMany (word => word.ToCharArray())	'z', 'e', 'r', 'o', 'o', 'n', 'e', 't', 'w', 'o', 't', 'h', 'r', 'e', 'e', 'f', 'o', 'u', 'r'

words.SelectMany
  ((word, index) =>
    Enumerable.Repeat(word, index))
	"one", "two", "two", "three",
	"three", "three", "four", "four",
	"four", "four"

A.11 Quantifiers

The quantifier operators (see table A.11) all return a Boolean value, using immediate execution:

- All checks whether all the elements in the sequence satisfy a specified condition.
- Any checks whether any of the elements in the sequence satisfy a specified condition, or if no condition is specified, whether there are any elements at all.
- Contains checks whether the sequence contains a particular element, optionally specifying a comparison to use.

Table A.11   Quantifier examples

Expression	Result
`words.All(word => word.Length > 3)`	`false` ("one" and "two" have exactly three letters)
`words.All(word => word.Length > 2)`	`True`
`words.Any()`	`true` (the sequence is not empty)
`words.Any(word => word.Length == 6)`	`false` (no six-letter words)
`words.Any(word => word.Length == 5)`	`true` ("three" satisfies the condition)
`words.Contains("FOUR")`	`False`
`words.Contains("FOUR",` `  StringComparer.OrdinalIgnoreCase)`	`True`

A.12   *Filtering*

The two filtering operators are `OfType` and `Where`. For details and examples of the `OfType` operator, see the conversion operators section (A.3). The `Where` operator (see table A.12) has overloads so that the filter can take account of the element's index. It's unusual to require the index, and the `where` clause in query expressions doesn't use this overload. `Where` always uses deferred execution.

Table A.12   Filtering examples

Expression	Result
`words.Where(word => word.Length > 3)`	`"zero", "three", "four"`

`words.Where`
`  ((word, index) =>`
`   index < word.Length)`
	`"zero",  // length=4, index=0`
	`"one",   // length=3, index=1`
	`"two",   // length=3, index=2`
	`"three", // length=5, index=3`
	`// Not "four", length=4, index=4`

A.13   *Set-based operations*

It's natural to be able to consider two sequences as sets of elements. The four set-based operators all have two overloads, one using the default equality comparison for the element type, and one where the comparison is specified in an extra parameter. All of them use deferred execution.

The `Distinct` operator is the simplest—it acts on a single sequence, and just returns a new sequence of all the distinct elements, discarding duplicates. The other operators also make sure they only return distinct values, but they act on two sequences:

- `Intersect` returns elements that appear in both sequences.
- `Union` returns the elements that are in either sequence.
- `Except` returns the elements that are in the first sequence but not in the second. (Elements that are in the second sequence but not the first are *not* returned.)

For the examples of these operators in table A.13, we'll use two new sequences: abbc ("a", "b", "b", "c") and cd ("c", "d").

Table A.13 Set-based examples

Expression	Result
abbc.Distinct()	"a", "b", "c"
abbc.Intersect(cd)	"c"
abbc.Union(cd)	"a", "b", "c", "d"
abbc.Except(cd)	"a", "b"
cd.Except(abbc)	"d"

A.14 Sorting

We've seen all the sorting operators before: OrderBy and OrderByDescending provide a "primary" ordering, while ThenBy and ThenByDescending provide subsequent orderings for elements that aren't differentiated by the primary one. In each case a projection is specified from an element to its sorting key, and a comparison (between keys) can also be specified. Unlike some other sorting algorithms in the framework (such as List<T>.Sort), the LINQ orderings are *stable*—in other words, if two elements are regarded as equal in terms of their sorting key, they will be returned in the order they appeared in the original sequence.

The final sorting operator is Reverse, which simply reverses the order of the sequence. All of the sorting operators (see table A.14) use deferred execution, but buffer their data.

Table A.14 Sorting examples

Expression	Result
words.OrderBy(word => word)	"four", "one", "three", "two", "zero"

// Order words by second character
words.OrderBy(word => word[1])
	"zero", "three", "one", "four", "two"

// Order words by length;
// equal lengths returned in original
// order
words.OrderBy(word => word.Length)
	"one", "two", "zero", "four", "three"

words.OrderByDescending (word => word.Length)	"three", "zero", "four", "one", "two"

// Order words by length and then
// alphabetically
words.OrderBy(word => word.Length)
    .ThenBy(word => word)
	"one", "two", "four", "zero", "three"

Table A.14   Sorting examples *(continued)*

Expression	Result

`// Order words by length and then`
`// alphabetically backwards`
`words.OrderBy(word => word.Length)`
`    .ThenByDescending(word => word)`
	`"two", "one", "zero", "four",`
	`"three"`

`words.Reverse()`	`"four", "three", "two", "one",` `"zero"`

index

INDEX